ANNUAL REPORT

OF THE U.S. COMMISSION ON INTERNATIONAL RELIGIOUS FREEDOM

Commissioners

Dr. Katrina Lantos Swett
Chair

Dr. Robert P. George
Dr. James J. Zogby
Vice Chairs

Ambassador Mary Ann Glendon
Dr. M. Zuhdi Jasser
Dr. Daniel I. Mark
Rev. Thomas J. Reese, S.J.
Hon. Hannah Rosenthal
Hon. Eric P. Schwartz
Ambassador David N. Saperstein, *ex officio, non-voting member*

Ambassador Jackie Wolcott
Executive Director

Professional Staff

Judith E. Golub, *Director of Government and Media Relations*
Paul Liben, *Executive Writer*
Knox Thames, *Director of Policy and Research*

Dwight Bashir, *Deputy Director for Policy and Research*
Elizabeth K. Cassidy, *Deputy Director for Policy and Research*

Sahar Chaudhry, *Senior Policy Analyst*
Catherine Cosman, *Senior Policy Analyst*
Tiffany Lynch, *Senior Policy Analyst*
Tina L. Mufford, *Policy Analyst*

Thomas Kraemer, *Manager of Administration*
Kalinda M. Stephenson, *Government and Media Relations Associate*
Travis Horne, *Government and Media Relations Assistant*

U.S. Commission on International Religious Freedom
732 North Capitol Street, NW, Suite A714
Washington, DC 20401
202–523–3240 (phone)
202–523–5020 (fax)
www.uscirf.gov

TABLE OF CONTENTS

INTRODUCTION

"I will follow anyone . . . and remind everyone . . . of the fate . . . of the . . . Yazidi . . . No one mentions your tears, sadness or slow death! But we feel your fallen tears, your beheaded bodies, your raped dignity."

–Widad Akrawi,
Iraqi-born human rights activist

"How in the 21st century could people be forced from their houses just because they are Christian or Shi'ite or Sunni or Yazidi?"

–Baghdad Chaldean Catholic Patriarch Louis Sako,
July 2014 sermon in Baghdad

"The Assad regime made no effort to protect the al-Hasakeh province . . . [ISIL] launched a surprise attack. . . . along the Khabor on February 23 . . . , kidnapped 265 men, women, and children, sold 30 young women as sex slaves, and executed all captured Syriac defense forces. . . . Upon securing control of . . . Tel Hormizd, [ISIL] informed [the elders] that all crosses must be removed . . . In fighting for control of Tel Tamr, they seized the Saint Circis Church and burned its Bibles and broke its cross. . . . "

–Testimony of Bassam Ishak,
Syriac National Council of Syria, before the Tom Lantos Human Rights Commission, March 18, 2015

"The devastating attack on the Grand Mosque in Kano, Nigeria . . . was almost certainly the work of Boko Haram, which . . . has targeted the Muslim 'establishment' in Nigeria . . . ."

–Tim Lister, *CNN, November 30, 2014*

"Madagali in Adamawa . . . was overrun . . . Christian men were caught and beheaded; the women were forced to become Muslims and were taken as wives for [Boko Haram]."

–Father Gideon Obasogie,
Director of Social Communications, Catholic Diocese of Maiduguri, Nigeria, cited in December 12, 2014 article from www.churchinneed.org web site

"Almost all of the 436 mosques in the Central African Republic have been destroyed by . . . fighting between Christians and Muslims, the U.S. ambassador to the United Nations [Samantha Power] said. . . . At least 5,000 people have been killed since CAR exploded into unprecedented sectarian violence in December 2013. Nearly 1 million of [its] 4.5 million residents have been displaced, many of [them] Muslim."

–Cara Anna,
Associated Press, March 18, 2015

"During my last visit [to Burma] in January 2015, I witnessed how dire the situation has remained in Rakhine State. The conditions in Muslim IDP [internally displaced person] camps are abysmal and I received heart-breaking testimonies from Rohingya people telling me they had only two options: stay and die or leave by boat."

–Yanghee Lee,
UN Special Rapporteur on the situation of human rights in Myanmar, March 2015 presentation to UN Human Rights Council

Humanitarian crises fueled by waves of terror, intimidation, and violence have engulfed an alarming number of countries in the year since the release of the U.S. Commission on International Religious Freedom's (USCIRF) prior Annual Report last May. The previous quotations highlight five of these nations – Iraq, Syria, Nigeria, Central African Republic, and Burma – and the horrific loss of human life, freedom, and dignity that has accompanied the chaos.

A horrified world has watched the results of what some have aptly called violence masquerading as religious devotion.

In both Iraq and Syria, no religious group has been free of ISIL's depredations in areas it has conquered. ISIL has unleashed waves of terror upon Yazidis and Christians, Shi'a and Sunnis, as well as others who have dared to oppose its extremist views. When ISIL last June overtook Mosul, Iraq's second largest city, it immediately murdered 12 dissenting Sunni clerics, kidnapped Christian priests and nuns, and leveled ancient houses of worship. The recent discovery of mass graves underscores the extent of the atrocities ISIL has perpetrated on foes of its reign.

More than half a million Mosul residents have fled their homes. When ISIL seized Sinjar, the Yazidis' ancestral homeland, 200,000 were forced to flee. In Syria, ISIL's horrors are replicated by those of other religious extremist groups and the Assad government.

Yazidis and Christians have borne the worst brunt of the persecution by ISIL and other violent religious extremists. From summary executions to forced conversions, rape to sexual enslavement, abducted children to destroyed houses of worship, attacks on these communities are part of a systematic effort to erase their presence from the Middle East.

Photo Removed Due to Copyright Restrictions

"Displaced Yazidis fleeing violent Islamic State forces in Sinjar town make their way towards the Syrian border" –*Reuters*

Photo Removed Due to Copyright Restrictions

"Ethnic Rohingya refugees from Myanmar wave as they are transported by a wooden boat to a temporary shelter in Krueng Raya in Aceh Besar" –*Reuters*

In Nigeria, Boko Haram has attacked both Muslims and Christians. From mass murders at churches and mosques to mass kidnappings of children from schools, Boko Haram has cut a wide path of terror across vast swaths of Nigeria.

There is perhaps no more visible testament to the human toll of these depredations than the millions of people who have been forced to flee their homes. In Iraq, 2 million people were internally displaced in 2014 as a result of ISIL's offensive. More than 6.5 million of Syria's pre-civil-war population now is internally displaced, and more than 3.3 million more are refugees in neighboring states. In Nigeria, Boko Haram's rampages are responsible for the displacement of more than one million individuals. In Central African Republic, a million or more people have been driven from their homes. And in Burma, 140,000 Rohingya Muslims and at least 100,000 largely Kachin Christians remain internally displaced.

By any measure, the horrors of the past year speak volumes about how and why religious freedom and the protection of the rights of vulnerable religious communities matter. Those responsible for the horrors have made the case better than anybody can.

And so it should come as no surprise that in the pages of this report, we have recommended that the United States designate all five of these nations – Iraq, Syria, Nigeria, Central African Republic, and Burma – as "countries of particular concern," or CPCs under the International Religious Freedom Act. We are identifying their governments as well as others as either perpetrating or tolerating some of the worse abuses of religious freedom in the world.

"Investigations following the bombing of Kano Central Mosque, the main mosque in north Nigeria's biggest city Kano, killing at least 81 people" – *Reuters*

For humanitarian reasons alone, the world dare not remain silent in the face of the long trail of abuses committed in these and other countries.

But there is another reason as well. In August 2014, Archbishop Jean-Benjamin Sleiman, Latin-rite Archbishop of Baghdad, had this to say: "Unless there is peace . . . , I do not think that Europe will be calm. This . . . does not stop at territorial boundaries. . . ."

The Archbishop's words proved tragically prophetic. Five months later, in January 2015, the same forces of violent religious extremism plaguing the Archbishop's country struck the Hyper Cacher kosher supermarket and the Charlie Hebdo newspaper in Paris. The victims of the supermarket attack were murdered simply because they were Jews and the victims of the assault on the newspaper were killed because their attackers considered them blasphemers deserving punishment.

All nations should care about abuses beyond their borders not only for humanitarian reasons but because what goes on in other nations rarely remains there. Standing for the persecuted against the forces of violent religious extremism is not just a moral imperative; it is a practical necessity for any country seeking to protect its security and that of its citizens.

So what can the United States and like-minded nations do?

First, the humanitarian crises of the past year require continued emergency action. The United States government should be commended for its actions which helped save numerous Yazidis from murder or enslavement at the hands of ISIL or starvation as they were driven from their homes. The need, however, remains enormous, especially when it comes to the sheer number of

"Internally displaced persons on an armed AU peacekeeping convoy escorting Muslims in the Central African Republic" – *Reuters*

refugees and displaced people created by the forces of religious radicalism.

Second, emergency help, while essential to protect lives and communities from current danger, is not enough. In the long run, there is only one permanent guarantor of the safety, security, and survival of the persecuted and the vulnerable. It is the full recognition of religious freedom as a sacred human right which every nation, government, and individual must fully support and no nation, government, or individual must ever violate.

In addition, since religious freedom does not exist in a vacuum, the fundamental problems of corruption and unequal sharing of national resources and opportunities must be dealt with. And legal systems must protect the rights of both the majority and minorities.

The stories of both Iraq and Syria offer an especially grim lesson on this score. In both countries, religious minorities appeared safe for a while, but owed their safety to the whim of strongmen – Saddam Hussein and Bashar Assad – who offered protection for their own purposes.

"Lone parishioner sits in church after a small Christmas Eve service in Baghdad" – *Reuters*

In both nations, the rule of a strongman took the place of rule of law. But to rely on the favor of a single ruler, regime, or party is to live precariously. The question is what transpires when those in control pass from the scene or decide that protecting an embattled minority no longer serves stated or unstated interests. In the blink of an eye, a minority's safety and security can vanish.

Rulers, regimes, and parties may come and go, but when a society commits itself to religious freedom, the security of religious communities – as well as that of dissenters from religion – is guaranteed no matter who holds power.

To be sure, embedding religious freedom and other human rights in a society often can seem a herculean task, but it is a vital one.

And so we must stand tall for religious freedom as an antidote to religious extremism, an aid to security, and a universal right of humanity.

2015 ANNUAL REPORT OVERVIEW

The U.S. Commission on International Religious Freedom (USCIRF), created by the International Religious Freedom Act of 1998 (IRFA) as an entity separate and distinct from the State Department, is an independent, bipartisan U.S. government advisory body that monitors religious freedom worldwide and makes policy recommendations to the President, Secretary of State, and Congress. USCIRF bases these recommendations on its statutory mandate and the standards in the Universal Declaration of Human Rights and other international documents. The 2015 Annual Report represents the culmination of a year's work by Commissioners and professional staff to document abuses on the ground and make independent policy recommendations to the U.S. government.

The 2015 Annual Report covers the period from January 31, 2014 through January 31, 2015, although in some cases significant events that occurred after the reporting period are mentioned. The Annual Report addresses 33 countries around the world and is divided into four sections.

The first section focuses on the U.S. government's implementation of the International Religious Freedom Act. It provides recommendations for specific actions that the Administration can take to bolster current efforts to advance freedom of religion or belief abroad. It also recommends legislative activity by Congress to provide additional tools to equip U.S. diplomats to better advocate for religious freedom.

The second section highlights countries that USCIRF concludes meet IRFA's standard for "countries of particular concern," or CPCs, and recommends for designation as such. IRFA requires the U.S. government to designate as a CPC any country whose government engages in or tolerates particularly severe violations of religious freedom that are systematic, ongoing and egregious. In its most recent designations in July 2014, the State Department designated nine countries as CPCs. In 2015, USCIRF has concluded that 17 countries meet this standard.

> In 2015, USCIRF recommends that the Secretary of State re-designate the following nine countries as CPCs: Burma, China, Eritrea, Iran, North Korea, Saudi Arabia, Sudan, Turkmenistan, and Uzbekistan. USCIRF also finds that eight other countries meet the CPC standard and should be so designated: Central African Republic, Egypt, Iraq, Nigeria, Pakistan, Syria, Tajikistan, and Vietnam.

The 2015 Annual Report recognizes that non-state actors, such as transnational or local organizations, are some of the most egregious violators of religious freedom. For example, in the Central African Republic and areas of Iraq and Syria, the governments are either non-existent or incapable of addressing violations committed by non-state actors. USCIRF has concluded that the CPC classification should be expanded to allow for the designation of countries such as these, where particularly severe violations of religious freedom are occurring but a government does not exist or does not control its territory. Accordingly, USCIRF's CPC recommendations reflect that approach.

The third section highlights countries USCIRF categorized as Tier 2, which includes countries where the violations engaged in or tolerated by the government are serious and are characterized by at least one of the elements of the "systematic, ongoing, and egregious" standard, but do not fully meet the CPC standard.

> In 2015, USCIRF places the following ten countries on Tier 2: Afghanistan, Azerbaijan, Cuba, India, Indonesia, Kazakhstan, Laos, Malaysia, Russia, and Turkey.

Lastly, there are brief descriptions of other countries that USCIRF monitored during the year: Bahrain, Bangladesh, Belarus, Cyprus, Kyrgyzstan, and Sri Lanka.

USCIRF TIER 1 & TIER 2 COUNTRIES

Tier 1 CPC Countries Designated by State Department & Recommended by USCIRF	Tier 1 CPC Countries Recommended by USCIRF	Tier 2 Countries
Burma China Eritrea Iran North Korea Saudi Arabia Sudan Turkmenistan Uzbekistan	Central African Republic Egypt Iraq Nigeria Pakistan Syria Tajikistan Vietnam	Afghanistan Azerbaijan Cuba India Indonesia Kazakhstan Laos Malaysia Russia Turkey

IRFA IMPLEMENTATION

IRFA's History

The International Religious Freedom Act of 1998 was a landmark piece of legislation, seeking to make religious freedom an important priority in U.S. foreign policy. Congress passed the Act unanimously in October 1998 and it was signed into law by President Bill Clinton that same month. Members of Congress believed that this core human right was being ignored and that a greater emphasis would make for smarter diplomacy and reflect the unique role that religious freedom played in the formation of the United States. Rather than creating a hierarchy of rights as some critics have argued, IRFA established parity – it ensured religious freedom would be considered by U.S. policymakers alongside the other pressing issues of the day, and not be forgotten or ignored.

To accomplish this, the Act did several things. First, it created special mechanisms inside and outside the executive branch. Inside the executive branch, the law created the position of Ambassador-at-Large for International Religious Freedom (a political appointee nominated by the President and confirmed by the Senate), to head an Office of International Religious Freedom at the State Department (the IRF Office). It also urged the appointment of a Special Adviser for this issue on the

recommendations for U.S. policy to the President, Secretary of State, and Congress.

Second, IRFA required monitoring and reporting. It mandated that the State Department prepare an annual report on religious freedom conditions in each foreign country (the IRF Report), in addition to the Department's annual human rights report. The law also required the State Department to maintain a religious freedom Internet site, as well as lists of religious prisoners in foreign countries. And it required that USCIRF issue its own annual report setting forth its findings on the worst violators of religious freedom and providing independent recommendations for U.S. policy.

Third, IRFA established consequences for the worst violators. The law requires the President – who has delegated this power to the Secretary of State – to designate annually "countries of particular concern," or CPCs, and to take action designed to encourage improvements in those countries. Under IRFA, CPCs are defined as countries whose governments either engage in or tolerate "particularly severe" violations of religious freedom. A menu of possible actions is available, ranging from negotiating a bilateral agreement, to imposing sanctions, to taking a "commensurate action," to issuing a waiver. While a CPC designation

Outside of the executive branch, IRFA created USCIRF, an independent U.S. government advisory body mandated to review religious freedom conditions globally and make recommendations for U.S. policy. . .

White House National Security Council staff. Outside of the executive branch, IRFA created USCIRF, an independent U.S. government advisory body mandated to review religious freedom conditions globally and make

remains in effect until removed, sanctions tied to a CPC action expire after two years, if not renewed.

Fourth, IRFA included religious freedom as an element of U.S. foreign assistance, cultural exchange, and international broadcasting programs.

> IRFA defines "particularly severe" violations of religious freedom as "systematic, ongoing, egregious violations of religious freedom, including violations such as—(A) torture or cruel, inhuman, or degrading treatment or punishment; (B) prolonged detention without charges; (C) causing the disappearance of persons by the abduction or clandestine detention of those persons; or (D) other flagrant denial of the right to life, liberty, or the security of persons."

Fifth, IRFA sought to address perceived deficiencies in U.S. government officials' knowledge and understanding of the issue. It mandated that State Department Foreign Service Officers and U.S. immigration officials receive training on religious freedom and religious persecution. It also required immigration officials to use the State Department's annual IRF Report as a resource in adjudicating asylum and refugee claims involving religious persecution.

Finally, IRFA sought assessments of whether recently-enacted immigration law reforms were being implemented consistent with the United States' obligations to protect individuals fleeing persecution, including but not limited to religious persecution. The law authorized USCIRF to appoint experts to examine whether asylum seekers subject to the process of Expedited Removal were being erroneously returned to countries where they could face persecution or detained under inappropriate conditions. Expedited Removal is a mechanism enacted in 1996 whereby foreign nationals arriving in the United States without proper documentation can be returned to their countries of origin without delay, but also without the safeguard of review by an immigration judge, unless they can establish that they have a "credible fear" of persecution.

Religious Freedom Violations under IRFA

IRFA brought an international approach to U.S. religious freedom advocacy. The Act did not use the First Amendment to the U.S. Constitution to measure other countries' activities, but rather looked to international instruments. IRFA specifically defined violations of religious freedom as "violations of the internationally recognized right to freedom of religion and religious belief and practice" as articulated in the UN Universal Declaration of Human Rights (UDHR), the UN International Covenant on Civil and Political Rights, (ICCPR), the Helsinki Accords, and other international instruments and regional agreements.

IRFA also did not limit violations to government actions. It recognized that religious freedom violations also can occur through government inaction against abuses by private actors. The 1998 statute does not, however, adequately address one of the 21st century's major challenges to freedom of religion or belief: the actions of non-state actors in failing or failed states. IRFA focused on government action or inaction, but in many of the most pressing situations today, transnational or local organizations are the egregious persecutors and governments are either incapable of addressing the violations or non-existent. In these situations, allowing the United States to designate the non-state actors perpetrating particularly severe violators of religious freedom would broaden the U.S. government's ability to engage the actual drivers of persecution. Such a step was taken with the Taliban, which was in effect named a CPC from 1999-2003 despite the United States' not recognizing its control of Afghanistan. Naming these countries or groups would reflect reality, which should be the core point of the CPC process.

The Act also allows the United States to take certain actions against specific foreign officials who are responsible for or directly carried out particularly severe religious freedom violations. IRFA bars the entry of such individuals to the United States, but the provision has been invoked only once: in March 2005, it was used to exclude then-Chief Minister Narendra Modi of Gujarat state in India due to his complicity in riots in his state in 2002 that resulted in the deaths of an estimated 1,100 to 2,000 Muslims. USCIRF continues to urge the Departments of State and Homeland Security to develop a lookout list of aliens who are inadmissible to the United States on this basis. The IRF Office has worked to identify people inadmissible under U.S. law for religious freedom violations, and USCIRF has provided information about several such individuals to the State Department.

Separate from the IRFA framework, in 2014 the State Department explicitly and publicly tied entry into the United States to concerns about violent activity. Secretary of State John Kerry announced during a visit to Nigeria that the United States would deny entry to any persons responsible for engaging in or inciting violence during Nigeria's election, including by declaring them ineligible for American visas. He said specifically that, "perpetrators of such violence would not be welcome in the United States of America." While not mandated by IRFA, USCIRF supports this approach.

Directly related to identifying and barring from entry severe religious freedom violators, IRFA also requires the President to determine the specific officials responsible for violations of religious freedom engaged in or tolerated by governments of CPC countries, and, "when applicable and to the extent practicable," publish the names of these officials in the Federal Register. Despite these requirements, no names of individual officials from any CPC countries responsible for particularly severe religious freedom violations have been published to date.

Apart from the inadmissibility provision discussed above, Congress at times has imposed targeted sanctions on specific individuals for severe religious freedom violations. Based on a USCIRF recommendation, Congress included sanctions on human rights and religious freedom violators in the 2010 Iran sanctions act, the Comprehensive Iran Sanctions and Divestment Act (CISADA, P.L. 111–195). This was the first time Iran sanctions specifically included human rights violators. President Obama has now imposed such sanctions (visa bans and asset freezes) by executive order on 16 Iranian officials and entities, including eight identified as egregious religious freedom violators by USCIRF. Also based on a USCIRF recommendation, the Senate included Chechen President Ramzan Kadyrov on the list of gross human rights violators in the Sergei Magnitsky Rule of Law Accountability Act (P.L. 112–208), which imposes U.S. visa bans and asset freezes on designated Russian officials. Kadyrov has engaged in abuses against Muslims and has been linked to politically-motivated killings.

With respect to these issues, USCIRF recommends that the State Department:

- Make greater efforts to ensure foreign government officials are denied entry into the United States due to their inadmissibility under U.S. law for their responsibility for religious freedom violations abroad;

- Train consular sections of all embassies on this entry requirement, and direct them that the application of this provision is mandatory; and

- Announce a policy that all individuals applying for entry to the United States will be denied entry if they are involved in or incite violence against members of religious communities.

USCIRF recommends that Congress:

- Expand the CPC classification to allow for the designation of countries where particularly severe violations of religious freedom are occurring but a government does not exist or does not control its territory; and

- Expand the CPC classification to allow the naming of non-state actors who are perpetrating particularly severe violations of religious freedom.

Institutional Issues

IRFA intended the Ambassador-at-Large for International Religious Freedom to be the highest-ranking U.S. official on religious freedom abroad, coordinating and developing U.S. policy regarding freedom of religion or belief, while also serving as an *ex officio* member of USCIRF. There have been four Ambassadors-at-Large since IRFA's enactment: Robert Seiple (May 1999 to September 2000); John Hanford (May 2002 to January 2009); Suzan Johnson Cook (May 2011 to October 2013); and David Saperstein (January 2015 to the present).

Under IRFA, the Ambassador-at-Large is to be a "principal adviser to the President and the Secretary of State regarding matters affecting religious freedom abroad." However, since the position was established, every administration, including the current one, has situated the Ambassador-at-Large in the Bureau of Democracy, Human Rights, and Labor (DRL) and thus under its Assistant Secretary, even though the State Department's organizational guidelines consider an Ambassador-at-Large to be of higher rank than an Assistant Secretary. Other Ambassadors-at-Large report to the Secretary, such as those for Global Women's Issues, Counterterrorism, and War Crime Issues, as well as the AIDS Coordinator.

Religious freedom advocates, including USCIRF, have long been concerned about the low placement of the Ambassador-at-Large for International Religious Freedom within the State Department hierarchy. Secretary of State Kerry committed to Congress at a public hearing that the Ambassador-at-Large will have direct and regular access to him, which would fulfill IRFA's intention that the Ambassador be "a principal advisor to the President and Secretary of State" on matters relating to religious freedom. In addition, the Office of International Religious Freedom should be strengthened, including by enlarging its staff, deepening its expertise, and providing dedicated programmatic funds for religious freedom promotion and protection.

The Ambassador-at-Large now sits among a crowded field of officials whose mandates overlap. Issues of religious freedom play a part in other U.S. government efforts to engage religious communities and to promote human rights more generally. This has become more apparent as various administrations created special State Department positions to focus on particular countries or issues where religious freedom is implicated, such as a Special Envoy for Sudan, a Special Representative to Afghanistan and Pakistan, a Special Representative to Muslim Communities, and a Special Envoy to the Organization of Islamic Cooperation. In addition, Congress created the position of Special Envoy to Monitor and Combat Anti-Semitism. In 2014, Congress passed, and President Obama signed into law, a bill creating the position of Special Envoy to Promote Religious Freedom of Religious Minorities in the Near East and South Central Asia at the State Department.

In addition, the State Department during the Obama Administration took steps to improve its ability to engage with religious actors. The IRF Office staff oversaw initial efforts to track U.S. government religious engagement globally, and the IRF Office co-chaired a special working group with civil society on religion and global affairs. From this process, the working group issued a white paper recommending, among other things, the creation of a special State Department office for religious engagement, modeled on similar offices in other agencies like USAID. In August 2013, the State Department created a new Office of Faith-Based Community Initiatives, headed by a Special Advisor, Shaun Casey. (The position and office titles have since been changed to Special Representative and Office for Religion and Global Affairs.) According

to the announcement, the Office will "set Department policy on engagement with faith-based communities and . . . work in conjunction with bureaus and posts to reach out to those communities to advance the Department's diplomacy and development objectives," and will "collaborate regularly with other government officials and offices focused on religious issues, including the Ambassador-at-Large for International Religious Freedom and the Department's Office of International Religious Freedom." The Special Representative for Muslim Communities and the Special Envoy to the Organization of Islamic Cooperation were moved into the Office for Religion and Global Affairs, as was the Special Envoy to Monitor and Combat Anti-Semitism, who formerly was situated in the DRL Bureau.

With respect to these issues, USCIRF recommends that the Secretary of State:

- Per IRFA's mandate that the Ambassador-at-Large for International Religious Freedom be "a principal adviser" to the President and the Secretary of State on religious freedom issues, and considering the proliferation of related positions and offices, task the Ambassador-at-Large with chairing an inter-bureau working group with all the religiously-oriented positions and programs to ensure consistency in message and strategy;

- Move under the leadership of the Ambassador-at-Large for International Religious Freedom the positions of Special Envoy to Monitor and Combat Anti-Semitism and Special Envoy to Promote Religious Freedom of Religious Minorities in the Near East and South Central Asia (should the latter be filled); and

- Provide the Office of International Religious Freedom with resources and staff similar to other offices with global mandates, as well as with increased programmatic funds for religious freedom promotion and protection.

USCIRF recommends that Congress:

- Annually specify that funds from the State Department's Human Rights Democracy Fund (HRDF) be allocated for religious freedom programming managed by the Office of International Religious Freedom.

Annual Reports

IRFA requires that the State Department submit the IRF Report "on September 1 of each year or the first day thereafter on which the appropriate House of Congress is in session." It also requires that USCIRF, based on its review of the IRF Report and other sources, submit its Annual Report by May 1.

However, a recent change by the State Department in its reporting calendar and release date has affected USCIRF's ability to review the IRF Report and still meet the mandated May 1 deadline. In 2010, the State Department decided to consolidate the reporting periods of its various reports on different human rights issues, in order to minimize the impact on limited staff resources. As a result, the period covered in each IRF Report was shifted from a mid-year (July 1 to June 30) to a calendar-year (January 1 to December 31) cycle. It also decided to release the IRF Report in March or April, rather than comply with the September timeframe established in IRFA.

It should be noted that, although IRFA mandated both the State Department and USCIRF to report annually on international religious freedom, the two entities' annual reports are significantly different. The State Department reports on every country in the world, while USCIRF reports on selected countries, generally those exhibiting the worst conditions. Further, the State Department's reports focus primarily on religious freedom conditions, while USCIRF's country chapters discuss conditions, analyze U.S. policy, and

when issuing their reports. As discussed above, however, the State Department's change of the reporting period to harmonize the timing of various human reports changed the release date of the IRF Report.

With respect to these issues, USCIRF recommends that:

- In light of the State Department's change in the release date of its report, USCIRF and the State Department meet to discuss the timing of their reports.

The CPC Mechanism

In IRFA's 16-year existence, the State Department has made CPC designations on 10 occasions: October 1999, September 2000, October 2001, March 2003, September 2004, November 2005, November 2006, January 2009, August 2011, and July 2014. As is evident from these dates, for a number of years the designations generally were made annually, but after 2006, designations became infrequent. While IRFA does not set a specific deadline, the Act indicates that CPC designations should occur soon after the State Department releases its annual IRF Report, as the decisions are to be based on that review and on USCIRF recommendations. In August 2011 and July 2014, the Obama Administration made CPC designations in conjunction with the IRF Report. Ambassador-at-Large Saperstein has also stated his commitment to have an annual CPC designation process.

State Department and USCIRF reports "are significantly different" as "USCIRF's country chapters discuss conditions, analyze U.S. policy, and make policy recommendations."

---

make policy recommendations. USCIRF's Annual Reports also assess the executive branch's implementation of IRFA and discuss religious freedom issues in multilateral organizations.

IRFA created a system in which the State Department's and USCIRF's annual reports would be issued approximately four months apart, and the State Department and USCIRF would consider each other's findings

As noted earlier, while a CPC designation remains in effect until it is removed, associated Presidential actions expire after two years if not renewed. The last three CPC designations occurred after the two-year mark from the previous designations had passed.

In addition to CPC designations being infrequent, the list has been largely unchanged. Of the nine countries designated as CPCs in July 2014, most had been named as CPCs for over a decade: Burma, China, Iran, and Sudan for 15 years; North Korea for 13 years; Eritrea and Saudi Arabia for 10 years; and Uzbekistan for eight years. Additionally, removal from the CPC list has been rare. Since IRFA's inception, only one country has been removed from the State Department's CPC list due to diplomatic activity: Vietnam (a CPC from 2004 to 2006). Three other CPC designees were removed, but only after military intervention led to the fall of those regimes: Iraq (a CPC from 1999 to 2004), the Taliban regime of Afghanistan (a "particularly severe violator" from 1999 to 2003), and the Milosevic regime of the Serbian Republic of Yugoslavia (a "particularly severe violator" from 1999 to 2001).

Besides requiring the naming of violators, IRFA provides the Secretary of State with a unique toolbox to promote religious freedom effectively. The Act includes a menu of options for countries designated as CPCs and a list of actions to encourage improvements in countries that violate religious freedom but do not meet the CPC threshold. The specific policy options to address severe violations of religious freedom in CPC countries include sanctions (referred to as Presidential actions in IRFA) that are not automatically imposed. Rather, the Secretary of State is empowered to enter into direct consultations with a government to bring about improvements in religious freedom. IRFA also permits the development of either a binding agreement with a CPC-designated government on specific actions it will take to end the violations giving rise to the designation or the taking of a "commensurate action." The Secretary may further determine that pre-existing sanctions are adequate

STATE'S DESIGNATIONS OF COUNTRIES AND REGIMES AS CPCS

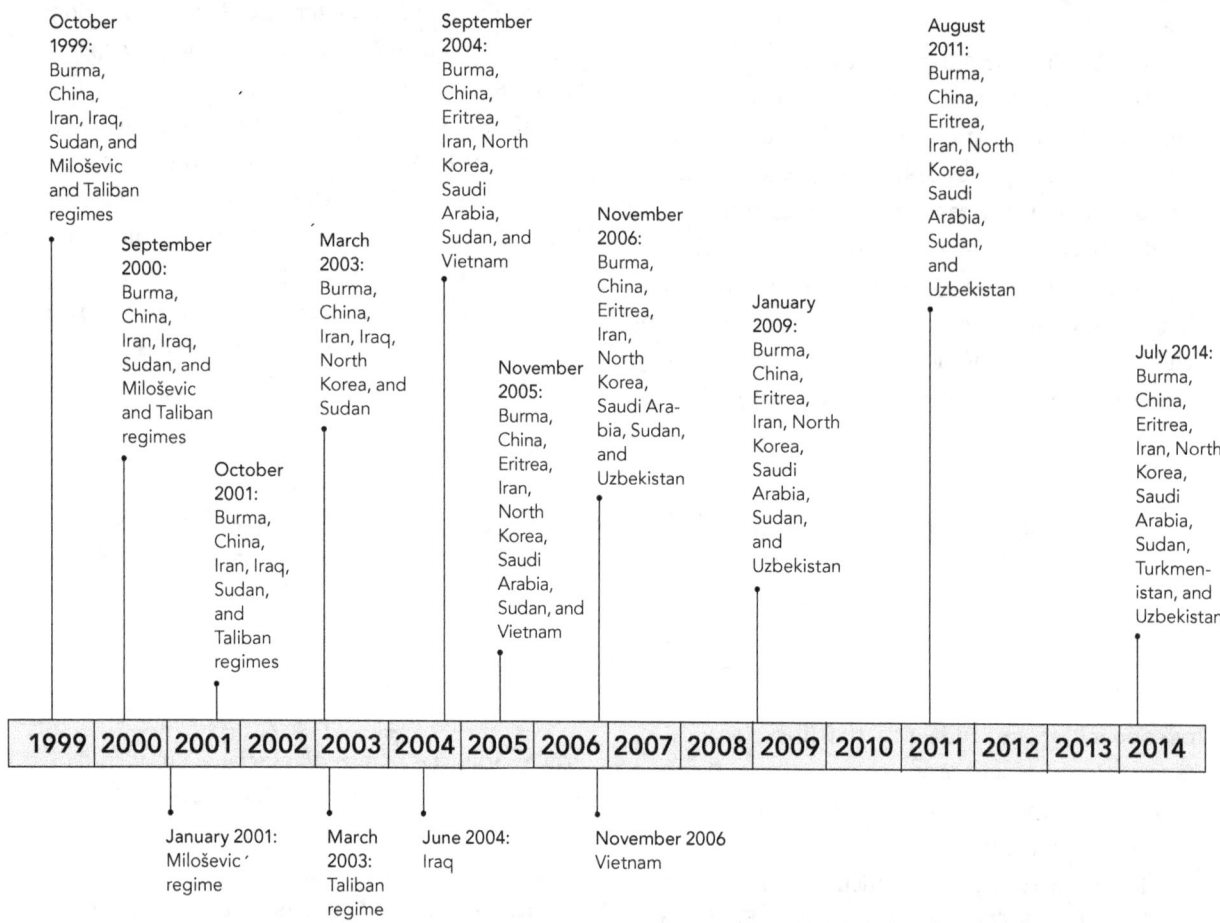

Source: GAO analysis of Department of State information

or waive the requirement of taking action to advance the purposes of the Act or the national interests of the United States.

However, in addition to designating the same countries for years, administrations generally have not levied new Presidential actions in accordance with CPC designations, with the State Department instead relying on pre-existing sanctions. While the statute permits such reliance, relying on pre-existing sanctions – or "double hatting" – has provided little incentive for CPC-designated governments to reduce or halt egregious violations of religious freedom.

The Presidential actions for the nine currently-designated CPC countries are shown in the table immediately below. Because of the indefinite waivers for Saudi Arabia, Turkmenistan, and Uzbekistan, the United States has not implemented a unique policy response tied to the CPC designation and particularly severe violations of religious freedom.

USCIRF welcomes Ambassador-at-Large Saperstein's commitment to have an annual CPC process. The CPC list should also expand and retract as conditions warrant, and the use of Presidential actions should be more dynamic. Of the current nine countries designated as CPCs, six have "double-hatted" sanctions, and three have indefinite waivers. The "double hatting" of sanctions can be the appropriate action in some circumstances. Yet specifically tailored actions can be more precise, either broadly structured or narrowly crafted to target specific government officials or provinces, if acute situations are highly localized. Indefinite waivers of penalties undermine the effectiveness of efforts to advance religious freedom, as they signal a lack of U.S. interest and communicate to the designated country that there never will be consequences for its religious freedom abuses.

Federal Register Notices / Vol. 79, No. 185 / Wednesday, September 24, 2014

Pursuant to section 408(a) of the International Religious Freedom Act of 1998 (Pub. L. 105–292), as amended (the Act), notice is hereby given that, on July 18, 2014, the Secretary of State, under authority delegated by the President, has designated each of the following as a "Country of Particular Concern" (CPC) under section 402(b) of the Act, for having engaged in or tolerated particularly severe violations of religious freedom: Burma, China, Eritrea, Iran, Democratic People's Republic of Korea, Saudi Arabia, Sudan, Turkmenistan, and Uzbekistan.

The Secretary simultaneously designated the following Presidential Actions for these CPCs:

- For **Burma**, the existing ongoing arms embargo referenced in 22 CFR 126.1(a) pursuant to section 402(c)(5) of the Act;

- For **China**, the existing ongoing restriction on exports to China of crime control and detection instruments and equipment, under the Foreign Relations Authorization Act of 1990 and 1991(Public Law 101–246), pursuant to section 402(c)(5) of the Act;

- For **Eritrea**, the existing ongoing arms embargo referenced in 22 CFR 126.1(a) pursuant to section 402(c)(5) of the Act;

- For **Iran**, the existing ongoing travel restrictions based on serious human rights abuses under section 221(a)(1)(C) of the Iran Threat Reduction and Syria Human Rights Act of 2012, pursuant to section 402(c)(5) of the Act;

- For **North Korea**, the existing ongoing restrictions to which North Korea is subject, pursuant to sections 402 and 409 of the Trade Act of 1974 (the Jackson-Vanik Amendment) pursuant to section 402(c)(5) of the Act;

- For **Saudi Arabia**, a waiver as required in the "important national interest of the United States," pursuant to section 407 of the Act;

- For **Sudan**, the restriction on making certain appropriated funds available for assistance to the Government of Sudan in the annual Department of State, Foreign Operations, and Related Programs Appropriations Act, currently set forth in section 7042(j) of the Department of State, Foreign Operations, and Related Programs Appropriations Act, 2014 (Div. K, Pub.L. 113–76), and any provision of law that is the same or substantially the same as this provision, pursuant to section 402(c)(5) of the Act;

- For **Turkmenistan**, a waiver as required in the "important national interest of the United States," pursuant to section 407 of the Act; and

- For **Uzbekistan**, a waiver as required in the "important national interest of the United States," pursuant to section 407 of the Act.

Along with an annual CPC process, the IRFA toolbox provides many options for diplomatic action. U.S. diplomatic engagement cannot and should not solely rely on naming CPCs, but rather use a concert of action including: diplomatic engagement; consultations about possible CPC action; CPC designations; binding agreement negotiations; presidential actions; and/or a waiver for the narrowest of circumstances. Past practice provides only a few

• Hold annual oversight hearings on IRFA implementation in the House and Senate.

Guidance

With multiple offices and positions dealing with issues that relate to or overlap with religious freedom, crafting a specific strategy outlining the need to promote

The CPC list should also expand and retract as conditions warrant, and the use of Presidential actions should be more dynamic.

examples of these tools being used together to bring about change in a country of concern. An annual CPC designation process should be the center of all IRF-related work, driving and energizing other areas of U.S. diplomacy, but should not be the sum total of all activity.

With respect to these issues, USCIRF recommends that the State Department:

• Use all of IRFA's tools, including "country of particular concern" designations, in a continuity of action;

• Publicly declare the results of its annual review of religious freedom conditions and make annual designations of "countries of particular concern" for particularly severe violations of religious freedom;

• Ensure that the CPC list expands and contracts as conditions warrant;

• Wherever possible, when Presidential Actions or commensurate actions are taken as a consequence of CPC designations, undertake specific efforts to emphasize the importance of religious freedom to the United States, and in particular avoid "double-hatted" sanctions; and

• Limit the use of waivers to a set period of time and subject them to review for renewal.

USCIRF recommends that Congress:

• Take steps through legislative action to require the State Department to make annual CPC designations, should the State Department fail to do so; and

freedom of religion or belief internationally across U.S. government agencies would set an important tone and give direction to U.S. efforts.

In February 2015, the President issued his second National Security Strategy, which touched on religious freedom. In a section entitled "Advance Equality," the Strategy said:

American values are reflective of the universal values we champion all around the world–including the freedoms of speech, worship, and peaceful assembly; the ability to choose leaders democratically; and the right to due process and equal administration of justice. We will be a champion for communities that are too frequently vulnerable to violence, abuse, and neglect– such as ethnic and religious minorities; people with disabilities; Lesbian, Gay, Bisexual, and Transgender (LGBT) individuals; displaced persons; and migrant workers.

The National Security Council issued a more specific strategy about religious engagement in July 2013, which includes a component on religious freedom and human rights. This positive initiative, on which USCIRF staff informally advised, connected religious freedom work to other related issues of conflict prevention and to engaging religious leaders on development goals. A document specifically tailored to the issue of religious freedom would further this effort.

In addition to a national strategy to guide U.S. efforts, elected leaders and U.S. officials need to communicate clearly and regularly that religious freedom is a foreign policy priority for the United States. For instance, during his January 2015 visit to India, President Obama gave a major speech highlighting the need for religious tolerance and freedom, and he reiterated the point at the February 2015 National Prayer Breakfast in Washington, DC. Notably, the Prime Minister of India subsequently gave a major address about these concerns. As this example demonstrates, one of the most direct ways to stress the importance of religious freedom is in high-profile

With respect to these issues, USCIRF recommends that:

- Each administration issue a strategy to guide U.S. government efforts to protect and promote religious freedom abroad and set up a process to oversee its implementation;

- The President, the Secretary of State, Members of Congress, and other U.S. officials consistently stress the importance of international religious freedom in

Crafting a specific strategy outlining the need to promote freedom of religion or belief internationally across U.S. government agencies would set an important tone and give direction to U.S. efforts.

public events. Both the U.S. government bureaucracy and foreign governments will notice such presentations by the President, the Secretary of State, Congressional leaders, and other high-ranking U.S. officials.

Action also is needed after communication. Public advocacy should be tied to a country-specific action plan or strategy for advancing religious freedom. This is especially important for countries designated as CPCs, as well as those recommended by USCIRF for CPC designation or on USCIRF's Tier 2 list. Such actions would include scheduling trips for embassy officials, including the U.S. ambassador, to visit oppressed religious communities or sites of violence. The United States should also insist that discussions on freedom of religion or belief and religious tolerance be included in various bilateral strategic dialogues and summits, such as the strategic dialogues with Russia, Pakistan, or Indonesia, or the meetings of the U.S.-Nigeria Bi-National Commission. Concerns about freedom of religion or belief should also be interwoven into negotiations over trade agreements, like the Trans-Pacific Partnership.

It is also essential to ensure that U.S. officials and elected leaders raise religious freedom issues during visits to key countries of concern. It is important for foreign leaders to hear directly from visiting delegations that restrictions on religious freedom are hindering bilateral cooperation and the overall relationship.

their public statements as well as in public and private meetings in the United States and abroad; and

- In consultation with USCIRF, the State Department develop and implement country-specific strategies for advancing religious freedom, interfaith harmony, mutual respect, and reconciliation, to ensure that official statements are followed by concrete actions.

Training

Training is needed to equip U.S. officials to speak on these issues and develop action plans. IRFA calls for American diplomats to receive training on how to promote religious freedom effectively around the world. In the past few years, training for Foreign Service Officers on issues of religious freedom has increased, but remains voluntary. The Foreign Service Institute (FSI) continued to offer a multi-day Religion and Foreign Policy course. USCIRF staff has been repeatedly invited to speak about the role of the Commission, but the overall focus could include a greater emphasis on promoting freedom of religion or belief. USCIRF also regularly speaks to regional studies classes to discuss the Commission's findings on countries of interest.

By contrast, DHS has made training on religious persecution and IRFA mandatory for all new refugee and asylum officers, and USCIRF and IRF Office representatives regularly speak to these classes. Over the years, USCIRF also has participated in, as well as submitted materials for, training sessions on religious freedom and religious persecution for Department of Justice immigration judges. Training on religious freedom issues in the military education system remains minimal, despite the many schools, military service colleges, and universities providing professional military education. With American service members increasingly engaging governments and societal leaders in religious contexts, training on international standards of freedom of religion or belief would better equip them to carry out their mission.

With respect to these issues, USCIRF recommends that the U.S. government:

- Make training on international religious freedom mandatory for State Department officials, including education on what it is, its importance, and how to advance it; Require such training at three intervals in each diplomat's career – the "A-100" class for incoming diplomats, Area Studies for midcareer officials, and a class for all ambassadors and deputy chiefs of missions; and

- Train relevant members of the military on the importance of religious freedom and practical ways to best promote it as an aspect of U.S. foreign policy.

USCIRF recommends that Congress:

- If necessary, require the Foreign Service Institute and the military to provide training on international religious freedom and on the best practices to promote it as an aspect of U.S. foreign policy, so that Foreign Service Officers, U.S. service members, and military chaplains can use globally recognized religious freedom standards when engaging in-country with religious leaders and government and military officials.

Ensuring Funding for Religious Freedom Programming

IRFA also envisaged the funding of religious freedom programs, authorizing foreign assistance to promote and develop "legal protections and cultural respect for religious freedom." In Fiscal Year (FY) 2008, for the first

time, $4 million was carved out from the Human Rights Democracy Fund (HRDF) for specific DRL grants on religious freedom programming. While no specific earmark or carve-out was made in subsequent years, the IRF Office has continued to receive HRDF funds. In March 2015, Ambassador Saperstein reported to Congress that the IRF Office receives approximately five percent of DRL's HRDF funding (approximately $3.5 million) annually. These funds support religious freedom programs currently operating in 16 countries. Ambassador Saperstein also reported in March 2015 that five new programs using FY 2014 funds would soon begin operations.

While IRFA authorizes the expenditures of funds for grant making to promote religious freedom, there is no annual appropriation of funds specifically for this purpose. Funding for religious freedom work need not come solely from the human rights bureau. Other potential funding sources include the State Department's Middle East Partnership Initiative (MEPI) and the U.S. Agency

> *While IRFA authorizes the expenditures of funds for grant making to promote religious freedom, there is no annual appropriation of funds specifically for this purpose.*

for International Development's (USAID) Bureau for Democracy, Conflict, and Humanitarian Assistance. Appropriation measures have signaled the importance of such funding. For instance, the Consolidated and Further Continuing Appropriations Act of 2015 (P.L. 113-325) directed that appropriated funds for democracy programs "shall be made available to support freedom of religion, including in the Middle East and North Africa."

In statute, report language, and discussions, Congress has at times tasked USCIRF to develop recommendations for challenging issues. In addition to the Expedited Removal Study, one such congressional tasking resulted in USCIRF's study about what Pakistan's education system teaches about religious minorities in that country. Another example was the special fellowship program that was funded for two years to enable scholars to focus on freedom of religion or belief.

With respect to these issues, USCIRF recommends that the State Department:

- Continue to designate specific HRDF funds to the IRF Office for grant making.

USCIRF recommends that Congress:

- Support State Department grants related to religious freedom programming, and call for entities that receive federal funds, including MEPI, USAID, the National Endowment for Democracy, and U.S. Institute of Peace, to devote resources for religious freedom programming;

- Encourage USAID to prioritize programs that develop and disseminate, especially in countries of concern, educational and teacher training materials that focus on international human rights standards and religious freedom and the centrality of interfaith understanding to achieving development objectives; and

- Urge that the National Endowment for Democracy and other entities that receive federal funding solicit competitive proposals on specific international religious freedom programming.

The Treatment of Asylum Seekers in Expedited Removal

As authorized by IRFA, USCIRF conducted a major research study in 2003 and 2004 on the U.S. government's treatment of asylum seekers in Expedited Removal. The Departments of Homeland Security (DHS) and Justice (DOJ) cooperated with the Commission, whose designated experts had unrestricted access to the internal workings of Expedited Removal.

USCIRF's February 2005 report, The Treatment of Asylum Seekers in Expedited Removal (the Study), found serious flaws placing legitimate asylum seekers at risk of being returned to countries where they could face persecution. It also found that asylum seekers were being inappropriately detained under prison-like conditions and in actual jails. To address these problems, the Study made a series of recommendations, none requiring Congressional action, to the responsible agencies within DHS and DOJ. The recommendations were geared to help protect U.S. borders and ensure fair and humane treatment for bona fide asylum seekers, mirroring the two goals of the 1996 immigration reform law that established Expedited Removal.

USCIRF has continued to monitor the implementation of these recommendations and has issued several follow-up reports finding progress in some areas but no changes in others. Moreover, since the time of the Study, DHS has expanded Expedited Removal from a port-of-entry program to one that covers the entire land and sea border of the United States. In addition, over the past several fiscal years, the number of individuals claiming a fear of return in Expedited Removal has increased sharply. As a result, the continuing flaws in the system now potentially affect even more asylum seekers.

In 2014, in anticipation of the 10th anniversary of the 2005 Study's release, USCIRF has been reviewing the current situation of asylum seekers in expedited removal, as an update to the original study. USCIRF staff has visited ports of entry, border posts, asylum offices, and immigration detention facilities in southern California (July 2014), New York and New Jersey (September 2014), Florida and Puerto Rico (November 2014) and south Texas (February 2015) to tour facilities, meet with officials and detainees, and observe processing. In addition, USCIRF staff has met with DHS officials in Washington, DC, and with non-governmental experts. USCIRF anticipates issuing in 2015 a special report assessing implementation of the study's recommendations and discussing the changes in expedited removal over the past decade.

With respect to these issues, USCIRF recommends that the Departments of Homeland Security and Justice

- Implement the recommendations from the 2005 Expedited Removal Study that remain either wholly or partly unimplemented, including by:

  - addressing the serious flaws identified in the initial interviews of arriving aliens;

  - allowing asylum officers to grant asylum at the credible fear stage in appropriate cases;

  - not detaining asylum seekers after credible fear has been found unless absolutely necessary and, if asylum seekers must be detained, doing so only in civil conditions;

  - codifying the existing parole policy into regulations; and

- increasing detainees' access to legal representation and in-person hearings.

USCIRF recommends that Congress:

- In light of Expedited Removal's expansion since the Study and the recent increase in claims of fear, consider authorizing and funding USCIRF to conduct another comprehensive study on the treatment of asylum seekers in Expedited Removal.

Multilateral Efforts

IRFA specifically cites U.S. participation in multilateral organizations as an avenue for advancing religious freedom. Both the United Nations (UN) and the Organization for Security and Cooperation in Europe (OSCE) have conventions and agreements that protect freedom of religion or belief and related rights, including assembly and expression. UN and OSCE mechanisms can be used to advance religious freedom or call attention to violations, on which USCIRF has engaged over the years.

United Nations

At the UN Human Rights Council, the Universal Periodic Review (UPR) process allows states to assess the human rights performance of every UN member state, and thereby provides an opportunity for the United States and other like-minded countries to ask questions and make recommendations about religious freedom. This is particularly important when countries designated as "countries of particular concern" under IRFA are reviewed. Country-specific resolutions in the Human Rights Council and the UN General Assembly

focuses on religious freedom as a thematic issue. That position was created in 1986, at the initiative of the United States. The UN Special Rapporteur on Freedom of Religion or Belief – currently Professor Heiner Bielefeldt of Germany – monitors freedom of religion or belief worldwide, communicates with governments about alleged violations, conducts country visits, and issues reports and statements. Some of the Council's country-specific Special Procedures also have drawn attention to religious freedom violations in the countries they cover, such as the current UN Special Rapporteur on the Human Rights Situation in Iran, Ahmed Shaheed. In addition, the specially-created Commissions of Inquiry on North Korea and on Eritrea focused on the severe religious freedom abuses in those nations.

For a number of years, the UN Human Rights Council and General Assembly were the centers of a problematic effort by the Organization of Islamic Cooperation (OIC) and some of its members to seek an international legal norm restricting speech that defamed religions, particularly Islam. In a welcome change, the OIC no longer is sponsoring the flawed and divisive defamation-of-religions resolutions. They were replaced in 2011 by a new, consensus approach (often referred to as the Resolution 16/18 approach, after the first such resolution) that focuses on positive measures to counter religious intolerance and protect individuals from discrimination or violence, rather than on criminalizing expression.

Nevertheless, USCIRF remains concerned that some OIC members continue to support a global anti-blasphemy law. Many OIC member states continue to have and enforce repressive domestic blasphemy and religious defamation laws. These laws result in gross human rights abuses and exacerbate

---

UN and OSCE mechanisms can be used to advance religious freedom or call attention to violations, on which USCIRF has engaged over the years.

---

provide other opportunities to highlight religious freedom concerns.

The Human Rights Council's system of independent experts, or Special Procedures, is another important mechanism, particularly the Special Rapporteur who

religious intolerance, discrimination, and violence, the very problems that the OIC claims it is trying to address. In addition, some OIC countries continue to refer publicly to the defamation-of-religions concept and call for international laws against it, including in the context of the "Istanbul Process," a series of international meetings launched in 2011 to discuss the implementation of the Resolution 16/18 approach. The Arab League also has been considering a regional model law against the defamation of religions.

With respect to these issues, USCIRF recommends that the State Department:

- Continue to use the UN Human Rights Council's Universal Periodic Review process, as well as country-specific resolutions in both the Human Rights Council and the UN General Assembly, to shine a light on religious freedom violations in specific countries, especially those designated as CPCs under IRFA;

- Continue its vigorous support of the mandate and work of the UN Special Rapporteur on Freedom of Religion or Belief, including by working to secure sufficient assistance to support the Rapporteur in carrying out this volunteer position;

- Work for the creation of additional country-specific Special Rapporteur positions, especially for CPC countries;

- Remain vigilant against any renewed efforts at the UN to seek legal limitations on offensive or controversial speech about religion that does not constitute incitement to violence, and continue to press countries to adhere to the Resolution 16/18 approach, including by repealing blasphemy laws.

OSCE

The Organization for Security and Cooperation in Europe (OSCE), comprised of 57 participating States from Europe, the former Soviet Union, Mongolia, the United States, and Canada, continues to be an important forum for holding those states to extensive international standards on freedom of religion or belief and to combat hate crimes, discrimination, xenophobia, intolerance, and anti-Semitism. In recent years, however, some OSCE-participating States, led by Russia, have sought to curtail the OSCE's human rights activities in favor of a security focus and have tried to limit the participation of NGOs, particularly in the annual Human Dimension (HDim) meeting in Warsaw, Europe's largest human rights conference.

In 2012, the OSCE's Office of Democratic Institutions and Human Rights (ODIHR) re-launched its Advisory Panel of Experts on Freedom of Religion or Belief. The Panel reviews proposed or enacted legislation against international and OSCE commitments, and provides expert opinions and guidelines. The Panel previously was composed of 60 persons nominated by OSCE countries, including a 15-member Advisory Council appointed by the ODIHR Director. The restructure resulted in a much smaller panel with 12 members. In 2014, ODIHR issued guidelines, on which the Panel advised, about OSCE norms on recognizing religious or belief communities. As part of its continuing cooperation with other international organizations, the ODIHR Director and the UN High Commissioner for Human Rights signed a joint declaration in June 2014 to increase their combined work to promote and protect human rights, democracy, the rule of law, tolerance, non-discrimination, and gender equality.

In early 2015, ODIHR hired a new advisor on freedom of religion or belief for its staff, filling a position vacant for some years. The advisor will be placed in the Human Rights Section, instead of the Tolerance Unit. USCIRF had recommended this move, as religious freedom is not merely an issue of tolerance but also encompasses a full range of human rights concerns, such as the freedoms of assembly, association, and expression.

Since their inception in 1992, OSCE Field Operations have become a key feature of the organization, including in the human rights sphere. Each has its own mandate drawn up with the host government, but more recent mandates provide decreased scope for human rights activities. At present, there are six field offices in South East Europe, two in Eastern Europe, three in the South Caucasus and five in Central Asia. The OSCE office in Tajikistan worked with the host country government and civil society to build local human rights capacity. In May 2014, the OSCE office in Turkmenistan held a training session for government officials by British specialists on international religious freedom standards. Freedom of religion or belief was also the focus of training courses for lawyers, human rights defenders, and journalists in Armenia in April and May of 2014. Despite Azerbaijan's sharply deteriorating record on freedom of religion or belief, the

OSCE office in Baku cooperated with the Azerbaijani government to co-sponsor a 2014 religious tolerance conference. The head of the OSCE Baku office also has made public statements supporting the government of Azerbaijan's positions on religious tolerance and religious freedom. ODIHR should make greater efforts to ensure consistency on issues of religious freedom and related human rights, including by providing training for staff.

The OSCE recently has also become more involved in efforts to counter violent extremism and terrorism in the name of religion. For example, in 2008, the ODIHR issued a manual to familiarize states' senior policy makers with basic international human rights standards to which they must adhere in efforts to combat terrorism and extremism. In 2014, the OSCE held regional anti-terrorism training meetings in Tajikistan and Kazakhstan, while in November 2014 ODIHR organized a training session for police in combating terrorism. In March

Working with Like-Minded Nations

There are increasing opportunities for the U.S. government to work in concert with like-minded nations around freedom of religion or belief. The United States is no longer the only player in this field. The United Kingdom's foreign ministry and parliament have increased their focus, the European Union issued guidelines for its diplomats in the field on promoting freedom of religion or belief, and the European Parliament established a working group on the subject. Canada also created an ambassadorial position on religious freedom. The Austrians, Dutch, Italians, Norwegians, and Germans also have focused specifically on religious freedom over the past five years. Recently, USCIRF has taken the lead in fostering increased collaboration between the United States, Canada, and a number of European countries in promoting freedom of religion or belief. This effort is now expanding to other parts of the world.

There are increasing opportunities for the U.S. government to work in concert with like-minded nations around freedom of religion or belief.

2015, ODIHR held a "train-the-trainer" session on respecting human rights in combating violent extremism, as well as an experts' meeting on human rights and responding to foreign fighters.

With respect to these issues, USCIRF recommends that the State Department:

- Urge ODIHR to empower the new Advisory Panel to act independently and issue reports or critiques and conduct activities without undue interference by ODIHR or participating States;

- Request that the new advisor on freedom of religion or belief be adequately resourced to effectively monitor religious freedom abuses across the OSCE area and to provide training for staff of OSCE field offices; and

- Encourage OSCE missions to fully integrate religious freedom and related human rights into counter-terrorism training and other relevant programs.

In early 2014, USCIRF Commissioners and staff met with members of the British All Parties Parliamentary Group on Freedom of Religion or Belief in London and cosponsored with the European Parliament Working Group on Freedom of Religion or Belief (EPWG) an unprecedented joint event in the European Parliament. In Brussels, the event USCIRF cosponsored with the EPWG filled the room to its maximum capacity of 200 people. In November 2014, USCIRF, working alongside a group of parliamentarians from Brazil, Canada, Norway, Turkey, and the United Kingdom, helped launch a new parliamentary network, the Inter-Parliamentary Platform for Freedom of Religion or Belief, at the Nobel Peace Center in Oslo, Norway. Over 30 MPs signed the Charter for Freedom of Religion or Belief, pledging to advance religious freedom for all. A direct outcome of the meeting was the creation of a caucus in the Brazilian Congress to promote international religious freedom. In addition, the parliamentary group has sent letters to the Prime Minister of Pakistan, the President of Burma, and the North Korean ambassador to the United Nations relating to religious freedom issues in those countries.

Paired with any parliamentary effort should be coordinated inter-governmental activities. Officials from the United States, Canada, the United Kingdom, and the EU External Action Service have recognized this need. Efforts are beginning to coordinate joint demarches on countries of common concern, as well as to share information about how governments fund religious freedom work in the field. While coordinating government action may pose challenges, the power of many voices is sure to have greater impact.

With respect to these issues, USCIRF recommends that the State Department:

- Continue to work with other governments and parliaments interested in promoting international religious freedom to share information and coordinate activities.

The Role of Congress

Congress has an important role to play to ensure that religious freedom remains a priority to the U.S. government. Hearings are a particularly useful tool, as they signal Congressional interest in international religious freedom. For example, subcommittees of the House of Representatives Committee on Foreign Affairs have held hearings focusing on holding accountable countries of particular concern, the issuance of the

protecting religious freedom abroad. The Tom Lantos Human Rights Commission has held several hearings on religious freedom, including religious minorities in India, religious and indigenous communities in Vietnam, prisoners of conscience, and religious minorities in Iran. Holding annual Congressional oversight hearings on IRFA implementation in both the House and Senate would reinforce Congressional interest in the issue.

As religious freedom problems are interwoven into some of the most difficult foreign policy challenges facing the United States, both houses of Congress should ensure that religious freedom issues are included in specific country hearings and ambassadorial confirmation hearings. In addition, Members of Congress should continue to use appropriations bills and supporting report language to express congressional concerns to both our own government and other governments. While creating the new Senate Human Rights Caucus is an important step, creating a Senate caucus on international religious freedom, similar to the existing House caucus, would also serve an important function.

Another example of congressional action is the Defending Freedoms Project, an initiative of the Tom Lantos Human Rights Commission, in conjunction with USCIRF and Amnesty International USA. Through the project, Members of Congress advocate on behalf of prisoners abroad, work toward their release, and shine a spotlight on the laws and policies that have led to their incarceration. The goal of this

Congress has an important role to play to ensure that religious freedom remains a priority to the U.S. government.

State Department's IRF Report and USCIRF's Annual Report, as well as country-specific religious freedom issues. The National Security Subcommittee of the House Oversight and Government Reform Committee for two years in a row has held a hearing on protecting international religious freedom. The Senate Appropriations Subcommittee on State, Foreign Operations and Related Programs held a hearing in March 2015 on

project is to help set free these prisoners and increase attention to and support for human rights and religious freedom.

With respect to these issues, USCIRF recommends that:

- Both the House and Senate hold annual oversight hearings on IRFA implementation, as well as hearings on religious freedom-specific issues, and ensure that religious freedom is raised in country-specific hearings and ambassadorial confirmation hearings; and

- During delegation trips abroad, Members of Congress examine conditions of religious freedom for all faiths/beliefs, and meet with individuals and organizations that promote religious freedom and related human rights, targeted religious communities, and people detained for their religious beliefs or religious freedom advocacy.

Dissenting Statement of Vice Chair James J. Zogby:

I voted against some of the recommendations in this chapter because I cannot support USCIRF calling on Congress to micro-manage the way the State Department and the White House National Security Council organize their staff and set their priorities.

We are united in our commitment to advance religious freedom but recommending that important offices of the Executive Branch play musical chairs with the positions they currently have in place or that they add more chairs to the game both exceeds our mandate and has the potential of making an admittedly cumbersome and sometime confusing bureaucracy even more cumbersome and confusing.

We can advocate that attention be paid to advancing religious freedom, but it is up to the President and the Secretary of State - not USCIRF - to decide how the Executive Branch should configure their offices and expend their resources in furthering that goal.

Additional Statement of Chair Katrina Lantos Swett, with whom Vice Chair Robert P. George and Commissioners Mary Ann Glendon, M. Zuhdi Jasser, and Daniel I. Mark join:

As I conclude my second term as USCIRF Chair and enter my final year as a Commissioner, I want to thank USCIRF's dedicated team for their diligence, hard work, and professionalism. The Annual Report is a task of herculean proportions, with USCIRF analysts gathering facts and data from numerous sources around the world, vetting the data, and drafting the chapters and recommendations. Based on those drafts and working with staff, Commissioners are able to produce what I

have consistently referred to as the "gold standard" of U.S. government reports on religious freedom. As the Government Accountability Office found when surveying non-governmental organizations, our report is highly valued and sought after because of its impartiality, factual nature, and inventive and creative ideas for how the U.S. government could better position itself in the 21st century to advance religious freedom.

In addition, I have had the opportunity to travel with Commissioners and USCIRF analysts to Bahrain, Egypt, Nigeria, Pakistan, Saudi Arabia, and elsewhere. I have been repeatedly impressed by USCIRF staff with their knowledge of the issues relating to international religious freedom, their contacts with U.S. government officials and NGOs, their nonpartisan approach to the issue, and their dedication to help ensure that the United States more effectively advances this fundamental freedom for all persons everywhere. Our government is well served by this team of dedicated public servants including USCIRF's able Executive Director, Ambassador Jackie Wolcott.

Additional Statement of Commissioners Eric P. Schwartz and Hannah Rosenthal and Vice Chair James J. Zogby:

Our chapter on implementation of the International Religious Freedom Act (IRFA) addresses many aspects of the legislation, but it does not address in great detail the operations or overall effectiveness of the U.S. Commission on International Religious Freedom itself, which, of course, was created by the IRFA legislation. We believe that the Commission has played an important role in keeping issues of religious freedom on the policy agenda, and in keeping faith with victims of abuses around the world. But we also believe there are ways that the Commission can be more effective in its work. We hope the upcoming reauthorization discussion will provide an opportunity to explore several important issues in our efforts to protect religious freedom, such as whether we are most effectively critiquing, engaging and, where appropriate, complementing the work of the Department of State and the Administration, whether we can enhance Commissioner-Commission staff relations and safeguard staff professionalism, independence and impartiality over time, how we should address new challenges posed by non-state actors, and how we might better engage issues of religious reconciliation even as we continue to focus on issues of basic rights. We look forward to considering these and other issues in the months to come.

TIER 1

2015 COUNTRY REPORTS: CPCS DESIGNATED BY THE STATE DEPARTMENT AND RECOMMENDED BY USCIRF

–BURMA

–CHINA

–ERITREA

–IRAN

–NORTH KOREA

–SAUDI ARABIA

–SUDAN

–TURKMENISTAN

–UZBEKISTAN

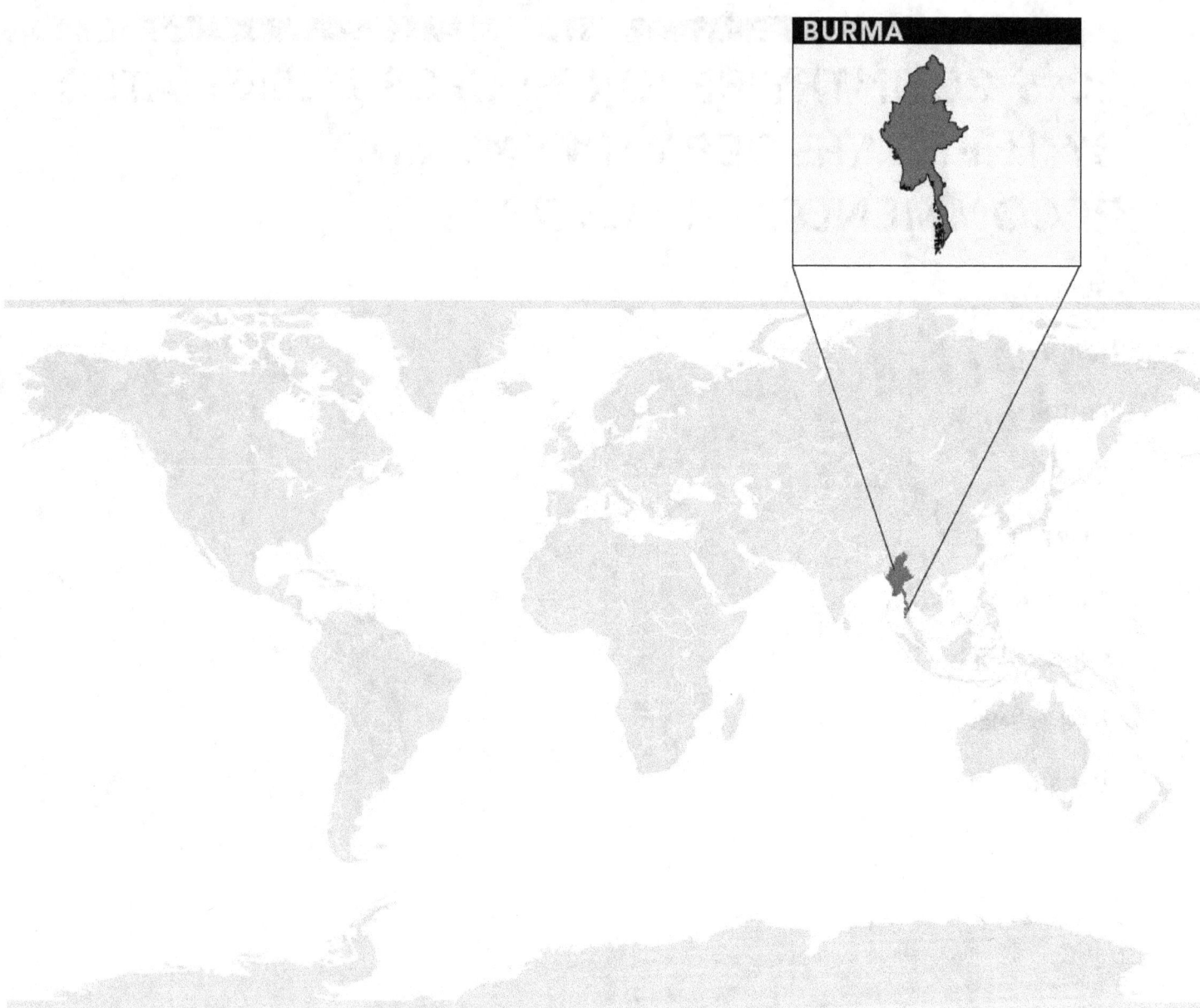

BURMA

Key Findings

In 2014, religious and ethnic minorities in Burma continued to experience intolerance, discrimination, and violence, particularly Rohingya Muslims. Bigotry and chauvinism against religious and ethnic minorities grew more pervasive, in some cases provoked by religious figures within the Buddhist community, while the Burmese government demonstrated little willingness to intervene, investigate properly, or prosecute those responsible for abuses in a timely and transparent manner. While the government, at times, denounced violence and incitement, its lack of strong and consistent leadership to condemn intolerance enabled abuses to continue relatively unchecked. Throughout 2014, the expansion of Internet availability and social media played a role in propagating expressions of hatred and spurring violence directed against minority populations. The introduction of four discriminatory race and religion bills in 2014 could well further entrench such prejudices. Based on these systematic, egregious, and ongoing violations, USCIRF continues to recommend in 2015 that Burma be designated as a "country of particular concern," or CPC, under the International Religious Freedom Act (IRFA). The State Department has designated Burma a CPC since 1999, most recently in July 2014.

Background

In August 2014, USCIRF conducted a commissioner-level visit to Burma, issuing a special report of its findings in November 2014. The visit not only confirmed USCIRF's concerns about religious freedom violations against religious and ethnic minorities, especially Rohingya Muslims, but also underscored the appropriateness of Burma's designation as a CPC.

Burma has undertaken notable political reforms in a relatively short period of time, a process likely to receive even more scrutiny as the 2015 general elections approach. However, these steps have not yet improved conditions for religious freedom and related human rights in the country, nor spurred the Burmese government to curtail those perpetrating abuses. The vast majority of the population – nearly 90 percent – is Buddhist; four percent is Muslim; four percent is Christian; and the remainder is animist or follows other faiths or beliefs. Constitutional protections for religious freedoms in Burma are not sufficient to protect those of

> *Rather than reforming current laws to strengthen or expand protections for religious rights, the government has facilitated the development of legislation that would further impinge on these freedoms.*

minority religious faiths from discrimination, violence, or targeted crimes. Rather than reforming current laws to strengthen or expand protections for religious rights, the government has facilitated the development of legislation that would further impinge on these freedoms. For example, at the prompting of nationalist Buddhists and with the support of the central government, Burma's 2015 session of parliament opened with consideration of a package of four race and religion bills that would further restrict religious freedom and discriminate against all minority faiths in matters of conversions, marriages, and births. Critics argue the bills are a means to restrict the rights of Muslims, but they also restrict the rights of women, the very constituency the architects of the legislation are purporting to protect. A combined 180 women's groups and civil society organizations in Burma delivered a statement in January 2015 in strong opposition to all four bills. Some of those who have spoken publicly against these bills have been harassed and even received death threats.

Politically, the absence thus far of a national reconciliation agreement with ethnic minority groups and lack of meaningful constitutional reform looms over Burma's government as it heads into the critical 2015 general elections. The 2014 census, Burma's first in more than 30 years, largely excluded Rohingya Muslims if they identified their ethnicity as Rohingya, and counts of ethnic minorities were not conducted in large parts of Kachin State. President Thein Sein did not make good on his pledge for the government to release all political prisoners by the end of 2013, and has left unfulfilled a number of other commitments made publicly to President Barack Obama and others. USCIRF met with representatives of both an ad hoc religious affairs advisory group created by the president and the Ministry of Religious Affairs, and found their contradictory perspectives on issues of religious freedom to be concerning.

Visits to Burma and expressions of concern by high-level UN representatives about religious and ethnic minorities were met with rebukes, protests, and even vitriolic language from Rakhine State and national-level officials, as well as Buddhist monks.

Religious Freedom Conditions 2014–2015

Anti-Muslim Violence and the Plight of Rohingya Muslims

In northern Rakhine State in January 2014, violence directed at Rohingya Muslims resulted in the deaths of at least 40 people. The government's investigation concluded that only a policeman was killed in the violence, effectively denying the civilian Rohingya deaths despite detailed information provided by Médecins Sans Frontières (MSF) and others. MSF's role in reporting publicly the killings contributed to its nearly year-long expulsion from Burma. Other international organizations have had difficulty trying to provide assistance to Rohingya Muslims in Rakhine State, mostly due to the reactions of frustrated Rakhine Buddhists who view such aid to Rohinga Muslims as one-sided when the entire state faces poverty and low development.

Inter-communal violence in Mandalay in July 2014 resulted in the deaths of two men – one Muslim and one

Buddhist – as well as several injuries and vandalized property, including the burning of a mosque and several Qur'ans inside. The incident was spurred by a blog post about an alleged rape, later proven to be fabricated, that was circulated online and posted to the Facebook page of extremist monk U Ashin Wirathu. Notably, the violence, which led to a city-wide curfew, could have been much worse had it not been for the efforts of the Mandalay Peace Keeping Committee, a non-governmental group comprised of religious and community leaders of various faiths, and others who intervened during the riots to prevent the situation from deteriorating further. USCIRF visited Mandalay and met with the Peace Keeping Committee.

Displacement from past inter-communal violence continues, including of Rohingya and other Muslims

> *Inter-communal violence in Mandalay in July 2014 resulted in the deaths of two men – one Muslim and one Buddhist – as well as several injuries and vandalized property, including the burning of a mosque and several Qur'ans inside.*

throughout Rakhine State since June 2012 and of both Muslims and Buddhists in the city of Meiktila since March 2013. USCIRF's visit to the camps for internally displaced persons in Meiktila revealed that much progress remains in finding a durable solution for both communities.

Rohingya Muslims in Burma face a unique level of discrimination, disenfranchisement, and the denial of basic rights. The government denies them citizenship, which precludes them from ever attaining equal status in law or practice. They also are denied the right to self-identify as Rohingya because many, including the government, claim that they are illegal "Bengali" immigrants. In fact, a partially implemented pilot verification program in Rakhine State forced Rohingya Muslims to identify as Bengali if they wanted to apply for citizenship, or face indefinite confinement in camps with limited rights, mobility, and access to services.

Government representatives at both the central level and within Rakhine State have reacted strongly to the use of the term Rohingya by the international community, particularly the United Nations. Rohingya Muslims are also now among those who will be ineligible to vote in the constitutional referendum expected in May 2015 and likely the general elections later in the year. More than 100,000 Rohingya are estimated to have fled Burma by boat since 2012, seeking a better life but often facing trafficking, exploitation, and deplorable living conditions.

Abuses Targeting Ethnic Minority Christians

Predominantly Christian areas, such as Kachin and Chin States, continue to experience discriminatory practices. Continuing the long-standing practice of removing crosses, in January 2015, the government of Chin State ordered the removal of a cross and sought charges against a Chin man they accuse of erecting it. Chin groups are among those publicly opposed to the package of race and religion bills, noting that the religious conversion bill would give Buddhist state officials the power to approve or disapprove religious conversions even though the vast majority of the state's population is Christian. In January 2015, two Kachin Christian women who were volunteering as teachers with the Kachin Baptist Convention were raped and murdered in Shan State. At the time of this report's writing, the police investigation was still ongoing; an investigation conducted by the Kachin Baptist Convention determined villagers where the women lived were not involved. Those in the Kachin community believe the act was carried out by the Burmese army, which has used sexual and gender-based violence as weapons of war in ethnic areas in the past. Some have speculated the two women may have been targeted because of their work as Christian missionaries. The U.S. government was among the many voices calling on Burmese officials to investigate and bring the perpetrators to justice.

Religious Intolerance and Expressions of Hate

Expressions of intolerance toward Muslims by senior political and Buddhist leaders are on the rise in Burma, particularly among those who seek to advance anti-Muslim agendas of hate and discrimination. The growing use of social media to communicate messages of intolerance has exacerbated tensions and encouraged violence. However, intolerance is not only limited to online platforms or attacks on Muslims; those rejecting anti-Muslim hatred and discrimination have also been targeted. For example, former National League for Democracy (NLD) official Htin Lin Oo is facing criminal charges of religious defamation and hurting religious feelings for speaking out, in his capacity as a writer, against religious nationalism and the use of Buddhism for extremist purposes in a public speech at an October 2014 literary event. After drawing the ire of Buddhist monks for allegedly insulting the faith, NLD relieved him of his position within the party and he was formally detained and indicted in December 2014. He faces three years in jail.

U.S. Policy

In 2014, Burma chaired the Association of Southeast Asian Nations (ASEAN). Owing to the United States' participation in the ASEAN Regional Forum and the East Asia Summit, the year saw high-profile visits to the country by both President Obama and Secretary of State

> *Expressions of intolerance toward Muslims by senior political and Buddhist leaders are on the rise in Burma, particularly among those who seek to advance anti-Muslim agendas of hate and discrimination.*

John Kerry, as well as other high ranking U.S. government officials. Human rights and religious freedom issues were regularly raised both publicly and privately by the Administration during these visits, including President Obama's trip in November 2014 and during the U.S.-Burma Human Rights Dialogue held in January 2015. Ahead of President Obama's visit, the Administration announced it was placing parliamentarian Aung Thaung on the list of "specially designated nationals" as a means to sanction him for his role in undermining reforms in Burma, including his assumed role in activities that have inflamed religious and ethnic tensions, such as violence against Muslims.

The United States provides a variety of assistance programs to Burma, primarily in the areas of economic and democratic development. Although the U.S. arms embargo on Burma is still in effect, the Obama Administration has sought to begin military-to-military cooperation. In response, the U.S. Congress put in place congressional oversight of this cooperation through the National Defense Authorization Act of 2015, which restricts the Department of Defense's engagement to areas such as human rights training programs and cooperation on humanitarian aid and disaster relief. Moreover, the 2015 Omnibus Spending Bill expressly prohibits funding under foreign military financing and international military education and training. Critics have suggested that military cooperation with Burma is premature given that the military is still an entrenched part of the government and due to the ongoing military incursions into ethnic minority areas in the absence of a nationwide ceasefire agreement.

The U.S. government has designated Burma as a CPC since 1999, most recently in July 2014. The long-standing Presidential action for this designation, the existing arms embargo referenced above, remains in place. In USCIRF's meetings in Naypyidaw during the August 2014 trip, parliamentarians inquired about the possibility of Burma being removed from the CPC list. One of these same parliamentarians also directed this question to the deputy minister for foreign affairs during a debate in the Upper House in February 2015. However, the discussion centered on accusing the United States of trying to control Burma, rather than the steps the country could take to improve conditions for religious freedom. Although the debate mischaracterized the intent and purpose of the CPC designation, the fact that it occurred indicates a certain discomfort with the classification. Burma's Minister of Foreign Affairs, U Wunna Maung Lwin, conveyed a similar uneasiness with international scrutiny in his September 2014 address to the UN General Assembly, when he prematurely suggested Burma has addressed "all major concerns related to human rights" and should be removed from the UN Human Rights Council's agenda.

Recommendations

In light of the lack of momentum on human rights related reforms in Burma, the United States and the international community should continue to press the government of Burma to prioritize religious freedom and related human rights. Respecting the rights and dignity of religious and ethnic minorities, particularly Rohingya Muslims, is critical to the reform process, and the United States should continue to stress this consistently at every level of its engagement with Burma. In addition to recommending the U.S. government sustain pressure on the government of Burma at the highest levels and continue to designate Burma as a CPC, USCIRF recommends the U.S. government should:

- Enter into a binding agreement with the government of Burma, as authorized under section 405(c) of IRFA, setting forth mutually-agreed commitments that would foster critical reforms to improve religious freedom and establish a pathway that could lead to Burma's eventual removal from the CPC list, including but not limited to the following:

  - taking concrete steps to end violence and policies of discrimination against religious and ethnic minorities, including the investigation and prosecution of those perpetrating or inciting violence; and

  - lifting all restrictions inconsistent with international standards on freedom of religion or belief;

- Engage the government of Burma, the Buddhist community and especially its leaders, and religious minorities on issues of religious freedom, tolerance, inclusivity, and reconciliation to assist them in promoting understanding among people of different religious faiths and to impress upon them the dangers of de-linking political improvements from improvements in religious tolerance and religious freedom;

- Use the term Rohingya, both publicly and privately, in respect for the Rohingya Muslim community's right to identify as they choose;

- Encourage crucial legal and legislative reform that strengthens protections for religious and ethnic minorities, including citizenship for the Rohingya population through the review, amendment, or repeal the 1982 Citizenship Law or some other means, and support the proper training of local government officials, lawyers, judges, police, and security forces tasked with implementing, enforcing, and interpreting the rule of law;

- Continue to support the unconditional release of all persons detained for the peaceful exercise of religious freedom and related human rights;

- Continue to use the leverage of the "specially designated nationals" list by the Treasury Department's Office of Foreign Asset Control (OFAC) with respect to individuals who have participated in human rights abuses, including religious freedom violations, such as by instigating, carrying out, or supporting publicly anti-Muslim violence and discrimination;

- Apply section 604(a) of IRFA to deny visas to or admission into the United State by Burmese government officials responsible for or known to have directly carried out particularly severe violations of religious freedom; and

- Renew beyond May 2015 the designation of a National Emergency with Respect to Burma pursuant to the International Emergency Economic Powers Act, 50 U.S.C. 1701-1706, based on the ongoing nature of intercommunal violence and humanitarian crises throughout Burma.

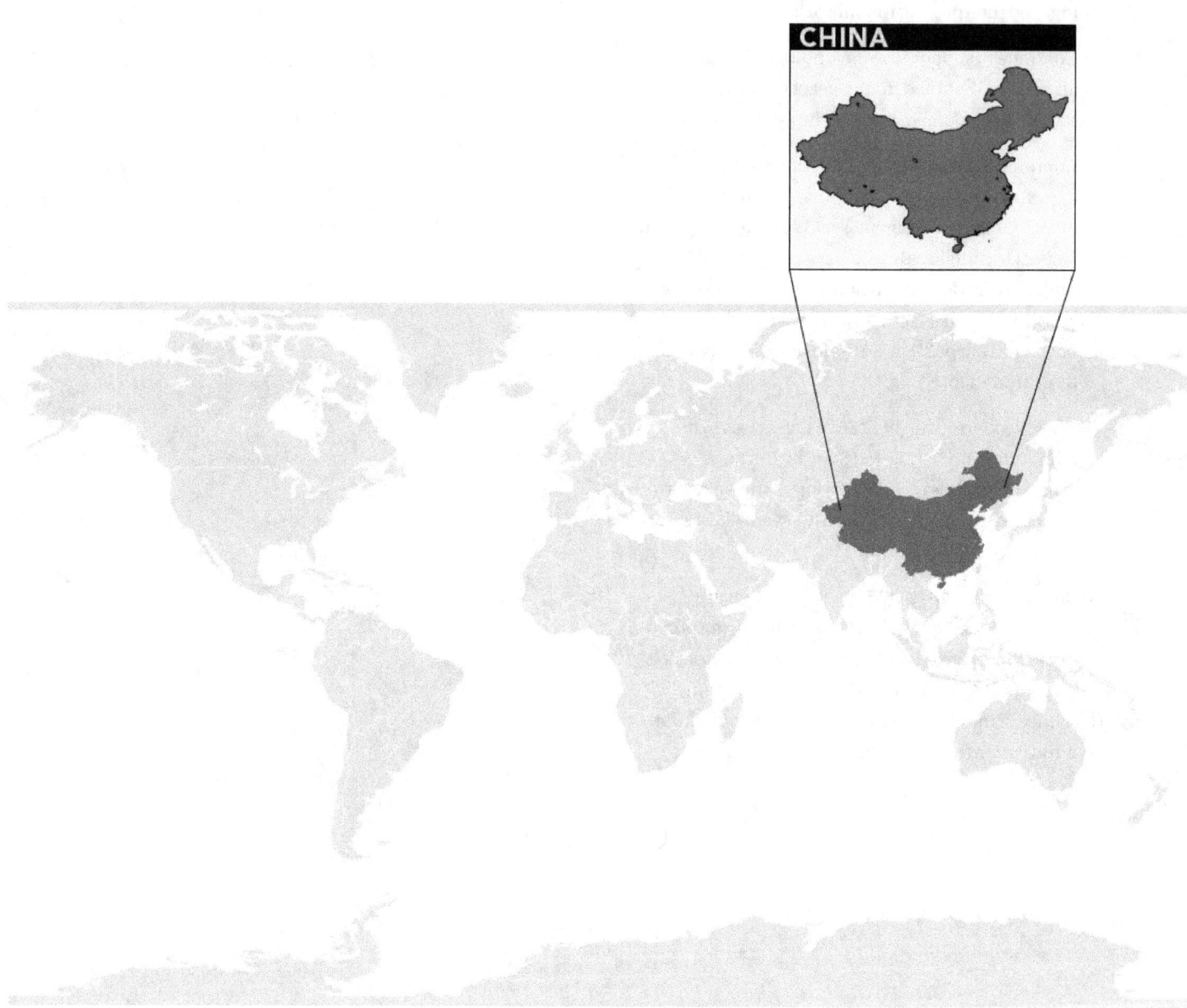

CHINA

Key Findings

In 2014, the Chinese government took steps to consolidate further its authoritarian monopoly of power over all aspects of its citizens' lives. For religious freedom, this has meant unprecedented violations against Uighur Muslims, Tibetan Buddhists, Catholics, Protestants, and Falun Gong practitioners. People of faith continue to face arrests, fines, denials of justice, lengthy prison sentences, and in some cases, the closing or bulldozing of places of worship. Based on the alarming increase in systematic, egregious, and ongoing abuses, USCIRF again recommends China be designated a "country of particular concern," or CPC, under the International Religious Freedom Act (IRFA). The State Department has designated China as a CPC since 1999, most recently in July 2014.

Background

The Chinese Constitution states that it guarantees freedom of religion. However, only so-called "normal religions" – those belonging to one of the five state-sanctioned "patriotic religious associations" associated with the five officially-recognized religions (Buddhism, Taoism, Islam, Catholicism, and Protestantism) – can register with the government and legally hold worship services and conduct religious activities. The government and Chinese Communist Party are officially atheist, with more than 700 million persons unaffiliated with any religion or belief. However, religious followers are strong and reportedly on the rise: more than 294 million practice folk religions, more than 240 million Buddhism, 68 million Christianity, and nearly 25 million Islam. The Chinese government monitors strictly religious activities, including by those recognized by the state, but unregistered groups and their members are especially vulnerable. For example, although Christianity is state-sanctioned, the government continues to engage in severe violations of religious freedom against both registered and unregistered Catholics and Protestants. Some have characterized the new wave of persecution against Christians that swept through China in 2014 as the most egregious and persistent since the Cultural Revolution. Nevertheless, the number of religious followers, of Christianity in particular, is considered to be growing.

In the name of fighting terrorism, Chinese officials' increased religious persecution of Uighur Muslims in the autonomous region of Xinjiang has gone hand-in-hand with the growing number of violent episodes there, creating a perpetual cycle of government repression, violent Uighur reprisals, and deadly force by the Chinese police. Both central and regional government officials have undertaken pre-emptive security and punitive legal measures.

The Chinese communist regime, which celebrated its 65th anniversary in October 2014, views ideologies that promote freedom of speech, civil society, genuine rule of law, and human rights as directly undermining

> *People of faith continue to face arrests, fines, denials of justice, lengthy prison sentences, and in some cases, the closing or bulldozing of places of worship.*

its control. As a result, all-around repression in China worsened in 2014, including the government's aggressiveness in controlling Tibet, Xinjiang, and even Hong Kong, as well as stricter controls on the Internet and social media and targeting of human rights defenders, civil society activists, journalists and academics. For example, Pu Zhiqiang, a prominent human-rights lawyer, was charged in June 2014 with creating a disturbance, inciting ethnic hatred, and separatism based on his postings on Sina Weibo, a popular blog service; he was detained just prior to the 25th anniversary of the Tiananmen Square incident. Other human rights defenders also face arbitrary detention, harassment, intimidation, or imprisonment. Another human rights lawyer, Gao Zhisheng, was finally released in August 2014 but remains under constant surveillance and has been denied freedom of movement to seek proper medical care or to be reunited with his family, who fled to the United States.

Religious Freedom Conditions 2014–2015

Uighur Muslims

On May 25, 2014, just days after Uighur suicide bombings at an Urumqi marketplace killed 39 people and injured nearly 100, Chinese President Xi Jinping announced a campaign against terrorism in Xinjiang that has led to a wide-scale crackdown on religious expression. Hundreds or thousands of Uighur Muslims have been detained in security sweeps, and many prosecuted on charges of "endangering state security," which potentially carry the death penalty. Local authorities' efforts to suppress so-called "religious extremism" also have resulted in Uighur Muslims being detained and sentenced to jail

fasted were arrested and detained. Also in 2014, a Chinese court sentenced Ilham Tohti, a respected Uighur Muslim scholar, to life in prison for alleged separatism. Central and regional government authorities conflate religion with extremism, assigning the terrorist label to all Uighur Muslims in an attempt to justify their draconian and extrajudicial actions with what they assert is a legitimate war against terrorism.

Tibetan Buddhists

Since 2008, the Chinese government has imposed harsh policies of repression on Buddhists across the Tibetan plateau, including harassment, imprisonment, and torture. In March 2014, Goshul Lobsang died shortly following his release from prison after suffering extreme malnourishment and brutal torture, such as regular injections and stabbings; he was imprisoned for his role in organizing a protest in 2008. Also in 2014, religious leader Khenpo Kartse was sentenced to two-and-a-half years in prison for allegedly protecting a fugitive monk. The government's campaign of repression also has involved the destruction of religious structures and restrictions that have forced younger monks out of monasteries. Self-immolations have continued, and in

> *Central and regional government authorities conflate religion with extremism, assigning the terrorist label to all Uighur Muslims in an attempt to justify their draconian and extrajudicial actions with what they assert is a legitimate war against terrorism.*

for religious attire, unofficial publications of Islamic teachings, religious gatherings, and religious activities. In addition, during the year numerous mosques were raided, "illegal" imams and religious personnel detained or dismissed, and unofficial Islamic publications confiscated. In 2014, Xinjiang authorities again banned the observance of Ramadan throughout that region, and reportedly enforced the ban more thoroughly than in past years. In some locations, local authorities forbade party officials and public servants from holding *iftar* dinners breaking the day's fast or held festivities unrelated to Ramadan as a test to determine if Muslims would comply with the fasting ban; in some cases, individuals who

recent years more than 130 Tibetan Buddhists, including monks and nuns, have set themselves on fire in acts of protest. Moreover, the Chinese government continued its ongoing vilification of the Dalai Lama, including accusing him of seeking Tibetan independence, which he has repeatedly denied. While there were indications the Chinese government may allow him to visit Tibet, its insistence on selecting the next Dalai Lama continued to strain the relationship.

Protestants and Catholics

In a striking development, at least 400 churches were torn down or had crosses forcibly removed and/or demolished in 2014, a notable increase over previous years. Most of these incidents occurred in Zhejiang Province and included both underground and state-sanctioned churches, though incidents were reported in other places as well. In Zhejiang Province, these actions can be attributed to the "Three Rectifications and One Demolition" campaign, the provincial government's March 2013 plan purportedly aimed at building code violations and illegal structures. Many religious believers in Zhejiang, particularly Christians, regarded the campaign as directly targeting their religion. The city of Wenzhou, home to China's largest Christian community, known as "China's Jerusalem," saw a particularly high number of demolitions. Registered churches in Wenzhou also faced demolitions, including the Protestant Wuai Church and the Liushi and Longgangshan Catholic Churches. In general, conditions faced by registered and unregistered churches across the country vary widely and are often subject to the inconsistent discretion of local and/or provincial officials.

Leaders and members of both registered and unregistered churches have faced increased harassment and

(In the past, China has refused to allow papal aircraft to fly through its airspace; it is common practice for sitting popes to send messages to the countries over which they fly.) However, shortly thereafter, a Chinese Foreign Ministry spokesperson reiterated calls for the Vatican to cut ties with Taiwan and to stop interfering in China's internal affairs in the name of religion. Moreover, according to a 2015 working plan of the State Administration of Religious Affairs, China still insists on electing and ordaining bishops completely independent of the Holy See.

Falun Gong

The year 2014 marked the 15th anniversary of the Chinese government's ban on Falun Gong, a practice officials consider to be an "evil cult." In fact, Falun Gong heads the expanded list of cults the government issued in 2014. Since the ban, Falun Gong practitioners have been imprisoned and subjected to torture, such as psychiatric experiments and organ harvesting from executed prisoners. In October 2014, Falun Gong practitioner Wang Zhiwen was released after 15 years in prison, but was immediately detained in what the

---

Leaders and members of both registered and unregistered churches have faced increased harassment and arbitrary arrests.

---

arbitrary arrests. Typically leaders of house churches are more vulnerable to these types of charges, but in 2014 pastors of sanctioned churches also faced detention or arrest. The Chinese government generally claimed these actions were to maintain social order, but there were multiple reports that Christians and religious activists were unfairly targeted. In July 2014, Pastor Zhang Shaojie of the Nanle County Christian Church, a registered church in Henan Province, was convicted on trumped-up charges and sentenced to 12 years in prison. The government also began classifying house church leaders as alleged "cult" leaders.

Pope Francis has opened the door for improved relations with China, reportedly inviting President Xi Jinping to the Vatican. Additionally, the Chinese government granted the Pope permission to fly through Chinese airspace following his January 2015 trip to the Philippines.

Chinese government refers to as a "legal education center." (In these centers, also referred to as brainwashing centers, torture reportedly is common.) Although this extrajudicial detention was temporary, his freedom of movement is still restricted, impacting his ability to seek proper medical treatment for the effects of the torture he endured while in prison. Li Chang, Yu Changxin and Ji Liewu are among the countless Falun Gong practitioners who remain imprisoned. While China in 2014 reportedly ended its deplorable system of "re-education through labor," a form of extrajudicial detention used for many Falun Gong practitioners, other forms of extralegal detention remain, including secretive "black jails."

Targeting of "Cults"

Under Article 300 of China's Criminal Law, those who participate in so-called "superstitious sects or secret societies or weird religious organizations" or other similar activity are subject to imprisonment. In 2014, the Chinese government took its broadest steps yet to designate and criminalize some groups as "cult organizations." On June 3, 2014, the government published a list of 20 "cults" and began a sweeping crackdown against these organizations. House churches were targeted because they lack any official protection. In September 2014, more than 100 Christians were arrested during a raid on a house church in Foshan City, Guangdong Province, with eyewitnesses claiming that more than 200 officials took part in the raid. As part of the "anti-cult" effort, China's government issued a directive to "eradicate" unregistered churches over the course of the next decade, resulting in unregistered church members facing an increased number of arrests, fines, and church closures in 2014.

Forced Repatriation of North Korean Refugees

The release in 2014 of the report of the UN Commission of Inquiry on Human Rights in the Democratic People's Republic of Korea (COI) brought swift and sustained international condemnation of North Korea's abysmal human rights record. China fared little better in the report's findings due to its longstanding position that North Koreans entering China without permission are economic migrants ineligible for refugee status. The COI found that North Koreans repatriated from China experience persecution, torture, arbitrary detentions, and other unspeakable atrocities. By undertaking forced repatriations, the COI determined that China violates its international obligations regarding the principle of non-refoulement. At the 69th session of the UN General Assembly in fall 2014, China was one of the few countries to side with North Korea during both debates and votes on a resolution condemning North Korea's human rights record. The resolution expressed concern about the violations documented in the COI report, including religious freedom violations, and noted the ill-treatment of North Koreans repatriated from other countries.

U.S. Policy

There are several strategic bilateral and multilateral issues that influence the U.S.-China relationship. For example, the ongoing maritime territorial disputes in the East China and South China Seas impact how the two countries relate to one another as well as with other regional stakeholders in East and Southeast Asia. The relationship is also influenced by the Obama Administration's Asia "pivot" or "rebalance", particularly on issues such as trade, the economy, military, and commerce. Mistrust exists on both sides: China is skeptical of U.S. intentions on Taiwan, the Dalai Lama, and the Trans-Pacific Partnership; and the United States is wary of Chinese cyber-espionage, military modernization, and troubling human rights record. As the United States seeks to integrate China more fully into a rules-based global economy, China continues to tightly control its domestic and foreign markets, and tension between the two countries remains in their trade relationship.

In a noteworthy example of cooperation between the two powers on a global issue, the United States and China in November 2014 announced a joint agreement to reduce carbon and other emissions in an unprecedented climate change and clean energy plan.

The United States approaches foreign assistance to China as a means to support programs that protect U.S. interests, such as promoting human rights and the rule of law, supporting environmental protection, addressing pandemic diseases, and assisting Tibetan communities. These programs are primarily administered through the State Department and the U.S. Agency for International Development through its regional mission in Bangkok, as well as other U.S. agencies. The Chinese government remains suspicious of any foreign funding, particularly support to local non-governmental organizations.

The regular meetings of the U.S.-China Strategic and Economic Dialogue (S&ED) provide another avenue for cooperation and frank discussion between the two countries. At the sixth session of the S&ED held in July 2014, Secretary of State John Kerry reportedly raised human rights concerns in a number of discussions, including the issues of religious freedom and repression of ethnic minorities in Tibet and Xinjiang, noting the linkages between human rights and counterterrorism.

The United States has raised a number of human rights issues with China both publicly and privately, including individual cases. However, human rights advocates urge the United States to do more, and to do so publicly. The United States has publicly expressed concern on several key issues, including: government censorship and crackdowns on press freedoms and free speech, including on the Internet and social media, and often under the rubric of fighting terrorism; the denial of rights to ethnic and religious minorities; excessive detentions and arrests; and Beijing's proposed counterterrorism law and its potential impact on U.S. technology companies. In return, the Chinese government has criticized human rights in the United States in light of racial tensions and the release of the U.S. Senate report on torture.

China regularly condemns U.S. reports critical of its religious freedom and human rights record, including the CPC designation assigned by the State Department since 1999. Secretary Kerry re-designated China as a CPC in July 2014, thereby also extended the existing sanctions under section 423 of IRFA relating to exports of certain items.

Recommendations

The U.S.-China relationship is complex, nuanced, and continuously impacted by ever-changing bilateral and global dynamics. Navigating diplomacy within this ebb and flow is challenging, but this underscores the importance of delivering a consistent, recurring message on religious freedom and related human rights in China. In addition to recommending the U.S. government continue to designate China as a CPC, USCIRF recommends the U.S. government should:

- Continue to raise consistently religious freedom concerns at the U.S.- China Strategic and Economic Dialogue and other high-level bilateral meetings with Chinese leaders, encourage Chinese authorities to refrain from conflating peaceful religious activity with terrorism or threats to state security, and use the U.S.-China Human Rights Dialogue as a mechanism to further high-level discussions and reach concrete agreements;

- Urge the Chinese government to release prisoners of conscience who have been detained, sentenced, or placed under house arrest for the peaceful exercise of their faith, and continue to raise individual prisoner cases;

- Initiate a "whole-of-government" approach to human rights diplomacy with China in which the State Department and National Security Council staff develop a human rights action plan for imple-

mentation across all U.S. government agencies and entities, including developing targeted talking points and prisoner lists, and providing support for all U.S. delegations visiting China;

- Increase staff attention to U.S. human rights diplomacy and the rule of law, including the promotion of religious freedom, at the U.S. Embassy in Beijing and U.S. consulates in China, including by gathering the names of specific officials and state agencies who perpetrate religious freedom abuses;

- As permitted by IRFA and to more directly convey U.S. concerns about severe religious freedom violations in China, impose targeted travel bans and other penalties on specific officials who perpetrate religious freedom abuses;

- Press China to uphold its international obligations to protect North Korean asylum seekers crossing its borders, including by allowing the UN High Commissioner for Refugees (UNHCR) and international humanitarian organizations to assist them and by ending repatriations, which are in violation of the 1951 Refugee Convention and Protocol and/or the Convention Against Torture; and

- Encourage the Broadcasting Board of Governors to use appropriated funds to advance Internet freedom and protect Chinese activists by supporting the development and accessibility of new technologies and programs to counter censorship.

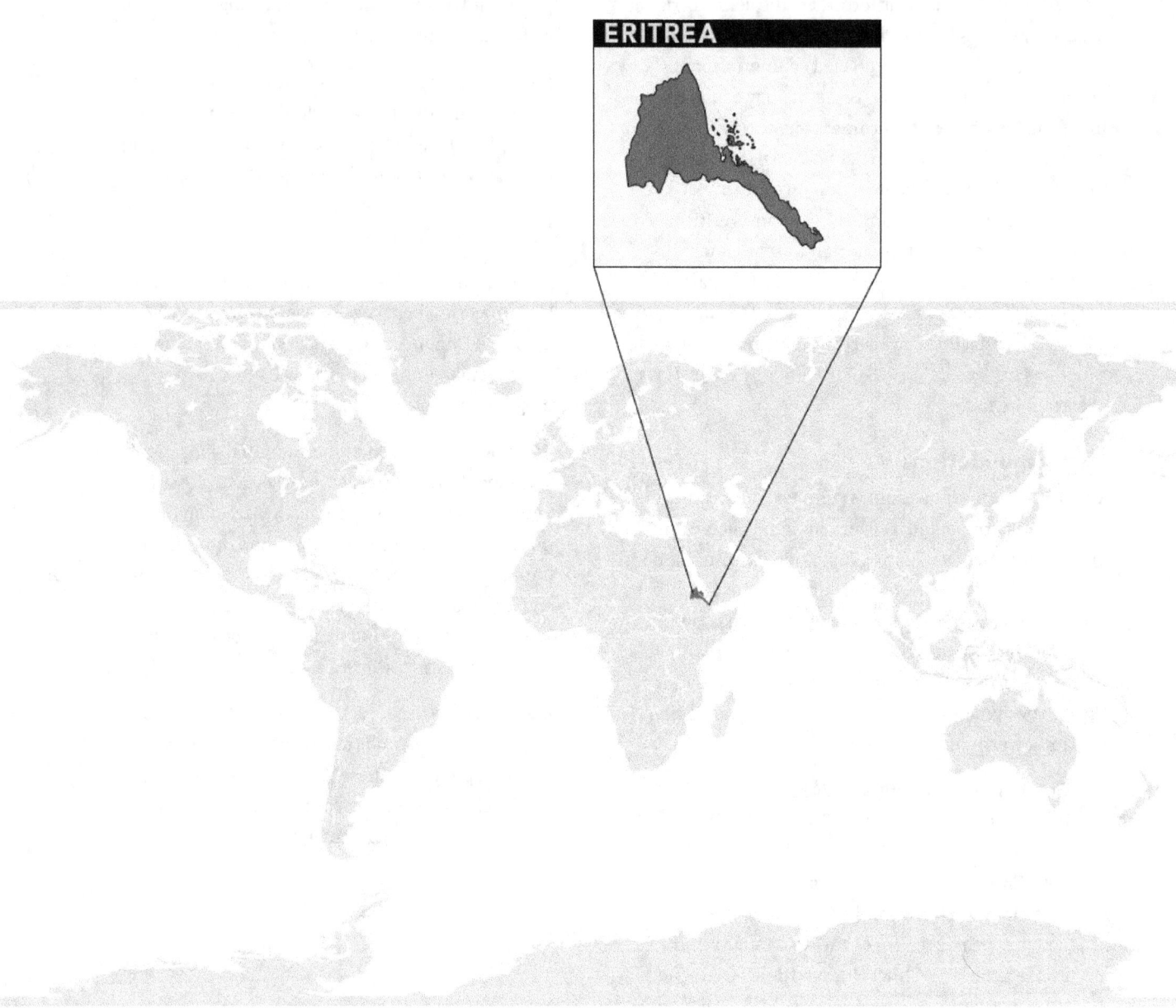

ERITREA

ERITREA

Key Findings

Systematic, ongoing, and egregious religious freedom violations continue in Eritrea. Violations include torture or other ill-treatment of religious prisoners, arbitrary arrests and detentions without charges, a prolonged ban on public religious activities, and interference in the internal affairs of registered religious groups. The religious freedom situation is particularly grave for Evangelical and Pentecostal Christians and Jehovah's Witnesses. The government dominates the internal affairs of the Orthodox Church of Eritrea, the country's largest Christian denomination, and suppresses Muslim religious activities and those opposed to the government-appointed head of the Muslim community. In light of these violations, USCIRF again recommends in 2015 that Eritrea be designated as a "country of particular concern," or CPC, under the International Religious Freedom Act (IRFA). Since

of Eritreans are imprisoned for their real or imagined opposition to the government, and torture and forced labor are extensive. No private newspapers, political opposition parties, or independent non-governmental organizations exist, and independent public gatherings are prohibited. The government requires all physically- and mentally-capable people between the ages of 18 and 70 to perform national service, including military training and/or service, which is full time and indefinite. The national service requirement does not include a provision or alternative for conscientious objectors. Persons who fail to participate in the national service are detained, sentenced to hard labor, abused, and have their legal documents confiscated.

In 2002, the government increased its control over religion by imposing a registration requirement on all religious groups other than the four officially-recognized religions: the Coptic Orthodox Church of Eritrea;

> *President Isaias and his circle maintain absolute authority and suppress all independent activity. Thousands of Eritreans are imprisoned for their real or imagined opposition to the government, and torture and forced labor are extensive.*

2004, USCIRF has recommended, and the State Department has designated, Eritrea as a CPC, most recently in July 2014.

Background

President Isaias Afwerki and the Popular Front for Democracy and Justice (PFDJ) have ruled Eritrea since the country gained independence from Ethiopia in 1993. President Isaias and his circle maintain absolute authority and suppress all independent activity. Thousands

Sunni Islam; the Roman Catholic Church; and the Evangelical Church of Eritrea, a Lutheran-affiliated denomination. The requirements mandated that the non-preferred religious communities provide detailed information about their finances, membership, activities, and benefit to the country.

There are no reliable statistics of religious affiliation in Eritrea. The Pew Charitable Trust estimates that Orthodox Christians comprise approximately 57 percent of the population, Muslims 36 percent, Roman Catholics 4 percent, and Protestants, including Evangelical

Lutherans, Baptists, Presbyterians, Jehovah's Witnesses, Pentecostals, and others, 1 percent.

No religious group has been registered since the registration requirement was imposed in 2002, although the Baha'i community, Presbyterian Church, Methodist Church, and Seventh-day Adventists have all submitted the required applications when the registration law was first enacted. As a result of the registration requirement and the government's inaction on applications, unregistered religious communities lack a legal basis on which to practice their faiths publicly, including holding services or weddings. The government's campaign against religious activities by persons belonging to unregistered denominations frequently targets Evangelical and Pentecostal Christians and Jehovah's Witnesses, the latter of whom are denied citizenship by an October 1994 Presidential Decree. Eritrean security forces routinely arrest followers of these faiths, including at clandestine prayer meetings and religious ceremonies.

Religious Freedom Conditions 2014-2015
Torture and Other Abuses

The government regularly tortures and beats political and religious prisoners, however, religious prisoners are sent to the harshest prisons and receive some of the cruelest punishments. Released religious prisoners have reported to USCIRF and other human rights monitors that they were confined in crowded conditions, such as in 20-foot metal shipping containers or underground barracks, and subjected to extreme temperature fluctuations. Evangelicals and Pentecostals released from prison report being pressured to recant their faith in order to be freed. Persons detained for religious activities, in both short-term and long-term detentions, are not formally charged, permitted access to legal counsel, accorded due process, or allowed family visits. Prisoners are not permitted to pray aloud, sing, or preach, and religious books are banned.

Religious Prisoners

The government continued to arrest and detain followers of unregistered religious communities. While the country's closed nature makes exact numbers difficult to determine, recent estimates suggest 1,200 to 3,000 persons are imprisoned on religious grounds in Eritrea, the vast majority of whom are Evangelical or Pentecostal Christians. Reports of torture and other abuses of religious prisoners as described above continue. Known religious prisoners include: the government-deposed Eritrean Orthodox Patriarch Abune Antonios, who protested government interference in his church's affairs and has been under house arrest since 2007; 64 Jehovah's Witnesses detained without trial, including three who have been imprisoned for more than 20 years (see list in appendix); more than 180 Muslims detained for opposing the state's appointment of the Mufti of the Eritrean Muslim community; and other reformist members of the Orthodox clergy. During the past year, there were reports of deaths of religious prisoners who were denied medical care or subjected to other ill treatment.

Repressive Environment

The government controls the internal affairs of the four recognized religions, including appointing religious

> *The government's campaign against religious activities by persons belonging to unregistered denominations frequently targets Evangelical and Pentecostal Christians and Jehovah's Witnesses, the latter of whom are denied citizenship by an October 1994 Presidential Decree.*

leaders and controlling religious activities. The recognized groups are required to submit activity reports to the government every six months. Since December 2010, the Eritrean Department of Religious Affairs has reportedly instructed these groups to not accept funds from co-religionists abroad, an order with which the

Eritrean Orthodox Church reportedly said it would not comply. Despite community protests, the Department of Religious Affairs also appoints the Mufti of the Eritrean Muslim community and hundreds of Muslims who protested this appointment remain imprisoned. In a reversal of policy, in 2010 the Eritrean government began requiring all clergy, including those from registered religious communities, to participate in national military service regardless of their conscientious objections to such service. In this reporting period, USCIRF received reports that Eritrean officials visiting the United States pressured diaspora members only to attend Eritrean government-approved Orthodox churches in this country.

U.S. Policy

Relations between the United States and Eritrea remain poor. The U.S. government has long expressed concern about Eritrea's human rights practices and its activities in the region, including its longstanding conflict with Ethiopia. The government of Eritrea expelled USAID in 2005, and U.S. programs in the country ended in

in the country. The Commission has not been allowed into Eritrea to conduct its research, but has been meeting with Eritrean diaspora, refugees, experts, and human rights activists outside of the country. Its final report is due in June 2015.

The State Department designated Eritrea a CPC under IRFA in September 2004. When renewing the CPC designation in September 2005 and January 2009, the State Department announced the denial of commercial export to Eritrea of defense articles and services covered by the Arms Export Control Act, with some items exempted. The Eritrean government subsequently intensified its repression of unregistered religious groups with a series of arrests and detentions of clergy and ordinary members of the affected groups. The State Department most recently re-designated Eritrea as a CPC in July 2014, and continued the presidential action of the arms embargo, although since 2011 this has been under the auspices of UN Security Council resolution 1907 (see below).

U.S. policy toward Eritrea is also concentrated on the country's activities to destabilize the Horn of

---

The U.S. government has long expressed concern about Eritrea's human rights practices. . .

---

fiscal year 2006. Eritrea receives no U.S. development, humanitarian, or security assistance. Since 2010, the government has refused to accredit a new U.S. ambassador to the country; in response the U.S. government revoked the credentials of the Eritrean ambassador to the United States.

U.S. government officials routinely raise religious freedom abuses when speaking about human rights conditions in Eritrea. The United States was a co-sponsor of a 2012 UN Human Rights Council resolution that successfully created the position of Special Rapporteur on the situation of human rights in Eritrea. In July 2014, the United States supported the creation of a Commission of Inquiry on Human Rights in Eritrea to investigate systematic violations of human rights, recommend how to improve conditions and ensure accountability, and raise awareness of the situation

Africa. In December 2009, the United States joined a 13-member majority on the UN Security Council in adopting Resolution 1907, sanctioning Eritrea for supporting armed groups in Somalia and failing to withdraw its forces from the Eritrean-Djibouti border following clashes with Djibouti. The sanctions include an arms embargo, travel restrictions, and asset freezes on the Eritrean government's political and military leaders, as well as other individuals designated by the Security Council's Committee on Somalia Sanctions. In April 2010, President Obama announced Executive Order 13536 blocking the property and property interests of several individuals for their financing of al-Shabaab in Somalia, including Yemane Ghebreab, the former head of political affairs and senior advisor on Somali issues for the Eritrean president. In December 2011, the United States voted in favor of

UN Security Council Resolution 2023, which calls on UN member states to implement Resolution 1907's sanctions and ensure that their dealings with Eritrea's mining industry do not support activities which would destabilize the region.

UN resolution 1907 also condemns Eritrea's two-percent tax on Eritreans living outside of the country, which it noted is used "for purposes such as procuring arms and related materiel for transfer to armed opposition groups." The Eritrean government relies heavily on this tax to boost its poor economy and fund national defense. U.S. government officials, the UN Somalia and Eritrea Monitoring Group, and Eritrean diaspora in the United States and other coun-

in 22 CFR 126.1(a), USCIRF recommends that the U.S. government should:

- Continue to use diplomatic channels to urge the government of Eritrea to: release unconditionally and immediately detainees held on account of their peaceful religious activities, including Ortho- dox Patriarch Abune Antonios; implement the constitutional guarantees of freedom of thought, conscience, and religion; institute a voluntary registration process for religious groups and promptly register those groups that comply with the requirements issued in 2002; and extend an official invitation for visits by the Commission of Inquiry on Human Rights in Eritrea, Special Rapporteur on

. . . use diplomatic channels to urge the government of Eritrea to: release unconditionally and immediately detainees held on account of their peaceful religious activities, including Orthodox Patriarch Abune Antonios . . .

tries report that those who refuse to pay are subject to threats, intimidation, and coercion, and their families in Eritrea are also harassed. In 2011, the United King- dom suspended collection of this tax stating that it may contravene the Vienna Convention on Diplomatic Relations. In 2012 the Eritrean consulate in Ottawa, Canada agreed to stop collecting the tax after Canadian threats to remove the Eritrean Ambassador. This move corresponds with Canadian efforts to make it illegal to finance the Eritrean military in compliance with UNSC Resolution 1907. The Netherlands and Germany are also considering ending the collection of the diaspora tax within their territories.

Recommendations

In response to the policies and practices of Eritrea's gov- ernment, the U.S. government should press for imme- diate improvements to end religious freedom violations in Eritrea and advance religious freedom through sanctions and other bilateral and multilateral efforts. In addition to recommending that the U.S. government should continue to designate Eritrea as a CPC and main- taining the existing, ongoing arms embargo referenced

human rights in Eritrea, the UN Special Rapporteur on Freedom of Religion or Belief, the UN Working Group on Arbitrary Detention and International Red Cross;

- Work to limit the Eritrean government's ability to levy and forcibly collect a diaspora tax on Eritreans living in the United States by imposing visas bans on Eritrean officials who violate UN resolution 1907 and/or engage in human rights abuses related to the collection of the diaspora tax in the United States, and partner with other countries with Eritrean diaspora communities to ban similar forced taxes;

- Encourage unofficial dialogue with Eritrean authorities on religious freedom issues by pro- moting a visit by U.S. and international religious leaders to facilitate dialogue with all of Eritrea's religious communities, and expand the use of educational and cultural exchanges, such as the Fulbright Program, the International Visitor Pro- gram, and lectures by visiting American scholars and experts;

- Work with other nations, especially those with mining interests in Eritrea and large Eritrean diaspora communities, to draw attention to religious freedom abuses in Eritrea and advocate for the unconditional and immediate release of religious prisoners, including Orthodox Patriarch Abune Antonios; and

- Increase assistance to the Office of the UN High Commissioner for Refugees (UNHCR) and non-governmental organizations to provide support to Eritrean refugees with psychosocial needs due to torture and other ill-treatment.

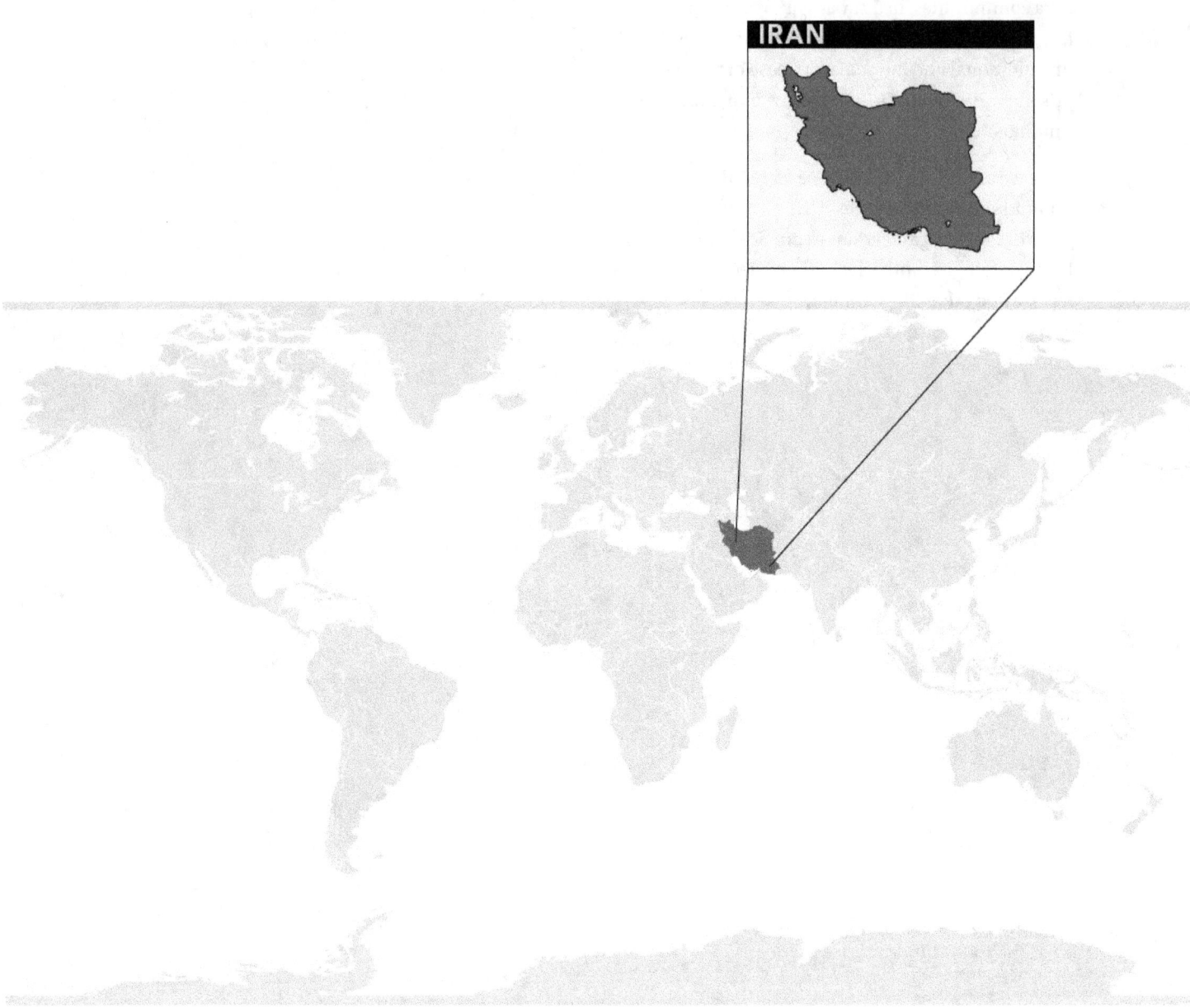

IRAN

Key Findings

Poor religious freedom conditions continued to deteriorate in 2014, particularly for religious minorities, especially Baha'is, Christian converts, and Sunni Muslims. Sufi Muslims and dissenting Shi'a Muslims also faced harassment, arrests, and imprisonment. Since President Hassan Rouhani assumed office in August 2013, the number of individuals from religious minority communities who are in prison because of their beliefs has increased. The government of Iran continues to engage in systematic, ongoing, and egregious violations of religious freedom, including prolonged detention, torture, and executions based primarily or entirely upon the religion of the accused. While Iran's clerical establishment continued to express anti-Semitic sentiments, the level of anti-Semitic rhetoric from government officials has diminished over the past year. Since 1999, the State Department has designated Iran as a "country of particular concern," or CPC, under the International Religious Freedom Act (IRFA), most recently in July 2014. USCIRF again recommends in 2015 that Iran be designated a CPC.

Background

The Islamic Republic of Iran is a constitutional, theocratic republic that proclaims the Twelver (Shi'a) Jaafari School of Islam to be the official religion of the country. The constitution recognizes Christians, Jews, and Zoroastrians as protected religious minorities, and five seats in the parliament are reserved for these groups (two for Armenian Christians, one for Assyrian Christians, and one each for Jews and Zoroastrians). Nevertheless, the government of Iran discriminates against its citizens on the basis of religion or belief, as all laws and regulations are based on unique Shi'a Islamic criteria. Since the 1979 revolution, many members of minority religious communities have fled in fear of persecution. Killings, arrests, and physical abuse of detainees have increased in recent years, including for religious minorities and Muslims who dissent or express views perceived as threatening the government's legitimacy. The government continues to use its religious laws to silence reformers, including human rights defenders and journalists, for exercising their internationally-protected rights to freedom of expression and religion or belief.

Since his June 2013 election, President Hassan Rouhani has not delivered on his campaign promises to strengthen civil liberties for religious minorities. Physical attacks, harassment, detention, arrests, and imprisonment continued. Even some of the constitutionally-recognized non-Muslim minorities – Jews, Armenian

> *Since President Hassan Rouhani assumed office in August 2013, the number of individuals from religious minority communities who are in prison because of their beliefs has increased.*

and Assyrian Christians, and Zoroastrians – face harassment, intimidation, discrimination, arrests, and imprisonment. Some majority Shi'a and minority Sunni Muslims, including clerics who dissent, were intimidated, harassed, and detained. Dissidents and human rights defenders were increasingly subject to abuse and several were sentenced to death and even executed for the capital crime of "enmity against God."

Religious Freedom Conditions 2014–2015
Muslims

Over the past few years, the Iranian government has imposed harsh prison sentences on prominent reformers from the Shi'a majority community. Authorities charged many of these reformers with "insulting Islam," criticizing the Islamic Republic, and publishing materials that allegedly deviate from Islamic standards. Dissident Shi'a cleric Ayatollah Mohammad Kazemeni Boroujerdi continued to serve an 11-year prison sentence, and the government has banned him from practicing his clerical duties and confiscated his home and belongings. He has suffered physical and mental abuse while in prison. According to an October 2014 UN report on human rights in Iran, some 150 Sunni Muslims are in prison on charges related to their beliefs and religious activities. More than 30 are on death row after having been convicted of "enmity against God" in unfair judicial proceedings. Leaders from the Sunni community have been unable to build a mosque in Tehran and have

severe religious freedom violations. The government views Baha'is, who number at least 300,000, as "heretics" and consequently they face repression on the grounds of apostasy. Since 1979, authorities have killed or executed more than 200 Baha'i leaders, and more than 10,000 have been dismissed from government and university jobs. Although the Iranian government maintains publicly that Baha'is are free to attend university, the de facto policy of preventing Baha'is from obtaining higher education remains in effect. Approximately 750 Baha'is have been arbitrarily arrested since 2005.

As of February 2015, there are more than 100 Baha'is being held in prison solely because of their religious beliefs. These include seven Baha'i leaders – Fariba Kamalabadi, Jamaloddin Khanjani, Afif Naemi,

. . . President Hassan Rouhani has not delivered on his campaign promises to strengthen civil liberties for religious minorities.

reported widespread abuses and restrictions on their religious practice, including detentions and harassment of clerics and bans on Sunni teachings in public schools. Iranian authorities have destroyed Sunni religious literature and mosques in eastern Iran.

Iran's government also continued to harass and arrest members of the Sufi Muslim community, including prominent leaders from the Nematollahi Gonabadi Order, while increasing restrictions on places of worship and destroying Sufi prayer centers and hussainiyas (meeting halls). Over the past year, authorities have detained hundreds of Sufis, sentencing many to imprisonment, fines, and floggings. In May 2014, approximately 35 Sufis were convicted on trumped-up charges related to their religious activities and given sentences ranging from three months to four years in prison. Another 10 Sufi activists were either serving prison terms or had cases pending against them. Iranian state television regularly airs programs demonizing Sufism.

Baha'is

The Baha'i community, the largest non-Muslim religious minority in Iran, long has been subject to particularly

Saeid Rezaie, Mahvash Sabet, Behrouz Tavakkoli, and Vahid Tizfahm – as well as Baha'i educators and administrators affiliated with the Baha'i Institute for Higher Education. Over the past year, dozens of Baha'is were arrested throughout the country, including in Tehran, Isfahan, Mashhad, and Shiraz. Violent incidents targeting Baha'is and their property continued. In February 2014, three Baha'is were stabbed and nearly killed in a religious hate crime. No one has been charged. In April 2014, Iranian authorities began destroying a historic Baha'i cemetery in Shiraz. In October 2014, nearly 80 Baha'i-owned shops in Kerman Province were forcibly closed. In 2014, pro-government print and online media outlets published nearly 4,000 anti-Baha'i articles, a significant increase from recent years. The government's draft Citizens' Rights Charter, released in November 2013, includes protections for the recognized minorities but excludes Baha'is from any legal protections.

Christians

Over the past year, there were numerous incidents of Iranian authorities raiding church services, threatening church members, and arresting and imprisoning worshipers and church leaders, particularly Evangelical Christian converts. Since 2010, authorities arbitrarily arrested and detained more than 500 Christians throughout the country. As of February 2015, approximately 90 Christians were either in prison, detained, or awaiting trial because of their religious beliefs and activities.

During the reporting period, human rights groups inside Iran reported a significant increase in the number of physical assaults and beatings of Christians in prison. Some activists believe the assaults, which have been directed against converts who are leaders of underground house churches, are meant to intimidate others who may wish to convert to Christianity. In December 2014, authorities raided a number of private Christmas services and arrested more than a dozen church members in Tehran. In October 2014, three Christian converts – Silas Rabbani, Abdolreza Haghnejad, and Behnam Irani – were sentenced to six years in prison in remote parts of the country for bogus charges of "action against national security" and "creating a network to overthrow the system." In December, the sentences were dropped against the three and Rabbani and Haghnejad were released. Irani continues to serve a separate six year sentence. Christian convert Farshid Fathi, who was arrested in 2010 and sentenced in 2012 to six years in prison for his religious activities, was beaten by security officials and injured during a April 2014 raid at Evin Prison. In August, he was transferred to Rajai Shahr Prison outside Tehran and in December he was given an additional one-year prison sentence in connection with the April prison raid.

Iranian-born American pastor Saeed Abedini continues to serve an eight-year prison term after being convicted in 2013 for "threatening the national security of Iran" for his activity in the Christian house church movement. While in Evin Prison since September 2012, Pastor Abedini spent several weeks in solitary confinement and was physically and psychologically abused. In November 2013, he was transferred to the Rajai Shahr Prison, which is known for its harsh and unsanitary conditions. In March 2014, prison authorities beat Pastor Abedini after which he was hospitalized for nearly two months to receive treatment for the injuries sustained from the beatings. In May 2014, Pastor Abedini was beaten a second time when he was released from the hospital and returned to prison.

Jews and Zoroastrians

Although not as pronounced as in previous years, the government continued to propagate anti-Semitism and target members of the Jewish community on the basis of real or perceived "ties to Israel." In 2014, high-level clerics continued to make anti-Semitic remarks in mosques, and the government reinstated a Holocaust denial conference, which had been cancelled in 2013. Numerous programs broadcast on state-run television advance anti-Semitic messages. Official government discrimination against Jews continues to be pervasive, fostering a threatening atmosphere for the approximately 20,000 member Jewish community. In a positive development, as of February 2015, the government no longer requires Jewish students to attend classes on the Sabbath. In recent years, members of the Zoroastrian community – numbering between 30,000 and 35,000 people – have come under increasing repression and discrimination. At least four Zoroastrians convicted in 2011 for propaganda of their faith, blasphemy, and other trumped-up charges remain in prison.

Human Rights Defenders and Journalists

Iranian authorities regularly detain and harass journalists, bloggers, and human rights defenders who say or write anything critical of the Islamic revolution or the

In the past year, an increasing number of human rights lawyers who defended Baha'is and Christians in court were imprisoned or fled the country.

Iranian government. In the past year, an increasing number of human rights lawyers who defended Baha'is and Christians in court were imprisoned or fled the country.

U.S. Policy

The U.S. government has not had formal diplomatic relations with the government of Iran since 1980, although the United States has participated in negotiations with Iran over the country's nuclear program as part of the group of countries known as the P5+1 (China, France,

Russia, United Kingdom, United States and Germany). U.S. law prohibits nearly all trade with Iran. The United States has imposed sanctions on Iran because of its sponsorship of terrorism, refusal to comply with International Atomic Energy Agency regulations regarding its nuclear program, and for severe human rights and religious freedom violations. According to the State Department, these sanctions are intended to target the Iranian government, not the people of Iran.

On July 1, 2010, President Barack Obama signed into law CISADA, the Comprehensive Iran Sanctions, Accountability, and Divestment Act (P.L. 111-195), which highlights Iran's serious human rights violations, including suppression of religious freedom. CISADA requires the President to submit to Congress a list of Iranian government officials or persons acting on their behalf responsible for human rights and religious freedom abuses, bars their entry into the United States, and freezes their assets. In August 2012, the President signed into law the Iran Threat Reduction and Syria Human Rights Act of 2012 (H.R. 1905 / P.L. 112-239), which enhances the scope of human rights-related sanctions contained in CISADA. Issuing its first sanction for human rights abuses since President Rouhani's election in June 2013, the U.S. Treasury Department on May 23, 2014 announced sanctions against the former governor of Tehran and current head of the Tehran Provincial Public Security Council, Morteza Tamaddon, for being involved in censorship and other activities limiting the freedoms of expression and assembly. During his tenure as governor, Tamaddon orchestrated in 2011 a series of coordinated arrests and abuses against Christian converts.

During the past year, U.S. policy on human rights and religious freedom in Iran included a combination of public statements, multilateral activity, and the imposition of unilateral sanctions on Iranian government officials and entities for human rights violations. During the reporting period, high-level U.S. officials in multilateral fora and through public statements urged the Iranian government to respect its citizens' human rights, including the right to religious freedom. In December 2014, for the 12th year in a row, the U.S. government co-sponsored and supported a successful UN General Assembly resolution on human rights in Iran, which passed 78 to 35, with 69 abstentions. The resolution condemned the Iranian government's poor human rights record, including its religious freedom violations and continued abuses targeting religious minorities.

During the year, President Obama and Secretary of State John Kerry used public occasions to call for the release of Iranian-American pastor Saeed Abedini. In early February 2015, the President called for Mr. Abedini's release at the National Prayer Breakfast. In January, President Obama met with Naghmeh Abedini, Mr. Abedini's wife, and stated that securing her husband's release was a "top priority."

On July 28, 2014, the Secretary of State re-designated Iran as a country of particular concern. The Secretary designated the following Presidential Action for Iran: "the existing ongoing travel restrictions based on serious human rights abuses under section 221(a)(1)(C) of the Iran Threat Reduction and Syria Human Rights Act of 2012, pursuant to section 402(c)(5) of the Act." The previous designation made in 2011 cited a provision under CISADA as the Presidential Action. The Iran Threat Reduction and Syria Human Rights Act does not contain a specific provision citing religious freedom violations as CISADA does.

Recommendations

In addition to recommending that the U.S. government should continue to designate Iran as a CPC, USCIRF recommends that the U.S. government should:

- Ensure that violations of freedom of religion or belief and related human rights are part of multilateral or bilateral discussions with the Iranian government whenever possible, and continue to work closely with European and other allies to apply pressure through a combination of advocacy, diplomacy, and targeted sanctions;

- Continue to speak out publicly and frequently at the highest levels about the severe religious freedom abuses in Iran, press for and work to secure the release of all prisoners of conscience, and highlight the need for the international community to hold authorities accountable in specific cases;

- Continue to identify Iranian government agencies and officials responsible for severe violations of religious freedom, freeze those individuals' assets, and bar their entry into the United States, as delineated under the Comprehensive Iran Sanctions, Account-ability, and Divestment Act of 2010 (CISADA);

- Call on Iran to cooperate fully with the UN Special Rapporteur on the Human Rights Situation in Iran, including allowing the Special Rapporteur – as well as the UN Special Rapporteur on Freedom of Religion or Belief – to visit, and continue to support an annual UN General Assembly resolution condemning severe violations of human rights, including freedom of religion or belief, in Iran and calling for officials responsible for such violations to be held accountable; and

- Use appropriated funds to advance Internet freedom and protect Iranian activists by supporting the development and accessibility of new technologies and programs to counter censorship and to facilitate the free flow of information in and out of Iran.

The U.S. Congress should:

- Reauthorize the Lautenberg Amendment, which aids persecuted Iranian religious minorities and other specified groups seeking refugee status in the United States, and work to provide the President with permanent authority to designate as refugees specifically-defined groups based on shared characteristics identifying them as targets for persecution on account of race, religion, nationality, membership in a particular social group, or political opinion.

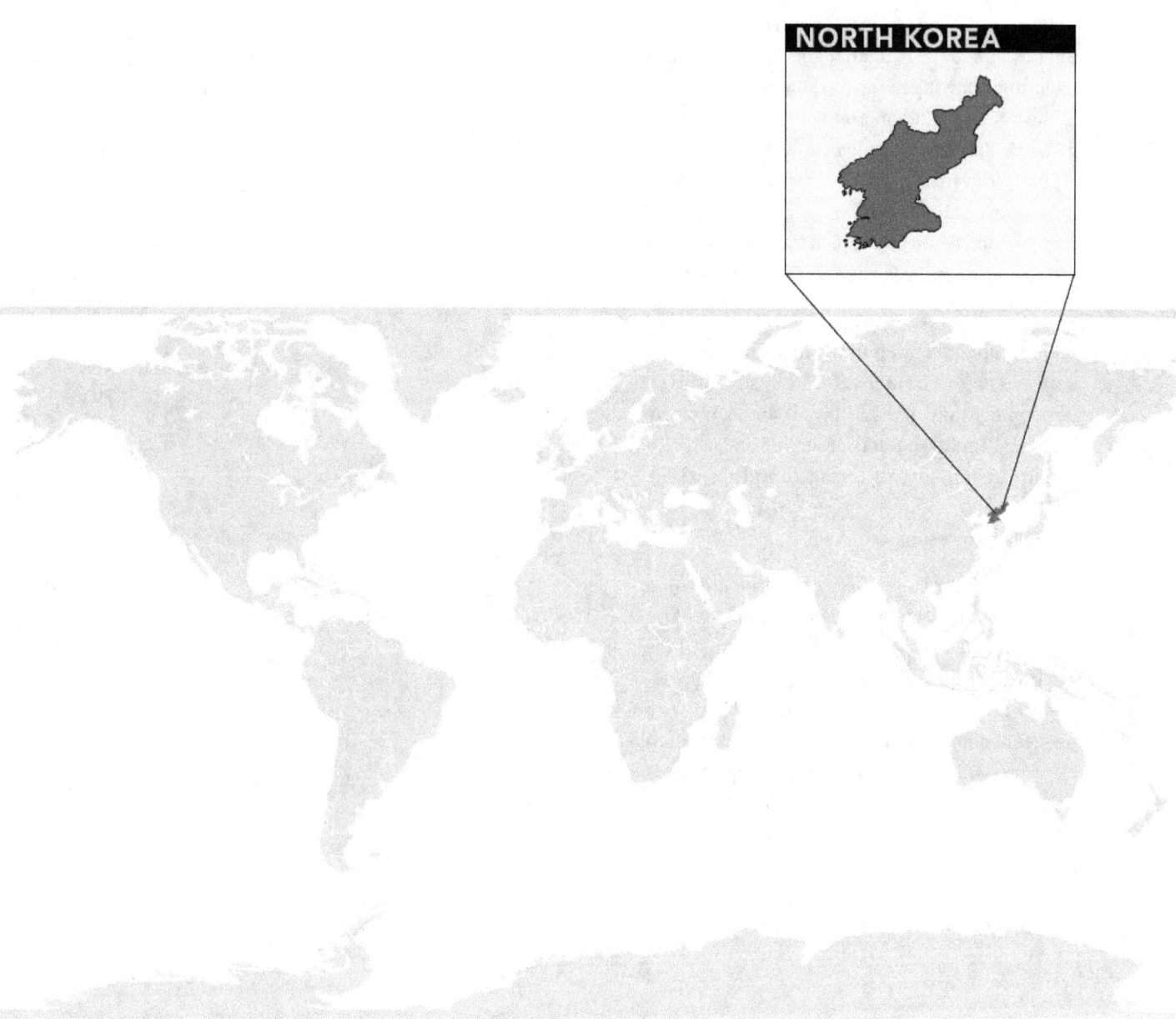

NORTH KOREA

NORTH KOREA

Key Findings

North Korea remains one of the most oppressive regimes in the world and among the worst violators of human rights. The government tightly controls all political and religious expression and activities, and it punishes those who question the regime. Genuine freedom of religion or belief is non-existent. Individuals secretly engaging in religious activities are subject to arrest, torture, imprisonment, and sometimes execution. North Koreans suspected of contacts with South Koreans or with foreign missionaries, particularly in China, or caught possessing Bibles, reportedly have been executed. Thousands of religious believers and their families are imprisoned in labor camps, including those forcibly repatriated from China. While it is challenging to document the full scope and scale of the government's repression of religious freedom, growing

its people with the *Juche* ideology, the Kim family cult of personality, which requires absolute obedience to the Kim family and to the overall state. This pseudo-religious, socialist mentality suppresses the expression of individualized thought, belief, and behavior. North Korea has traditions of Buddhism and Confucianism, and before the Korean War had a sizeable Christian population, earning Pyongyang the nickname "the Jerusalem of Asia." Today, reliable figures of religious adherents are difficult to obtain. Although the constitution purports to grant freedom of religious belief, it requires approvals for the construction of religious buildings and the holding of religious ceremonies. North Korea classifies families based on their expressions of loyalty to the state, a system known as *songbun*. Religious believers are assigned to the lowest ratings, making them vulnerable to harassment and persecution. Anyone caught violating the state's strict

> *Thousands of religious believers and their families are imprisoned in labor camps, including those forcibly repatriated from China.*

information available through firsthand accounts from defectors and refugees makes it clear that the violations taking place are systematic, ongoing, and egregious. Thus, USCIRF again recommends in 2015 that North Korea be designated a "country of particular concern," or CPC, under the International Religious Freedom Act (IRFA). The State Department has designated North Korea a CPC since 2001, most recently in July 2014.

Background

North Korea has long maintained absolute control through systematic repression and the cultivation of widespread political fear. The government indoctrinates

religious regulations faces imprisonment, torture, and even death. Figures are difficult to ascertain, but estimates suggest up to 200,000 North Koreans are currently suffering in labor camps, tens of thousands of whom are incarcerated for religious activity.

In February 2014, the Commission of Inquiry on Human Rights in the Democratic People's Republic of Korea (COI) established by the UN Human Rights Council released its comprehensive report documenting the systematic, widespread, and grave violations of human rights in North Korea. The report concluded that Pyongyang's abuses are "without any parallel in the contemporary world." It found "an almost complete denial of the right to freedom of thought, conscience, and religion, as well as of the rights to freedom of opinion, expression, information, and association."

Religious Freedom Conditions 2014–2015
Government Control and Repression of Christianity

While all forms of religion or belief not expressly sanctioned and operated by the state are restricted, Christians experience the most severe persecution. The government of North Korea imposes extreme consequences on those caught practicing Christianity, which it associates with

caught practicing Christianity. Generally, state officials monitor closely missionaries during their stay, making them especially vulnerable to harassment, and the government is known to sentence to hard labor foreigners who undertake religious acts. In late May 2014, South Korean Baptist missionary Kim Jung-wook was sentenced to life imprisonment in a labor camp for alleged espionage for attempting to establish up to 500 underground churches. North Korean leader Kim Jong-un also reportedly ordered the execution of 33 North Koreans who associated with Kim Jung-wook for allegedly

> *While all forms of religion or belief not expressly sanctioned and operated by the state are restricted, Christians experience the most severe persecution.*

the United States and Western ideology and therefore considers particularly threatening. Although Christianity is not explicitly criminalized, in practice Christians detained for their religious beliefs are generally treated as political prisoners, receive little to no justice when facing conviction, and endure particularly harsh conditions during incarceration. It is estimated that tens of thousands of Christians in North Korea are currently in prison camps facing hard labor or execution.

The few state-controlled churches that do exist are widely considered to be artificial and established for international propaganda. The government permits a limited number of Christian churches to operate that are reserved for the elite and foreigners. Pyongyang contains one Catholic Church, two Protestant churches, and a Russian Orthodox Church. However, the government tightly controls these congregations. For example, the Vatican reported that its invitation to North Korea's state-run Korean Catholic Association to attend Mass during the Pope's August 2014 visit to South Korea was declined by North Korea authorities. Although underground churches exist, state security agents are trained to infiltrate and target these groups; prisoners are often tortured to draw confessions that will lead to the infiltration of underground churches and their followers.

The treatment of foreign missionaries in North Korea illustrates the government's response to those

attempting to overthrow the government. Original source information about the purported execution order is limited, and the fate of the 33 Christians is unknown.

Former prisoners have described the atrocious treatment of those incarcerated in North Korea's infamous penal labor camps, known as *kwan-li-so*. Prisoners are forced to engage in demanding physical labor with little food, resulting in malnourishment and chronic illness, and are subject to prolonged periods of severe mental and physical torture. Individuals accused of engaging in religious activities and other political prisoners experience some of the harshest conditions because they are singled out as exceptionally dangerous to the state.

North Korean Refugees in China

In recent years, China has tightened security along the border with North Korea, making it even more dangerous for North Koreans who attempt to flee their country to escape persecution and famine. Pursuant to China's longstanding position, North Koreans entering China without permission are considered economic migrants and thus not eligible for refugee status determinations. Reportedly, those receiving the worst punishment upon being forcibly repatriated to North Korea are individuals suspected of becoming Christian, interacting with missionaries, or engaging in other religious activities. The UN Commission of Inquiry also found that some

Chinese officials provide information about those it apprehends to North Korea. In a letter responding to the COI, China challenged the Commission's claims that North Koreans forcibly repatriated are subjected to detention and torture, arguing that China has seized North Korean citizens who have crossed the border multiple times. Nonetheless, the COI report presented strong evidence that returnees risk harsh punishment. International law specifically prohibits the deportation of a person to another state when there are reasonable grounds to believe that they will be subjected to torture or persecution upon return.

U.S. Policy

The United States does not have diplomatic relations with North Korea and has no official presence within the country. U.S. officials have publicly stated that the United States is open to engagement and substantive dialogue with North Korea, both bilaterally and through the Six-Party process, on the issue of denuclearization.

own report unequivocally rejecting the COI's critiques and recommendations and stating that human rights are a matter of state sovereignty. It also sent its foreign minister to the opening session of the General Assembly for the first time in 15 years and submitted its own General Assembly resolution on human rights. Following the international condemnation and the ineffectiveness of its diplomatic response, in October 2014 the government unexpectedly released American prisoner Jeffrey Fowle, who was accused of leaving a Bible in a public place. In November 2014, North Korea released two more U.S. prisoners: Matthew Miller and Kenneth Bae, the latter a missionary serving a 15-year sentence to hard labor for allegedly undermining the government. While Mr. Fowle's release occurred during the period following the opening session of the General Assembly and the high-level side meeting on North Korea, Mr. Miller and Mr. Bae's release took place just days before passage of the UN resolution by the General Assembly's human rights committee, which

> *Individuals accused of engaging in religious activities and other political prisoners experience some of the harshest conditions because they are singled out as exceptionally dangerous to the state.*

The U.S. policy of "strategic patience" with North Korea has opened the door for enhanced engagement with important regional stakeholders, such as South Korea and Japan, as well as Australia and the European Union, including on human rights issues. For example, at the UN in September 2014, Secretary of State John Kerry addressed a high-level side meeting on human rights in North Korea with his counterparts from Japan and South Korea, among others. However, 2014 saw several developments that challenged U.S. attempts to achieve improvements in human rights and religious freedom.

First, with the February 2014 release of the COI report, North Korea denied the report's claims and sought to blame the United States for orchestrating both the report and the subsequent UN General Assembly resolution. North Korea continued its pointed attacks against the United States by issuing its

resulted in North Korea threatening nuclear tests. In December 2014, following the release of the U.S. Senate report, North Korea called on the UN to add the issue of CIA torture to its agenda.

Second, North Korea was linked to the late November 2014 digital break-in at Sony Pictures Entertainment. The hacking was accompanied by a warning that company secrets would be revealed if the hackers' demands were not obeyed. Although it denies involvement, North Korea was reportedly linked to the hack as a retaliation for *The Interview*, the movie about a fictional assassination plot on Kim Jong-un. The United States responded with new economic sanctions targeting 10 senior North Korean officials, and Congress is considering measures to broaden additional sanctions against North Korea.

Recommendations

With the attention the COI report brought on North Korea throughout 2014, the government has increasingly felt the need to respond to criticisms of its human rights abuses. The United States has been integral in these efforts and should pursue further opportunities with the UN or through bilateral or multi-lateral partnerships to continue bringing attention to these grave violations. In addition to recommending the U.S. government continue to designate North Korea as a CPC, USCIRF recommends the U.S. government should:

- Call for a follow-up UN inquiry within five years to track the findings of the 2014 report by the Commission of Inquiry on Human Rights in the Democratic People's Republic of Korea and assess any new developments, and suggest a regularization of such analysis similar to and in coordination with the Universal Periodic Review process;

- Include, whenever possible, both the Special Envoy for North Korean Human Rights Issues and the Ambassador-at-Large for International Religious Freedom in bilateral discussions with North Korea in order to incorporate human rights and religious freedom into the dialogue, and likewise incorporate human rights and religious freedom concerns into discussions with multilateral partners regarding denuclearization, as appropriate;

- Coordinate efforts with regional allies, particularly Japan and South Korea, to raise human rights and humanitarian concerns, and specific concerns regarding freedom of religion or belief, and press for improvements, including closure of the infamous penal labor camps;

- Explore innovative ways to expand existing radio programming transmitting into North Korea and along the border, as well as other forms of information technology, such as mobile phones, thumb drives, and DVDs, as well as improved Internet access so that North Koreans have greater access to independent sources of information;

- Encourage Chinese support for addressing the most egregious human rights violations in North Korea, and raise regularly with the government of China the need to uphold its international obligations to protect North Korean asylum seekers in China, including by allowing the UN High Commissioner for Refugees (UNHCR) and international humanitarian organizations to assist them and by ending repatriations, which are in violation of the 1951 Refugee Convention and Protocol and/or the United Nations Convention Against Torture; and

- Implement fully the provisions of the North Korean Human Rights Act, and use authorized funds to promote increased access to information and news media inside North Korea and greater capacity of NGOs to promote democracy and human rights, protect and resettle refugees, and monitor deliveries of humanitarian aid.

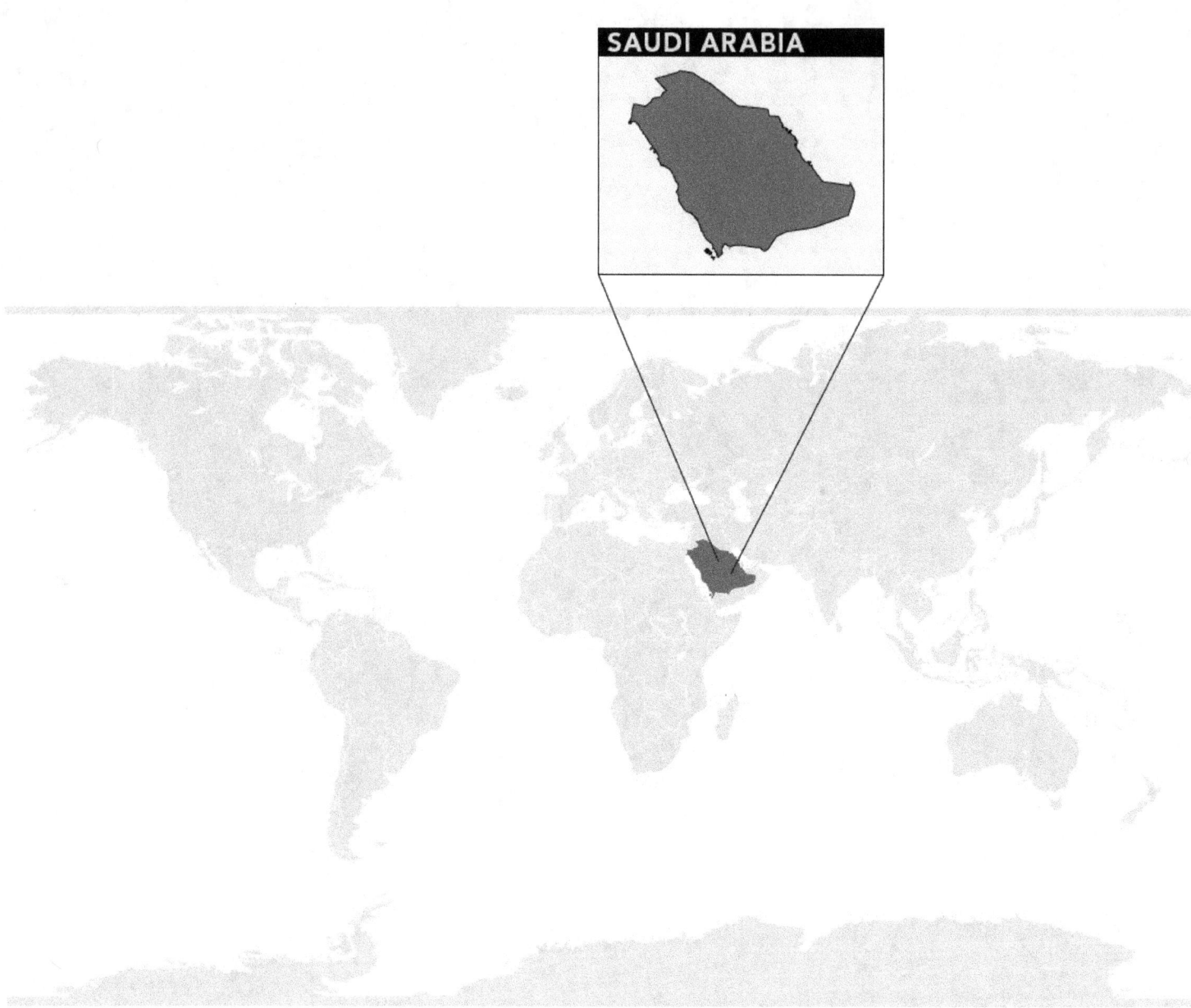

SAUDI ARABIA

Key Findings

Despite the fact that Saudi Arabia remains unique in the extent to which it restricts the public expression of any religion other than Islam, there were some improvements in religious freedom, including further progress on revisions to public school religious textbooks. The government privileges its own interpretation of Sunni Islam over all other interpretations and prohibits any non-Muslim public places of worship in the country. It continues to prosecute and imprison individuals for dissent, apostasy, blasphemy, and sorcery, and a new 2014 law classifies blasphemy and advocating atheism as terrorism. In addition, authorities continue to repress and discriminate against dissident clerics and members of the Shi'a community. Based on these

lims. In recent years, the Saudi government has made improvements in policies and practices related to freedom of religion or belief; however, it persists in restricting most forms of public religious expression inconsistent with its particular interpretation of Sunni Islam. Saudi officials base this on their interpretation of *hadith* and state that this is what is expected of them as the country that hosts the two holiest mosques in Islam, in Mecca and Medina. This policy violates the rights of other Sunni Muslims who follow varying schools of thought, Shi'a and Ismaili Muslims, and both Muslim and non-Muslim expatriate workers.

While the government has taken some steps to address its legitimate concerns of combatting religious extremism and countering advocacy of violence in

> The [Saudi] government privileges its own interpretation of Sunni Islam over all other interpretations and prohibits any non-Muslim public places of worship in the country.

severe violations of religious freedom, USCIRF again recommends in 2015 that Saudi Arabia be designated as a "country of particular concern," or CPC, under the International Religious Freedom Act (IRFA). Although the State Department has designated Saudi Arabia a CPC repeatedly since 2004, most recently in July 2014, an indefinite waiver has been in place since 2006 on taking an otherwise legislatively mandated action as a result of the CPC designation.

Background

Saudi Arabia is officially an Islamic state with approximately eight to 10 million expatriate workers of various faiths, including at least one to two million non-Mus-

sermons and educational materials, other government actions continue to restrict peaceful religious activities and expression by suppressing the religious views and practices of Saudi and non-Saudi Muslims who do not conform to official positions. Furthermore, the government has not codified the protection of private religious practice for non-Muslim expatriate workers in the country, which fosters a sense of insecurity.

On January 23, 2015, King Abdullah passed away. He was succeeded immediately by his half-brother, Crown Prince Salman bin Abdulaziz al-Saud. In various remarks, King Salman stated that he would continue many of his predecessor's policies, advance a Saudi foreign policy committed to the teachings of Islam, and maintain the country's Shari'ah legal system. He also announced a significant reshuffling of several cabinet-level positions, including appointing new Ministers of Justice, Education, and Islamic Affairs, and a new head of the Commission for the Promotion of Virtue and Prevention of Vice (CPVPV), among others.

Religious Freedom Conditions 2014–2015
Recent Improvements

USCIRF has noted some improvements in recent years that include: curtailing the powers of the CPVPV; promoting a "culture of dialogue" and understanding between Muslim religious communities inside the Kingdom and advancing inter-religious dialogue in international fora; improving conditions for public religious expression by Shi'a Muslims in the Eastern Province; continuing efforts to counter extremist ideology inside the Kingdom; and making further revisions to remove intolerant passages from textbooks and curriculum.

Restrictions on Shi'a Muslims and Dissidents

Sporadic arrests and detentions of Shi'a Muslim dissidents continued. For many years, particularly since 2011, the government has detained and imprisoned Shi'a Muslims for participating in demonstrations or calling for reform; holding small religious gatherings in private homes; organizing religious events or celebrating religious holidays; and reading religious materials in private homes or *husseiniyas* (prayer halls). Saudi officials often cite security concerns to justify cracking down on religious minorities and Muslim dissidents. The Shi'a community also faces discrimination in education, employment, the military, political representation, and the judiciary.

During the past year, several Shi'a clerics received lengthy prison terms or death sentences. For example, in October 2014, Nimr al-Nimr, a prominent Shi'a cleric who has criticized the government, was sentenced to death by a Specialized Criminal Court. The Specialized Criminal Court is a non-shari'ah court that tries terrorist-related crimes, although human rights activists also have been tried in these courts. Al-Nimr's brother and legal advocate, Mohamed, reportedly was arrested after announcing the verdict on Twitter. Nimr Al-Nimr had been arrested in July 2012 and was convicted on a range

of unfounded charges, including "inciting sectarian strife," disobeying the government, and supporting rioting. According to reports, days after al-Nimr's sentencing, a Saudi court sentenced two individuals to death for participating in Shi'a protests, saying it imposed the penalty "as a deterrent to others." A third person was jailed for 12 years. In August 2014, Tawfiq al-Amr, a Shi'a cleric from the al-Ahsa governorate, was sentenced to eight years in prison, followed by a 10-year travel ban, and barred from delivering sermons. According to human rights groups, a Specialized Criminal Court convicted him on charges of defaming Saudi Arabia's ruling system, ridiculing its religious leaders, inciting sectarianism, calling for change, and "disobeying the ruler." Al-Amr was arrested in 2011 following a series of public speeches calling for reforms in the Kingdom.

Dissident Sunni Muslims also encountered repression. For example, in November 2014, Mikhlif al-Shammari, a Sunni Muslim writer and activist, was convicted by a criminal court and sentenced to two years in prison and 200 lashes for, in part, visiting prominent Shi'a leaders in the Eastern Province and promoting reconciliation between Sunni and Shi'a Muslims. The Specialized Criminal Court previously convicted him in 2013 in a separate trial on charges of "sowing discord" and criticizing Saudi officials, for which he received a five-year prison sentence and a 10-year travel ban.

Violence against Shi'a Muslims

During the past year, Shi'a worshippers were targeted by violent extremists. In November, during Ashura celebrations in the Eastern Province of al-Ahsa, masked gunmen shot and killed at least seven Shi'a worshippers and wounded more than a dozen. After a violent gun battle that resulted in the death of two police officers and two gunmen, authorities arrested more than 15 suspected perpetrators, including several others already in jail on terrorism charges. Authorities linked the incident to the armed group ISIL (the Islamic State of Iraq and the Levant). At the end of the reporting period, an investigation was ongoing. In addition, Minister of Interior Mohammed bin Naif traveled to the site of the attack and visited family members of the victims; he also announced that the government would provide compensation to the families of those who were killed. At the funeral for the victims, tens of thousands of

Sunni and Shi'a Muslims demonstrated in solidarity against sectarianism.

Apostasy, Blasphemy, and Sorcery Charges

The Saudi government continues to use criminal charges of apostasy and blasphemy to suppress discussion and debate and silence dissidents. Promoters of political and human rights reforms, and those seeking to debate the role of religion in relation to the state, its laws, and society, typically have been the targets of such charges.

In February 2015, after the end of the reporting period, a General Court reportedly sentenced to death a Saudi man for apostasy. According to multiple reports, the unidentified man allegedly posted a video of himself on a social networking site tearing pages from a Quran while making disparaging remarks. The court used this video as evidence to convict him and justify the death sentence.

In May 2014, a Saudi appeals court sentenced blogger Raif Badawi to 10 years in prison and 1,000 lashes, and fined him $1 million SR ($266,000 USD) for, among other charges, insulting Islam and religious authorities. The sentence called for Badawi – the founder and editor of a Web site that served as an online forum for diverse views to be expressed freely – to be lashed 50 times a week for 20 consecutive weeks. On January 9, 2015, Badawi received his first set of 50 lashes. Immediately after the flogging was carried out, several governments, including the United States, and numerous international human rights groups and individuals condemned the implementation of the sentence. Badawi has not received additional floggings, due in part to the international outrage and in part to a medical doctor's finding that he could not physically endure more lashings. At

Saudi Supreme Court in January 2015. Badawi's lawyer, Waleed Abu al-Khair, was sentenced in July 2014 by a Specialized Criminal Court to 15 years in jail on various trumped-up charges related to his work as a human rights defender.

In June 2014, two Saudi men, Sultan Hamid Marzooq al-Enezi and Saud Falih Awad al-Enezi, were released from prison after being arrested under the pretext of drug charges and spending more than two years in prison without charges. Although formal charges were not filed, reports suggested the two men were held for committing the capital crime of apostasy for converting to the Ahmadi interpretation of Islam.

Individuals arrested for sorcery – a crime punishable by death – continued to be prosecuted during the reporting period. In June 2014, the Saudi Ministry of Justice announced that prosecutors had filed 191 cases of alleged sorcery between November 2013 and May 2014. In August, authorities reportedly beheaded a Saudi man, Mohammed bin Bakr al-Alawi, in the al-Jawf Province for allegedly practicing sorcery. His death sentence had been upheld by an appeals court and the Supreme Judiciary Council. In February 2014, King Abdullah pardoned a female Indonesian domestic worker, Ati Bt Abeh Inan, who had been on death row for more than 10 years following a 2003 sorcery conviction.

New Law Classifies Blasphemy, Advocating Atheism as Acts of Terrorism

Saudi Arabia's new terrorism law, the Penal Law for Crimes of Terrorism and its Financing, and a series of subsequent royal decrees create a legal framework that criminalizes as terrorism virtually all forms of peaceful dissent and free expression, including criticizing the gov-

Saudi Arabia's new terrorism law . . . criminalizes as terrorism virtually all forms of peaceful dissent and free expression, including criticizing the government's interpretation of Islam or advocating atheism.

the end of the reporting period, Badawi continued to languish in prison, where he has been held since June 2012. Badawi's case reportedly was referred to the

ernment's interpretation of Islam or advocating atheism. Under the new law, which went into effect in February 2014, a conviction could result in a prison term ranging from three to 20 years. The Interior Ministry's March 2014 regulations state that, under the new law, terrorism includes "[c]alling for atheist thought in any form, or calling into question the fundamentals of the Islamic religion on which this country is based." While Saudi Shari'ah courts already permit judges to criminalize various forms of peaceful dissent, the new law provides an additional mechanism to classify as terrorism actions considered blasphemous or to be advocating for atheism.

Abuses by the CPVPV

The Commission for the Promotion of Virtue and Prevention of Vice (CPVPV), which reports to the King and is not subject to judicial review, officially enforces public morality and restricts public religious manifestations and practice by both Saudis and non-Saudis. In recent years, the public presence of the CPVPV has diminished. Nevertheless, in 2014, members of the CPVPV periodically overstepped their authority in parts of the

USCIRF found that there were improvements concerning the removal of intolerant content. USCIRF subsequently requested seven additional textbooks, which it hopes to review in the future. USCIRF had not received these books by the end of the reporting period. The Saudi government acknowledged that some of the high school-level textbooks were still in the process of being revised.

In recent years, a Saudi royal decree banned the financing outside Saudi Arabia of religious schools, mosques, hate literature, and other activities that support religious intolerance and violence toward non-Muslims and non-conforming Muslims. Nevertheless, some literature, older versions of textbooks, and other intolerant materials reportedly remain in distribution in some countries around the world despite the Saudi government's policy that it would attempt to retrieve previously-distributed materials that teach hatred toward other religions and, in some cases, promote violence. For example, some of the

USCIRF found that there were improvements concerning the removal of intolerant content [from Saudi textbooks].

country. In 2013, a law was passed limiting the jurisdiction of the CPVPV. Despite the fact that the CPVPV is not allowed to engage in surveillance, detain individuals for more than 24 hours, arrest individuals without police accompaniment, or carry out any kind of punishment, its members have been accused over the past year of beating, whipping, detaining, and otherwise harassing individuals. USCIRF continues to call for the dissolution of the CPVPV.

Improvements in Saudi Textbooks, Yet Continued Dissemination of Intolerant Materials

During the reporting period, USCIRF's longstanding request was largely fulfilled when the Saudi Embassy in Washington, DC provided most textbooks used in public schools in the Kingdom during the 2013-2014 school year. After an analysis of some of the relevant religious textbooks that had been cited previously as containing inflammatory language advocating hatred and violence,

older books justified violence against apostates, sorcerers, and homosexuals, and labeled Jews and Christians "enemies of the believers;" another high school textbook presented the "Protocols of the Elders of Zion" – a notorious forgery designed to promote hostility toward Jews – as an authentic document. Concerns also remain about privately-funded satellite television stations in the Kingdom that continue to espouse sectarian hatred and intolerance.

U.S. Policy

Despite a series of challenges in recent years, U.S.-Saudi relations remain close. For years, the U.S. government's reliance on the Saudi government for cooperation on counterterrorism, regional security, and energy supplies has limited its willingness to press the Saudi government to improve its poor human rights and religious freedom record. Since 2012, the U.S. government has notified Congress of more than $24 billion in proposed arms sales to the Kingdom. During the past year, shared concerns over Islamist terrorism, particularly advances by ISIL, and Iranian regional ambitions provided a renewed impetus for increased strategic cooperation. As a result, there are concerns that the United States has been reluctant to jeopardize important bilateral initiatives by pushing publicly for political and human rights reforms, despite opportunities that arose during the year, such as two high-profile visits to the Kingdom by President Obama. However, in January 2015, the State Department issued a public statement urging the Saudi government to cancel the flogging against blogger Raif Badawi and to review his case and sentence.

According to the State Department, U.S. policy seeks to press the Saudi government "to respect religious freedom and honor its public commitment to permit private religious worship by non-Muslims, eliminate discrimination against minorities, promote respect for non-Muslim religious belief, and combat violent extremism." The U.S. government continues to encourage the Saudi government's efforts to remove intolerant passages advocating violence in textbooks, and it continues to include Saudi officials in exchange and U.S. visitor programs that promote religious tolerance and interfaith dialogue. In addition, according to the U.S. Ambassador to Saudi Arabia, as of mid-2014, more than 83,000 Saudi students were studying in American colleges and universities, the highest figure to date.

In September 2004, consistent with USCIRF's recommendation, the State Department designated Saudi Arabia a CPC for the first time. In 2005, a temporary waiver was put in place, in lieu of otherwise legislatively mandated action as a result of the CPC designation, to allow for continued diplomatic discussions between the U.S. and Saudi governments and "to further the purposes of IRFA." In July 2006, the waiver was left in place indefinitely when the State Department announced that ongoing bilateral discussions with Saudi Arabia had enabled the U.S. government to identify and confirm a number of policies that the Saudi government "is pursuing and will continue to pursue for the purpose of promoting greater freedom for religious practice and increased tolerance for religious groups." USCIRF has concluded that full implementation by the Saudi government of these policies would diminish signifi-

cantly the government's institutionalized practices that negatively affect freedom of religion and belief. The measures that Saudi Arabia confirmed as state policies included the following:

- Revise and update textbooks to remove remaining intolerant references that disparage Muslims or non-Muslims or that promote hatred toward other religions or religious groups, a process the Saudi government expected to complete in one to two years [no later than July 2008].

- Prohibit the use of government channels or government funds to publish or promote textbooks, literature, or other materials that advocate intolerance and sanction hatred of religions or religious groups.

- Control distribution of Saudi educational curricula to ensure that unauthorized organizations do not send them abroad.

- Ensure Saudi embassies and consulates abroad review and destroy any material given to them by charities or other entities that promote intolerance or hatred.

- Guarantee and protect the right to private worship for all, including non-Muslims who gather in homes for religious practice.

- Address grievances when the right to private worship is violated.

- Ensure that customs inspectors at borders do not confiscate personal religious materials.

- Ensure that members of the CPVPV do not detain or conduct investigations of suspects, implement punishment, violate the sanctity of private homes, conduct surveillance, or confiscate private religious materials.

- Hold accountable any CPVPV officials who commit abuses.

- Bring the Kingdom's rules and regulations into compliance with human rights standards.

On July 28, 2014, the State Department re-designated Saudi Arabia a CPC but kept in place a waiver of any action citing the "important national interest of the United States," pursuant to section 407 of IRFA.

Recommendations

USCIRF urges the U.S. government to address religious freedom issues actively and publicly with the Saudi government and to report openly on the government's success or failure to implement genuine reforms, in order to ensure that the Saudi government's initiatives will result in substantial, demonstrable progress. Specifically, USCIRF recommends that the U.S. government should:

- Continue to designate Saudi Arabia a CPC, no longer issue a waiver, and press the Saudi government to take concrete action towards completing reforms confirmed in July 2006 in U.S.-Saudi bilateral discussions; provide a detailed report on progress and lack of progress on each of the areas of concern;

- At the highest levels, press for and work to secure the release of Raif Badawi, his lawyer Waleed Abu al-Khair, and other prisoners of conscience, and press the Saudi government to end state prosecution of individuals charged with apostasy, blasphemy, and sorcery;

- Undertake and make public an annual assessment of the relevant Ministry of Education religious textbooks to determine if passages that teach religious intolerance have been removed;

- Press the Saudi government to publicly denounce the continued use around the world of older versions of Saudi textbooks and other materials that promote hatred and intolerance, to include the concepts of tolerance and respect for the human rights of all persons in school textbooks, and to make every attempt to retrieve previously distributed materials that contain intolerance;

- Press the Saudi government to continue to address incitement to violence and discrimination against disfavored Muslims and non-Muslims, including by prosecuting government-funded clerics who incite violence against Muslim minority communities or individual members of non-Muslim religious minority communities;

- Press the Saudi government to ensure equal rights and protection under the law for Shi'a Muslim citizens;

- Press the Saudi government to remove the classification of advocating atheism and blasphemy as terrorist acts in its 2014 terrorism law;

- Include Saudi religious leaders, in addition to government officials, in exchanges and U.S visitor programs that promote religious tolerance and interfaith dialogue; and

- Work with the Saudi government to codify non-Muslim private religious practice, and permit foreign clergy to enter the country to carry out worship services and to bring religious materials for such services.

The U.S. Congress should:

- Require the State Department to issue a public progress report on efforts and results achieved by the Saudi government to implement religious freedom reforms announced in July 2006.

Dissenting Statement of Vice Chair James J. Zogby:

I did not disagree with designating Saudi Arabia as a "country of particular concern" (CPC) because as the report makes clear Saudi Arabia does not allow "public expression of any religion of any religion other than Islam."

Where I strongly disagree is with USCIRF's decision to call on the Department of State to remove the waiver provision that defers any action that might be taken as a result of Saudi Arabia's CPC status.

What I would have preferred was a recommendation that would have coupled the CPC designation with a full review of the progress or lack of progress the Saudi government has made in implementing the 2006 "US-Saudi Discussions on Religious Practice and Tolerance."

That 2006 discussion paper included 32 specific areas where the Saudi government committed to make reforms. Saudi officials have said that they are making these reforms, not because of outside pressures, but because these are changes they know they need to make to move their country forward. Annually we report, in piecemeal fashion, on some of the progress the government has made in a number of these areas: removal of both intolerant literature from their schools and intolerant speech from their mosques, insuring the right to private worship, creating a Human Rights Commission, etc. What we are lacking is a comprehensive review of just how much progress made and a list of the areas that still need to be addressed.

What the State Department should do is go back to the 2006 discussion paper and treat its 32 items as a check list. They should go through it with their Saudi interlocutors and report, in detail, on progress or lack of progress made in each case. In some instances, such engagement may provide opportunities for U.S. officials or USCIRF to offer assistance or new ideas to help Saudi officials find a way to move forward. In an effort to achieve progress, engagement with Saudi officials is the preferred and most effective course of action. On the other hand, should we move to end the waiver and enact the punitive measures that might flow from this action, we would risk shutting off further discussion. This would prove to be counterproductive.

Additional Statement of Commissioners Eric P. Schwartz and Thomas J. Reese, S.J.:

We strongly supported and voted for the CPC designation, but we write to comment on the Commission recommendation to urge the Administration to remove the waiver provision, which, pursuant to the IRFA legislation, effectively constitutes a recommendation to impose sanctions absent a U.S.-Saudi "binding agreement" to improve religious freedom. To be sure, we believe that both a readiness to impose sanctions and the imposition of sanctions can send important signals to offending governments and help bring critical pressure to bear in efforts to improve conditions related to human rights and religious freedom. Commissioner Schwartz notes further that, as a White House and State Department official, he was in general quite reliably on the side of those supporting sanctions as a tool to promote human rights. In short, we should impose sanctions when we have a fair degree of confidence that, over time, they will strengthen the position of human rights activists or help to change behavior of offending governments. But sanctions can also be ineffective or sometimes even counterproductive. Policy goals can be frustrated if the sanctions have little economic impact, permit a government easily to stoke nationalist or religious fervor against perceived outside interference, or are imposed when our influence is uncertain. Thus, their possible imposition

merits careful discussion of costs and benefits. In this case, Commissioners did not subject their decision to such careful consideration, and, in the absence of such deliberation, we were not prepared to support elimination of the waiver.

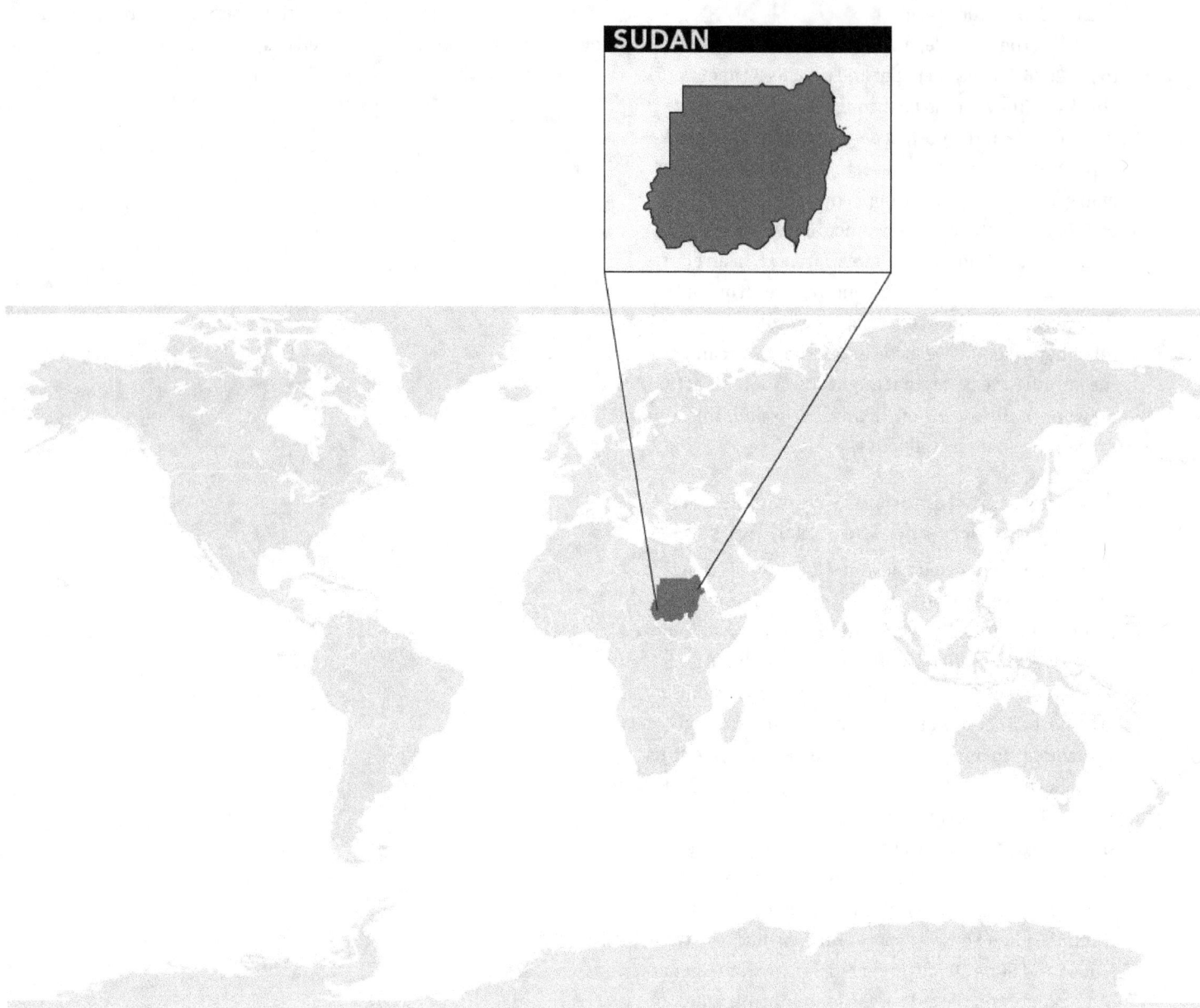

SUDAN

Key Findings

The government of Sudan, led by President Omar Hassan al-Bashir, continues to engage in systematic, ongoing, and egregious violations of freedom of religion or belief. These violations are the result of President Bashir's policies of Islamization and Arabization. The government of Sudan prosecutes persons accused of apostasy, imposes a restrictive interpretation of Shari'ah (Islamic law) and applies corresponding *hudood* punishments on Muslims and non-Muslims alike, and harasses the country's Christian community. President al-Bashir and other National Congress Party (NCP) leaders continue to state that the country will be governed by Shari'ah law. In 2015, USCIRF again recommends that Sudan be designated as a "country of particular concern," or CPC, under the International Religious Freedom Act (IRFA). The State Department has designated Sudan as a CPC since 1999, most recently in July 2014.

Background

More than 97 percent of the Sudanese population is Muslim. The vast majority of Sudanese Muslims belong to different Sufi orders, although Shi'a Muslims and Sunni Muslims who follow the Salafist movement are

For more than 20 years, the 1991 Criminal Code, the 1991 Personal Status Law of Muslims, and state-level "public order" laws have restricted religious freedom for all Sudanese.

These laws contradict Sudan's constitutional and international commitments to freedom of religion or belief and related human rights. The 1991 Criminal Code imposes the ruling NCP's interpretation of Shari'ah law on Muslims and Christians: it allows death sentences for apostasy, stoning for adultery, cross-amputations for theft, prison sentences for blasphemy, and floggings for undefined "offences of honor, reputation and public morality," including undefined "indecent or immoral acts." Prohibitions and related punishments for "immorality" and "indecency" are implemented through state level Public Order laws and enforcement mechanisms; violations carry a maximum penalty of 40 lashes, a fine, or both.

Government policies and societal pressure promote conversion to Islam. The government is alleged to tolerate of the use of humanitarian assistance to induce conversion to Islam; routinely grants permits to construct and operate mosques, often with government funds; and provides Muslims preferential access

For more than 20 years, the 1991 Criminal Code, the 1991 Personal Status Law of Muslims, and state-level "public order" laws have restricted religious freedom for all Sudanese.

also present. Christians are estimated at three present of the population and include Coptic, Greek, Ethiopian, and Eritrean Orthodox; Roman Catholics; Anglicans; Presbyterians; Seventh-day Adventists; Jehovah's Witnesses; and several Pentecostal and evangelical communities.

to government employment and services and favored treatment in court cases against non-Muslims. The Sudanese government prohibits foreign church officials traveling outside Khartoum and uses school textbooks that negatively stereotype non-Muslims. Permission to build churches is impossible to obtain, and destruction of churches has increased since 2011.

Religious Freedom Conditions 2014–2015

Implementation of Apostasy Prohibitions

Conversion from Islam is a crime punishable by death. Suspected converts to Christianity face societal pressures, and government security personnel intimidate and sometimes torture those suspected of conversion. Since 2011, more than 170 persons have been arrested and charged with apostasy; almost all recanted their faith in exchange for having the charges dropped and being released from prison.

On May 15, 2014, the government of Sudan sentenced Meriam Yahia Ibrahim Ishag to death by hanging because, although she said she was raised a Christian, a family member said she was raised a Muslim and thus was guilty of apostasy for converting. In addition, because the court did not recognize her marriage to a Christian man, she also was found guilty of adultery and sentenced to 100 lashes. While imprisoned in the Omdurman Federal Women's Prison with her two-year-old son, Meriam give birth on May 27 to a baby girl. On June 23, an appeals court cancelled the apostasy charges and death sentence and ordered her

ongoing. Throughout the reporting period, the lawyers were harassed and threatened with death for being "un-Islamic."

Application of Shari'ah Law Provisions

The government continued to apply the Shari'ah-based provisions of the 1991 Criminal Code and Public Order laws, although there were fewer reported incidents during this reporting period. As in previous years, there were several known amputation sentences for those found guilty of theft. Dozens of Muslim and Christian women were flogged or fined for "indecent" dress. What constitutes indecent dress is not defined by law, but is left to the discretion of arresting officers and prosecuting judges. Under the guise of protecting morality, the Public Order Laws also prohibit the co-mingling of unmarried men and women, which is deemed "prostitution."

Destruction and Confiscation of Churches

The Sudanese Minister of Guidance and Religious Endowments announced in July 2014 that the government no longer will issue permits for the building of new

---

On May 15, 2014, the government of Sudan sentenced Meriam Yahia Ibrahim Ishag to death by hanging because, although she said she was raised a Christian, a family member said she was raised a Muslim and thus was guilty of apostasy for converting.

---

release from prison, finding that she was not an apostate. The next day, she and her family were detained at Khartoum's airport as they sought to leave the country. From June 27 until July 24, when she was permitted to leave Sudan, Meriam, her American citizen husband, and their two children took refuge at the U.S. Embassy in Khartoum.

In October, Meriam's lawyers challenged the constitutionality of the prohibition on conversion from Islam contained in article 126 of the 1991 criminal code. They argue that it violates article 38 of the interim constitution, which guarantees freedom of religion or belief and states that "no person shall be coerced to adopt such faith, that he/she does not believe in." The case is

churches, alleging that the current number of churches is sufficient for the Christians remaining in Sudan after South Sudan's 2011 secession. In 2014, Sudanese authorities bulldozed the Sudanese Church of Christ. In the last few years, at least 11 churches have been attacked either by government officials or societal actors.

Throughout this reporting period, the government of Sudan continued efforts to confiscate church property. In 2014 and early 2015, both the Bahri Evangelical Church and an Anglican church in Khartoum continued legal battles to maintain ownership of their churches and the land they occupy. On December 2, Sudanese authorities partially destroyed the Bahri Evangelical Church and arrested 37 congregants protesting the action. They were later released. Authorities also arrested Rev. Yat Michael and Rev. Peter Yein for "instigating Sudanese citizens against their government;" the two clergymen remain detained.

U.S. Policy

The United States remains a pivotal international actor in Sudan. U.S. government involvement was vital to achieving the Comprehensive Peace Agreement (CPA) that ended the North-South civil war and to bringing about the referendum on South Sudan's independence, as well as ensuring that its result was recognized. The U.S. government continues multilateral and bilateral efforts to bring peace to Southern Kordofan, Blue Nile, and Darfur, including supporting African Union peace talks.

In 1997, President Bill Clinton utilized the International Emergency Economic Powers Act (IEEPA) to sanction Sudan, based on its support for international terrorism, efforts to destabilize neighboring governments, and prevalent human rights and religious freedom violations. These sanctions imposed a trade

mitment to promote freedom of expression through access to communications tools."

Neither country has had an ambassador to the other since the late 1990s, after the U.S. Embassy bombings in East Africa and U.S. airstrikes against al-Qaeda sites in Khartoum, but successive U.S. administrations have appointed special envoys to Sudan. The current U.S. Special Envoy to Sudan and South Sudan is Donald E. Booth.

In February 2015, Sudanese Foreign Minister Ali Kharti and Presidential Assistant Ibrahim Ghandour made separate trips to Washington, DC. After the Ghandour visit, U.S. Deputy Assistant Secretary of State for Democracy, Human Rights and Labor Steve Feldstein was granted permission to travel to Sudan. From February 22-26, DAS Feldstein met with Sudanese government leaders and representatives of non-governmental organizations in Khartoum, as well as civil society activists, humanitarian groups, and internally displaced persons (IDPs) in Blue Nile State.

The international attention to the Meriam Ibrahim case and her marriage to a U.S. citizen led to increased

---

The international attention to the Meriam Ibrahim case and her marriage to a U.S. citizen led to increased U.S. public advocacy about religious freedom conditions. . .

---

embargo on the country and a total asset freeze on the government. Since 1997, an arms embargo, travel bans, and asset freezes have been imposed in response to the genocide in Darfur. With the 1999 designation of Sudan as a CPC, the Secretary of State has utilized IRFA to require U.S. opposition to any loan or other use of funds from international financial institutions to or for Sudan. In an attempt to prevent sanctions from negatively impacting regions in Sudan under assault by the NCP government, the sanctions have been amended to allow for increased humanitarian activities in Southern Kordofan State, Blue Nile State, Abyei, Darfur, and marginalized areas in and around Khartoum. In February 2015, the United States allowed the exportation countrywide of communication hardware and software, including computers, smartphones, radios, digital cameras, and related items, as part of a "com-

U.S. public advocacy about religious freedom conditions in Sudan in this reporting period. The White House, Secretary of State John Kerry, the U.S. Embassy in Khartoum, the State Department, and Members of Congress vigorously advocated on Meriam Ibrahim's behalf. On May 14, the United States, Canada, the United Kingdom, and the Netherlands issued a joint statement expressing their concern over the apostasy ruling and noting an individual's right to change faith. U.S. Embassy officials observed her May 15 hearing and offered her refuge before she could leave the country. DAS Feldstein met with religious leaders and raised religious freedom concerns with Sudanese officials during his February 2015 trip to the country.

U.S. government assistance programs in Sudan support conflict mitigation efforts, democracy promotion, and emergency food aid and relief supplies. The United

States remains the world's largest donor of food assistance to Sudan, providing needed aid, either directly or through third parties, to persons from Darfur, Abyei, Southern Kordofan, and Blue Nile.

Recommendations

With the Bashir regime taking steps that would move Sudan toward a more repressive state, the U.S. government should increase efforts to encourage reforms and discourage regressive behavior. The normalization of relations with Sudan and any lifting of U.S. sanctions must be preceded by demonstrated, concrete progress

- Create a Commission on the Rights of Non-Muslims to ensure and advocate religious freedom protections for non-Muslims in Sudan;

- Issue a decree ending the use of corporal punishments for hudood offenses that violate "public order" as enumerated in the 1991 Criminal Code Act and state-level public order laws; and

- Hold accountable any person who engages in violations of freedom of religion or belief, including attacking houses of worship, attacking or discriminating against a person because of their

With the Bashir regime taking steps that would move Sudan toward a more repressive state, the U.S. government should increase efforts to encourage reforms and discourage regressive behavior.

by Khartoum in implementing peace agreements, ending abuses of religious freedom and related human rights, and cooperating with efforts to protect civilians. In addition to recommending that Sudan continue to be designated as a CPC, USCIRF recommends the U.S. government should:

- Seek to enter into a binding agreement with the government of Sudan, as defined in section 405(c) of IRFA, which would set forth commitments the government would undertake to address policies leading to violations of religious freedom, including but not limited to the following:

  - End prosecutions and punishments for apostasy;

  - Maintain all of the provisions respecting the country's international human rights commitments and respect for freedom of religion or belief currently in the interim constitution;

  - Lift government prohibitions on church construction, issue permits for the building of new churches, and create a legal mechanism to provide compensation for destroyed churches and address future destructions if necessary;

religious affiliation, and prohibiting a person from fully exercising their religious rights.

- Work to ensure that Sudan's future, permanent constitution includes protections for freedom of religion or belief, respect for international commitments to human rights, and recognition of Sudan as a multi-religious, multi-ethnic, and multi-cultural nation;

- Continue to support national dialogue efforts with civil society and faith-based leaders and representatives of all relevant political parties;; educate relevant parties to the national dialogue about international human rights standards, including regarding freedom of religion or belief; and work with opposition parties and civil society to resolve internal disputes related to freedom of religion or belief;

- Encourage and support civil society groups to monitor implementation of the Public Order Regime and advocate for its repeal; and

- Urge the government in Khartoum to cooperate fully with international mechanisms on human rights issues, including by inviting further visits by the UN Special Rapporteur on Freedom of Religion or Belief, the Independent Expert on the Situation of Human Rights in Sudan, and the UN Working Group on Arbitrary Detention.

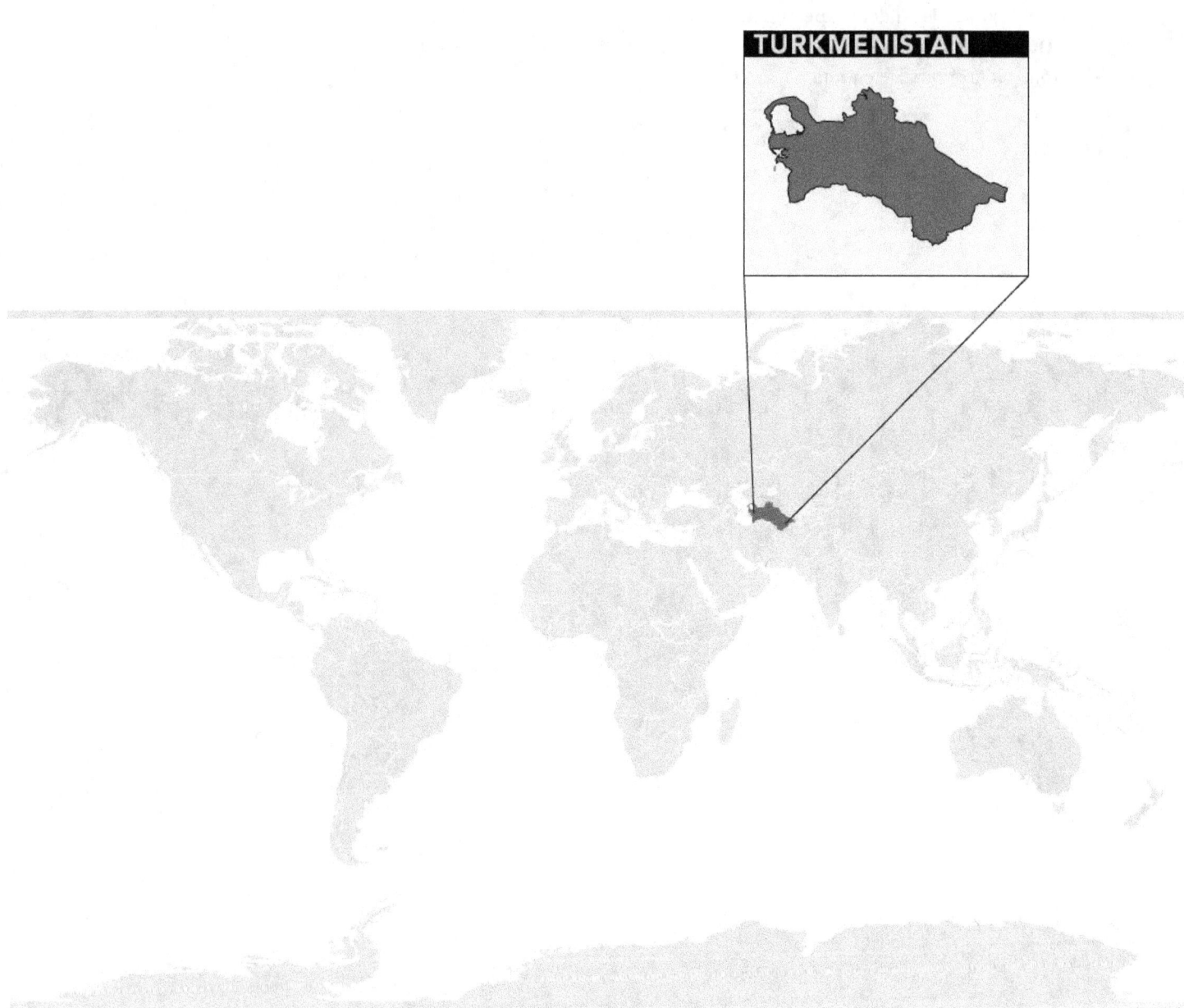

TURKMENISTAN

Key Findings

In a climate of pervasive government information control, particularly severe religious freedom violations persist in Turkmenistan. Police raids and harassment of registered and unregistered religious groups continued. The country's laws, policies, and practices violate international human rights norms, including those on freedom of religion or belief, and new administrative code provisions increased the penalties for most "illegal" religious activities. Turkmen law does not allow a civilian alternative to military service, and at least one Jehovah's Witness conscientious objector is known to be detained. In light of these severe violations, USCIRF recommends in 2015 that the U.S. government again designate Turkmenistan as a "country of particular concern," or CPC, under the International Religious Freedom Act (IRFA). In July 2014, the State Department designated Turkmenistan a CPC for the first time. USCIRF has recommended CPC designation for Turkmenistan since 2000.

Background

Turkmenistan has an estimated total population of 5.1 million. Official Turkmen data on religious affiliation are not available; the U.S. government estimates that the country is about 85 percent Sunni Muslim, nine percent Russian Orthodox, and a two percent total that includes number of ethnic Turkmen. The small number of Shi'a Muslims is mostly ethnic Iranians, Azeris, or Kurds on the Iranian border or on the Caspian Sea. The Jewish community consists of approximately 400 Jews.

Turkmenistan is the most closed country in the former Soviet Union. The country's first president, Saparmurat Niyazov, who died in late 2006, oversaw one of the world's most repressive and isolated states. Turkmenistan's public life was dominated by Niyazov's quasi-religious personality cult set out in his book, the *Ruhnama*, which was imposed on the country's religious and educational systems. After assuming the presidency in early 2007, President Gurbanguly Berdimuhamedov ordered the release of 11 political prisoners, including the former chief mufti; placed certain limits on Niyazov's personality cult; set up two new official human rights commissions; and registered 13 minority religious groups. He eased police controls on internal travel and allowed Turkmenistan to become slightly more open to the outside world.

Since that early period, President Berdimuhamedov has not reformed the country's oppressive laws, maintains a state structure of repressive control, and has reinstituted a pervasive presidential personality cult. Turkmenistan's constitution purports to guarantee religious freedom, the separation of religion from the state, and equality regardless of religion or belief.

> *Turkmenistan is the most closed country in the former Soviet Union.*

Jehovah's Witnesses, Jews, and evangelical Christians. While most Russians and Armenians belong to the Russian Orthodox Church, a significant number attend unregistered religious meetings as do an increasing

The 2003 religion law, however, contradicts these provisions. Despite minor reforms in 2007, this law sets intrusive registration criteria and bans any activity by unregistered religious organizations; requires that the government be informed of all foreign financial support; forbids worship in private homes; allows only clerics to wear religious garb in public; and places severe and discriminatory restrictions on religious education. The government-appointed Council on Religious Affairs (CRA) supervises religious matters; it controls the hiring, promoting, and firing of Sunni Muslim and Russian Orthodox clergy; censors religious texts; and oversees the activities of all registered groups. CRA members include only government officials and Sunni Muslim and Russian Orthodox Church representatives. A new demonstrations law enacted in March 2015 potentially allows for limited public rallies, including by registered religious organizations. Rallies must be at least 200 meters from government buildings and cannot be funded by individuals or foreign governments, RFE/RL reported.

A new Internet law was published in December 2014; it is now illegal for citizens to insult or slander Turkmenistan's president in web postings, RFE/RL reported. While the law states there are plans to ensure free access to the worldwide web for Turkmen Internet users, in 2015 the Turkmen government reportedly has engaged in a campaign to dismantle private satellite cables.

In 2014 and early 2015, Turkmen border guards reportedly were killed by the Taliban on the Turkmen-Afghan border. This region of Afghanistan also reportedly includes some Turkmen who allegedly are Islamic State sympathizers, giving rise to concern about possible religious radicalism spreading across the border into Turkmenistan.

Religious Freedom Conditions 2014–2015
Punishments for Religious and Human Rights Activities

In January 2014, new administrative code provisions increased the penalties for most "illegal" religious activi-

fines, for religious and human rights activities. In recent years, Muslims, Protestants, and Jehovah's Witnesses were detained, fined, imprisoned or internally exiled for their religious beliefs or activities. Most religious prisoners of conscience are held at Seydi Labor Camp in the Lebap Region desert, where they face harsh conditions, including torture. The government of Turkmenistan denies the International Committee of the Red Cross access to the country's prisons.

An unknown number of Muslim prisoners of conscience remain jailed. In February 2015, five prisoners convicted of "Wahhabism" were sent to Seydi Labor Camp, where reportedly prison guards brutally beat them. The NGO Forum 18 News Service could not determine if the five men were jailed for non-violent religious practice or for crimes, since in Central Asia the term "Wahhabi" is commonly used to describe any devout Muslim. In December 2014, a group of about 10 Muslim religious prisoners were transferred from that labor camp to the high-security prison in Ovadan-Depe. Reports have faded of a dissident imam who spent years in a psychiatric hospital; this news drought also applies to dozens of other political and religious prisoners, according to the NGO coalition known as "Prove they are Alive."

On a positive note, in October 2014 two known religious prisoners of conscience were released under presidential amnesty from a labor camp in eastern Turkmenistan, Forum 18 reported. In February 2015, Protestant Umid Gojayev, imprisoned at Seydi Labor Camp for "hooliganism," also was freed under amnesty.

Government Control over Religious Activities

The secret police, anti-terrorist police units, local government, and local CRA officials continued to raid registered and unregistered religious communities. It is illegal for unregistered groups to rent, purchase, or

The government continues to impose harsh penalties . . . for religious and human rights activities.

ties. The government continues to impose harsh penalties, such as imprisonment, forced drug treatment, and

construct places of worship, and even registered groups must obtain scarce government permits. A decree banned publication of religious texts inside Turkmenistan and only registered groups can legally import such texts. In September 2014 in Dashoguz, Jehovah's Witness Bibi Rahmanova was detained for a month and physically abused for distributing religious texts; she received a four-year suspended sentence on trumped-up charges of assaulting a police officer, according to Forum 18. Forum 18 also reported that a Protestant outside Ashgabat was fined in September 2014 after a relative was

Ruslan Narkuliyev was released, Forum 18 reported.

Registration of Religious Groups

Since 2005, some small religious groups have been registered, such as the Baha'i, several Pentecostal groups, Seventh-Day Adventists, several Evangelical churches, and the Society for Krishna Consciousness. In 2010, Turkmenistan told the UN Human Rights Committee there were 123 registered religious groups,

---

The government interferes in the internal leadership and arrangements of religious communities

---

found to have electronic versions of religious texts. The religion law also bans private religious education.

The government continues to deny international travel for many citizens, especially those travelling to religious events. For the approximately 110,000 mainly Russian Orthodox who have dual Russian-Turkmen citizenship, it is easier to meet with their coreligionists abroad and for clerical training. Muslims, however, are not allowed to travel abroad for religious education, and the government also restricts *hajj* participation. In 2014, it requested a quota of 650 Turkmen Muslims to make the pilgrimage to Mecca, according to Forum 18. While this number was an increase over the usual 188, it is still less than a seventh of the country's quota. Muslims often must wait up to 11 years to reach the top of the *hajj* waiting list.

Conscientious Objectors

Turkmen law has no civilian alternative to military service for conscientious objectors. Reportedly such a bill was drafted in 2013 but not enacted. Those who refuse to serve in the military can face up to two years of jail. Until 2009 the Turkmen government had given suspended sentences, but since then conscientious objectors have been imprisoned. Jehovah's Witness conscientious objector Soyunmurat Korov is being involuntarily held in an Ashgabat military hospital. On a positive note, in October 2014, six imprisoned conscientious objectors were amnestied and released by presidential order, and in February 2015, Jehovah's Witness conscientious objector

100 of which are Sunni and Shi'a Muslim and 13 Russian Orthodox. Some groups have decided not to register due to the onerous and opaque process, while certain Shi'a Muslim groups, the Armenian Apostolic Church, some Protestant groups, and the Jehovah's Witnesses have faced rejection of numerous registration applications.

Government Interference in Internal Religious Affairs

The Turkmen government interferes in the internal leadership and organizational arrangements of religious communities. In early 2013, the President named a new Grand Mufti. The government also has replaced imams who had formal Islamic theological training from abroad with individuals lacking such education, as it is official policy not to name imams if they have had foreign theological training. Local secret police officers reportedly require Muslim and Orthodox clerics to report regularly on activities.

U.S. Policy

For the past decade, U.S. policy in Central Asia was dominated by the Afghan war. The United States has key security and economic interests in Turkmenistan due to its proximity to and shared populations with Afghanistan and Iran, and its huge natural gas supplies. Although officially neutral and in the Northern Distribution Network for the delivery of supplies to U.S. troops and International Security Assistance Forces (ISAF) in Afghanistan, the country has allowed U.S. flights with non-lethal supplies to refuel at the Ashgabat International Airport.

The United States is training Turkmenistan's fledgling navy, and holding exchange programs on English language and naval administration. During counter-terrorism operations, U.S. Special Operations Forces reportedly have been allowed to enter Turkmenistan on a "case-by-case" basis, with the Turkmen government's permission. The U.S government also has encouraged a joint Turkmenistan-Afghanistan-Pakistan-India project, known as "TAPI," to construct a major gas pipeline, scheduled to begin in 2015. This project could help stabilize the Turkmen gas export market and create economic and political bonds with energy-poor South Asian markets.

Initiated five years ago by the State Department, the Annual Bilateral Consultations (ABC's) are a regular mechanism for the United States and Turkmenistan to discuss a wide range of bilateral issues, including regional security, economic and trade relations; social and cultural ties; and human rights. As part of the ABC process, Assistant Secretary of State for South and Central Asian Affairs Nisha Desai Biswal led an interagency delegation to Ashgabat, Turkmenistan, in January 2014 for the third U.S.-Turkmen ABC. While in Ashgabat, Assistant Secretary Biswal met with senior Turkmenistan officials, but it is not in the public record if she also met with representatives of civil society or religious groups. Religious freedom concerns traditionally have been raised in these forums.

The United States funds programs in Turkmenistan that support: civil society organizations; training on legal assistance; Internet access and computer training; capacity building for civil servants, as well as exchange programs. In recent years, however, the Turkmen government has barred many students from participating in U.S.-funded exchange programs and in 2013 it ordered the Peace Corps to stop its 20-year-operations in the country. The U.S. government continues to support three American Corners that provide free educational materials and English language opportunities in Dashoguz, Mary, and Turkmenabat. The American Corners Program is a worldwide Department of State-sponsored initiative that was started over 10 years ago.

The State Department announced the designation of Turkmenistan as a "country of particular concern" in late July 2014 when it released its annual report on international religious freedom. The State Department cited "concerns about the detention and imprisonment of religious minorities, the rights of religious groups to register, the lack of public access to registration procedures, and restrictions on importing religious literature." In September 2014, a waiver of a Presidential action was tied to the designation.

Recommendations

The recent CPC designation positions the U.S. government to negotiate commitments to improve religious freedom, while establishing a pathway to eventually de-list Turkmenistan based on concrete reforms. In addition to recommending that the U.S. government continue to designate Turkmenistan as a CPC, USCIRF recommends that the U.S. government should:

- Negotiate a binding agreement with the government of Turkmenistan under section 405(c) of IRFA to achieve specific and meaningful reforms, with benchmarks that include major legal reform, an end to police raids, prisoner releases, and greater access to foreign coreligionists; should an agreement not be reached, the waiver of Presidential actions should be lifted;

- Ensure that the U.S. Embassy maintains active contacts with human rights activists and press the Turkmen government to ensure that every prisoner has greater access to his or her family, human rights monitors, adequate medical care, and a lawyer;

- Raise concerns about Turkmenistan's record on religious freedom and related human rights in bilateral meetings, such as the ABCs, as well as appropriate international fora, including the UN and OSCE; encourage the UN Regional Centre for Preventive Diplomacy for Central Asia (UNRCCA) to enhance the human rights aspect of its work;

- Urge the Turkmen government to agree to another visit by the UN Special Rapporteur on Freedom of Religion or Belief, as well as visits from the Rapporteurs on Independence of the Judiciary and on Torture, set specific visit dates, and provide the full and necessary conditions for their visits;

- Encourage the Broadcasting Board of Governors to increase radio broadcasts and Internet programs to Turkmenistan on religious freedom, including the informative new Islam and Democracy website, as well as information on human rights and basic education, to help overcome decades of isolation;

- Continue to press for resumption of the U.S. Peace Corps program; and

- Use funding allocated to the State Department under the Title VIII Program (established in the Soviet-Eastern European Research and Training Act of 1983) for research, including on human rights and religious freedom in former Soviet states, and language training.

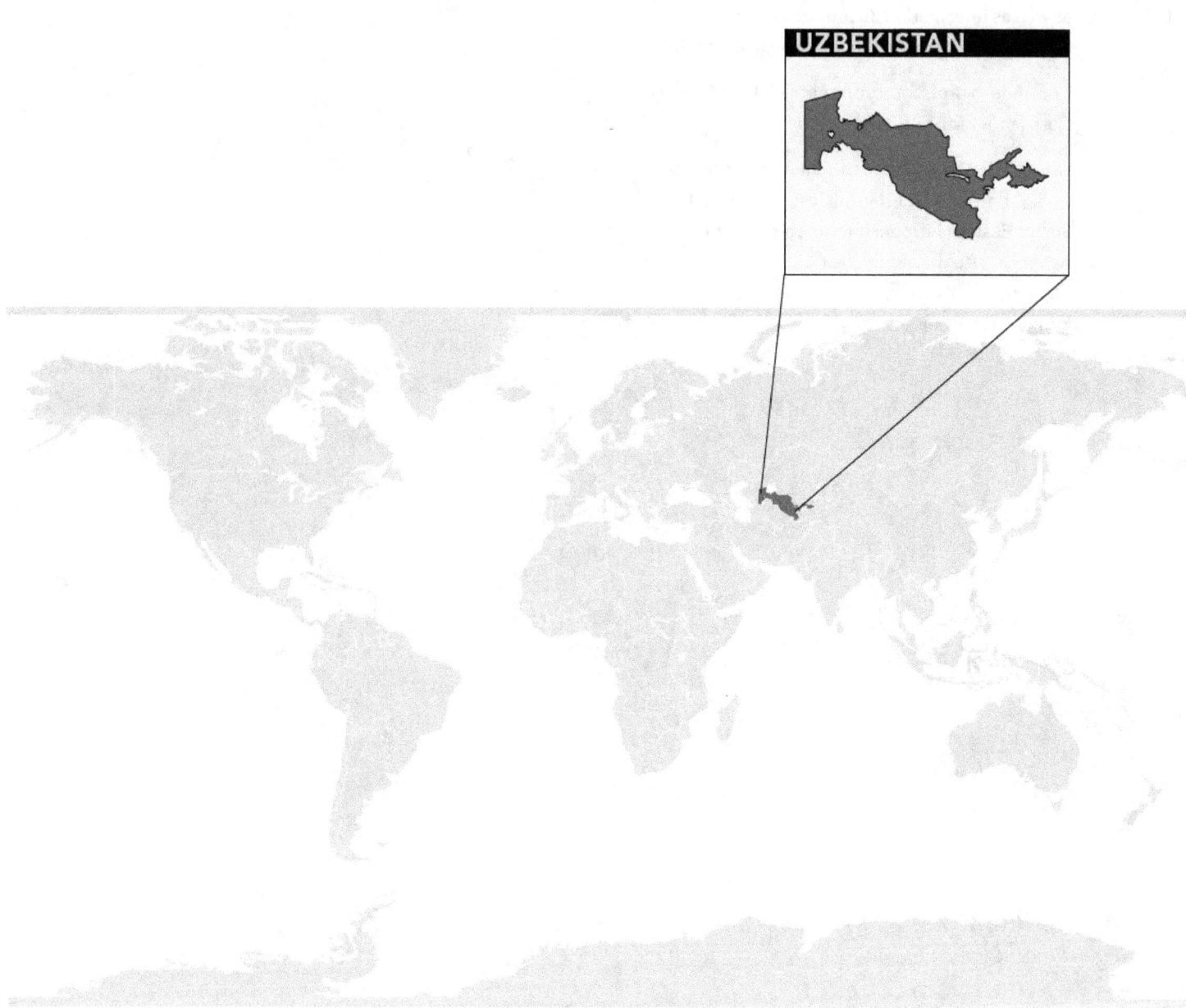

UZBEKISTAN

Key Findings

Particularly severe violations of freedom of religion or belief continue in Uzbekistan through government efforts to enforce a highly restrictive religion law and to impose severe restrictions on all independent religious activity. The government imprisons individuals who do not conform to officially-prescribed practices or who it claims are extremist, including as many as 12,000 Muslims. Based on these systematic, egregious, ongoing violations, USCIRF again recommends in 2015 that Uzbekistan be designated a "country of particular concern," or CPC, under the 1998 International Religious Freedom Act (IRFA). While the State Department has so designated Uzbekistan since 2006, most recently in July 2014, it has also indefinitely waived taking any punitive action since 2009.

Background

With an estimated total of 28.7 million people, Uzbekistan is the most populous post-Soviet Central Asian state. According to local data, 93 percent of its population is Muslim, mostly Hannafi Sunni with about one percent Shi'a, mostly in Bukhara and Samarkand. Some four percent is Russian Orthodox. The other three per-

of all religious groups and facilitates Uzbek government control of religious activity, particularly of the majority Muslim community. The law criminalizes unregistered religious activity; requires official approval of the content, production and distribution of religious publications; bans minors from religious organizations; and allows only clerics, and not laypeople, to wear religious clothing in public. Many religious groups are unable to meet registration requirements, which include a permanent representation in eight of the country's 13 provinces. In 2014, a detailed new censorship decree went into effect banning materials that "distort" beliefs or encourage individuals to change religions.

The Uzbek government actively represses individuals, groups, and mosques that do not conform to officially-prescribed practices or for alleged association with extremist political programs. While Uzbekistan faces security threats from groups using violence in the name of religion, the government has arbitrarily used vague anti-extremism laws against peaceful religious adherents and others who pose no credible security threat. In addition, the Uzbek government's harsh campaign against independent Muslims continues. Particular targets include those linked to the May 2005 protests in

The government has arbitrarily used vague anti-extremism laws against peaceful religious adherents . . .

cent includes Roman Catholics, ethnic Korean Christians, Baptists, Lutherans, Adventists, Pentecostals, Jehovah's Witnesses, Buddhists, Baha'is, Hare Krishnas, and atheists. An estimated 6,000 Ashkenazi and 2,000 Bukharan Jews are in Tashkent and other cities.

Uzbekistan's 1998 Law on Freedom of Conscience and Religious Organizations severely limits the rights

Andijon of the conviction of 23 businessmen for alleged membership in the banned Muslim group *Akromiya*; 231 are still imprisoned in connection with the Andijon events; 10 prisoners have died. The Uzbek government continues to pressure countries to return Uzbek refugees who fled after the Andijon tragedy.

Religious Freedom Conditions 2014-2015

New Surveillance Regime

A new law that went into effect in August 2014 established a Preventive Register that lists all previous convicts for at least one-year of "preventative measures." It authorizes state agencies to prolong Register listings beyond one year and allows local authorities to work with unofficial informers to "prevent the activity of unregistered religious groups."

Application of Extremism Laws

The Uzbek government continued its decade-long policy of arresting and imprisoning, some for as long as 20-year terms, individuals who reject state control over religious practice or for their suspected religious affiliation. Many are denied due process and are tortured; some are detained in psychiatric hospitals. Observers estimate that upwards of 12,000 Uzbek Muslims are in jail on these related charges. In 2013, approximately 200 religious believers were arrested, according to the Uzbek Initiative Group of Independent Human Rights

also cannot leave Uzbekistan for an unknown period. In an RFE/RL Uzbek interview, Hamidov reportedly praised his prison conditions. The other five – Rashid Sharipov, Akmal Abdullayev, Ahmad Rakhmonov, Ahmadjon Primkulov, and Kudratullo (last name unknown) – were pardoned only after they repented and asked President Karimov for forgiveness, thereby in effect admitting their guilt, according to the independent Forum 18 News Service. They were jailed because they met to study the writings of Turkish Muslim theologian Said Nursi. There are unconfirmed reports that other religious prisoners were amnestied in the run-up to the March presidential election in Uzbekistan.

A prominent Uzbek imam, known as Shaykh Abdullah Bukhoroy, a critic of Uzbekistan's government viewed as a radical Islamist, was shot dead in Istanbul on December 10, 2014. In 2014, President Karimov urged religious leaders to protect Uzbeks from the influence of those who wish to establish an Islamic caliphate, according to RFE/RL. The Uzbek government has also used state television to justify its overly broad anti-extremism policies. For example, in late 2014, Uzbek state

---

. . . [U]pwards of 12,000 Uzbek Muslims are in jail . . .

Defenders. The government claims that many detainees are associated with extremist groups that it labels "Wahhabi" or "jihadist," but often without evidence of use or advocacy of violence. These terms can refer to a range of Muslim individuals or groups, including violent extremists, political opponents, those with foreign education, and others.

In 2014, several Muslims, including Tajik citizen Zuboyd Mirzorakhimov and Uzbek citizen Zoirjon Mirzayev, were sentenced to five-year prison terms after police found Qur'anic verses and allegedly "extremist" sermons on their cell phones; as of July 2014, the Tajik citizen was held practically incommunicado in a Tashkent Investigation Prison, 10 months after sentencing.

In February 2015, the Uzbek government amnestied six known Muslim prisoners of conscience, including Hairulla Hamidov, a well-known sports journalist and Muslim commentator. As a release condition, Hamidov had to write an apology to President Islam Karimov; he

TV ran a half-hour show on what it alleged is a new method of treason. The program focused on six Uzbek citizens who were granted refugee status in Norway but had returned to Uzbekistan and were in detention. The show made unfounded allegations not only that the six were religious extremists but also homosexuals who had belonged to a supposed underground religious extremist organization reportedly led by an imam in Oslo.

Detention Conditions

The Uzbek human rights group *Ezgulik* has reported on torture of female detainees, including many jailed for religious beliefs. Despite the Uzbek government's claims, torture remains endemic in prisons, pretrial facilities, and police precincts, and reportedly includes the threat or use of violence, including rape, and the use of gas masks to block victims' air supply. Torture allegedly is used to force adults and children to renounce their religious beliefs or to make confessions. In early 2013, the International Committee for the Red Cross halted its work in Uzbekistan due to lack of official cooperation. Despite a UN Committee Against

a car from two Baptists who refused to pay court fines for religious activity.

In May 2014, police and tax officials raided a Protestant-run drug and alcohol rehabilitation center in

In February 2015, the Uzbek government amnestied six known Muslim prisoners of conscience . . .

Torture appeal, Muslim believer Khayrullo Tursonov was returned by Kazakhstan to Uzbekistan; sentenced to a 16-year term in June 2013, he is now in a TB-infected camp. Nilufar Rahimjanova, 37, died in detention in September 2014 in the women's labor camp near Tashkent, according to Forum 18 News Service. She was three years into a 10-year prison term. Reportedly, she was jailed to punish her Iran-based husband and her Tajikistan-based father, both Muslim theologians.

Restrictions on Muslims

The Uzbek government tightly controls Islamic institutions and prohibits their independent practice. In the Ferghana Valley, the government has confiscated several mosques and banned children from attendance. The government-controlled Muslim Spiritual Board oversees the training, appointment, and dismissal of imams, and censors the content of sermons and Islamic materials. Despite these restrictions, attendance at registered official mosques is high, and the country's former chief mufti, Muhammad Sodiq Muhammad Yusuf, runs a popular website that includes reports on human rights outside Uzbekistan.

Charges against Non-Muslims

The government often brands evangelical Protestants and Jehovah's Witnesses as "extremists" for practicing religion outside of state-sanctioned structures, and they face massive fines, detention, and arrest for "illegal religious activity." Authorities raid meetings of registered and unregistered Christian and Baha'i groups. In three known cases in 2014, local officials supported imams' refusals to allow non-Muslim burials in secular state-owned cemeteries, Forum 18 reported. In May 2014, court bailiffs in the Samarkand region confiscated

Tashkent, closing the center and evicting 20 residents. Criminal charges for alleged financial crimes were brought against the center's founder, Vladislav Sekan; a teacher, Pyotr Tikhomirov, was fined for "illegally" storing religious texts. Both belong to Tashkent's Full Gospel Presbyterian Church. Sekan, who fled the country with his family in June 2014, told Forum 18 that he believed the prosecution was linked to his efforts to unite various Protestant churches in an alliance. In another incident in the same month, police raided an Adventist home in Samarkand; they seized religious texts and computers, reportedly in retaliation for a July registration application. The state-controlled media encourages prejudice against minority religious groups and has equated missionaries with religious extremists.

Restrictions on Religious Materials

The Council on Religious Affairs (CRA) censors religious materials. The religion law prohibits the importing, storing, producing, and distributing of unapproved religious materials. Members of religious communities reportedly destroy their own sacred texts due to fear of confiscation during police raids. In 2013, a CRA official told Forum 18 that Uzbek law only allows religious texts to be read inside buildings of registered religious groups. In May 2014, a Tashkent court fined a couple for "illegally storing" religious texts at home and ordered the books destroyed. In another case, police ignored a court order to return confiscated texts. In July 2014, a Baptist from Taskhent was detained after he posted posters with Bible verses; a court ordered property destruction and a fine. In August 2014 in Navoi, police, without a warrant, searched the home of Baptists while they were worshipping, seized all religious texts from another Baptist home, and warned them not to store Christian texts. The government also maintains an extensive list of banned international websites, particularly on human rights and religious freedom.

Restrictions on Religious Instruction and Travel

Religious instruction is limited to officially-sanctioned religious schools and state-approved instructors, and only six registered religious communities have met the requirement to conduct religious education that they must have eight legally-registered regional branches. In 2013, a woman was fined for her 12-year-old son's "illegal" religious education; he took art lessons from two Protestants. Private religious education is punished. In 2010 Muslim religion teacher Mehrinisso Hamdamova was sentenced to seven years' imprisonment for teaching women about Islam; as previously reported, she continues to need medical attention. The government also restricts international travel for religious purposes, and has a long list of those banned from such travel.

U.S. Policy

Uzbekistan is Central Asia's most populous country and shares borders with the four other former Soviet Republics in Central Asia as well as Afghanistan. It is central to the regional rail system built during the Soviet period that also connects with Russia. Because of this centrality, in recent years, U.S. policy in Uzbekistan has focused on the country's key position in the Northern Distribution Network (NDN), a supply route for U.S. and international forces in Afghanistan. Uzbekistan is the NDN hub, but at times has not been cooperative. Uzbekistan's NDN role will remain important in 2015 as the withdrawal of U.S. combat forces accelerates.

In 2004, Congress prohibited U.S. assistance to the Uzbek central government unless the Secretary of State reports that Uzbekistan is making substantial progress in meeting human rights commitments, establishing a multi-party system, and ensuring free and fair elections. Since 2004, some U.S. aid to Uzbekistan had been withheld due to a lack of progress on democratic reforms. In 2008, Congress adopted a measure blocking Uzbek officials from entering the United States if they are deemed responsible for the 2005 Andijon violence or other human rights violations.

In recent years, however, military assistance has increased. As of 2009, Uzbekistan reportedly has allowed "case-by-case" counter-terrorism operations on its territory. In 2010, Congress permitted expanded military education and training programs for Uzbekistan. In 2012, the State Department certified on national security grounds that military aid to Uzbekistan should resume for six months, despite its human rights assessment citing numerous concerns, such as severe limitations on religious freedom, persistent torture, and no independent probe into the 2005 Andijon events. Such aid includes training border troops and possibly providing military supplies. In a January 2015 VOA interview, Deputy Assistant Secretary of State (DAS) for South and Central Asia Affairs Dan Rosenblum said that as of late 2014 Uzbekistan had received excess U.S. military mine-resistant and armored vehicles under the Excess Defense Articles program to support the country's counter-terrorism and counter-narcotics efforts.

The United States instituted Annual Bilateral Consultations (ABCs) with each Central Asian state in 2009. The most recent U.S.-Uzbekistan ABC was in Tashkent in December 2014. The U.S. delegation was led by Assistant Secretary of State for South and Central Asia Affairs Nisha Desai Biswal. DAS Rosenblum told the VOA that the human rights issues discussed included prison conditions, treatment of prisoners, restrictions on civil society and media, labor rights, and religious freedom. According to Rosenblum, the ABC for the first time also included an NGO roundtable on prison conditions. He also informed USCIRF staff that the U.S. delegation called for the release of specific religious and political prisoners.

Since 2006, the State Department has designated Uzbekistan as a "country of particular concern," or CPC, for its systematic, egregious, ongoing violations of religious freedom. The CPC designation was most recently renewed in July 2014. The State Department continued its policy of indefinitely waiving any action as a consequence of CPC designation, stating that this waiver is in the "important national interest of the United States" pursuant to IRFA section 407.

Recommendations

In addition to recommending that the U.S. government continue to designate Uzbekistan as a CPC, USCIRF recommends that the U.S. government should:

- Work to establish a binding agreement with the Uzbek government, under section 405(c) of IRFA, on steps it can take to be de-listed from the CPC list; should negotiations fail or Uzbekistan not uphold its promises in the agreement, lift the waiver on taking any action in consequence of the CPC designation, in place since January 2009, and impose sanctions, as contemplated in the IRFA legislation;

- Consider making U.S. assistance, except humanitarian assistance and human rights programs, contingent on the Uzbek government's adoption of specific actions to improve religious freedom conditions and comply with international human rights standards, including reforming the 1998 religion law and permitting an international investigation into the 2005 Andijon events;

- Press for UN Human Rights Council scrutiny of the human rights situation in Uzbekistan, as well as raise concerns in other multilateral settings, such as the OSCE, and urge the Uzbek government to agree to visits by UN Special Rapporteurs on Freedom of Religion or Belief, the Independence of the Judiciary, and Torture, set specific visit dates, and provide the full and necessary conditions for such a visit;

- Ensure that U.S. statements and actions are coordinated across agencies so that U.S. concerns about religious freedom and related human rights are reflected in its public statements and private interactions with the Uzbek government, including calls for the release of religious prisoners; ensure that the U.S. Embassy maintains appropriate contacts with human rights activists and press the Uzbek government to ensure that every prisoner has greater access to his or her family, human rights monitors, adequate medical care, and a lawyer;

- Maintain the two-day duration of the Annual Bilateral Consultations to allow full discussion of relevant issues, particularly human rights and religious freedom;

- Encourage the Board for Broadcasting Governors to ensure continued U.S. funding for the Uzbek Service of the Voice of America and for RFE/RL's Uzbek Service website, Muslims and Democracy and consider translating this RFE/RL Uzbek Service material into other relevant languages;

- Use funding allocated to the State Department under the Title VIII Program (established in the Soviet-Eastern European Research and Training Act of 1983) for research, including on human rights and religious freedom in former Soviet states, and language training.

TIER 1

2015 COUNTRY REPORTS:
CPCS RECOMMENDED BY USCIRF

–CENTRAL AFRICAN REPUBLIC

–EGYPT

–IRAQ

–NIGERIA

–PAKISTAN

–SYRIA

–TAJIKISTAN

–VIETNAM

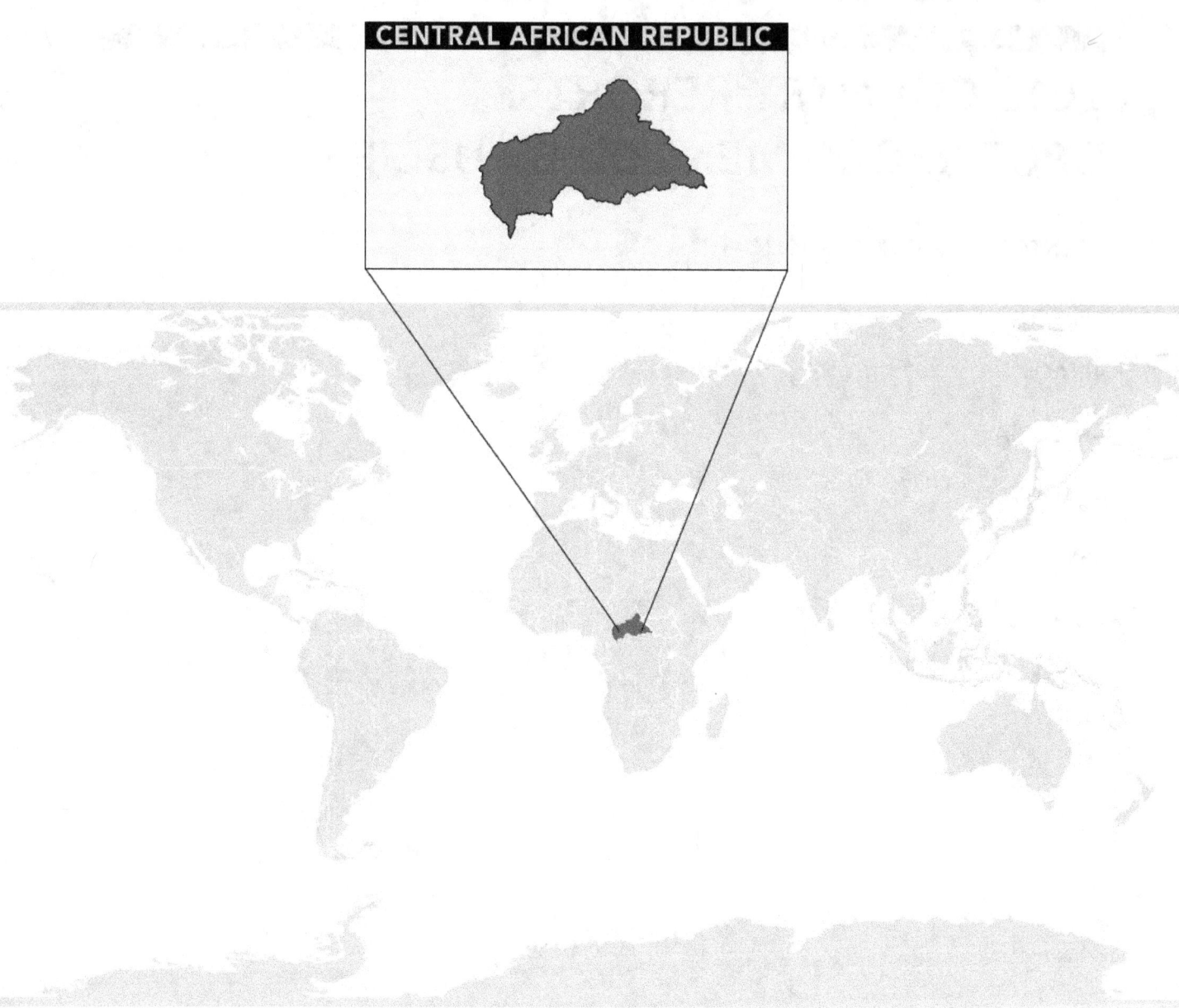

CENTRAL AFRICAN REPUBLIC

CENTRAL AFRICAN REPUBLIC

Key Findings

Militias formed along opposing Muslim and Christian lines in the Central African Republic (CAR) have engaged in systematic, ongoing, and egregious violations of freedom of religion or belief. For much of 2014, CAR was engulfed in a religious conflict after a 2013 coup resulted in rampant lawlessness and the complete collapse of government control. The ethnic cleansing of Muslims and the sectarian violence in CAR in this reporting period meet the International Religious Freedom Act's (IRFA) definition of particularly severe violations of religious freedom meriting "country of particular concern," or CPC, designation. While IRFA's language focuses CPC designations on governmental action or inaction, its spirit is to bring U.S. pressure and attention to bear to end egregious violations of religious freedom and broaden the U.S. government's ability to engage the actual drivers of persecution. As such, USCIRF recommends CPC designation for the Central African Republic in 2015.

Background

The Central African Republic has a long history of political strife, coups, and severe human rights abuses. However, severe religious freedom violations and sectarian violence are new to the majority-Christian country. The rise of religious freedom violations and sectarian violence in the CAR started with the December 2012 political rebellion by a coalition of majority-Muslim armed rebels, the Séléka. The Séléka rebel alliance united four northern rebel groups angered by the government's failure to implement previous peace deals calling for economic development for the country's marginalized northeast and army jobs for former rebel fighters. Large numbers of Chadian and Sudanese foreign fighters and diamond sellers also supported the rebels, hoping to increase their access to CAR's lucrative natural resources. Despite a brief peace agreement, the Séléka took the capital, Bangui, in March 2013 and deposed President François Bozizé. Subsequently, Séléka leader Michel Djotodia proclaimed himself President. As rulers, Séléka leaders and soldiers committed crimes against humanity, including enforced disappearances, illegal detention, torture, and extrajudicial killings of political opponents, many of whom ended up in mass graves. The Séléka also, at times, engaged in targeted attacks on churches and Christian communities while sparing mosques and Muslims.

In June 2013, deposed president Bozizé, former Central African Armed Forces (FACA) soldiers, and members of Bozizé's inner circle met in Cameroon and France to plan his return to power. They recruited existing self-defense militias (known as the anti-balaka), FACA soldiers, and other aggrieved non-Muslims to carry out their plans. As part of their effort to return to power, Bozizé and his supporters framed the upcoming fighting as an opportunity to avenge Séléka attacks on non-Muslims. Christian fears about their rights under a Muslim leader were compounded by military aircrafts transporting wounded Séléka to Khartoum and a letter from President Djotodia to the Organization of Islamic Cooperation asking for support in return for helping to institute Islamic governments in CAR and other regional countries.

The fighting between the Séléka and anti-balaka started in September 2013. The situation dramatically deteriorated on December 5, 2013, when the anti-balaka attacked Muslim neighborhoods in Bangui. The ensuing fighting led to a large-scale conflict in which civilians were targeted based on their religious identity. In January 2014, at a meeting of Central African and neighboring states, President Djotida was forced to resign. Two weeks later, Catherine Samba Panza, then mayor of Bangui, was voted in as Interim President by the country's Parliament. Sectarian violence continued to escalate for the first half of 2014, but slowed after the country's de facto partition between the Séléka and the anti-balaka and the signing of the Brazzaville peace accords on July 23.

The fighting now is largely within and between the militias for land and resource control. However, after over a year of violence between Muslims and Christians, the country has become religiously divided. Muslims who took refuge in peacekeeper-protected enclaves remain there for fear of being attacked by the anti-balaka should they leave. Sporadic killings and skirmishes based on religious identity continue. The ethnic cleansing campaign in Muslim areas resulted in 99 percent of the capital's Muslim residents leaving Bangui, 80 percent of CAR's Muslim population fleeing to neighboring countries, and 417 of the country's 436 mosques being destroyed in 2014.

In an effort to stabilize the country, the African Union (AU), European Union, and France deployed peacekeepers to Bangui and outside of the capital in late 2013 and early 2014. The AU troops were absorbed into the enhanced 10,000 troop United Nations Multidimensional Integrated Stabilization Mission in the Central African Republic (MINUSCA) peacekeeper mission on September 15, 2014. Government officials, the police, and judiciary have neither the infrastructure nor the resources to stop the fighting or to bring to justice the perpetrators of violence. CAR transitional authorities are in the process of drafting a new constitution.

Religious Freedom Conditions 2014–2015
Violations by the anti-balaka

The International Criminal Court (ICC) and the United Nations both opened investigations into reports of genocide in the CAR in this reporting period. In December 2014, the United Nations Commission of Inquiry on the Central African Republic (COI) issued a report finding a "pattern of ethnic cleansing committed by the anti-balaka in the areas in which Muslims had been living." The anti-balaka began their ethnic cleansing campaign with the December 5, 2013 attack on Bangui. The COI found that, although purportedly fighting to return Bozizé to power, the anti-balaka deliberately targeted Muslims and forcibly transferred them out of their villages. Bozizé is reported to have told supporters to kill Muslims.

The anti-balaka have killed hundreds of Muslim civilians since January 2014. The arrival of French and AU troops in Bangui and their Séléka demobilization efforts in early 2014 left the Muslim population without protection and vulnerable to attack. Within months, CAR's western and northwestern cities, towns, and villages were emptied of their Muslim residents. Anti-balaka fighters deliberately killed Muslims because of their religious identity or told them to leave the country or die. The anti-balaka even killed Muslims fleeing the violence, including those in humanitarian-assisted evacuation convoys. In March, the United Nations and Chadian peacekeepers operated convoys to help Muslims safely leave the country. The program was stopped by transitional president Catherine Samba-Panza, who did not want the government to be held responsible for the ethnic cleansing of Muslims. The UN reports that 99 percent of the capital's Muslim residents have left Bangui, and 80 percent of the entire country's Muslim population has fled to Cameroon or Chad. Prior to the start of the conflict in December 2012, Muslims comprised 15 percent of CAR's population. According to Human Rights Watch, the remaining Muslims live in peacekeeper-protected enclaves and are vulnerable to attack if they leave.

In addition to the targeted killing of Muslims, the anti-balaka systematically destroyed mosques and Muslim homes and businesses. U.S. Permanent Representative to the United Nations Samantha Power reported, after her trip to the Central African Republic in March 2015, that 417 of the country's 436 mosques have been destroyed.

Violations by the Séléka

The UN Commission of Inquiry determined that Séléka soldiers engaged in widespread rape, looting of non-Muslim properties, targeted killing of Christians, and the systematic killing of non-Muslim civilians in Bossangoa in 2013. During their rebellion and after the March 2013 coup, Séléka fighters attacked Christian priests, pastors, nuns, church buildings, and other Christian institutions. The militia specifically looted churches but not mosques, and protected Muslim residents while killing or raping Christian residents. However, the COI did not find that the Séléka engaged in the ethnic cleansing of CAR's Christian community.

U.S. Policy

U.S.-Central African Republic relations historically have been limited. USAID does not have a presence in the country. U.S. Embassy Bangui has closed multiple times due to instability. Current U.S. policy focuses on assisting the CAR and supporting international efforts to prevent mass atrocities and provide security, humanitarian assistance, justice, rule of law, and national reconciliation. The U.S. government supports the transitional government, UN peacekeeping mission, and African and international mediating efforts.

As part of U.S. and international efforts to bring justice to the CAR, on May 13, 2014, President Barack Obama issued Executive Order 13667 sanctioning the following persons for threatening the stability of the Central African Republic: former president François Bozizé, former transitional president Michel Djotodia, Séléka leaders Nourredine Adam and Abdoulaye Miskine, and anti-balaka "political coordinator" Levy Yakite. The sanctions block these individuals' property and financial interests in the United States.

In 2014, the United States provided more than $145 million in humanitarian assistance, $100 million to support international peacekeepers, and $7.5 million in conflict mitigation, interfaith messaging, and human rights programs. U.S. Permanent Representative to the United Nations Samantha Power and Assistant Secretary of State for African Affairs Linda Thomas-Greenfield travelled to the Central African Republic in 2014, and the United States facilitated high-level inter-religious exchanges in this reporting period all aimed to prevent and end mass atrocities, increase interfaith dialogue, and encourage national reconciliation efforts.

Future U.S. programming, based on the State Department's FY2016 budget request to Congress, will focus on re-establishing and professionalizing a functioning criminal justice system; supporting efforts to end impunity for serious crimes; training and professionalizing the CAR's law enforcement forces and prison system; training the CAR's military; and building capacity for military and police from contributing countries deploying to the country.

U.S. policy in the CAR is led by Special Representative for the Central African Republic Ambassador W. Stuart Symington and U.S. Embassy Bangui Chargé d'Affaires David Brown, who previously served as a Special Advisor on CAR in Washington, D.C. Prior to Brown's appointment as Chargé in September 2014, the Embassy had been closed since the start of the conflict in December 2012.

Recommendations

In addition to recommending that the United States designate the Central African Republic a "country of particular concern" for systematic, ongoing and egregious violations of freedom of religion or belief, USCIRF recommends that the U.S. government should:

- Include issues related to ending sectarian violence, reducing interfaith tensions, and ensuring the rights of religious freedom and religious minorities in all engagements with CAR authorities, UN officials, and MINUSCA contributing countries;

- Continue to speak out regularly against sectarian violence and gross human rights abuses by the Séléka and the anti-balaka;

- Sanction additional Séléka and anti-balaka members responsible for organizing and/or engaging in sectarian violence, ethnic cleansing, and crimes against humanity;

- Support rule of law reform and continue funding programs to re-establish and professionalize the CAR's judiciary;

- Support and fund the formation of the Special Criminal Court, a hybrid court composed of CAR judges and international judges, to prosecute persons accused of committing ethnic cleansing, crimes against humanity, and other gross human rights abuses;

- Work with CAR transitional authorities, religious leaders, and other civil society representatives to ensure that international standards of freedom of religion or belief are included in the CAR's new constitution;

- Encourage CAR transitional authorities and interfaith leaders to undertake initiatives to ensure that CAR Muslims have a future in the country, by issuing statements that Muslims are full and equal citizens, including Muslims in constitution drafting and national reconciliation dialogues, and aiding the rebuilding of destroyed mosques and Muslim properties;

- Continue to support interfaith dialogues and efforts by religious leaders and their U.S. faith-based partners to rebuild social cohesion; and

- Continue to support humanitarian assistance for refugees and displaced persons, as well as rebuilding projects.

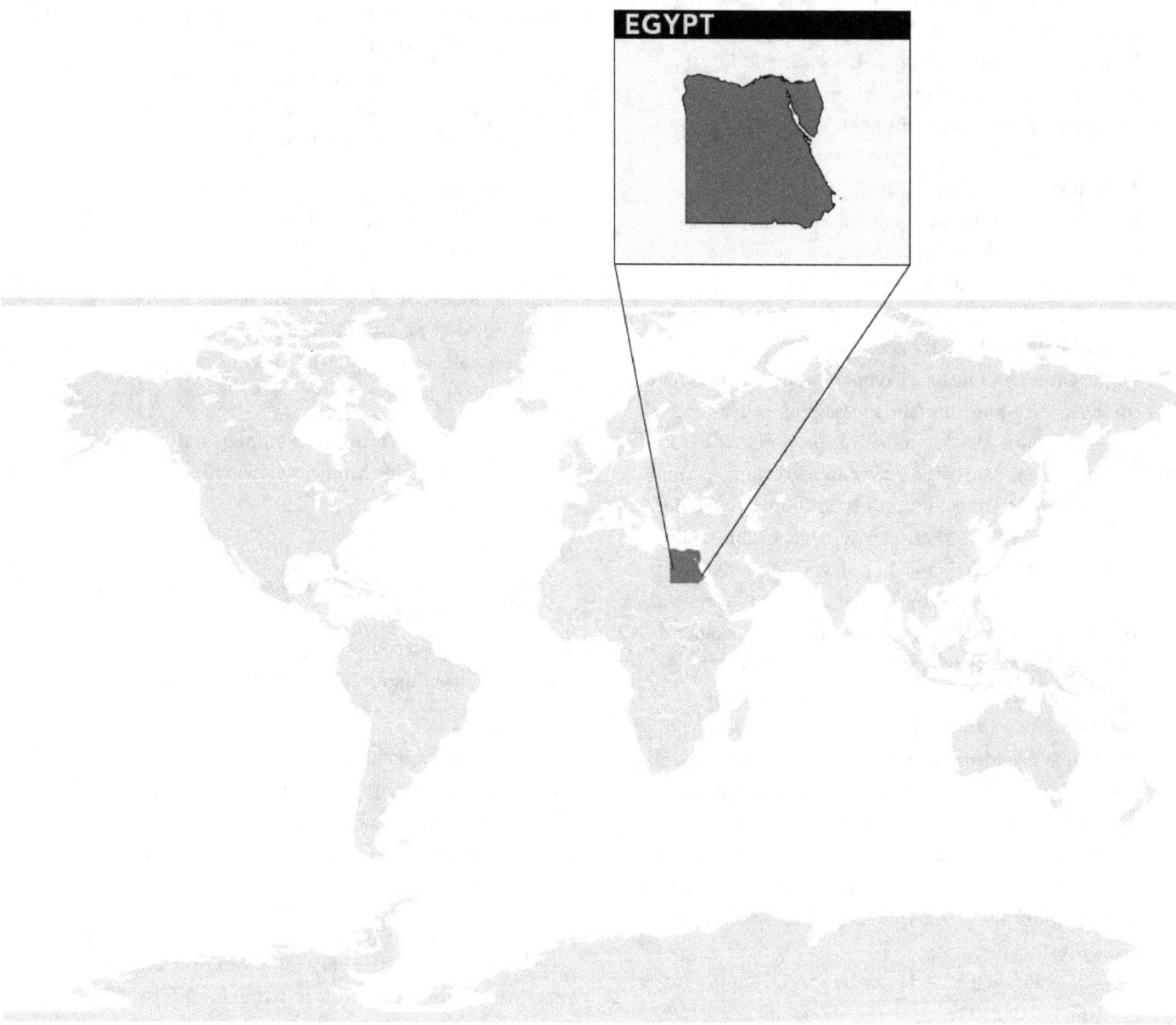

EGYPT

Key Findings

Since he assumed office in June 2014, President Abdel Fattah al-Sisi has made several important public statements and gestures encouraging religious tolerance and has urged changes to religious curricula, a significant shift in tone and rhetoric from his predecessors. In particular, President al-Sisi delivered a speech to senior Muslim religious authorities at Al Azhar University calling for reforms; he was the first head of state to attend a Coptic Christmas Eve mass; and he offered condolences in person to Coptic Pope Tawadros after the killing of 21 Copts in Libya. In addition, there was a decrease in the number of targeted, sectarian attacks when compared to the previous year. Nevertheless, the Egyptian government has not adequately protected religious minorities, particularly Coptic Orthodox Christians and their property, from periodic violence. Discriminatory and repressive laws and policies that restrict freedom of thought, conscience, and religion or belief remain in place. Egyptian courts continue to prosecute, convict, and imprison Egyptian citizens for blasphemy, and new government initiatives to counter atheism emerged during the year. While the 2014 constitution includes improvements regarding freedom of religion or belief, the interpretation and implementation of relevant provisions remain to be seen, in part due to the lack of an elected parliament. Based on these concerns, for the fifth year in a row, USCIRF recommends in 2015 that Egypt be designated a "country of particular concern," or CPC, under the International Religious Freedom Act (IRFA). USCIRF will continue to monitor the situation closely to determine if positive developments warrant a change in Egypt's status in next year's annual report.

Background

During the reporting period, Egypt continued its volatile political transition following the July 2013 ouster of former president Mohamed Morsi by the military, led by then-General Abdel Fattah al-Sisi. The interim government continued to implement a roadmap to amend the constitution and to hold presidential and parliamentary elections. In January 2014, a new constitution was approved overwhelmingly by referendum, and in May, al-Sisi was elected president with nearly 97 percent of the vote with a turnout of 47.5 percent of eligible Egyptian voters. Parliamentary elections, originally scheduled for March and April 2015, were delayed indefinitely after the Supreme Constitutional Court ruled that the law on electoral constituencies was unconstitutional because it did not guarantee fair representation. Some of the improved religious freedom provisions in the constitution cannot be implemented until a new parliament is seated.

Despite President al-Sisi urging religious tolerance and moderation in several public statements during the year, including in a January 2015 speech

> *Egyptian courts continue to prosecute, convict, and imprison Egyptian citizens for blasphemy, and new government initiatives to counter atheism emerged during the year.*

at Al Azhar University, the government's efforts to combat extremism and terrorism have had a chilling impact on civil society activities in the country. Among the consequences have been severe limits on dissent and criticism of the government, resulting in a poor human rights situation overall, including for freedom of religion or belief. Sympathizers and members of the Muslim Brotherhood, journalists, and opposition figures continue to be harassed, jailed, and given harsh prison terms, including death sentences for Brotherhood members and other Islamists, sometimes on legitimate, but also on unfounded, security charges. Conditions for Coptic Orthodox Christians remained precarious, as most perpetrators of attacks in recent years have not been convicted, including from large-scale incidents that occurred between 2011 and 2013. Small communities of Baha'is and Jehovah's Witnesses remain banned and anti-Semitism persists in state-controlled and semi-official media.

Religious Freedom Conditions 2014–2015
Government Control of Islamic Institutions

The government increased its control over all Muslim religious institutions, including mosques and religious endowments. Egyptian officials have justified this regulation as necessary to counter extremism and terrorism. In February 2015, an administrative court upheld a September 2013 decree by the Ministry of Religious Endowments that prevents imams who are not graduates of Al-Azhar from preaching in licensed and unlicensed mosques. The ruling, which resulted in the closure of thousands of small mosques, bans unlicensed mosques from holding Friday prayers and requires Friday sermons to follow government "talking points." The government appoints and pays the salaries of all Sunni Muslim imams and monitors sermons.

Coptic Christians, Violence and Continued Impunity

In January 2015, President al-Sisi became the first Egyptian head of state to attend a Coptic Christmas Eve mass at the St. Mark's Coptic Orthodox Cathedral in Cairo, and in February, he met with and offered condolences to Coptic Pope Tawadros at the cathedral after the killing by ISIL of 21 Copts in Libya. While the Coptic community in general welcomed these and other symbolic gestures, repressive laws and discriminatory policies against Copts remained in place, including blasphemy charges and convictions, limits on building and maintaining churches, limits on conversion from Islam, and lack of accountability for violent attacks.

Over the past year, the number and severity of violent incidents targeting Copts and their property decreased significantly when compared to the previous year; however, sporadic violence continued, particularly in Upper Egypt. In some parts of the country, Egyptian security services increased protection of churches during significant religious holidays, which lessened the level of fear and insecurity among members of the Coptic community. Following the unprecedented violence in the summer of 2013, including against Coptic churches and their property, the Egyptian government formed a fact-finding commission to investigate the attacks and pledged to hold accountable those responsible for the violence and to rebuild the dozens of churches that were destroyed. In November 2014, the Egyptian government released an executive summary of its report, which found 52 churches were completely destroyed, another 12 damaged, and numerous Christian-owned properties destroyed. The report also found that 29 people died in sectarian-related killings, without any specific details surrounding the deaths. At the end of the reporting period, according to human rights groups, 10 percent of the destroyed churches and Christian properties were in the process of being rebuilt.

In December 2014, some 40 perpetrators who were found responsible for attacks on five churches in Assiut, Upper Egypt, were sentenced to prison terms ranging from one to 15 years. Some other cases are ongoing, and perpetrators have yet to be brought to justice. In some cases, police have not conducted adequate investigations, sometimes due to fear of retribution against them by violent extremists. The inability to protect Copts and other religious minorities, and successfully prosecute those responsible for violence, continued to foster an atmosphere of impunity.

Blasphemy Law and Limits on Religious Expression

Article 98(f) of the Egyptian Penal Code prohibits citizens from "ridiculing or insulting heavenly religions or inciting sectarian strife." Authorities use this "contempt-of-religion," or blasphemy, law to detain, prosecute, and imprison members of religious groups whose practices deviate from mainstream Islamic beliefs or whose activities are alleged to jeopardize "communal harmony" or insult Judaism, Christianity, or Islam. In January 2015, President al-Sissi issued a decree that permits the government to ban any foreign publications it deems offensive to religion.

Blasphemy cases have increased since 2011, and this trend continued during the reporting period.

While the majority of charges are leveled against Sunni Muslims, the majority of those sentenced by a court to prison terms for blasphemy have been Christians, Shi'a Muslims, and atheists, mostly based on flawed trials. In June 2014, separate courts in Luxor imposed blasphemy sentences of up to six years in prison on four individuals, including Coptic Christian Kirollos Shawqi Atallah, who was sentenced to six years for posting photos on a Facebook page deemed defamatory to Islam. In February 2014, a court sentenced Amr Abdullah, an Egyptian Shi'a, to five years in prison with labor on charges of blasphemy and defaming the Prophet Mohammed's companions for attempting to observe the Shi'a Ashura holiday at the al-Hussein mosque in Cairo. Bishoy Armia, previously known as Mohamed Hegazy, a Christian convert who was among the first to legally change his religion from Islam to Christianity, was sentenced in June 2014 to five years in prison for working as a journalist and reporting on anti-Christian activities in Minya, Upper Egypt. In July, he also was charged with "insulting Islam," charges that were previously filed against him in 2009. In December 2014, an appeals court dropped some of the charges, however, at the end of the reporting period, Armia remained in prison on the blasphemy charge.

Egyptian atheists saw a rise in blasphemy charges over the past year, as well as growing societal harassment and various Egyptian government campaigns to counter atheism. In December 2014, Dar al-Ifta, a Justice Ministry entity that issues religious edicts, published a survey claiming that Egypt was home to 866 atheists, supposedly the "highest number" of any country in the Middle East. Two officials from the office of the Grand Mufti – who heads Dar al-Ifta – publicly called this a "dangerous development." In June 2014, the Ministries of Religious Endowments and Sports and Youth initiated a national campaign to combat the spread of atheism among Egyptian youth. In March 2014, a high-level Ministry of Interior official publicly stated that a special police task force would be formed to arrest a group of Alexandria-based atheists who expressed their beliefs on Facebook and other social media platforms. In January 2015, Egyptian atheist student Karim Al-Banna was given a three-year prison sentence for blasphemy because a court found some of his Facebook posts to "belittle the divine." In March 2014, an Egyptian court upheld a three-year prison sentence on "contempt-of-religion" charges for Egyptian author Karam Saber for publishing a book questioning the existence of God.

Baha'is and Jehovah's Witnesses

Baha'is and Jehovah's Witnesses have been banned since 1960 by presidential decrees. As a result, Baha'is living in Egypt are unable to meet or engage in public religious activities. Al-Azhar's Islamic Research Center has issued fatwas over the years urging the continued ban on the Baha'i community and condemning its members as apostates. In December 2014, the Ministry of Religious Endowments held a public workshop to raise awareness about the "growing dangers" of the spread of the Baha'i Faith in Egypt. Since Baha'i marriage is not recognized, married Baha'is cannot obtain identity cards, making it impossible to conduct daily transactions like banking, school registration, or car ownership. In recent years, the government has permitted Jehovah's Witnesses to meet in private homes in groups of fewer than 30 people, despite the community's request to meet in larger numbers. Jehovah's Witnesses are not allowed to have their own places of worship or to import Bibles and other religious literature. Over the past year, security officials continued to harass and intimidate Jehovah's Witnesses by monitoring their activities and communications and by threatening the community with intensified repression if it does not provide membership lists.

Anti-Semitism and the Jewish Community

In 2014, material vilifying Jews with both historical and new anti-Semitic stereotypes continued to appear in Egypt's state-controlled and semi-official media. This material included anti-Semitic cartoons, images of Jews and Jewish symbols demonizing Israel or Zionism, comparisons of Israeli leaders to Hitler and the Nazis, and Holocaust denial literature. Egyptian authorities failed to take adequate steps to combat anti-Semitism in the state-controlled media. Egypt's once-thriving Jewish community is now only a small remnant consisting of fewer than 20 people. It owns communal property and finances required maintenance largely through private donations.

Egypt's Constitution

There are some encouraging changes in the January 2014 constitution that could bode well for religious freedom. Several problematic provisions from the 2012 constitution were removed: a provision that narrowly defined Islamic Shari'ah law; a provision potentially giving Al-Azhar a consultative role in reviewing legislation; and a provision that effectively banned blasphemy. In addition, a new provision, Article 235, requires the incoming parliament to pass a law governing the building and renovating of churches. This would potentially lift the longstanding requirement of governmental approval for building or repairing churches, which has served as a justification for sectarian-related violence targeting Christians. While Article 64 provides that "freedom of belief is absolute," like the 2012 constitution, this article limits the freedom to practice religious rituals and establish places of worship to only the "divine" religions: Islam, Christianity, and Judaism.

U.S. Policy

For many years, U.S. policy toward Egypt has focused on fostering strong bilateral relations, continuing security and military cooperation, maintaining regional stability, and sustaining the 1979 Camp David peace accords. Successive administrations have viewed Egypt as a key ally in the region. Egypt is among the top five recipients in the world of U.S. aid. The FY2015 Consolidated Appropriations Act provides Egypt with $1.3 billion in foreign military financing (FMF) and $150 million in economic support funds (ESF), the lowest level in more than three decades. During the reporting period, the Obama Administration publicly urged the Egyptian government to make progress on economic and political reforms, including on human rights concerns, although less so on specific religious freedom issues than it did in the three years following the January 25, 2011 revolution.

Public Law 113-235, the FY2015 Consolidated Appropriations Act, places conditions on U.S. assistance to Egypt related to limits on human rights, including religious freedom. Specifically, it requires the Secretary of State to certify that Egypt has taken steps to advance the democratic process, protect free speech, and protect the rights of women and religious minorities, among other things. However, the Act also authorizes the Secretary to provide assistance to Egypt without such certification if he or she determines that the assistance is important to the national security interests of the United States. At the end of the reporting period, the Secretary of State has not made a determination that would waive human rights-related certification requirements and allow for the provision of assistance.

According to the State Department, officials at all levels of the U.S. government raised a range of religious freedom concerns with Egyptian counterparts during the reporting period. When President Barack Obama met with President al-Sisi in September 2014 on the sidelines of the UN General Assembly, President Obama raised some human rights concerns, although it was not clear if any religious freedom issues were discussed. Despite USCIRF recommending since 2011 that Egypt should be designated a "country of particular concern," the State Department has not taken such action.

Recommendations

Egypt continues to experience both progress and setbacks during its transition, the success of which hinges on full respect for the rule of law and compliance with international human rights standards, including freedom of religion or belief. In addition to recommending that the U.S. government designate Egypt as a CPC, USCIRF recommends that the U.S. government should:

- Ensure that a portion of U.S. military assistance is used to help police implement an effective plan for dedicated protection for religious minority communities and their places of worship, and provide direct support to human rights and other civil society or non-governmental organizations to advance freedom of religion or belief for all Egyptians;

- Press the Egyptian government to undertake immediate reforms to improve religious freedom conditions, including: repealing decrees banning religious minority faiths; removing religion from official identity documents; and passing a law for the construction and repair of places of worship once a new parliament is formed;

- Urge the Egyptian government to revise Article 98(f) of the Penal Code, which criminalizes contempt of religion, and, in the interim, provide the constitutional and international guarantees of the rule of law and due process for those individuals charged with violating Article 98(f);

- Press the Egyptian government to prosecute perpetrators of sectarian violence through the judicial system, and to ensure that responsibility for religious affairs is not under the jurisdiction of the domestic security agency, which should only deal with national security matters such as cases involving the use or advocacy of violence; and

- Place particular emphasis, in its annual reporting to Congress on human rights and religious freedom, on the Egyptian government's progress on the protection of religious minorities, prosecution of perpetrators of sectarian violence, and the ability of Egyptian non-governmental organizations to receive outside funding from sources including the U.S. government.

Dissenting Statement of Vice Chair James J. Zogby

With this report, USCIRF is recommending that the Department of State designate Egypt as a "country of particular concern" (CPC). I strongly disagree. This is the wrong recommendation, for the wrong country, at the wrong time.

While the overall human rights situation in Egypt is deplorable and a matter of concern, the same cannot be said for the status of religious freedom in the country. Matters of political repression and the out-of-control actions of an overzealous judiciary, though quite serious, are beyond the scope of our Commission unless they directly impact issues of religious liberty.

As is noted in the opening sentences of USCIRF's report, when it comes to matters of religious freedom, there were significant developments in Egypt during this past year. President al Sisi made unprecedented outreach to Coptic Christians to affirm that they are "equal citizens," promising to protect their rights. And both the President and the Sheikh al Azhar have called for a "revolution in Islam" in order to help eliminate extremism. Even now major changes are being made in Egypt's educational materials and efforts are underway to limit the ability of extremists to develop congregations of followers. Furthermore, Coptic leaders with whom I have spoken have said that they feel more secure than they have in a long time.

The above report does include a number of other cases and charges against Egypt. Some of these are serious, but they do not reach the "systematic, ongoing, and egregious" standard required to declare Egypt a CPC. In light of these positive developments, it simply makes no sense for USCIRF to be asking the State Department to now give Egypt a CPC status when the State Department has not done so before.

The challenges facing the government of Egypt at this time are to: defeat the terrorist threat they are facing, rein in their judiciary, restore rights to civil society, grow the economy, and move quickly to complete their "road map" by electing a new parliament. This will do more to advance religious liberty than imposing the ill-timed and uncalled for sanctions that might result from a CPC designation.

Additional Statement of Commissioners Eric P. Schwartz and Thomas J. Reese, S.J.

We abstained on the Commission vote to urge the State Department to designate Egypt as a country of particular concern. We don't question whether abuses against religious freedom remain serious and substantial, or even whether a CPC designation is legally defensible. But by its act, the Commission urges the Department of State to impose a new, condemnatory measure on Egypt for violations of religious freedom and therefore send a signal that could be reasonably inferred to mean we believe the religious freedom situation is deteriorating. This strikes us as a peculiar time for the State Department to send such a message, in light of the fact that President Sisi has made, by the Commission's own account, "important public statements and gestures" supporting religious tolerance, and at a time in which "targeted, sectarian attacks," again by our own account, have diminished as compared to last year. We believe that recent developments made it possible for the Commission to defer from making a CPC recommendation to the State Department, and that is what we would have preferred. Let us be clear that we are no fans of the Sisi regime, which is guilty of systematic abuses of human rights that merit the strongest condemnation. But we also are not fans of making recommendations that, if implemented, would risk sending a confusing and counterproductive message. Of course, we will continue to monitor the situation in Egypt and hope to see improvements. And should conditions deteriorate, we'd be prepared to reconsider our position.

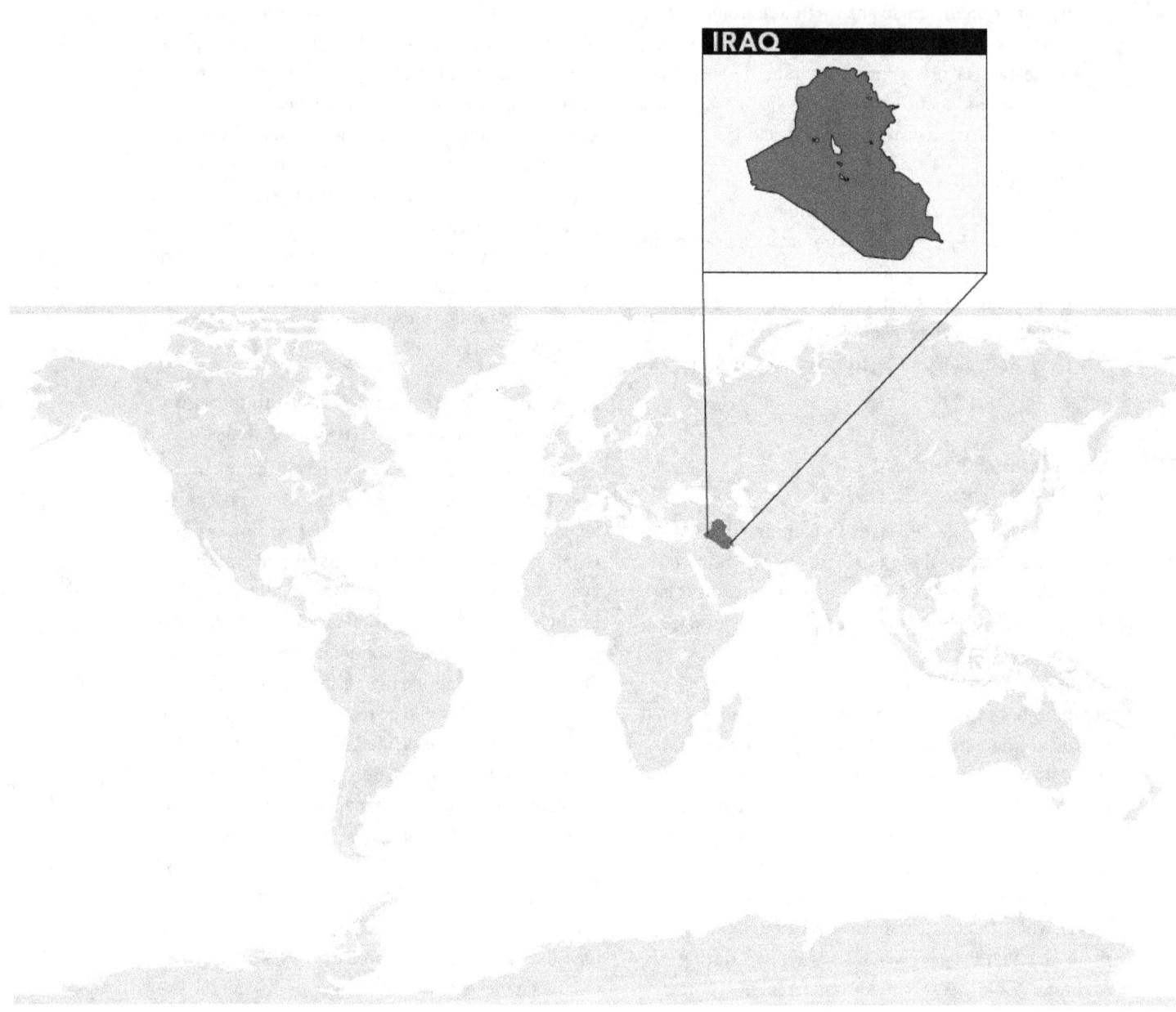

IRAQ

Key Findings

Iraq's overall human rights landscape, including for religious freedom, deteriorated significantly in 2014, especially in areas controlled by the U.S.-designated terrorist group the Islamic State of Iraq and the Levant (ISIL). In these areas the Iraqi government has little capacity to fight ISIL's advances or to protect religious communities from violent attack. ISIL targets all Iraqis who oppose its violent religious ideology, but the smallest non-Muslim minority communities, particularly Yazidis and Christians, suffered especially egregious and large-scale abuses. While ISIL was the most egregious perpetrator of religiously-motivated human rights and religious freedom violations in Iraq in the last year, the Iraqi government also contributed to the deterioration in religious freedom conditions. Security forces and Shi'a militias supported by the Iraqi government perpetrated grave human rights violations, particularly against Sunni Muslims. Millions of Iraqis are now refugees or are internally displaced. Based on these violations, perpetrated primarily by non-state actors but also by the state, USCIRF recommends in 2015 that the U.S. government designate Iraq as a "country of particu-

lar concern," or CPC, under the International Religious Freedom Act (IRFA). USCIRF has recommended CPC designation for Iraq since December 2008. Post-Saddam Iraq has never been designated as a CPC by the State Department.

Background

Under Saddam Hussein, the Iraqi government maintained religious peace through intimidation and terror while favoring the Sunni Muslim minority. With the fall of Saddam in 2003, sectarian conflict exploded. The Shi'a Muslim majority took control of the government and effectively froze out the Sunni Muslim population. The Iraqi government under Prime Minister Nouri al-Maliki often acted in an authoritarian and sectarian manner, for example, raiding and disbanding peaceful Sunni protests, targeting Sunni areas, citizens and politicians for security sweeps and arrests, mistreating Sunni prisoners, and marginalizing Sunnis from government and security positions. This background helped create the conditions that allowed ISIL to rise, spread, and ultimately control significant areas of northern and central Iraq. Despite al-Maliki's resignation and replacement in August by new Prime Minister Haider al-Abadi, Sunni resentment and reports of abuses against Sunni Muslims by security forces and allied Shi'a militias continue.

Over the past decade, many Iraqis, Muslim and non-Muslim alike, have been victimized by religious-ly-motivated violence. The Iraqi government has proven unable or unwilling to stop this violence or bring perpetrators to justice, creating a perpetual sense of insecurity for all religious communities, particularly the smallest ones. While the 2005 Iraqi constitution states that it guarantees equality and religious freedom to all Iraqis,

> *ISIL targets all Iraqis who oppose its violent religious ideology,*
> *but the smallest non-Muslim minority communities,*
> *particularly Yazidis and Christians,*
> *suffered especially egregious and large-scale abuses.*

these guarantees thus far have provided little actual protection, particularly, but not only, in the past year.

Even before ISIL's rise, the country's smallest religious communities – which include Catholics, Christian Orthodox, Protestants, Yazidis, and Sabean Mandae-

rights and religious freedom in Iraq and the region. ISIL espouses an extreme, violent religious ideology that allows for no religious diversity. While ISIL targets all Iraqis who oppose it, religious minority communities have suffered especially egregious, devastating, and

Despite al-Maliki's resignation and replacement in August by new Prime Minister Haider al-Abadi, Sunni resentment and reports of abuses against Sunni Muslims by security forces and allied Shi'a militias continue.

ans – were mere shadows of their already-small former presence. Pre-2003, non-Muslims amounted to only an estimated 3 percent of Iraq's population. They have long faced official and societal discrimination, and their small size and lack of militia or tribal structures have made it difficult for them to defend themselves against violence or protect their rights through the Iraqi political system. In 2013 the Christian population was estimated at 500,000, half the size estimated in 2003. Also in 2013, the Yazidis reported that since 2005 their population had decreased by nearly 200,000 to approximately 500,000, and the Mandaeans reported that almost 90 percent of their community had left the country or been killed, leaving just a few thousand. The size of these religious communities continue to decline as the crisis in Iraq deepens, with Iraqi Christian leaders now stating that their community only numbers around 250,000-300,000. Between 2003 and 2008, many members of Iraq's smallest minority communities were driven out of the country or fled to northern Iraq, including areas in the semi-autonomous Kurdistan region (KRG), as well as other nearby areas that are now under ISIL's control. The KRG areas have been the safest part of Iraq, but minorities in areas nearby that are disputed between the KRG and the Iraqi central government have reported pressure from Kurdish officials and political parties to support their territorial claims.

Religious Freedom Conditions 2014-2015
Violations by ISIL and other Non-State Actors

ISIL's rise, spread and ultimately its June 2014 declaration of a so-called "Islamic State," which cuts across Iraq and Syria, is particularly threatening for the future of human

large-scale abuses, including forced expulsion from their historic homelands, forced conversion, rape and enslavement of women and children, torture, beheadings, and massacres. ISIL's takeover of northern Iraq could well mark the end of the presence in that area of its ancient Yazidi and Christian communities.

In June 2014, ISIL took the northern city of Mosul, overrunning Iraqi forces there, who dropped their weapons and fled. ISIL issued an ultimatum that all Christians must convert to Islam, leave Mosul, pay a tax, or face death. The Christian community in Mosul dates back more than 1,700 years, with an estimated 30,000 living there before the ISIL offensive. In August, ISIL captured Qaraqosh, the largest Christian town in northern Iraq, prompting an estimated 100,000 Christians to flee, and an assault on the Christian town of al-Kosh also led to an exodus of Christians. Nearly all Christians are believed to have left ISIL-held territory, with most fleeing to the KRG region.

ISIL's August 2014 attack on the largely Yazidi town of Sinjar, located in the Nineveh province of northern Iraq, led to the massacre of Yazidis, Assyrian Christians, Shi'a and others, and the destruction of religious sites that date back centuries. Yazidi contacts told USCIRF that the Kurdish forces protecting the town abandoned them during the night when ISIL was approaching, leaving them defenseless. According to the UN, 200,000 civilians, mostly Yazidis, fled Sinjar town for the mountain, which ISIL forces surrounded. Men, women, and children were stranded on Mount Sinjar with no escape and little access to food, water, or shelter, except for limited airlifts provided by Iraqi and Kurdish Peshmerga forces. Reportedly, as many as 500 Yazidis were massacred by

ISIL and dozens died of starvation and dehydration. For Yazidis, the ISIL ultimatum was to convert or die; they are not considered "people of the book" and therefore not afforded the options to leave or pay a tax. In addition, thousands of Yazidi women and girls, including those who had not reached puberty, were kidnapped, raped, sold as sex slaves, or killed. The Kurdish Peshmerga, with the assistance of U.S. airstrikes, was finally able to break through ISIL's siege of Mt. Sinjar in December 2014. Peshmerga forces reported finding mass graves in the area.

ISIL also has killed Sunni Muslims who disagree with its extreme ideology. In October 2014, 150 Sunni

abuses committed by members of these groups against Sunni civilians. In an October 2014 report, Amnesty International named 'Asa'ib Ahl al-Haq, the Badr Brigades, the Mahdi Army, and Kata'ib Hizbullah as perpetrators of human rights abuses, including mass killings of Sunni civilians.

U.S. Policy

After the U.S. military withdrew from Iraq in December 2011, the U.S. presence in the country decreased significantly between 2012 and 2014. However, the rise of ISIL and the formation of a new Iraqi government in

ISIL's takeover of northern Iraq could well mark the end of the presence in that area of its ancient Yazidi and Christian communities.

Muslims from the Albu Nimr tribe were found in a mass grave, and in a separate case a few weeks earlier, 70 additional corpses from the same tribe were found. ISIL has also killed at least 12 Sunni clerics that rejected their extremist ideologies or attempted to assist or protect religious minorities.

Non-state actors other than ISIL have also perpetrated religiously-motivated attacks. As in previous years, 2014 saw a number of violent attacks targeting the country's Shi'a majority, including pilgrims celebrating important holidays. These presumably were carried out by Sunni extremist groups, though the actual perpetrator of specific attacks is rarely known. For example, on May 22, multiple attacks in and around Baghdad killed at least 35 Shi'a pilgrims traveling to a shrine in Kadhimiya and injured dozens.

Violations by the Iraqi Government

The Iraqi government, under both former Prime Minister al-Maliki and current Prime Minister Haider al-Abadi, also has committed human rights abuses, including torture and extrajudicial killings of Sunni prisoners and civilians. In addition, the government is funding and arming Shi'a militias to fight ISIL, which operate outside any legal framework and with impunity. Human rights groups and the United Nations have documented summary executions and other severe

2014 have led the United States to once again deepen its involvement, including but not limited to, increased humanitarian aid, air strikes, and training and assisting Iraqi forces.

After years of supporting the al-Maliki government, by mid-2014 U.S. officials reportedly felt that al-Maliki could no longer govern Iraq due to his and his government's sectarian and authoritarian actions, and pressured al-Maliki to step down to allow a new government to form. In August 2014, al-Maliki resigned and Haider al-Abadi was designated as Prime Minister by President Fuad Masum.

In August 2014, ISIL's offensive in northern Iraq that targeted Yazidis and other minority communities and threatened U.S. personnel in Erbil led to U.S. airstrikes, the first since the 2011 troop withdrawal. In addition, the U.S. military began airdrops of food and water to the thousands of people trapped on Mount Sinjar. The same month, the U.S. government announced that it would provide Iraqi Kurdistan's Peshmerga forces with light weaponry and ammunition and begin sending military advisers and trainers to assist Iraqi government forces. In addition, in August 2014, USAID deployed a Disaster Assistance Response Team (DART) to the region to coordinate U.S. humanitarian efforts in responding to the needs of newly displaced populations. According to a Congressional

Research Service February 2015 report, approximately 3,100 U.S. military non-combat personnel have been deployed to Iraq. The United States is now leading a coalition of 60 countries to combat ISIL's advance.

> *The Iraqi government, under both former Prime Minister al-Maliki and current Prime Minister Haider al-Abadi, also has committed human rights abuses, including torture and extrajudicial killings of Sunni prisoners and civilians.*

Many of the countries conduct their own airstrikes, train and provide weaponry to Iraqi and Kurdish forces, provide humanitarian aid, and are working to cut off ISIL's funding sources. In September 2014, President Obama appointed retired General John Allen as the U.S. Special Presidential Envoy for the Global Coalition to Counter ISIL.

In addition, the United States is leading the international effort to provide aid for civilians whom ISIL forced to flee their homes and are now internally displaced or refugees in neighboring countries. The Congressional Research Service has reported that the total U.S. government humanitarian funding to Iraq in FY2014 and FY2015 (as of December 19, 2014) was more than $213.8 million. The United States also continues to resettle Iraqi refugees to the United States. According to State Department statistics, 19,769 Iraqis were resettled to the United States in FY2014, the most from any single country.

In recent years, the U.S. government has made efforts to help address the problems facing Iraq's smallest religious and ethnic minorities. Since 2008, the State Department has designated officials in both Washington and Baghdad to coordinate its efforts on minority issues. In Washington, that responsibility is now held by the deputy to the Special Presidential Envoy for the Global Coalition to Counter ISIL. The United States also has funded civil society efforts to assist Iraq's minorities, such as the Support for Minorities in Iraq (SMI) program, which works with minority groups to help them better represent themselves in civil society. In addition, after the reporting period, Assistant Secretary of State for Democracy, Human Rights and Labor Tom Malinowski and Ambassador-at-Large for International Religious Freedom David Saperstein raised concerns about minority issues and abuses perpetrated by Iraqi militias on a February 2015 visit to Iraq.

Recommendations

In addition to recommending that the U.S. government designate Iraq as a CPC, USCIRF recommends that the U.S. government should:

- Call for or support a referral by the UN Security Council to the International Criminal Court to investigate ISIL violations in Iraq and Syria against religious and ethnic minorities, following the models used in Sudan and Libya, or encourage the Iraqi government to accept ICC jurisdiction to investigate ISIL violations in Iraq after June 2014;

- Ensure that the efforts of the Global Coalition to Counter ISIL include steps to protect and assist the region's most vulnerable religious and ethnic minorities and, where appropriate, assist Iraqi government and KRG security forces in efforts to provide security to protect likely targets of sectarian or religiously-motivated violence;

- Develop a government-wide plan of action to protect religious minorities in Iraq and help establish the conditions for them to return to their homes; charge the Ambassador-at-Large for International Religious Freedom with engaging with the Inter-Governmental Contact Group on Freedom of Religion or Belief to coordinate similar efforts by other governments;

- Urge the Iraqi government to create structures to oversee and hold to account Shi'a militias, so they do not violate the human rights of non-combatant Sunni Muslims or religious minorities, and to investigate and prosecute perpetrators when violations occur;

- Include in all military or security assistance to the Iraqi and Iraqi Kurdistan governments a requirement that security forces are integrated to reflect the country's religious and ethnic diversity, and provide training for recipient units on universal human rights standards and how to treat civilians, particularly religious minorities;

- Continue to task embassy officials with engaging religious minority communities, and work with Iraq's government and these communities and their political and civic representatives to help them reach agreement on what measures are needed to ensure their rights and security in the country;

- Urge the parties to include the protection of rights for all Iraqis and ending discrimination as part of negotiations between the KRG and the Iraqi government on disputed territories, and press the KRG to address alleged abuses against minorities by Kurdish officials in these areas;

- Focus U.S. programming in Iraq on promoting religious freedom and tolerance and ensure that marginalized communities benefit from U.S. and international development assistance; and

- Continue to prioritize the resettlement to the United States of vulnerable Iraqi refugees, including those who fled to Syria but are now refugees in a third country; interview applicants by video-conference when in-person interviews cannot be conducted for security reasons; and allocate sufficient resources to the Department of Homeland Security and other agencies to expeditiously process applications and conduct security background checks to facilitate resettlements without compromising U.S. national security.

Dissenting Statement of Vice Chair James J. Zogby

I disagree with the decision to name Iraq a "country of particular concern" for two reasons.

First, the main violators of religious freedom in Iraq today are non-state actors from the self-styled "Islamic State" (IS) to the armed sectarian militias that operate outside of the control of the central government. Both the IS and the armed sectarian militias have committed atrocities against those not of their faith, and the IS, in particular, has engaged in genocidal behavior towards Christians and other vulnerable religious minorities.

At present, the Administration is working with the Iraqi government to defeat the IS, to rebuild a non-sectarian army, and to implement political reforms that will create a more inclusive government. Declaring Iraq as a CPC does not contribute to this effort.

The second reason I am averse to making this designation is that it was hubris that led the Bush Administration to invade, occupy, and believe that it could restructure the governance of the country. The creation of the murderous sectarian militias took place on our watch in the middle of the last decade, as did the massive sectarian "cleansing" operations that resulted in the dislocation of one-fifth of the country's population and the forced exile of two-thirds of Iraq's Christian community.

The question we must ask now ourselves is: did we do everything in our power, when we left Iraq to insure that the country was on the path to national reconciliation and inclusive governance? Since the answer is clearly that we did not, it is, at best, insensitive for us to now declare the mess we left behind a "country of particular concern."

While the non-state actors in Iraq deserve our condemnation, what the Iraqi government now needs from us is the political and military support we are providing to defeat the IS and put their house in order.

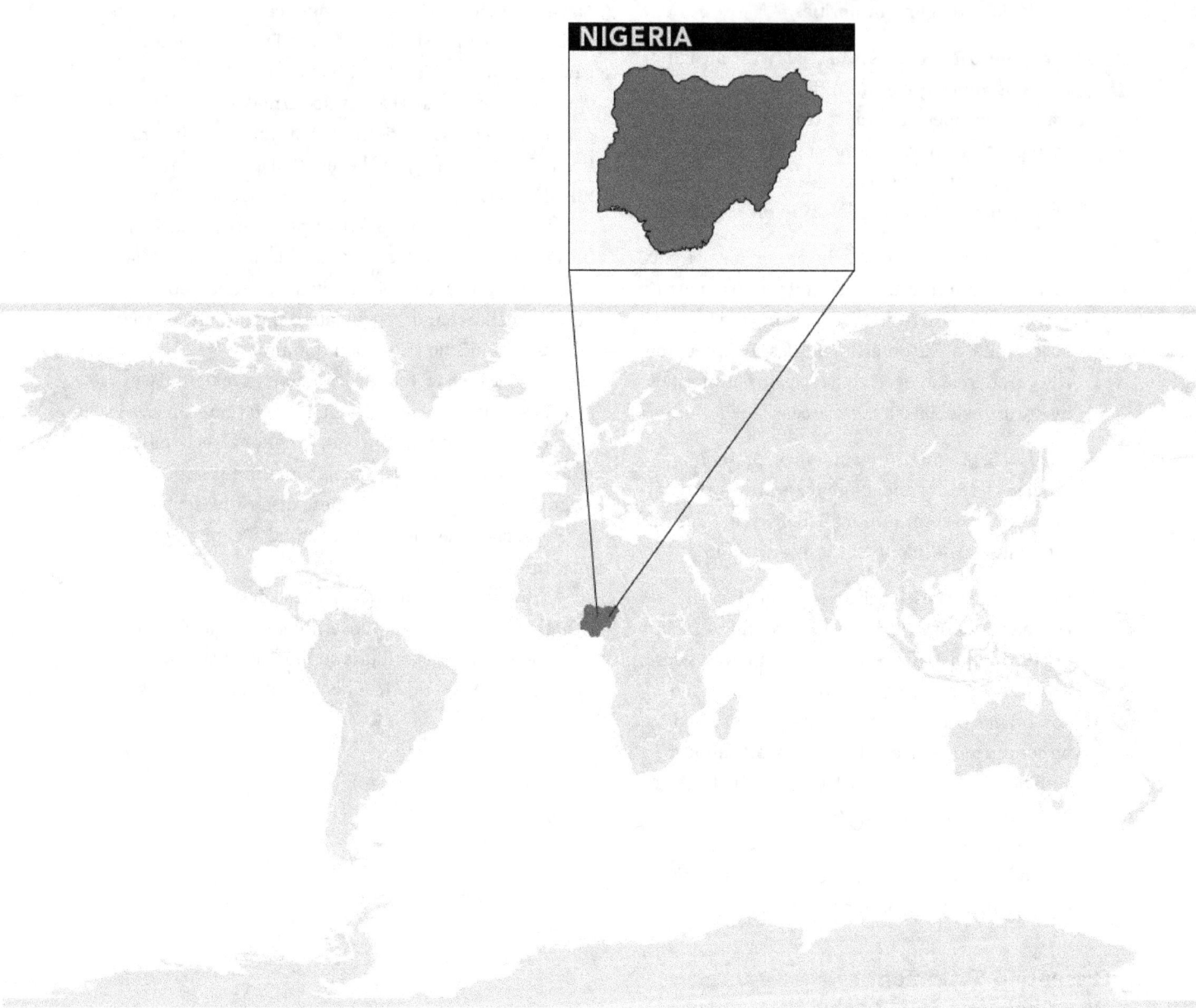

NIGERIA

Key Findings

Religious freedom conditions in Nigeria are being strained by Boko Haram's terrorist attacks against Christians and Muslims, recurring sectarian violence, and escalating interfaith tensions. While the Nigerian federal government does not engage in religious persecution, it fails to implement effective strategies to prevent or stop terrorism or sectarian violence and does not bring to justice those responsible for such violence. The Nigerian government's almost exclusively military approach to Boko Haram contributes to ongoing terrorism in the country. Boko Haram exploits sectarian fissures to manipulate religious tensions and destabilize Nigeria.

regions. Managing this diversity and developing a national identity has been, and continues to be, a problem for Nigerians and the Nigeria government, especially between its "Muslim North" and "Christian South." To address this challenge, the practice has been for presidential tickets to include candidates from both regions and to be religiously balanced. The charter of the ruling Peoples' Democratic Party requires its presidential candidates to switch between the north and south every eight years. Critics argue that President Goodluck Jonathan upset the regional alternation when he succeeded the late President Umaru Yar'Adua and continued to seek re-election in 2011 and 2015. During the 2011

Religious freedom conditions in Nigeria are being strained by Boko Haram's terrorist attacks against Christians and Muslims, recurring sectarian violence, and escalating interfaith tensions.

Based on these concerns, in 2015 USCIRF again recommends that Nigeria be designated as a "country of particular concern" or CPC, under the International Religious Freedom Act (IRFA). USCIRF first recommended Nigeria be designated a CPC in 2009; Nigeria was on the Commission's Tier 2 (Watch List) from 2002-2009. The State Department has not designated Nigeria a CPC.

Background

Nigeria's population of almost 180 million people is equally divided between Muslims and Christians. Religious identity frequently falls along regional, ethnic, political, and socio-economic lines and provides flashpoints for violence.

The return to democracy and elected leadership ended decades of corrupt military rule, but created a winner-take-all fight for presidential power between

and 2015 presidential elections, many in the north felt that it was still that region's turn for the presidency.

On March 28, 2015, Nigerians elected opposition candidate and northerner Major General (ret.) Muhammadu Buhari as president. It was Nigeria's first closely-contested presidential election between two major political parties, and led to Nigeria's first democratic transfer of power between parties. Fears of inter-religious violence like that which killed more than 800 persons in April 2011 were unrealized.

Since 1999, violence between Christian and Muslim communities in Nigeria, particularly in the Middle Belt states, has resulted in more than 18,000 people killed, hundreds of thousands displaced, and thousands of churches, mosques, businesses, homes, and other structures damaged or destroyed. Years of inaction by Nigeria's federal and state governments have created a climate of impunity.

Although the 1999 constitution provides for freedom of religion or belief, it also legally discriminates between persons whose ethnic group is deemed by state-level officials to be native to a particular area ("indigenes") and those considered to be from elsewhere ("settlers"). Indigene and settler identities can fall along religious lines, leading to ethno-religious violence over who controls local governments to determine indigene status and distribute corresponding education, employment, and property benefits. The constitution's federalism provisions also create an overly centralized rule-of-law system that hinders effective and timely police responses to sectarian violence and impedes prosecutions.

The Nigerian government does not actively perpetrate religious freedom abuses, but does tolerate northern and southern state laws and practices that

May 2014, Boko Haram garnered international attention with the abduction of more than 270 schoolgirls from the northeastern town of Chibok. The Council on Foreign Relations' Nigeria Security Tracker reports that from May 2011 through December 2014, Boko Haram killed more than 8,400 persons; another 7,900 were killed in fighting between Boko Haram and Nigerian security forces. The United Nations reported that by the end of 2014 more than 700,000 Nigerians were internally displaced and 142,000 sought refuge in Cameroon, Chad, and Niger.

In 2014, Boko Haram attacked Muslim and Christian religious leaders and religious ceremonies, police, military, schools, "non-conforming" Muslims, and Muslim critics. It bombed St. Charles Catholic Church in Kano, a Shi'a Muslim Ashura festival in Potiskum, and

The Nigerian government does not actively perpetrate religious freedom abuses, but does tolerate northern and southern state laws and practices that result in religious freedom violations.

result in religious freedom violations. The criminal codes of 12 Muslim-majority northern Nigerian states include Shari'ah law penalties and have been applied against Muslims and Christians. In the south, there have been reports of increased discrimination against Muslims. States habitually fail to implement announced programs or recommendations by government commissions to end sectarian violence.

Religious Freedom Conditions 2014–2015

Boko Haram

Boko Haram is a U.S.-designated Foreign Terrorist Organization (FTO) engaged in an insurgent campaign to overthrow Nigeria's secular government and impose what it considers "pure" Shari'ah law. The group declared an Islamic "Caliphate" in areas it controls in August 2014. After the close of this reporting period, Boko Haram pledged its allegiance to the Islamic State of Iraq and the Levant (ISIL) on March 8, 2015. Boko Haram opposes Nigeria's federal and northern state governments, political leaders, and Muslim religious elites and has worked to expel all Christians from the north. In

the Kano Central Mosque. The terrorists also attempted to assassinate presidential candidate Major General (ret.) Muhammadu Buhari and the Emir of Kano. Boko Haram routinely abducted hundreds of Nigerians to be slave laborers or wives. The terrorists successfully exploded two bombs in the greater Abuja area in 2014 and regularly bombed crowded markets and bus stations throughout the north. These attacks killed thousands of innocent civilians. Christian advocacy groups report that Boko Haram ordered Christian men to convert or die and forced abducted Christian women to convert.

The Nigerian government's military efforts against Boko Haram have been ineffective. From May 2013 through November 2014, the Nigerian government operated a state of emergency in Borno, Yobe, and Adamawa states, and deployed a Joint Task Force (JTF) composed of army, air force, police, state security, and intelligence officers to the three states to defeat Boko Haram. In this time period, Boko Haram expanded the territory it controlled to an area roughly the size of Belgium and ran incursions into neighboring Cameroon, Chad, and

Niger. As a result of inadequate government protection, civilians in Borno state formed vigilante groups to defend their villages from Boko Haram; at times these vigilante groups (known as the Civilian Joint Task Force) cooperated with the JTF.

Observers note that the military's heavy-handed techniques have been counterproductive. They fail to protect northeastern communities and at the same time alienate civilians from the central government, fueling recruitment or passive support for Boko Haram. The U.S. State Department, Human Rights Watch, Amnesty International, and Nigeria experts all report that security forces' actions often increased the death toll. Security forces are accused of excessive use of force, committing extra-judicial killings, mistreating detainees in custody, arbitrary arrests, and using collective punishments. The Nigerian Security Tracker reports that state security officers are solely responsible for an additional 5,000 deaths from May 2011 through December 2014. Nigerian officials deny these abuses and the federal government has not arrested or prosecuted one soldier for such abuses.

Corruption also hampered the military campaign against Boko Haram. Despite a Nigerian military budget of $5.8 billion, the U.S. State Department and Department of Defense report that the funding is "skimmed off the top" and there is low troop morale in the JTF. Soldiers are poorly trained and equipped, and at times are reported to run away or not engage a better armed and trained Boko Haram. Several military officers were prosecuted in this reporting period for failing to engage Boko Haram. The military did secure some successes in this reporting period. In the lead-up to Christmas, security forces successfully protected Christians by increasing their presence around houses of worship, strategically undertaking helicopter patrols, and banning vehicle movements in Borno and Yobe states. After the close of this reporting period, in February 2015, the

African Union approved an 8,700-troop Multi-National Joint Task Force (MNJTF) composed of soldiers from Benin, Cameroon, Chad, Niger, and Nigeria, which successfully re-captured dozens of towns. Nevertheless, Boko Haram suicide bombings continue to occur almost daily throughout the north, and the group appears to be returning to the urban, guerilla campaign that categorized much of its activities in 2012 and 2013.

The State Department and Nigeria experts also have criticized the Nigerian government for failing to implement a holistic response to the insurgency that includes counter- and de-radicalization programs and economic and social development initiatives. In May and September 2014, Nigerian National Security Advisor Colonel (ret.) Sambo Dasuki called for a "soft approach" to tackle Boko Haram that would include development and counter-radicalization programs for the northeast. In 2014, the Nigerian government announced northeast development, emergency relief, reconstruction,

> *. . . from May 2011 through December 2014, Boko Haram killed more than 8,400 persons; another 7,900 were killed in fighting between Boko Haram and Nigerian security forces.*

and rehabilitation programs, as well as a safe schools initiative. However, to date the Nigerian government has not shown a willingness to vigorously implement these types of initiatives as part of a broader campaign to defeat Boko Haram. There is no available evidence that development or reconstruction and rehabilitation programs are in effect. Only the safe schools initiative and emergency relief fund to support internally displaced persons have commenced. Further, the State Department reports that the Nigerian federal government does not support northern state-level education and employment initiatives.

Sectarian Violence

Since 1999, violence between Christian and Muslim communities in Nigeria, particularly in the Middle Belt states, has resulted in more than 18,000 people killed, hundreds of thousands displaced, and thousands of churches, mosques, businesses, homes, and other structures damaged or destroyed. Rarely are perpetrators of sectarian violence held accountable. With almost no consequence for violence, incidents regularly trigger retaliatory attacks. Human Rights Watch estimates that between January 2010 and December 2013, 2,000 to 3,000 Muslims and Christians in the Middle Belt were killed in revenge attacks on each other's communities.

Recurrent rural violence between predominately Christian farmers and predominately Muslim herders continued in 2014 with attacks in Bauchi, Benue, Kaduna, Plateau, and Taraba states that killed hundreds, displaced thousands, and destroyed a number of churches. While land disputes factor into this violence, religion is a significant catalyst in the attacks in the religiously-balkanized Kaduna and Plateau states. Southern Kaduna state has been especially prone to sectarian violence since the April 2011 elections. In the country's most deadly episode of Muslim-Christian violence in this reporting period, 147 people were

Northern State-Level Legal Problems

Twelve Muslim-majority northern Nigerian states apply their interpretation of Shari'ah law in their criminal codes. State governments in Bauchi, Zamfara, Niger, Kaduna, Jigawa, Gombe, and Kano funded and supported Hisbah, or religious police, to enforce such interpretations.

In January 2014, two Shari'ah courts in Bauchi State held a trial of 12 men accused of breaking national and Shari'ah laws on homosexuality. Their cases were heard in secret after an angry mob pelted the defendants with stones following a hearing, demanding their immediate execution. In March, four were convicted, given 15 lashes, and fined $125, and seven were secretly released on bail. A Christian suspect was tried in a secular court and later secretly released. Also in January, in a separate case, a man was publicly flogged and fined $5,000 after being convicted of homosexuality.

Christian leaders in the northern states report that those states' governments discriminate against Christians in denying applications to build or repair places of

> *Christian leaders in the northern states report that those states' governments discriminate against Christians in denying applications to build or repair places of worship, access to education, representation in government bodies and employment.*

killed and 285 houses and three churches were razed when suspected Muslim Fulanis launched attacks on Christian villages in Kaura Local Government Area, Kaduna State in March. No arrests or prosecutions of perpetrators were reported.

As in previous reporting periods, the Nigerian federal and state government response was ineffective, if present at all. When they did act, it typically involved tardy military deployments to stop violence, implementation of 24-hour curfews following some episodes, and a series of meetings and peace agreements. Security officers often were accused of excessive use of force and killing civilians. Starting on March 31, 2014, the Nigerian military executed a major internal security operation in Benue, Nasarawa, and Plateau states to stem the rural violence.

worship, access to education, representation in government bodies and employment.

Southern State-Level Legal Problems

Reports of discrimination against Muslims in southern states increased in 2014. Hundreds of northern Muslims were arrested throughout southern Nigeria in 2014 for being suspected Boko Haram members; most were later released. Further, northern Muslims in the southeast were required to register with the local governments. A Lagos High Court upheld a state ban on wearing the hijab in all Ogun state schools.

U.S. Policy

Nigeria is a strategic U.S. economic and security partner in Sub-Saharan Africa. Senior Obama Administration officials regularly visit the country, including trips by Secretaries of State Hillary Clinton and John Kerry and by other senior State Department officials. The United States is Nigeria's largest trading partner. Nigeria is the second largest recipient of U.S. foreign assistance in Africa and the United States is the largest bilateral donor to Nigeria; for fiscal year 2016 the State Department is requesting $607,498,000 for programs to support democratic governance, professionalization of the security services, counterterrorism initiatives, economic and agricultural production, and health and education services. Nigeria's importance to U.S. foreign policy was demonstrated in 2010 with the establishment of the U.S.-Nigeria Bi-National Commission.

Despite strong bilateral ties, the Nigerian-U.S. relationship deteriorated in 2014 due to disagreements over how to stop the Boko Haram insurgency. The United States has consistently urged the Nigerian government to expand its solely military approach to address problems of economic and political marginalization in the north. Additionally, senior U.S. officials frequently warn in private bilateral meetings and in public speeches that Nigerian security forces' excessive use of force in response to Boko Haram is unacceptable and counterproductive. Nigerian government officials believe that

their capture in June 2013. It also supported UN Security Council sanctions on Boko Haram to prohibit arms sales, freeze assets, and restrict movement. In May 2014, following the Chibok kidnappings, President Barack Obama sent to Abuja a multi-disciplinary team composed of humanitarian experts, U.S. military personnel, law enforcement advisors, investigators, and hostage negotiation, strategic communication, civilian security and intelligence experts to advise Nigerian officials and help secure the return the kidnapped girls. The Departments of State and Defense fund a $40 million Global Security Contingency Fund to train and equip Cameroon, Chad, Niger, and Nigeria to conduct a regional, cross-border strategy to stop Boko Haram. Nigeria receives additional security advice and assistance through its participation in other partnerships, initiatives, and programs. However, in compliance with the Leahy Amendment, U.S. security assistance to the Nigerian JTF is limited due to concerns of gross human rights violations by Nigerian soldiers. Finally, both USAID and the State Department support counter-radicalization communication programs in northeast Nigeria.

Throughout 2014 and early 2015, the U.S. government supported efforts to make the 2015 presidential, legislative, and gubernatorial elections free, fair, cred-

> *Despite strong bilateral ties, the Nigerian-U.S. relationship deteriorated in 2014 due to disagreements over how to stop the Boko Haram insurgency.*

the U.S. government is failing to provide it with adequate military support, and prematurely ended a U.S. training program of its army officers in November 2014 after the United States stopped selling helicopters to the country due to concerns about human rights abuses.

Despite these disagreements, the U.S. government has a large military assistance and anti-terrorism program in Nigeria to stop Boko Haram. The United States designated Boko Haram as a Foreign Terrorist Organization (FTO) in November 2013. It designated as terrorists Boko Haram leaders Abubakar Shekau, Abubakar Adam Kambar, and Khalid el Barnawi in June 2012, and offered a $7 million reward for information leading to

ible, and violence free. In February 2015, Secretary of State John Kerry met with President Jonathan and lead opposition presidential candidate Gen. Buhari in Abuja and warned that the U.S. government would deny entry visas to any individual who instigated electoral violence. The U.S. government provided capacity and technical assistance to the Independent National Elections Commission; funded electoral violence mitigation, political party development, and civic education programs; supported domestic and international observation missions; lobbied the media to refrain from sensational elections reporting and called on the political parties and candidates to renounce electoral violence.

Despite problems of sectarian violence, none of the Bi-National Commission working groups have addressed specifically issues of recurrent inter-religious violence and the culture of impunity. However, the State Department and USAID have implemented programs on conflict mitigation and improving interfaith relations in line with USCIRF recommendations. The State Department funds capacity-building initiatives for the Kaduna Interfaith Mediation Center (IMC) to address ethnic and religious violence across the country. USAID's TOLERANCE program works with the IMC to provide conflict mitigation and management assistance in northern and Middle Belt states in Nigeria. Additionally, the State Department's Office of International Religious Freedom funds the NGO Search for Common Ground to conduct interfaith conflict mediation programs in the Middle Belt and the Bureau of Democracy, Human Rights, and Labor supports an Open Society Foundation interfaith religious education and dialogue program.

Recommendations

Nigeria has the capacity to improve religious freedom conditions by more fully addressing Boko Haram and sectarian violence, and will only realize respect for human rights, lasting progress, security, stability, and prosperity as a democracy if it does so. Moreover, USCIRF is concerned that the charged rhetoric used by political and religious leaders could lead to an escalation of violence and a more divided, sectarian Nigeria. For these reasons, USCIRF recommends that the U.S. government designate Nigeria as a CPC. In addition to so designating Nigeria, USCIRF recommends that the U.S. government should:

- Seek to enter into a binding agreement with the Nigerian government, as defined in section 405(c) of IRFA, and be prepared to provide financial and technical support to help the Nigerian government commit to undertake reforms to address policies leading to violations of religious freedom, including but not limited to the following:

  - vigorously investigating, prosecuting, and bringing to justice perpetrators of all past and future incidents of sectarian violence and terrorism;

  - developing effective conflict-prevention and early-warning mechanisms at the local, state, and federal levels using practical and implementable criteria;

  - developing the capability to deploy specialized police and army units rapidly to prevent and combat sectarian violence in cities around the country where there has been a history of sectarian violence; and

  - taking steps to professionalize its police and military forces in its counter-terrorism, investigative, community policing, crowd control, and conflict prevention capacities by conducting specialized training for its military and security forces on human rights standards, as well as non-lethal responses to crowd control and quelling mob or communal violence;

- Hold a joint session of the U.S.-Nigeria Bi-National Commission working groups on good governance and security to address issues of Nigeria's recurrent sectarian violence and failure to prosecute perpetrators;

- Impose visa bans on persons who instigate sectarian violence;

- Urge the Nigerian government to create a Ministry of Northern Affairs and provide technical assistance to this new body to address the socio-economic disparities in the north that fuel the creation and continuation of Boko Haram;

- Advise the Nigerian government in the development of de-radicalization and community reintegration programs for youth and women enslaved by Boko Haram;

- Encourage and support through training and education efforts by the Nigerian government to provide additional security personnel to protect northern Christian minorities and clerics and Muslim traditional rulers who denounce and actively work to end the Boko Haram insurgency;

- Expand engagement with Middle Belt and northern religious leaders and elders on universal human rights, including freedom of religion or belief;

- Ensure that U.S-funded education efforts in northern Nigeria to increase access to schools and reform traditional Islamic schools include lessons on the promotion of freedom of religion or belief, tolerance, and human rights;

- Continue to support civil society and faith-based organizations at the national, regional, state, and local levels that have special expertise and a demonstrated commitment to intra-religious and interreligious dialogue, religious education, reconciliation and conflict prevention; and

- Support programs and institutions, particularly in areas where sectarian violence has occurred, that monitor, report on, and counter religiously-inflammatory language and incitement to violence, consistent with the right to freedom of expression.

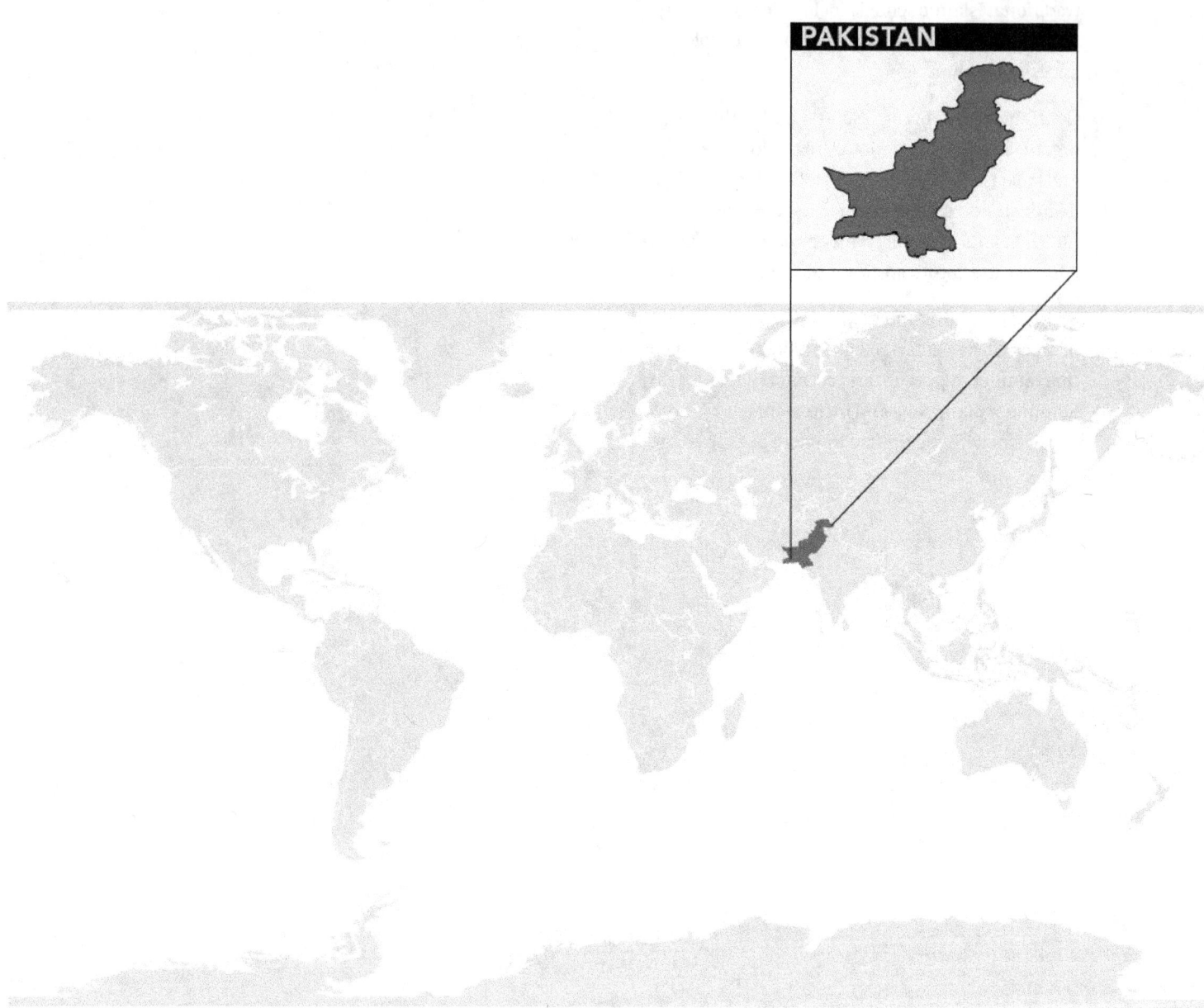

PAKISTAN

Key Findings

Pakistan represents one of the worst situations in the world for religious freedom for countries not currently designated by the U.S. government as "countries of particular concern." In the past year, the government grappled with a challenging security environment and initiated efforts to fight the Pakistani Taliban. However, despite these efforts, Pakistan continued to experience chronic sectarian violence targeting Shi'a Muslims, Christians, Ahmadi Muslims, and Hindus. Despite positive rulings by the Supreme Court, the government failed to provide adequate protection to targeted groups or to prosecute perpetrators and those calling for violence. Pakistan's repressive blasphemy laws and anti-Ahmadi laws continue to violate religious freedoms and to foster a climate of impunity. USCIRF again recommends in 2015 that Pakistan be designated a "country of particular concern," or CPC, under the International Religious Freedom Act (IRFA), as it has recommended since 2002.

Background

Pakistan is an ethnically and religiously diverse country of over 190 million people. The 1998 census of Pakistan found that 95 percent of the population identified as Muslim. Of that, 75 percent identified as Sunni, but that is divided among numerous Sunni sects and denominations. 25 percent of the Muslim population identified as Shi'a. Two to four million Ahmadis consider themselves Muslims, but Pakistani law does not recognize them as such. Non-Muslim faiths constitute roughly five percent of the population, and include Christians, Hindus, Parsis/Zoroastrians, Baha'is, Sikhs, Buddhists, and others. Shi'a, Christian, and Hindu groups believe their communities are larger than the census reported.

In 2014, the Pakistani Supreme Court took up the issue of violence against religious minorities on several occasions, going so far as to mandate the creation of special police forces and monitoring bodies. Despite

court oversight and democratic institutions, the Pakistani government engaged in and tolerated systematic, ongoing, and egregious violations of freedom of religion or belief. Pakistan's legal environment is particularly repressive due to its religiously discriminatory constitutional provisions and legislation, including its blasphemy laws. The government failed to protect citizens,

> *Pakistan represents one of the worst situations in the world for religious freedom . . . .*

minority and majority alike, from sectarian and religiously-motivated violence, and Pakistani authorities have not consistently brought perpetrators to justice or taken action against societal actors who incite violence.

In this climate, Prime Minister Nawaz Sharif and his party in parliament made condemnatory statements against acts of violence and established a commission on religious minorities under the Ministry of Religious Affairs. While prosecutions of perpetrators were generally rare, this year an anti-terror court did sentence to death an individual for the 2010 attacks on an Ahmadi mosque. An anti-terror court also remanded four individuals for the mob attack that killed a Christian couple in November 2014 over blasphemy allegations. In civilian courts, where the majority of these cases are heard, militants can intimidate judges and lawyers and perpetrators of mob attacks are frequently released on bail.

No action was taken to reform repressive laws, with observers noting that the National Assembly spent only 15 hours out of over 1000 to discuss rising violence against religious minorities. In addition, in contrast to the previous government, the Sharif government decreased the representation of religious minorities in positions of influence, as the interfaith harmony ministry remained folded into the ministry for religious affairs, which primarily deals with *hajj* participation. The Sharif government continued to recognize the Minorities Day holiday, established by the late Shahbaz Bhatti, the Minister of Minority Affairs who was assassinated in 2011, although the level of participation by government officials was low. The trial of Shahbaz Bhatti's murderers was suspended due to threats to prosecution witnesses made in the courtroom by militants.

In June 2014, after recurring attacks, the Pakistani military launched military operations against the Pakistani Taliban's base of operations in North Waziristan. In retaliation, the Pakistani Taliban attacked soft targets, such as Shi'a mosques, churches, and a school for the children of military officers in Peshawar. The December 16 school attack – which killed over 130 children, many execution style, and wounded scores – led Prime Minister Sharif to launch a National Action Plan, which was supported by the major political parties. The 20-point plan, *inter alia*, created military courts to try terrorists, emphasized actions taken to stop religious extremism and to protect religious minorities, and said an effort would be made to register *madrassas*.

After the reporting period, USCIRF Commissioners made the first ever Commissioner-level visit to Pakistan in March 2015. Commissioners met with high ranking Pakistani officials, including National Security Adviser Sartaj Aziz, as well as officials in the Ministries of Interior and Religious Affairs. Tragically, suicide bombers attacked two churches in Lahore the day the USCIRF delegation departed Pakistan.

Religious Freedom Conditions 2014-2015
Targeted Sectarian Violence

The Pakistani government's failure to effectively intervene against violence targeting the Shi'a minority community, as well as against Christians, Hindus and Ahamdis, continued during the reporting period. USCIRF found that from July 2013 to June 2014, 122 incidents of sectarian violence occurred, resulting in more than 1,200 casualties, including 430 deaths. Authorities have not consistently brought the perpetrators of such violence to justice. Early attempts in 2014 to negotiate peace with the Pakistani Taliban dissolved after repeated attacks, which spurred a major military offensive. The Pakistani Taliban

has been a major persecutor of religious minorities, as well as Sunni Muslims who disagree with their ideology, so the military offensive may limit their ability to use violence. However, the Pakistani Taliban may retaliate, as they have in the past, by targeting Shi'a Muslims and schools. Also, any military gains will likely be short-lived without a similar government effort on the civilian side to ensure arrests and prosecutions of perpetrators and instigators of religious violence.

Shi'a Muslims

During 2014, militants and terrorist organizations continued to target Shi'a processions and mosques, as well as social gathering places, with impunity. Police, if present, have failed to stop attackers before people are killed, and the government has not cracked down on the groups that repeatedly target Shi'a Muslims. The government has not successfully prosecuted the leader of Lashkar-e-Jhangvi, a banned terrorist organization behind many of the attacks, who is regularly released due to a purported lack of evidence.

Christians

Violence against Christians continued, with few concrete actions taken by federal or provincial officials to ensure their protection. For instance, after the 2013 mob attack on the Christian village Joseph Colony in Punjab, the provincial government provided some reparations but all of the attackers were released on bail. The only person serving a prison sentence is a Christian falsely accused of blasphemy, who was sentenced to death. Other attacks against Christians because of allegations of blasphemy continued (see below).

Ahmadis

During 2014, individual Ahmadis continued to be murdered in religiously-motivated attacks. In May 2014, a Canadian-American Ahmadi doctor visiting Pakistan to do relief work was murdered in front of his family. In July, three Ahmadis – a grandmother and her two grandchildren – were killed in an arson attack by a mob. In December, a major Pakistani television station aired an interview with religious scholars who referred to Ahmadis as "enemies." Days later, an Ahmadi was murdered; the community suspects motivation from the television broadcast. (See more about the unique legal repression of Ahmadis below.) In addition, local police repeatedly forced Ahmadis to remove Qur'anic scripture from mosques and minarets.

Hindus

Allegations of kidnappings of Hindu women, followed by forced conversions to Islam and forced marriages to Muslim men, continued to arise throughout 2014. Hindu women are particularly vulnerable to these crimes because Pakistani law does not recognize Hindu marriages. In March 2014, a mob set fire to a Hindu community center in southern Pakistan after allegations that a Hindu had desecrated a Qur'an. Four other Hindu temples were attacked that month elsewhere.

Forced Conversions

Forced conversion of Christian and Hindu girls and young women into Islam and forced marriage remains a systemic problem. The Movement for Solidarity and Peace in Pakistan estimates that hundreds of Christians and Hindus are victimized each year.

Blasphemy Laws

The country's blasphemy laws, used predominantly in Punjab province but also nationwide, target members of religious minority communities and dissenting Muslims. During the reporting period, five individuals were sentenced to death and one to life in prison,

their actions had blasphemed Islam. After the reporting period, the Punjab Prosecution Department and provincial judiciary announced that they had reviewed 262 blasphemy cases awaiting trial and recommended that 50 be reviewed for dismissal because the accused had been victimized by complainants. No religious minorities were included in the review.

Violence continued to be perpetrated around blasphemy allegations. In March 2014, a Pakistani Christian was murdered after being acquitted. In May, a leading human rights attorney, Rashid Rehman, was murdered in his office for defending a Muslim accused of blasphemy. In September, a leading Islamic scholar was gunned down after allegations of blasphemy. In November, a mob killed a Christian man and his pregnant wife accused of blasphemy by throwing them into a brick kiln. Also in November, a policeman killed a Shi'a Muslim with an axe while in custody due to allegedly blasphemous statements.

Blasphemy laws are inherently problematic and conflict with fundamental human rights protections. In Pakistan, they are particularly pernicious. The punishments are severe: death or life imprisonment. There is no clear definition of blasphemy, which empowers the accuser to decide if a blasphemous act has occurred. No proof of intent is required, nor must evidence be presented after allegations are made. Penalties for false allegations are not part of the blasphemy laws, though

The country's blasphemy laws, used predominantly in Punjab province but also nationwide, target members of religious minority communities and dissenting Muslims.

bringing the total of blasphemy prisoners in Pakistan to 38. In October, the Lahore High Court upheld the death sentence of Aasia Bibi, a Christian woman convicted of blasphemy in 2010 after a dispute with co-workers; she later wrote a letter from her windowless cell to the Pakistani President requesting a pardon. Many others have been charged with blasphemy and await trial. During 2014, charges were brought against the owner of a major Pakistani television station, as well as a popular Pakistan singer-turned imam, when individuals felt

they may exist in other criminal code provisions. The need for specific penalties was demonstrated when USCIRF asked government officials about instances where false allegations of blasphemy were prosecuted and they were not able to offer a single example.

Legal Restrictions on Ahmadis

Ahmadis are subject to severe legal restrictions, both in the constitution and criminal code, and suffer from officially-sanctioned discrimination. 2014 was the 40th anniversary of Pakistan's second amendment, which amended the constitution to declare Ahmadis to be "non-Muslims." Other discriminatory penal code provisions make basic acts of Ahmadi worship and interaction criminal offenses. They also are prevented from voting.

Education

Discriminatory content against religious minorities in provincial textbooks remains a concern. The provincial government of Khyber Pakhtunkhwa announced plans in October 2014 to restore problematic references to *jihad* that could support violence. More positively, the Sindh provincial Ministry of Education ordered the removal of all discriminatory passages about religious minorities. At the end of the year, it was unclear whether the positive or negative changes had been implemented. In addition, USCIRF received reports of preferential treatment for Muslim students, who can receive extra credit for memorizing the Qur'an, making it easier for them to obtain government jobs or university placement. This also discriminates against students from non-Muslim religions. USCIRF's 2011 study of Pakistani textbooks found that an alarming number of Pakistan's public schools and privately-run *madrassas* devalue religious minorities in both textbooks and classroom instruction. The *madrassa* education system generally relies on very old religious texts and for the most part does not educate children about the value of religious tolerance and diversity.

U.S. Policy

Pakistan plays a critical role in U.S. government efforts to combat al-Qaeda and in supporting U.S. and multinational forces in Afghanistan. However, with the drawdown of combat troops from Afghanistan, U.S. government reliance on Pakistan for transport of supplies and ground lines of communication to Afghanistan will decrease. Regardless, the United States will remain engaged with Pakistan, due to concerns about Pakistani links to terrorists and other militants opposed to the Afghan government, the country's nuclear arsenal, its contentious relationship with neighboring India, and other issues.

Overall U.S.-Pakistan relations have long been marked by strain, disappointment, and mistrust. Human rights and religious freedom have not been among the highest priorities in the bilateral relationship, although U.S. Embassy Islamabad has actively tracked cases and U.S. officials have raised concerns with Pakistani officials. The Strategic Dialogue, established between the United States and Pakistan in 2010, includes the topics of "economy and trade; energy; security; strategic stability and non-proliferation; law enforcement and counter-terrorism; science and technology, education; agriculture; water; health; and communications and public diplomacy," but not human rights. Although the Dialogue was dormant for some time due to challenges in the bilateral relationship, by the end of the reporting period select bilateral working groups reportedly were meeting. USCIRF has recommended the inclusion of a working group on religious tolerance, so as to create a positive forum to engage on issues of mutual concern.

The aid relationship with Pakistan is complex and changing. Congress has placed certification requirements on U.S. military assistance to Pakistan focusing on counterterrorism cooperation. The State Department notified Congress that the Obama Administration would waive the certification requirements in July 2014. Non-military U.S. aid dramatically increased in recent years, while military aid has ebbed and flowed over the decades of engagement. In October 2009, President Obama signed the Enhanced Partnership with Pakistan Act (also known as the Kerry-Lugar-Berman Act) authorizing an additional $7.5 billion ($1.5 billion annually over five years) in mostly non-military assistance to Pakistan. However, the $1.5 billion amount was only met in the first year, and the appropriated amount has been approximately one-third of that each year since. The Act expired in 2014. The Obama Administration's FY2015 request for aid to Pakistan totaled $882 million.

Recommendations

Promoting respect for freedom of religion or belief must be an integral part of U.S. policy in Pakistan, and designating Pakistan as a CPC would enable the United States to more effectively press Islamabad to undertake needed reforms. The forces that target religious minorities and members of the majority faith present a human rights and security challenge to Pakistan and the United States. USCIRF recommends that the U.S. government should:

- Designate Pakistan as a "country of particular concern," as required under IRFA, due to the government's engagement in and toleration of particularly severe violations of religious freedom, and work to reach a binding agreement with the Pakistani government on steps to be delisted and avoid Presidential actions; such an agreement should be accompanied by Congress appropriating resources for related capacity building through the State Department and USAID mechanisms;

- Press the Pakistani government to implement the Supreme Court decision to create a special police

- Encourage the government of Pakistan to launch a public information campaign about the historic role played by religious minorities in the country, their contributions to Pakistani society, and their equal rights and protections; either in parallel or independently, use the tools of U.S. public diplomacy to highlight similar themes;

- Urge the Pakistani government and provincial governments to review all cases of individuals charged with blasphemy in order to release those subjected

Promoting respect for freedom of religion or belief must be an integral part of U.S. policy in Pakistan . . . .

force to protect religious groups from violence and actively prosecute perpetrators, both individuals involved in mob attacks and members of militant groups;

- Recognize the unique governmental offices focusing on religious tolerance at the federal and provincial levels by including discussions on religious tolerance in U.S.-Pakistan dialogues or by creating a special track of bilateral engagement about government efforts to promote interfaith harmony;

- Urge the reestablishment of the Federal Ministry for Interfaith Harmony and the removal of the commission on religious minorities from the Ministry for Religious Affairs, giving both direct access to the cabinet and Prime Minister;

- Work with international partners to raise religious freedom concerns with Pakistani officials in Islamabad and in multilateral settings, and to encourage the Pakistani government to invite the UN Special Rapporteur on Freedom of Religion or Belief for a country visit;

- Encourage national textbook and curricula standards that actively promote tolerance towards members of all religions, both in government schools and the *madrassa* system overseen by the religious affairs ministry;

to abusive charges, as is underway in Punjab, while still also calling for the unconditional release and pardoning of all individuals sentenced to prison for blasphemy or for violating anti-Ahmadi laws;

- Work with federal and provincial parliamentarians to support the passage of marriage bills recognizing Hindu and Christian marriages;

- Call for the repeal of the blasphemy law and the rescinding of anti-Ahmadi provisions of law; until those steps can be accomplished, urge the Pakistani government to reform the blasphemy law by making blasphemy a bailable offense and/or by adding penalties for false accusations or enforcing such penalties found elsewhere in the penal code;

- Ensure that a portion of U.S. security assistance is used to help police implement an effective plan for dedicated protection for religious minority communities and their places of worship; and

- Provide USAID capacity-building funding to the provincial Ministries of Minority Affairs, and work with Pakistan's government and minority religious communities to help them reach agreement on measures to ensure their rights and security in the country.

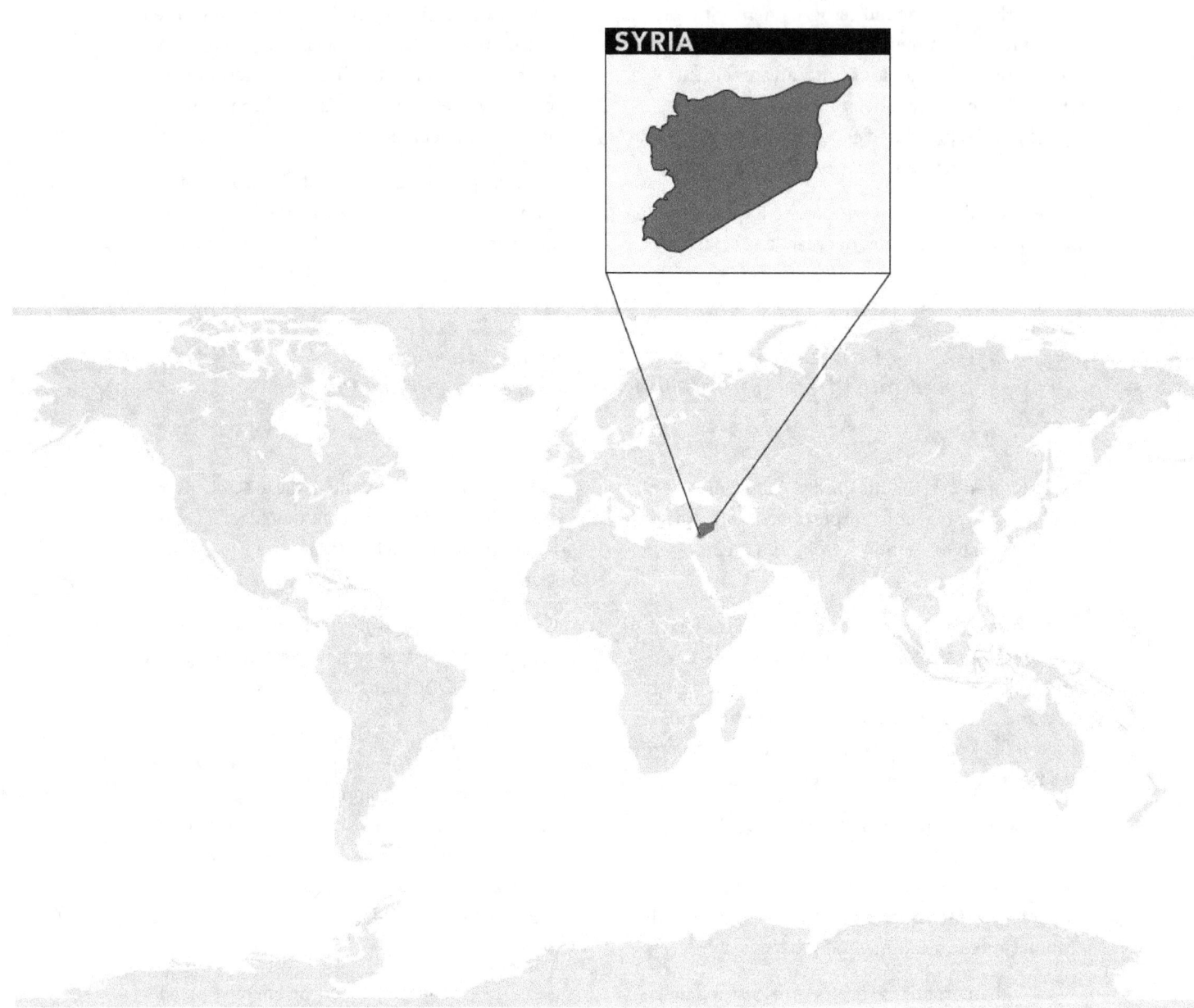

SYRIA

SYRIA

Key Findings

Syria's religious communities are largely deprived of religious freedom, and its history of religious diversity may be lost. After four years of conflict, religious diversity and freedom are victims of the actions of the al-Assad regime, as well as of internationally-recognized opposition fighters and U.S.-designated terrorist groups, in particular the Islamic State of Iraq and the Levant (ISIL). The Syrian crisis has evolved into a largely sectarian conflict. By the systematic targeting and massacre of primarily Sunni Muslims, the al-Assad regime created the environment in which ISIL could rise and spread, threatening the entire region and all religious communities that reject its violent religious ideology, with the smallest religious minority communities facing an existential threat. The al-Assad regime continues to target Sunni Muslim civilians and other individuals or groups that oppose it, including indiscriminately shelling civilian areas. Likewise, ISIL targets the regime, its supporters, religious minorities,

Background

The Syrian conflict began in March 2011 with peaceful protests by opponents of the al-Assad regime, mainly Sunni Muslims but also religious minorities. The initial protests were not overtly characterized by religious or sectarian undertones and sought repeal of the abusive emergency law, space for political parties, and President Bashar al-Assad's resignation. As the protests grew, al-Assad ordered an increasingly violent crackdown and he and his regime played on sectarian fears by utilizing religiously-divisive rhetoric. In support of the regime were U.S.-designated terrorist groups, such as Hezbollah and Shabiha. In opposition to the Assad regime, dozens of domestic and foreign groups, varying widely in goals, emerged. Some of these groups, including the U.S.-recognized National Coalition of Syrian Revolution & Opposition Forces (commonly known as the Syrian National Coalition (SNC)), espouse democratic reform. Others, such as ISIL, are motivated by religious ideologies espousing violence.

Now entering its fifth year, the conflict has become largely sectarian.

and any Muslims opposing its violent religious ideology. Well over half of Syria's pre-conflict population has fled to neighboring countries or is internally displaced. Moreover, it is not certain how many members of religious minority communities still live in Syria, a formerly religiously diverse country. Because of the actions of the al-Assad regime and non-state actors, in 2015 USCIRF recommends for the second year that Syria be designated a "country of particular concern," or CPC.

Now entering its fifth year, the conflict has become largely sectarian. Sunni Muslims generally associate all Alawites and Shi'a Muslims with the regime of President al-Assad, an Alawite himself, and many Alawites, Shi'a Muslims, Christians, and others believe that they will be killed by ISIL and other extremist Sunni groups if the al-Assad government falls.

Before the conflict, Syria's total population was approximately 22.5 million. Sunni Muslims constituted 74 percent; other Muslims, including Alawites, Ismailis, and Shi'a Muslims, were estimated at 13 percent of the total population; Druze were about three percent of the population; and various Christian groups, including Syriac, Armenian, and Greek Orthodox communities, were estimated at 10 percent.

Religious Freedom Conditions 2014–2015

Violations by al-Assad Regime and Affiliated Groups

The regime's atrocities have been indiscriminate, primarily targeting the Sunni Muslim population and where they live, creating an environment where internationally-recognized and protected human rights, including religious freedom, do not exist. The UN and

beheadings and mass murders, are widespread and well documented. Moreover, ISIL and other similar groups that control significant areas of Syria have been establishing systems that resemble governing structures, including creating Shari'ah courts that violate human rights, in areas they control.

Opposition Groups

During the reporting year, the SNC did not effectively or adequately represent religious minorities, and internal politics hampered its effectiveness and ability to agree on whether to reopen negotiations with the al-Assad regime. Reports that the Free Syrian Army, its affiliates,

The UN and most of the international community, including the United States, have found that the al-Assad regime has committed crimes against humanity.

most of the international community, including the United States, have found that the al-Assad regime has committed crimes against humanity. The regime and its supporters, including terrorist groups, utilize tactics such as extra-judicial killings, rape, torture, chemical weapons, indiscriminate shelling of civilian sites, including mosques and churches, and withholding food and other aid to maintain the regime's power.

Violations by ISIL and other Extremist and Terrorist Groups

ISIL, al-Qaeda, Khorasan, al-Nusra and numerous other extremist groups and radicalized individuals from across the globe are fighting in Syria in opposition to the regime or in support of the spread of their extreme, violent religious ideology. ISIL's declaration of a so-called "Islamic State" in June 2014 that cuts across Syria and Iraq is especially troubling for human rights and religious freedom. ISIL and other similar groups and individuals espouse violence and allow no space for religious diversity, targeting religious minority communities that have existed in Syria for centuries, as well as Muslims that reject their worldview. ISIL and four years of conflict have seriously damaged the country's religious diversity. Its gruesome attacks, including

and opposition fighters have committed human rights atrocities, including massacres of Shi'a Muslim civilians, surfaced in the last year. In addition, opposition military units on occasion have worked with terrorist groups to secure strategic areas, making it difficult for the international community to separate Sunni extremists associated with ISIL or other U.S.-designated terrorist groups from Sunni Muslims opposing the brutal al-Assad regime.

Refugees, Sectarian Spillover, and Internally-Displaced People

The duration of the conflict and the large populations of refugees in neighboring countries are causing sectarian tensions, and increasing the risk of sectarian violence and instability, in those countries. Most Syrian refugees reside in urban or rural areas, rather than official refugee camps, creating a significant burden for the host countries' economies and infrastructure. Increasingly refugees are facing societal harassment because they are perceived as taking jobs and using limited resources.

As of mid-January 2015, the Syrian crisis had led to more than 3.3 million registered refugees, mostly in Lebanon, Jordan, Turkey, Iraq, and Egypt, according to the UN refugee agency. Hundreds of thousands more are believed to be unregistered. More than three-quarters of the UN-registered refugees are women and children under the age of 17. Tens of thousands of babies have been born stateless, as they are ineligible for citizenship in the host countries where they were born. Additionally, Syrian refugees who fled to Iraq are once again finding themselves in a dangerous situation with conflict increasing there. In addition to the millions of refugees, an estimated 9.3 million people in Syria need basic assistance, such as food, water and shelter, including more than 6.5 million internally-displaced people.

U.S. Policy

U.S.-Syria relations have long been adversarial. Under the Hafez and Bashar al-Assad regimes, Syria has been on the U.S. list of state sponsors of terrorism since 1979. With the U.S. military presence in neighboring Iraq beginning in 2003, U.S.-Syria relations worsened. The

Coalition (formerly the Syrian Opposition Coalition) as the legitimate representative of the country's people and its offices in Washington, DC and New York as diplomatic missions, but it has stopped short of recognizing the Coalition as the official government of Syria.

The United States led in the creation of the Friends of Syria group, a collective of countries and organizations that periodically met outside of the UN Security Council to discuss the Syrian crisis. The group arose after Russia and China vetoed a number of Security Council resolutions that would have condemned the al-Assad regime's actions, and it met four times between 2012 and 2013. Most recently, China and Russia blocked a May 2014 UN Security Council Referral of Syria to the International Criminal Court. The United States also has been instrumental in the creation of the 60-nation Global Coalition to Counter ISIL. The United States and coalition members have been engaging in airstrikes

> *The duration of the conflict and the large populations of refugees in neighboring countries are causing sectarian tensions, and increasing the risk of sectarian violence and instability, in those countries.*

al-Assad regime failed to prevent foreign fighters from entering Iraq, refused to deport from Syria Iraqis supporting the insurgency, and continued to pursue weapons of mass destruction, among other U.S. concerns. For these reasons, in 2004 the U.S. levied economic sanctions under the Syria Accountability Act, which prohibits or restricts the export and re-export of most U.S. products to Syria. In 2008, sanctions prohibiting the export of U.S. services to Syria were added.

The regime's violent response to peaceful protestors in 2011 led to further sanctions, with the U.S. government designating groups and individuals complicit in human rights abuses and supporters of the al-Assad regime. In 2012, the United States closed its embassy in Damascus, and in March 2014 it ordered the Syrian embassy and consulates in the United States to close. Since the beginning of the Syrian conflict, the United States has called for the al-Assad regime to step down. The U.S. government has recognized the Syrian National

against ISIL-held territories in Syria. In addition, the United States has provided non-lethal aid and some light weaponry and funding to some groups fighting against ISIL in Syria. In January 2015, the Pentagon announced that several hundred U.S. military training personnel would be deployed to train and equip vetted Syrians beginning in spring 2015.

The United States is the largest donor to the international humanitarian response to the Syrian crisis. According to a February 2015 Congressional Research Service report, the United States allocated more than $3 billion to assist in the humanitarian crisis between September 2012 and mid-December 2014. As of early 2015, the U.S. government had resettled very few Syrian refugees to the United States, as compared to the scale of the crisis – only 450 since FY 2011. In December 2014, Assistant Secretary of State for Population, Refugees, and Migration Anne Richard said that the United States expected the resettlement of Syrians to "surge" in 2015 and beyond. In January 2015, Reuters reported that, according to a State Department official, 1,000-2,000 Syrian refugees were likely to be admitted in FY 2015 and a few thousand more in FY 2016.

Recommendations

All Syrians, including Sunni, Shi'a and Alawite Muslims, Christians, and the smallest communities, such as Yazidis and Druze, are living in bleak conditions and face a dire future. The prospect of achieving a post-conflict Syria that values religious diversity, minority rights, and religious freedom is fading, with an entire generation at risk from fighting, prolonged hunger, disease, poverty, and indoctrination into extremist ideologies. In addition to continuing to seek an end to the conflict, USCIRF recommends that the U.S. government should designate Syria as a CPC and should:

- Ensure that religious freedom and diversity are given a high priority in diplomatic planning and engagement that seeks to reach a political solution to the conflict;

- Encourage the Global Coalition to Counter ISIL, in its ongoing international meetings, to work to develop measures to protect and assist the region's most vulnerable religious and ethnic minorities, including by increasing immediate humanitarian aid, prioritizing the resettlement to third countries of the most vulnerable, and providing longer-term support in host countries for those who hope to return to their homes post-conflict;

- Ensure that U.S. government planning for a post-conflict Syria is a "whole-of- government" effort and includes consideration of issues concerning religious freedom and related human rights, and that USCIRF and other U.S. government experts on those issues are consulted as appropriate;

- Encourage the Syrian National Coalition to be inclusive of all religious and ethnic groups and provide training to members on international standards relating to human rights and religious freedom;

- Call for or support a referral by the UN Security Council to the International Criminal Court to investigate ISIL violations in Iraq and Syria against religious and ethnic minorities, and continue to call for an International Criminal Court investigation into crimes committed by the al-Assad regime, following the models used in Sudan and Libya;

- Initiate an effort among relevant UN agencies, NGOs, and like-minded partners among the Global Coalition to Counter ISIL to fund and develop programs that bolster intra- and inter-religious tolerance, alleviate sectarian tensions, and promote respect for religious freedom and related rights, both in neighboring countries hosting refugees (especially Lebanon, Jordan, Egypt and Turkey), and in preparing for a post-conflict Syria;

- Increase the U.S. refugee ceiling from 70,000 to at least 100,000, with additional reserves for the Middle East region.

- Consider issuing an exemption to U.S. immigration law's "material support bar" provision for Syrian refugees who supported specific U.S.-backed rebel groups or provided "support" by force or under duress to terrorist organizations, and properly apply existing exemptions, so that Syrians who pose no threat to the United States and are fleeing the al-Assad regime or terrorist groups are not erroneously barred from the U.S. refugee program;

- Allocate sufficient resources to the Department of Homeland Security and other agencies to expeditiously process applications and conduct security background checks to facilitate the resettlement of Syrian refugees in the United States without compromising U.S. national security; and

- Continue and increase funding and logistical support to the UN, humanitarian organizations, and refugee host nations (especially Lebanon, Jordan, Egypt and Turkey), and communities to provide humanitarian aid to refugees and internally displaced persons, and encourage other countries to do the same.

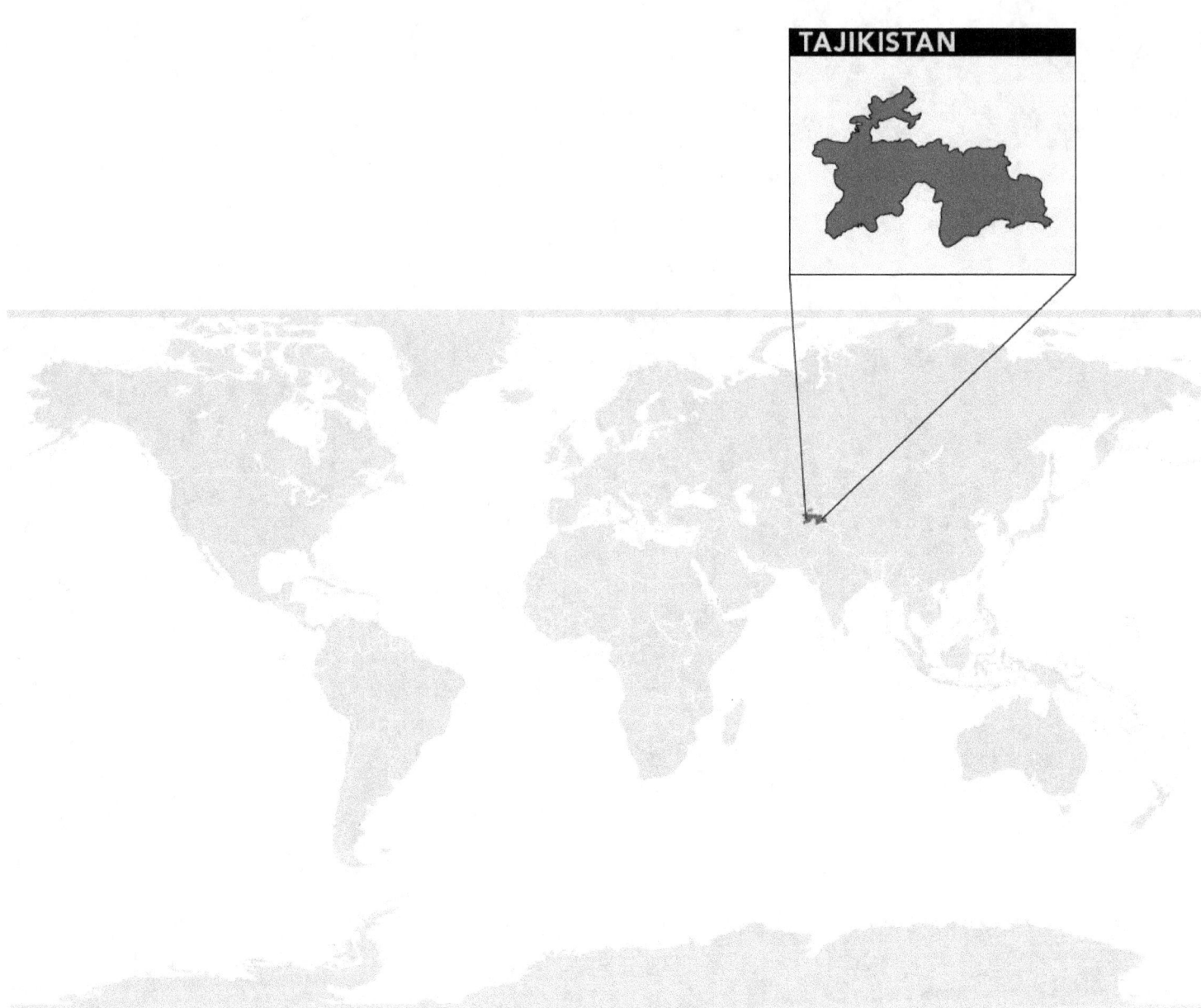

TAJIKISTAN

TAJIKISTAN

Key Findings

The government of Tajikistan suppresses and punishes all religious activity independent of state control, particularly the activities of Muslims, Protestants, and Jehovah's Witnesses. Numerous laws that severely restrict religious freedom have been implemented in the country since 2009. The government also imprisons individuals on unproven criminal allegations linked to Islamic religious activity and affiliation. Jehovah's Witnesses have been banned since 2007. Based on these concerns, as it has since 2012, USCIRF again recommends in 2015 that the U.S. government designate Tajikistan as a "country of particular concern," or CPC, under the International Religious Freedom Act (IRFA). Previously Tajikistan was on USCIRF's Tier 2 (formerly Watch List) since 2009.

Background

Tajikistan is an isolated and impoverished country that experienced a five-year civil war in the 1990s, which resulted in as many as 100,000 deaths; the official post-war amnesty included many Tajik officials responsible for torture. The government is weak and highly corrupt, and the country's economy leads the world in its dependence on remittances from migrant workers, mostly in Russia. After the Russian economy's

More than 90 percent of Tajikistan's estimated total population of 7.9 million is Muslim, most of whom belong to the Hanafi school of Sunni Islam; about four percent are Ismaili Shia. Most of the 150,000 Christians are Russian Orthodox, but there are also Baptists, Roman Catholics, Adventists, Lutherans, and Korean Protestants plus small numbers of Baha'is, Hare Krishnas, Jehovah's Witnesses, and fewer than 300 Jews. The legal environment in Tajikistan for religious freedom has deteriorated significantly since 2009, when a series of highly restrictive laws were passed and implemented. The 2009 religion law establishes onerous registration requirements for religious groups; criminalizes unregistered religious activity and private religious education and proselytism; sets strict limits on the number and size of mosques; allows state interference with the appointment of imams; requires official permission for religious organizations to provide religious instruction and communicate with foreign co-religionists; imposes state controls on the content, publication and import of religious materials; and restricts Muslim prayer to mosques, cemeteries, homes, and shrines.

In 2011 and 2012, administrative and penal code amendments set new penalties, including large fines and prison terms, for religion-related charges, such as organizing or participating in "unapproved" religious

Tajikistan is an isolated and impoverished country [with] . . . a weak and highly corrupt [government] . . .

downturn, many Tajik migrant workers returned home in 2014, giving rise to new social tensions. Tajikistan has good relations with Iran, its second-largest trading partner; these two countries also share common language and heritage.

meetings. Alleged organizers of a "religious extremist study group" face eight to 12-year prison terms. In addition, a 2011 law on parental responsibility banned minors from any organized religious activity except funerals. The State Department highlighted in its most recent International Religious Freedom (IRF) Report that "Tajikistan is the only country in the world in which the law prohibits persons under the age of 18 from participating in public religious activities."

Tajikistan's extremism law punishes extremist, terrorist, or revolutionary activities without requiring acts that involve violence or incitement to imminent violence. Trials under these charges lack due process and procedural safeguards. The Tajik government uses concerns over Islamist extremism to justify actions against individuals taking part in certain religious activities. According to public opinion polls conducted by the Tajik NGO Sharq Analytical Center, most Tajiks view poverty, not extremism, as the country's main problem. Little data on official bans of groups deemed extremist is public, but *Tabligh Jamaat* is prohibited.

Religious Freedom Conditions 2014–2015
Restrictions on Muslims

Tajik officials monitor mosques and their attendees for views they deem extremist or statements critical of the government; place restrictions on Muslim religious dress; control the age and the numbers of *hajj* (religious pilgrimage) participants; and indirectly control the selection and retention of imams and the content of sermons. The law prohibits the wearing of headscarves in educational institutions, and bans teachers younger

Rahmon also instructed the Council of Ulema to adopt a standard uniform for imams. The Sharq Analytical Center, reports that these policies have led to a sharp division between official and unofficial Muslim clergy, giving rise to popular mistrust of Muslim institutions.

Trials and Imprisonment of Muslims

During 2014, Tajik law enforcement officials continued to arrest and prosecute dozens of individuals for alleged links to banned Islamic groups or international terrorist networks. Due to Tajikistan's flawed judicial system, it is almost impossible to ascertain the accuracy of such charges. For example, in December 2014 Tajikistan's prosecutors said that nearly 50 young men from banned Islamist groups were arrested in the Sogd region for allegedly preparing to join jihadists in Syria. In February 2015, Tajikistan's Interior Minster claimed that 200 Tajik labor migrants in Russia had joined militants in Syria, RFE/RL reported, but others could not confirm that figure.

The Chairman of Tajikistan's Council of Ulema expressed concern in April 2014 over the increasing number of Tajik officials who reportedly have become adherents of Salafi or Shi'a Islam. The Sharq Analytical Center reports that Salafism is increasing in popularity among the Tajik political elite. A Tajik policeman, Captain Sharif Mirov was arrested in May 2014 for

[M]ost Tajiks view poverty, not extremism, as the country's main problem.

than 50 from wearing beards in public buildings. In 2014, the semi-official Council of Ulema announced it would start to allow women to attend mosques and would encourage female students at religious schools to become *imam-hatibs*, to work with female worshippers at mosques with women-only sections.

In 2014, the Ministry of Finance and the State Committee on Religious Affairs (SCRA) began paying the salaries of the imams of cathedral mosques. According to the Forum 18 News Service, these are the only mosques where the state allows sermons, which are prepared in advance by the Council of Ulema. President Emomali

allegedly inciting religious hatred by propagating Salafi Islam, reportedly the first such arrest in the country. The Deputy Head of the SCRA has called Salafis extremist because they pray differently and are argumentative about Islamic beliefs. In December 2014, the Tajik Supreme Court ruled that the Salafi Muslim movement is "extremist," and ordered Web sites blocked in the country, according to the independent Asia-Plus News Agency. Salafi Muslims now risk prosecution under three Criminal Code articles relating to extremism, which carry penalties between five and 12 years in jail, Forum 18 reported.

Tajikistan has the only legal Islamist political party in the former Soviet Union, the Islamic Renaissance Party (IRP), which was given such status as part of the country's post-civil war peace settlement. Government repression of Islamic practice is often intertwined with official efforts to suppress the IRP. In January 2014, Umedjon Tojiev, 34, an IRP member from the northern city of Isfara, died in a prison hospital under highly suspicious circumstances; he was arrested in October 2013 on charges of extremism.

Center, Central Asia's first Ismaili center, opened in Dushanbe in 2009, and Tajikistan announced that one of the world's largest mosques, funded by Qatar, will open in Dushanbe in 2017.

Restrictions on Religious Minorities

Jehovah's Witnesses were banned in 2007 for allegedly causing "discontent" and for conscientious objection to military service. Jehovah's Witnesses still face official harassment. Small Protestant and other groups cannot

---

Tajikistan has the only legal Islamist political party in the former Soviet Union.

After the reporting period, the IRP suffered a major election defeat, garnering only 1.5 percent in Tajikistan's March 1, 2015 vote, leaving it without any seats in parliament for the first time in 15 years. Five days after these much-criticized elections, a Tajik opposition leader, Umarali Kuvatov, was killed in Istanbul. The IRP and various Tajik human rights groups have reported on the torture of detainees and prisoners.

A leading Tajik human rights lawyer, Shukhrat Kudratov, was sentenced in January 2015, to nine years in prison on false charges of fraud and bribery, according to Human Rights Watch. He is known for taking on politically sensitive cases, including victims of police torture and those accused of "religious extremism;" he also works with the independent Asia-Plus News Agency.

Restrictions on Houses of Worship

Tajik law sets strict limits on the numbers of mosques permitted, and since 2008 the government has closed hundreds of unregistered mosques and prayer rooms and demolished three unregistered mosques in Dushanbe. The nation's only synagogue, located in Dushanbe, was bulldozed in 2008, although the Jewish community later was given a building by President Rakhmon's brother-in-law, one of Tajikistan's richest bankers, which it uses for worship but does not own. In July 2013, the SCRA fired the Chief Imam in Vossei of the Khatlon Region, Ubaydullo Khasanov, after he asked President Rakhmon for land to build a new mosque. In contrast, the Aga Khan Cultural

obtain legal status under onerous registration requirements. In June 2013, according to the State Department, authorities brought a second administrative case against the pastor of Grace Church in Khujand for an "illegal" chapel, "religious propaganda," and unregistered Bible studies. In another case, Forum 18 reported that in June 2014 an unnamed church was warned to stop allowing children to take part in worship meetings or face a three-month suspension of church activity.

Restrictions on Religious Literature

The government must approve the production, importation, export, sale, and distribution of religious materials by registered religious groups, which is in effect a ban on religious materials by unregistered religious groups. The Ministry of Culture has confiscated religious texts it deems inappropriate, including from Jehovah's Witnesses.

Restrictions on Religious Education

A state license is required for religious instruction, and both parents must give written permission for children to receive instruction. Only central mosques are allowed to set up educational groups. As of 2013, the activities of seven of the country's eight madrassas were suspended, according to the State Department. Tajik authorities now allow only one madrassa to operate, in Tursonzade, near Dushanbe. In December 2014, police in Vahdat near Dushanbe, arrested Komiljon Akhrorov and Sayidmumin Rashidov for teaching school-aged children at home about the Qur'an and Islam. In January 2015, the SCRA issued written warnings to various Protestant churches, threatening punishment unless they stopped allowing children to worship, according to Forum 18.

Civil Society and Religious Issues

Tajik civil society is subject to official pressure, and Tajik non-governmental organizations have expressed fear of reporting on religious freedom due to perceived dangers of involvement in that issue. In June 2014, Alexander Sodiqov, a Tajik citizen and University of Toronto graduate student who has written blogs that criticized Tajikistan's restrictive policies on religion, was arrested on charges of espionage while conducting foreign-funded research in the Ismaili-majority Gorno-Badakshan region near Afghanistan. After an international outcry, Sodiqov was allowed to leave Tajikistan in September 2014, but the espionage charges were not dropped.

U.S. Policy

Tajikistan is strategically important for the United States, partly because ethnic Tajiks are the second largest ethnic group in Afghanistan, the country's southern neighbor. Since 2010, the United States has expanded its cooperation with Central Asian states, including Tajikistan, to allow it to ship cargo overland via the Northern Distribution Network, which will be needed as U.S. and NATO troops in Afghanistan withdraw. In addition, Tajikistan has given U.S. Special Operations Forces permission to enter the country on a case-by-case basis during counter-terrorism operations. In 2014, the Tajik government expressed interest in an offer from the U.S. Defense Department of excess U.S. military equipment, for which Tajikistan would only pay transport costs.

Since 2010, the United States and Tajikistan have discussed bilateral policy and assistance issues through an Annual Bilateral Consultation (ABC). The State Department's stated priorities in Tajikistan include increasing respect for the rights of Tajikistan's citizens and strengthening sovereignty and stability. Assistant Secretary for South and Central Asian Affairs Nisha Desai Biswal led the U.S. delegation to the third ABC session, held in Tajikistan in June 2014. However, the ABC was reduced from two days to one, decreasing the time to discuss relevant issues. The State Department again visited Tajikistan in December 2014 and raised religious freedom concerns with Tajikistan's government and met with civil society representatives; higher-level religious freedom discussions occurred in February 2015. The State Department's annual IRF Reports have documented worsened religious freedom in Tajikistan. The U.S. assistance program in Tajikistan promotes improved legislation relating to civil society, the media, and speech; legal assistance to non-governmental organizations; and stronger non-state electronic media outlets.

Recommendations

In addition to recommending that the U.S. government designate Tajikistan as a CPC, USCIRF recommends that the U.S. government should:

- Press the Tajik government to bring the 2009 religion law and other relevant laws into conformity with international commitments, including those on freedom of religion or belief, and criticize publicly violations by the Tajik government of those commitments;

- Work with the international community, particularly during events on countering terrorism sponsored by the Organization on Security and Cooperation in Europe (OSCE), to ensure there is private and public criticism of Tajikistan's repressive approach to regulating religion and countering extremism, including its risk of radicalizing the country's population;

- Urge the Tajik government to agree to visits by UN Special Rapporteurs on Freedom of Religion or Belief, the Independence of the Judiciary, and Torture, set specific visit dates, and provide the full and necessary conditions for such a visit;

- Maintain two days of the ABC dialogues to allow a full discussion of all relevant issues, particularly human rights and religious freedom;

- Ensure that the U.S. Embassy continues to monitor the trials of individuals charged on account of their religious affiliation, maintains appropriate contacts with human rights activists, and presses the Tajik government to ensure that every prisoner has greater access to his or her family, human rights monitors, adequate medical care, and a lawyer;

- Ensure that U.S. assistance to the Tajik government, with the exception of aid to improve humanitarian conditions and advance human rights, be contingent upon the government establishing and implementing a timetable of specific steps to reform the religion law and improve conditions of freedom of religion or belief; and

- Use funding allocated to the State Department under the Title VIII Program (established in the Soviet-Eastern European Research and Training Act of 1983) for research, including on human rights and religious freedom in former Soviet states, and language training.

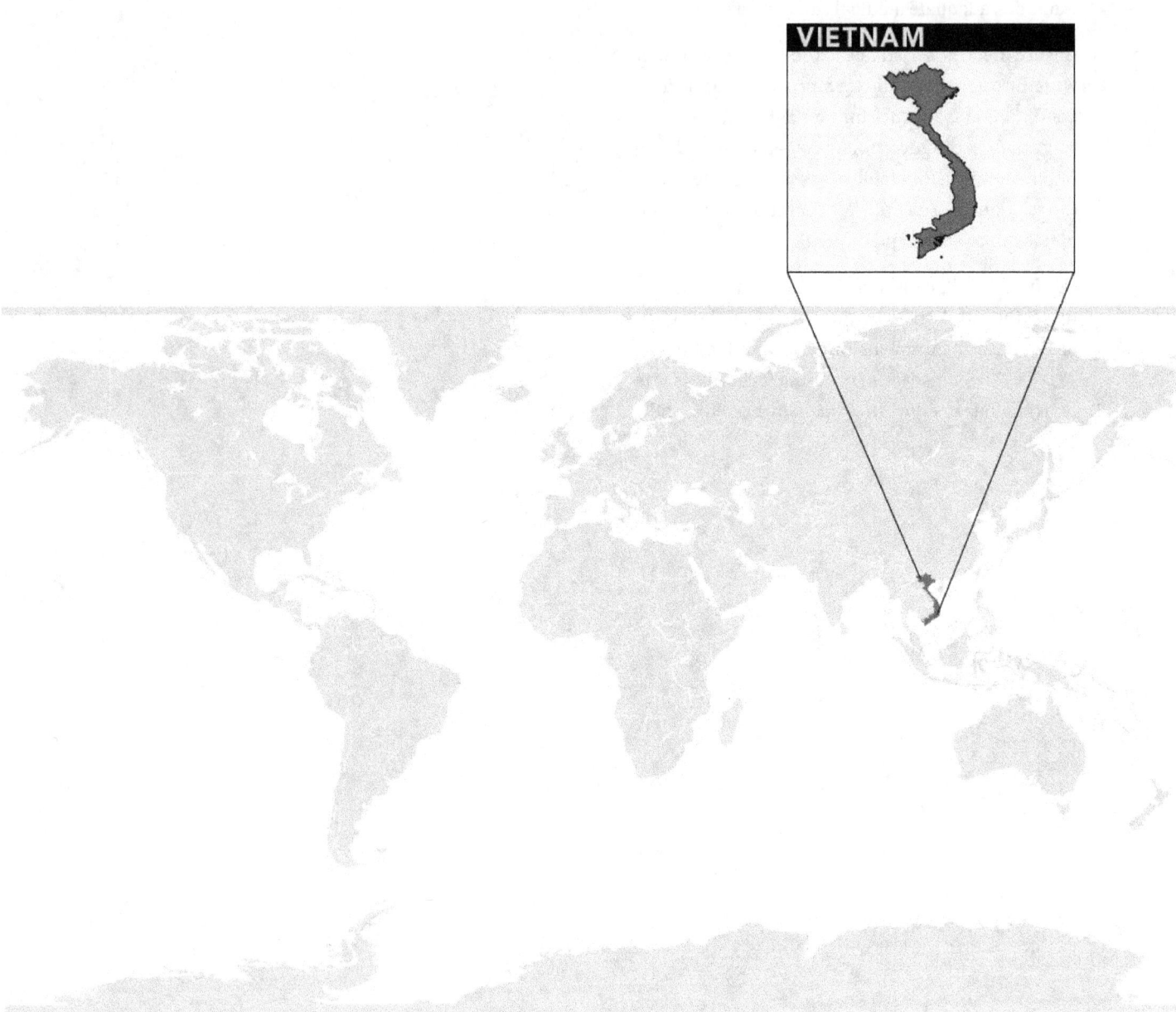

VIETNAM

Key Findings

The Vietnamese government continues to control all religious activities through law and administrative oversight, restrict severely independent religious practice, and repress individuals and religious groups it views as challenging its authority, including independent Buddhists, Hoa Hao, Cao Dai, Catholics, and Protestants. This occurs despite some improvements in the area of religious freedom, such as generally wider space for some religious communities to practice their faiths. Notably, the government requires religious organizations and congregations to register with a state-sanctioned entity in order to be considered legal. Individuals remain imprisoned for religious activity or religious freedom advocacy. Based on these severe violations, USCIRF again recommends in 2015 that Vietnam be designated as a "country of particular concern," or CPC, under the International Religious Freedom Act (IRFA). USCIRF has recommended that Vietnam be named a CPC every year since 2001.

Background

Vietnam's overall human rights record remains very poor, including relating to religious freedom. Accurate numbers of religious adherents in the country are difficult to ascertain, but the majority of Vietnam's 90 million citizens are Buddhist. More than six million are Catholic, Vietnam's second largest religious group,

Baha'is, Hindus and followers of other folk religions and beliefs.

The Communist government has moved decisively in recent years to repress perceived challenges to its regime, tightening controls on freedom of expression, association, religion, and assembly. Although the 2013 Constitution goes much further than its predecessor in protecting the right to freedom of religion or belief, other provisions create exceptions to those rights. In addition, other laws, decrees, and ordinances collectively restrict religious practices and create latitude for local officials to interpret and implement their own policies without federal influence. This inconsistency leads individuals to fear that the open practice of their faiths will result in harassment, attacks, or arrest. In 2013, the government implemented a new decree on religion (Decree 92) that provides clearer timetables for registration, but expands oversight of religious affairs and makes it more difficult for new religious groups to ever achieve legal status. Moreover, broadly-worded Penal Code provisions, such as Articles 88 and 258, ensnare countless human rights defenders, bloggers, journalists, religious leaders, and other activists whom the government accuses of acting against the state. At least 100-200 prisoners of conscience are detained in Vietnam, some for their religious activity or religious freedom advocacy.

In 2015, Vietnam is expected to produce a new law on religion that, as rumored, will supersede the 2004

At least 100-200 prisoners of conscience are detained in Vietnam, some for their religious activity or religious freedom advocacy.

---

and roughly one million or more are Protestant. Other minority religious groups include the Cao Dai, Hoa Hao, Khmer Krom Buddhists, ethnic Cham Muslims,

Ordinance on Beliefs and Religions and Decree 92. The UN Special Rapporteur on Freedom of Religion or Belief Heiner Bielefeldt visited Vietnam in July 2014, but had to curtail his visit due to state interference that violated the terms of reference agreed upon in advance with the Vietnamese government. His findings, released in January 2015, noted that the "... autonomy and activities of independent religious or belief communities, that is, unrecognized communities, remain restricted and unsafe, with the rights to freedom of religion or belief of such communities grossly violated in the face of constant surveillance, intimidation, harassment and persecution."

Religious Freedom Conditions 2014–2015
Buddhists

The Unified Buddhist Church of Vietnam (UBCV), the largest independent Buddhist organization in Vietnam, is not recognized by the state-sanctioned Vietnamese Buddhist Sangha, and by choosing to maintain its independence is considered an illegal entity.

Throughout 2014, officials in Da Nang City carried out efforts to take over the land belonging to the An Cu Temple. Similarly, in August, the Lien Tri Pagoda in Ho Chi Minh City was issued a government notice to close so that local officials could appropriate the property. Both locations have been sites of previous harassment. In January, UBCV monks and laypersons from the Long Quang Pagoda in Thua Thien Province were harassed and prevented from carrying out a celebratory service, with several subject to close police surveillance. Thich Quang Do,

the head of the UBCV, has been arrested numerous times, spent 10 years in exile, and is currently under house arrest. Throughout much of the year, police harassed Lê Công Cầu, leader of the UBCV-affiliated Buddhist Youth Movement, subjecting him to harsh interrogation before arresting him and placing him under house arrest.

Khmer-Krom Buddhists

Prominent Buddhist monks Venerable Lieu Ny and Venerable Thach Thuol, along with two of their students, Thach Phum Rich and Tra Quanh Tha, remain imprisoned for allegedly attempting to flee the country and for attempting to assist others in fleeing. The two monks have been outspoken critics of the government's treatment of the Khmer-Krom and the treatment of fellow monk, Venerable Ly Chanh Da. Laypersons reportedly have also been arrested for their support of Ven. Ly Chanh Da.

Cao Dai

Followers of the Cao Dai religion continued to experience harassment and obstacles to the peaceful practice of their faith. Several incidents occurred in Vinh Long Province where police and other government officials disrupted memorial services and other peaceful gatherings. Police prevented a member of the Cao Dai clergy from attending a July 2014 meeting of the Inter-Faith Council of Vietnam. Several followers were harassed and attacked upon leaving a ritual ceremony in Tay Ninh Province.

Catholics

Father Phan Van Loi testified before the Tom Lantos Human Rights Commission on March 26, 2014, via video conference because government surveillance and restrictions on his movement prevented him from traveling to give testimony in person. He described the difficulties, obstacles, harassment, and sometimes imprisonment priests and laypeople face when they

Local governments refuse to recognize Catholicism as a religion in the three northern provinces of Dien Bien, Son La, and Lai Chau, making it especially challenging for priests and their parishioners to practice their faith in these areas.

speak out about their beliefs. He also referenced the limitations and outright prohibitions on the Catholic Church imposed by current laws and government decrees on religion. Local governments refuse to recognize Catholicism as a religion in the three northern provinces of Dien Bien, Son La, and Lai Chau, making it especially challenging for priests and their parishioners to practice their faith in these areas.

Catholics continue to experience land confiscations, including parishioners from the Thai Ha Redemptorist Church in Dong Da District, who protested in Hanoi to object to the government filling in an existing lake on church property. Similarly, Con Dau parishioners near Da Nang City were forced to move their parish cemetery and in some cases have been evicted from their homes, disrupting the entire parish community. While some land rights disputes may be, in part, the result of local-level corruption or development projects, the religious identity of the targeted community and its status as a minority are also often factors.

On a positive note, in September, representatives of the Joint Vatican-Vietnam Working Group held another meeting in Hanoi as part of the group's efforts to restore diplomatic relations.

Hmong Protestants

During 2014, countless Hmong Protestant house churches continued to be denied registration, effectively consigning them to illegal status. In an ongoing effort to limit the freedom of Hmong Christians to practice their faith, local authorities continued to interfere with the way in which Hmong villagers honor and grieve their dead. In addition to destroying storage facilities which house supplies for Hmong funerals, authorities harassed and attacked villagers attempting to carry out funerals in accordance with their beliefs. In March 2014, Hoang Van Sang received an 18-month jail sentence for constructing a new funeral storage facility. Hmong villagers who marched in protest of Sang's sentence were stopped by police.

Montagnards (Degar)

Ethnic minority Montagnards, primarily from Vietnam's Central Highlands region, continued to face severe ethnic- and religious-based discrimination and violence, prompting some to flee Vietnam. During the year, Montagnards reported the police carrying out beatings, arrests, and forced renunciations of faith. In November, 13 Christian Montagnards fled persecution in Vietnam to seek refuge status in Cambodia, only to suffer harsh conditions while hiding in the Cambodian jungles. A UN team was able to meet with the group weeks later after first being blocked by local officials. Since then, dozens more have fled to Cambodia, and some forcibly returned to Vietnam by Cambodian officials, including small children. The UN High Commissioner for Refugees and the

Office of the UN High Commissioner for Human Rights both have urged the Cambodian government to abide by

> *Ethnic minority Montagnards, primarily from Vietnam's Central Highlands region, continued to face severe ethnic- and religious-based discrimination and violence, prompting some to flee Vietnam.*

their international obligations and allow the Vietnamese Montagnards to pursue refugee claims.

Mennonites

A Mennonite Christian center in Binh Duong Province was the site of repeated attacks throughout the year. In June 2014, 76 Mennonite Christians were attacked by more than 300 (some estimate closer to 500) police and security forces; the church itself was vandalized. In November, nine Mennonites, including two pastors, were arrested and the church vandalized once again. Three church employees were arrested, interrogated and beaten in early December. One of those arrested, a pastor, was ordered to end his role as pastor or face criminal charges. The three were eventually released but suffered additional harassment just outside the police station, and attacks on the church continued.

Hoa Hao

Early in 2014 in An Giang Province, several Hoa Hao worshippers who had gathered for a commemorative service were severely beaten. More than 300 police and thugs hired by the government carried out the attack on approximately 30 Hoa Hao followers; they later seized electronic and other equipment used during the ceremony and arrested 14 of the followers. The attack follows a similar one in the province less than one year earlier at the independent Hoa Hao Quang Minh Tu pagoda. Hoa Hao worshippers in Dong Thap Province experienced an even larger force of police and thugs in February 2014 as they attempted to visit Nguyen Bac Truyen, a former prisoner of conscience who had been recently arrested.

Prisoners

The ill-treatment and imprisonment of prisoners of conscience in Vietnam remains a key human rights concern, despite several releases during the year. Among them are countless individuals who have been harassed, beaten, detained, arrested, and imprisoned for their religious beliefs. Those still imprisoned include: Father Thaddeus Nguyen Van Ly, Mennonite Pastor Nguyen Cong Chinh, and Catholic intellectual and activist Francis Jang Xuan Dieu, for example.

Several prisoners of conscience were released in 2014, including prominent dissident Nguyen Van Hai, also

major source of clothing, footwear, furniture, and electrical machinery for the United States. The two are also part of the 12-nation negotiations of the Trans-Pacific Partnership (TPP), a regional free trade agreement. While the TPP talks are ongoing, the Obama Administration and some in Congress are concurrently pursuing the renewal of Trade Promotion Authority (TPA) that could grant the president greater flexibility when negotiating and approving trade agreements such as the TPP. Some members of Congress have raised concerns with a number of key components in the TPP, including agriculture, automotive markets, worker

> *The ill-treatment and imprisonment of prisoners of conscience in Vietnam remains a key human rights concern, despite several releases during the year.*

known as Dieu Cay. He was released in October 2014, coinciding with the visit of U.S. Assistant Secretary of State for Democracy, Human Rights, and Labor Tom Malinowski to Vietnam. Upon his release, Hai, like Cu Huy Ha Vu in April, was forced to leave the country and was immediately escorted onto a plane bound for the United States before he could inform his family of his release. Three others, Bui Thi Minh Hang, Nguyen Van Minh and Nguyen Thi Thuy Quynh, all well-known human rights defenders, received multi-year prison sentences in August.

U.S. Policy

The year 2015 marks the 20th anniversary of the normalization of ties between the United States and Vietnam. In 2013, the two countries entered into the U.S.-Vietnam Comprehensive Partnership, a framework for bilateral cooperation on a number of strategic issues, including trade and the economy, science and technology, defense and security, and human rights, among others. As part of their regular engagement on human rights, the two countries will conduct a session of the U.S.-Vietnam Human Rights Dialogue in Hanoi in May 2015. On January 1, 2014, Vietnam began its three-year term on the UN Human Rights Council.

The United States and Vietnam have a strong bilateral trade relationship, with Vietnam serving as a

rights, environmental protections, and human rights, among others, that are likely to be heavily debated during consideration of TPA.

In October 2014, the United States announced the partial easing of the arms ban with Vietnam with respect to maritime security. The State Department cited specific human rights improvements in Vietnam, including the release of prisoners of conscience and the registration of new church congregations. However, critics noted that Vietnam is still detaining numerous prisoners of conscience, including individuals imprisoned for their religious beliefs, and that registration figures pale in comparison to the thousands of congregations that either choose to remain independent or are denied registration, leaving them no choice but to operate illegally. Notably, Assistant Secretary Malinowski visited Vietnam shortly after the announcement and stressed the importance of Vietnam continuing to make progress on human rights.

The State Department designated Vietnam as a CPC in 2004 and 2005, but removed the designation in 2006 because of progress toward fulfilling a bilateral agreement to release prisoners, ban forced renunciations of faith, and expand legal protections for religious groups. USCIRF, however, has found that, the progress achieved through the bilateral agreement has been inconsistent and not fully realized, and that religious freedom violations in Vietnam have continued, and in some cases worsened. These ongoing violations in Vietnam serve as a cautionary tale of the potential for backsliding in religious freedoms when vigilance in monitoring such abuses ceases. Accordingly, USCIRF has continued to recommend CPC designation for the country.

Recommendations

The United States has a strategic interest in furthering its relationship and engagement with Vietnam, as does Vietnam in deepening ties with and support from the United States. Given Vietnam's past receptivity to constructive engagement on human rights, and specifically religious freedom, the United States should consider additional avenues to encourage improvements to religious freedom conditions, particularly for those groups and congregations that wish to remain independent from Vietnam's communist government. A formal framework with Vietnam that establishes a roadmap toward improved religious freedom conditions could strengthen the U.S. government's leverage to seek an end to such violations. Until such time that improvements are made, USCIRF recommends the U.S. government designate Vietnam as a CPC, as well as:

- Continue discussions with the government of Vietnam on the drafting of the new law on religion to urge that the measure both simplifies registration requirements for religious congregations and makes registration optional, and to ensure that those opting not to register have other appropriate means by which to operate legally;

- Encourage the government of Vietnam to acknowledge and address violations against religious communities perpetrated by state and non-state actors, and support the proper training of local government officials, lawyers, judges, and police and security forces tasked with implementing, enforcing, and interpreting the rule of law;

- Ensure that human rights and religious freedom are pursued consistently and publicly at every level of the U.S.-Vietnam relationship, including in the context of discussions relating to military, trade, or economic and security assistance, such as Vietnam's

participation in the Trans-Pacific Partnership, as well as in programs that address Internet freedom and civil society development, among others;

- Increase the frequency and visibility of U.S. government visits to remote, rural areas in Vietnam, including direct contact and communications with independent religious communities as appropriate;

- Encourage the U.S. Embassy in Hanoi and the U.S. Consulate General in Ho Chi Minh City to maintain appropriate contact, including through in-person visits, with Vietnamese prisoners of conscience to ensure that prisoners have regular access to their families, human rights monitors, adequate medical care, and proper legal representation, as specified in international human rights instruments; and

- Ensure the U.S.-Vietnam Human Rights Dialogue establishes concrete actions and outcomes relating to religious freedom, including the unconditional release of all prisoners of conscience arrested or otherwise detained for the peaceful practice of their beliefs, make those actions and outcomes part of a larger strategy of U.S engagement, and report to Congress on the trajectory of progress on these issues.

TIER 2

COUNTRIES

- AFGHANISTAN

- AZERBAIJAN

- CUBA

- INDIA

- INDONESIA

- KAZAKHSTAN

- LAOS

- MALAYSIA

- RUSSIA

- TURKEY

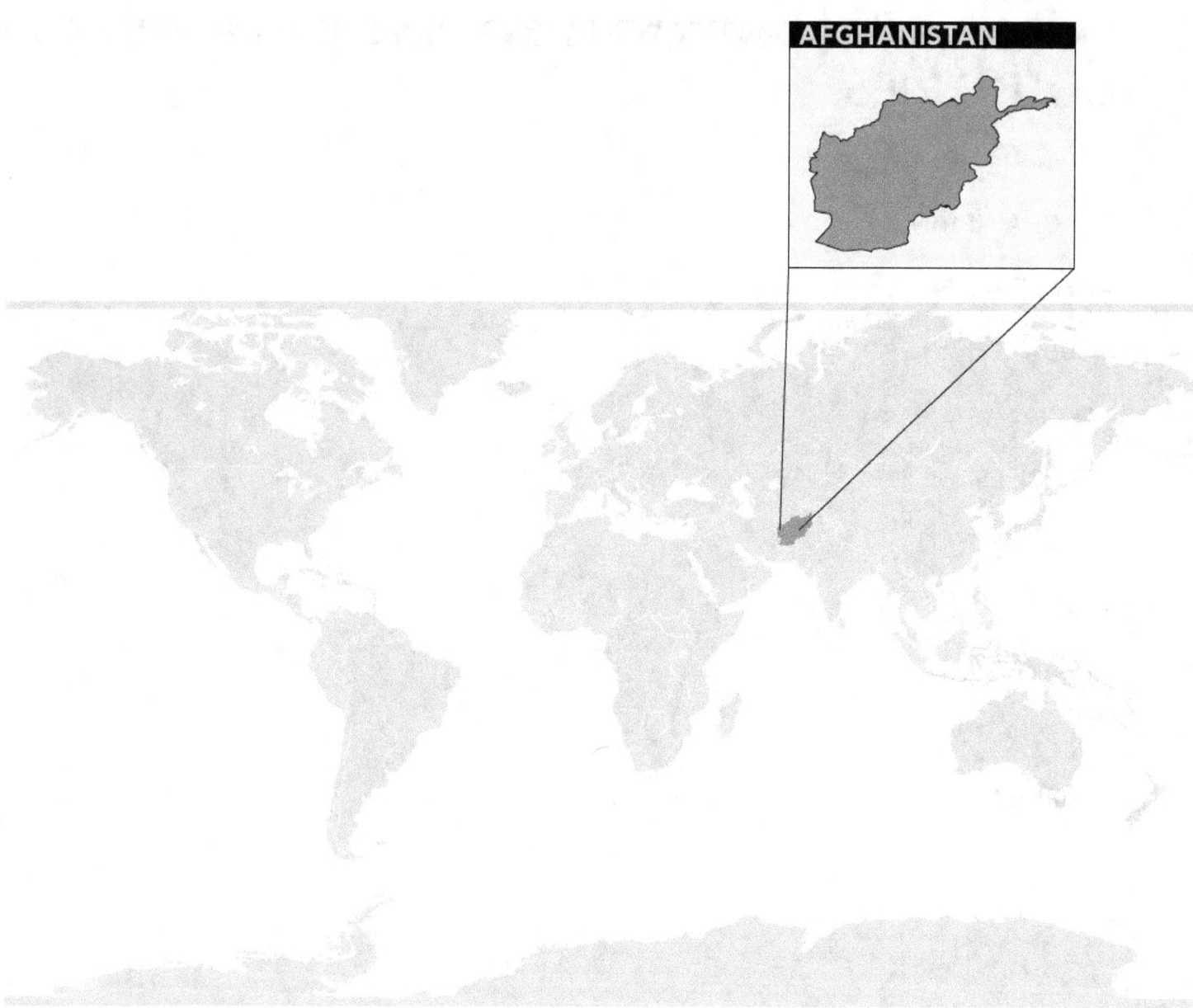

AFGHANISTAN

Key Findings

Religious freedom conditions continue to be exceedingly poor for Sunni Muslims who dissent from governmental and social orthodoxies, Shi'a Muslims, Hindus, and Sikhs, as well as the tiny Christian and Baha'i communities. During the reporting period the formal U.S. combat mission came to a close and a new Afghan government was established. The Taliban continued terrorist attacks in an attempt to demonstrate the government's inability to protect citizens against violence and intimidation. Taliban agents and sympathizers attacked three different Christian-based relief agencies for activity deemed "un-Islamic." Afghanistan's legal system remains deeply flawed, as the constitution explicitly fails to protect the individual right to freedom of religion or belief, and it and other laws have been applied in ways that violate international human rights standards. Based on these concerns, in 2015 USCIRF again places Afghanistan on Tier 2, where it has been since 2006.

Background

Afghanistan's population of around 30 million is comprised of numerous ethnic groups. According to U.S. government figures, Afghanistan is 42 percent Pashtun, 27 percent Tajik, nine percent Hazara, nine percent Uzbek, three percent Turkmen, two percent Baloch, and eight percent other groups. Regarding religious breakdown, 80 percent of the population identifies as Sunni Muslim, 19 percent as Shi'a, and 1 percent as other, including tiny Sikh, Hindu, and Christian communities. Shi'a Muslims generally come from the Hazara ethnic group, which the community believes comprises between 10 and 19 percent of the population. Hazaras traditionally have been harshly discriminated against and segregated from the rest of society for a combination of political, ethnic, and religious reasons.

Ashraf Ghani, a former World Bank official, was elected president of Afghanistan in a contested two-round campaign against Abdullah Abdullah. In a compromise to form a national unity government, Abdullah was named as the country's Chief Executive Officer (CEO). In a new development for this tradition-bound nation, President Ghani's wife, Rula Ghani, is Christian Lebanese-American by background and has expressed support for the French ban on face-covering veils.

President Ghani and CEO Abdullah oversee a constitutional and legal system that restricts religious freedom. The Afghan constitution fails to protect the individual right to freedom of religion or belief, allows ordinary laws to supersede other fundamental rights, and contains a repugnancy clause stating that no law can be contrary to the tenets of Islam. Governments have interpreted narrowly the repugnancy clause, which limits freedom of religion or belief. The penal code permits the courts to defer to Shari'ah law in cases involving matters that neither the penal code nor constitution explicitly address, such as apostasy and conversion, resulting in those charges being punishable by death. State-backed religious leaders and the judicial system are empowered to interpret and enforce Islamic principles and Shari'ah law, leading at times to arbitrary and abusive interpretations of religious orthodoxy.

Religious Freedom Conditions 2014–2015
Official Enforcement of Religious Norms

Within the legal context discussed above, a restrictive interpretation of Shari'ah law is prioritized over human rights guarantees and has resulted in abuses. One month after coming into office, the Council of Ministers chaired by CEO Abdullah tasked the Ministry of Interior and the Ministry of Culture to charge the English-language newspaper *Afghan Express* with blasphemy for publishing an article that reportedly questioned the existence of God. The Council's statement also declared that the new government would take strict actions against other articles deemed blasphemous. The newspaper issued an apology, citing a technical error. However, its owner and chief editor were arrested. It is unknown whether they remain in jail. This decision seems to be a continuation from former President Karzai's Council, which would periodically issue decrees directing action against activities deemed "un-Islamic."

Repression of Non-Muslim Religious Minorities

There were three major Taliban attacks on Christian-based relief agencies, which killed relief workers and their children. The Taliban justified two of the attacks by claiming the groups were proselytizing and hosting underground Christian worship sites for Afghans, allegations that were not confirmed. The violence demonstrated how Afghan Christians are forced to conceal their faith and cannot worship openly. In June 2014, Fr. Alexis Prem Kumar, who led Jesuit Refugee Services, was kidnapped. The Taliban released him in February 2015. There were no reports of Afghan Christians arrested by the government during the reporting period, but many have left for India, according to reports. The one known church in the country continues to operate on the grounds of the Italian embassy.

Afghanistan's small Baha'i community leads a covert existence, particularly since May 2007 when the General

Shi'a and other Muslims

The situation has improved since the end of Taliban rule for Afghanistan's Shi'a Muslim community, the largest religious minority in the country. During the reporting period, Shi'a Muslims generally were able to perform their traditional Ashura public processions and rituals without hindrance. Nevertheless, violence continues to be a threat. For instance in July 2014, Taliban insurgents killed 14 Shi'a Muslim Hazaras who were travelling on a bus. They were singled out from other passengers, bound, and shot on the side of the road. After the reporting period, 30 Shi'a Hazaras where kidnapped by gunmen. There have also been reports of the Afghan government deporting Uighur Muslims to China at the request of the Chinese government.

Women's Rights

Violence and discrimination against women continued throughout the reporting period, due in part to the Taliban's resurgence and in part to the strong influence of religious traditionalists. President Ghani in November told members of the Afghanistan Independent Human Rights Commission (AIHRC) that they could monitor his government's performance on human rights reforms and he pledged to promote women's rights. Women who seek to engage in public life often

---

The violence demonstrated how Afghan Christians are forced to conceal their faith and cannot worship openly.

Directorate of Fatwas and Accounts ruled the Baha'i faith blasphemous and converts to it apostates. Afghanistan's Jewish community is down to one member.

Hindus and Sikhs face discrimination, harassment and at times violence, despite being allowed to practice their faith in places of public worship. They have been represented in the parliament through Presidential appointments. The communities have declined over the past 30 years, due to instability and fighting; only one of the eight Sikh *gurdwaras* in Kabul is operating. Reports regularly arise of Afghan authorities and local residents preventing Sikhs from performing cremation ceremonies for their deceased.

are condemned as "immoral" and targeted for intimidation, harassment, or violence. However, President Ghani's wife, Rula Ghani, played a visible role during the campaign. President Ghani's proposed "unity cabinet" of 27 members had three women nominees who would head the ministries of Higher Education, Information and Culture, and Women's Affairs. Two of the three women nominees were reportedly chosen by CEO Abdullah; and one was chosen by President Ghani. Although President Ghani did not meet his promise to name four female cabinet members, his three nominees exceed the two women in former President Karzai's cabinet.

U.S. Policy

Afghanistan has been the focus of U.S. engagement in South Asia for over a decade. U.S. government efforts have focused on building a stable Afghanistan and fighting al-Qaeda and its affiliates. The past year saw two major milestones, the peaceful change in government and the transition of U.S. and international forces from a combat mission to a training mission, although U.S. forces are still authorized to conduct combat missions. The change in mission came after Afghanistan agreed to a Bilateral Security Agreement, which former President Karzai had resisted but President Ghani signed. As of this writing, U.S. forces number around 10,000, drastically down from a peak of 100,000. President Obama's original goal to shrink the force to around 5,000 by the end of 2015 was put off in response to President Ghani's request.

The United States helped resolve Afghanistan's highly contested 2014 presidential election, after allegations of fraud threatened to undermine the transition. In September 2014, a U.S.-brokered solution resulted in the creation of a unity government with Ashraf Ghani as President and Dr. Abdullah Abdullah as Chief Executive Officer, a new position. The governing coalition appears stable, but two factors – widespread corruption and Taliban attacks – threaten its longevity. Both President Ghani and CEO Abdullah have committed to stamp out corruption.

President Ghani has actively traveled to neighboring countries and countries that financially support his government in an attempt to restart negotiations with the Taliban. Many observers are concerned by the potential compromises that may be made in any peace deal with the Taliban. Taliban leader Mullah Omar has indicated he wants to see the imposition of religious law, which under the Taliban interpretation, would severely restrict religious minorities, dissenting members of the religious majority, and women's rights. U.S. officials have raised concerns about women's rights and minority rights in the past. However, Afghan law already imposes restrictions on fundamental human rights. It is unclear how much influence the United States and the international community would have over a settlement between the Ghani government and the Taliban on these issues.

While the number of combat troops is declining, Afghanistan's reliance on international aid has not changed. Afghanistan is very dependent on U.S. and foreign aid, a reality unlikely to change in the near future. According to the Congressional Research Service, since the overthrow of the Taliban the United States has provided approximately $93 billion in assistance to Afghanistan, and from that more than $56 billion to train and equip Afghan forces. The fiscal year 2014 appropriation was more than $6.1 billion and the FY2015 request is about $5.7 billion.

Recommendations

In the context of the withdrawal of international forces and the recent change in government, the threat of violence by the Taliban and other armed groups is a growing reality for all Afghans, but especially for religious minorities. To promote religious freedom and create civic space for diverse religious opinions on matters of religion and society in Afghanistan, USCIRF recommends that the U.S. government should:

- Raise directly with Afghanistan's president and CEO the importance of religious freedom, especially for dissenting Muslims, Muslim minorities, and non-Muslim religious groups;

- Revive the interagency U.S. government taskforce on religious freedom in Afghanistan and ensure religious freedom issues are properly integrated into the State and Defense Department strategies concerning Afghanistan;

- Include a special working group on religious tolerance in U.S.-Afghan strategic dialogues and the trilateral dialogues with the United States, Afghanistan, and Pakistan;

- Encourage the Afghan government to sponsor, with official and semi-official religious bodies, an initiative on interfaith dialogue that focuses on both intra-Islamic dialogue and engagement with different faiths; and

- Ensure that human rights concerns are integrated in the reconciliation process and that the parties to any peace agreement pledge to uphold the Universal Declaration of Human Rights and not just the Afghan constitution.

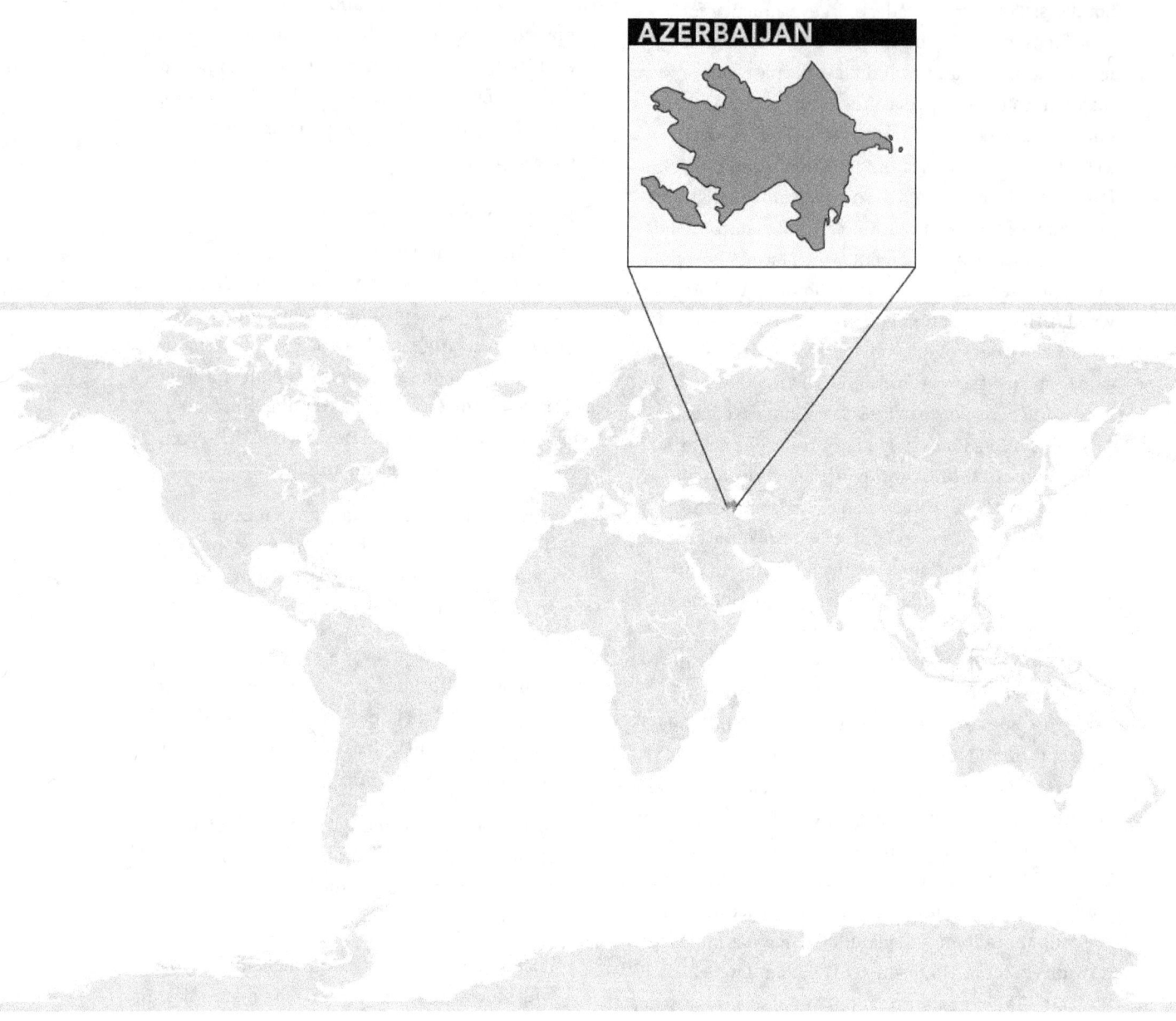

AZERBAIJAN

AZERBAIJAN

Key Findings

Despite societal religious tolerance in Azerbaijan, governmental respect for religious freedom continued to deteriorate in 2014, along with a sharp decline in respect for democratic norms. The past year witnessed a marked increase in arrests of civil society activists and members of religious groups. In addition, the government continued to levy penalties for violations of the restrictive 2009 religion law. Registration requests from religious groups were delayed or denied and religious groups closed. Peaceful religious believers, their defenders, and other activists have been detained, fined, and imprisoned on various charges. Based on these concerns, in 2015 USCIRF again places Azerbaijan on Tier 2, where it has been since 2013.

Background

Bordering Armenia, Georgia, Iran, and Turkey, Azerbaijan has a majority Shi'a Muslim population of nine million; some 13 million ethnic Azeris live in northern Iran. According to the State Department, 96 percent of Azerbaijan's population is Muslim, of whom about 65 percent are Shi'a Muslims and 35 percent Sunni Muslims. The remaining 4 percent of the population includes: Russian Orthodox, Armenian Orthodox, and other Christians (including Lutherans, Roman Catholics, Baptists, Molokans, and Seventh-day Adventists); some 20,000 Jews; Baha'is; and nonbelievers. Among Muslims and Russian Orthodox, religious identity is usually based on ethnicity. Shi'a Muslims, Sunni Muslims, Russian Orthodox, and Jews are officially seen as the country's "traditional" religious groups.

Pre-Soviet independent Azerbaijan was the world's first Muslim-majority secular parliamentary republic. After the USSR collapsed, Azerbaijan gained independence in 1991. The Nagorno-Karabakh war with Armenia ended in a 1994 cease-fire; Azerbaijan lost 16 percent of its land and gained 600,000 internally

> *Pre-Soviet independent Azerbaijan was the world's first Muslim-majority secular parliamentary republic.*

displaced persons. The OSCE Minsk Group, co-chaired by the United States, France, and Russia, mediates this conflict; clashes in August 2014 led to military fatalities on both sides.

The Aliev family, with roots in the Nakhichivan exclave, dominates Azerbaijan's politics. Heydar Aliev was the First Party Secretary of Soviet-era Azerbaijan from 1969 to 1982, and then president of independent Azerbaijan from 1993 until his 2003 resignation for health reasons. Aliev named his son, Ilham, as his party's sole candidate in a much-criticized 2003 presidential election. Term limits were lifted in 2009 and Ilham Aliev has been president ever since. The Azerbaijani government is viewed as corrupt and increasingly authoritarian.

During the reporting period, there was a marked increase in arrests and repression of civil society activists and peaceful members of religious groups in Azerbaijan. In 2014, the parliament also increased reporting requirements for NGOs and religious groups to the State Committee for Work with Religious Organizations (SCWRO), purportedly to prevent the spread of religious extremism and foreign missionary activity. These problematic actions occurred while Azerbaijan chaired the Council of Europe (CoE) Council of Ministers for six months in 2014. The CoE human rights chief, Nils Muiznieks, criticized Azerbaijan's government in

September 2014 for a "totally unacceptable" human rights situation" that "flies in the face" of CoE standards. In an August 2014 statement by the office of the UN High Commissioner for Human Rights, experts said they were "appalled" by "criminalization of rights activists" and called for their release.

Azerbaijan's 2009 religion law is used to limit religious freedom and to justify fines, police raids, detentions, and imprisonment. The law's provisions include: compulsory state registration with complex and intrusive requirements; no appeal for registration

In October 2014, an Azerbaijani NGO, Islam-Ittihad Association, won a case at the ECtHR challenging its 2003 dissolution. The ECtHR found that the government had violated the Association's rights to freedom of assembly and association by closing it down for organizing Muslim pilgrimages and criticizing the state-backed Caucasian Muslim Board (CMB). In November 2014, Azerbaijan's Supreme Court rejected an appeal by Baku's Fatima Zahra Sunni mosque against state-enforced legal liquidation. SCWRO officials claimed in late 2014 that Baptists and Adventists will be registered, but

Azerbaijan's 2009 religion law is used to limit religious freedom . . .

denials; religious activities limited to a community's registered address; extensive state controls on the content, production, import, export, and dissemination of religious materials; and required state-approved religious education to preach, teach religion, or lead ceremonies. Individuals or groups violating the religion law are subject to administrative fines. In 2010, fines for religious organizations increased 16-fold. In 2012, the CoE's Venice Commission and the Organization for Security and Co-operation in Europe (OSCE) issued a legal opinion finding that Azerbaijan's religion law failed to meet its international human rights commitments. In 2014, the European Court of Human Rights (ECtHR) found that Azerbaijan's 2009 religion law gives authorities "unlimited discretionary power" to define and prosecute "illegal" religious activity.

Religious Freedom Conditions 2014–2015
Government Control through Registration

Registration is mandatory, and religious groups denied registration or that refuse to register are deemed "illegal." Members of unregistered religious communities often face raids, confiscation of religious texts, and other penalties. Yet even registered religious groups are only allowed to conduct activity at their legal address and subject to other restrictions. The State Committee for Work with Religious Organizations claimed in February 2014 that the country's total number of registered religious groups was 588.

only if they liquidate and apply as new organizations; otherwise they face judicial liquidation.

Penalties for Religious Activity or Religious Freedom Advocacy

The Azerbaijani NGO Legal Protection and Awareness Society Public Union (LPASPU) has compiled a list of Muslims jailed for the non-violent practice of their faith or advocacy for religious freedom. Most were sentenced for publicly protesting what is in effect a ban on headscarves in school: 11 members of that group are still imprisoned, seven were released in 2014; two were pardoned by President Aliev in March 2015. The trial of lawyer Rasul Jafarov, LPASPU leader, began in January 2015 although witnesses' testimony did not support the official charges of financial manipulations; he was sentenced to 6.5 years. Leila and Arif Yunus, noted human rights activists who also drew attention to religious freedom, have been jailed since August 2014; their worsening health status is ignored in the penal system.

In November 2014, nine Sunni Muslims arriving to pray in a Sumgait home were detained for several hours; police claimed to have found weapons. In February 2015, a Baku court sentenced the home's owner, Zohrab Shikhaliyev (who offered his home for prayer because all local Sunni mosques were closed) to a six-month term on false weapons charges. Islamic theologian Taleh Bagirov, who publicly criticized the naming of a CMB imam to serve in his mosque, was sentenced in 2013 on fabricated drug charges and released in late 2014. The trial of three Muslims – Eldeniz Hajiyev, Ismayil Mammadov and Revan Sabzaliyev – for allegedly reading "illegal" religious literature and organizing an "illegal" religious group began in Baku in December 2014. If convicted, they face three to

Restrictions on Religious Minorities

Most Protestant denominations do not have legal status, including Baptists, Seventh-day Adventists, and Pentecostals, as well as Jehovah's Witnesses. Two Georgian Orthodox communities are registered, but Gakh region authorities restricted worship services to 30 minutes per day in three Georgian Orthodox churches. The

. . . Muslims [are] jailed for the non-violent practice of their faith . . .

five year prison terms. Muslim scholar and CMB press officer, Elshan Mustafaoglu, was sentenced on December 19, 2014 to four months of pre-trial detention, reportedly on treason charges. He had studied Islam in Iran and took part in the U.S. International Visitor Program in 2009. Jeyhun Jafarov, former host of a TV show on Islam, reportedly was arrested on unknown charges after the reporting period and sentenced to four months in pre-trial detention.

Additional Restrictions on Muslims

All Muslims in Azerbaijan are subject to official restrictions. All Muslim religious leaders are named by the state-backed CMB and must be citizens educated in Azerbaijan; all mosques must belong to the CMB; and only citizens can establish Islamic religious communities. By 2014, all Islamic communities that did not belong to the CMB lacked legal status and were vulnerable to police action. Police still enforce a 2008 decree that does not allow prayer outside of mosques. In 2010, the Ministry of Education introduced a school uniform, in effect banning the Islamic headscarf. In 2013 that ban was extended to universities, leading to petitions and unauthorized protests.

In 2014 the government and the CMB stepped up its apparent campaign to close Sunni places of worship. The Lezgin Mosque – one of two Sunni Muslim mosques open in Baku – was threatened with closure. In 2014, a Sunni mosque near Baku was put under new control; the SCWRO claims the mosque's first community dissolved by "choosing" to admit Shi'a members.

government has confiscated religious facilities without compensation. It uses Baku's renovated Armenian Apostolic Saint Gregory the Illuminator's Church as the archive for the Presidential Administration Department of Administration Affairs. The Culture Ministry runs a concert hall in Baku's confiscated Lutheran Church building; in October 2014 it limited rentals of that building to registered religious groups. Baku's Lutheran Church and New Life Pentecostal Church (two among the few registered non-Muslim religious groups) rent the building, but the unregistered Greater Grace Church was told by officials it no longer can do so.

Status of Conscientious Objection

When Azerbaijan joined the CoE in 2001 it promised to allow alternative service, but has yet to enact such a law. While the Constitution allows for alternative service, other laws set two-year prison terms for those who refuse military service. Jailed since October 2013, Jehovah's Witness Kamran Shikhaliev lost his court appeal in August 2014 against a one-year term in a military discipline unit where he must serve until August 2015.

Government Censorship of Religious Materials

Penalties for first-time violators of official restrictions and censorship of religious texts include up to two years in jail. A "conspiratorial" or organized group or a repeat offender faces a prison term of between two and five years; in February 2015, a Baku court ordered Jehovah's Witnesses Irina Zakharchenko and Valida Jabrayilova to be held for three months in a secret police investigation prison; they face up to a five-year term for offering religious literature without state permission.

Situation in the Nakhichevan Exclave

Residents of the Nakhichevan exclave face more severe religious freedom restrictions than elsewhere in Azerbaijan. Local Sunni Muslims have nowhere to pray. In November 2014, up to 200 Shi'a Muslims were arrested; according to Forum 18 News Service, up to 50 are detained and up to 50 mosques – particularly those officially seen as close to Iran – reportedly were closed. During the Shi'a Muslim Ashura commemoration, police outside mosques prevented children and students from entering. Many state employees reportedly are afraid to attend mosque. Baha'is, Adventists and Hare Krishnas are banned. The ancient Armenian cemetery near Juga village repeatedly has been vandalized since 2005.

U.S. Policy

The United States aims to encourage pro-Western democracy and to help build an open market economy in Azerbaijan. Other goals include promoting regional stability, primarily resolution of the Nagorno-Karabakh conflict; enhancing energy security, and fostering economic and political reforms. U.S. companies cooperate in offshore oil development with Azerbaijan. Azerbaijan supports the North Atlantic Treaty Organization (NATO) operations in Afghanistan by participating in the Northern Distribution Network and counters transnational threats, especially from Iran. U.S. assistance helps build capacity for maritime counterterrorism operations, especially in its Caspian Sea area, and provides military security training courses. U.S. civil society assistance in Azerbaijan focuses on small grants for civil-society and on civic dialogue.

Criticism by UN human rights bodies and international civil society groups of Azerbaijan's human rights record has sharply increased during the reporting period. In response to human rights criticism, in 2014 Azerbaijani government officials verbally attacked former U.S. Ambassador Richard Morningstar and Senate staff who were in Baku and met RFE/RL reporter, Khadija Ismayilova, who was later arrested. In February 2015, U.S. Assistant Secretary of State for European and Eurasian Affairs Victoria Nuland went to Azerbaijan to meet senior government officials to discuss bilateral relations on trade and investment; energy diversification; security and counter-terrorism; democracy and civil society, and the Nagorno-Karabakh conflict. During that one-day visit, she also held a brief meeting with civil society and announced the start of an ongoing U.S.-Azerbaijani dialogue on civil society and democracy to run in parallel with Council of Europe initiatives.

Recommendations

In order to promote freedom of religion or belief in Azerbaijan, USCIRF recommends that the U.S. government should:

- Urge the Azerbaijani government to reform its religion law to bring it into conformity with its international human rights commitments, as recommended by the Council of Europe's Venice Commission and the Organization for Security and Co-operation in Europe in 2012;

- Urge the Azerbaijani government to cease detention and imprisonment of members of religious groups, as well as activists, jailed for peaceful religious activity or religious affiliations;

- Ensure that the U.S. Embassy in Azerbaijan maintains appropriate contacts with human rights activists and press the government of Azerbaijan to ensure that every prisoner has regular access to his or her family, human rights monitors, adequate medical care, and a lawyer, as specified in international human rights instruments;

- Encourage public scrutiny of Azerbaijan's violations of international religious freedom and related human rights norms at the UN and Organization for Security and Cooperation in Europe, and urge the OSCE to engage these issues publicly;

- Urge the Azerbaijani government to agree to visits by UN Special Rapporteurs on Freedom of Religion or Belief, as well as Independence of the Judiciary and Torture; set specific visit dates; and provide the necessary conditions for such visits;

- Press the government of Azerbaijan to allow religious groups to operate freely without registration, and advocate for amendments to the religion law's registration process to make it voluntary;

- Specify freedom of religion as a grants category and area of activity in the Democracy and Conflict Mitigation program of the U.S. Agency for International Development and the Democracy Commission Small Grants program administered by the U.S. Embassy, and encourage the publicly-funded National Endowment for Democracy to make grants for civil society programs on tolerance and freedom of religion or belief; and

- Increase U.S. government-funded radio and Internet programs, particularly in Azeri, of objective information on relevant issues, such as religious freedom, including its role in U.S. foreign policy.

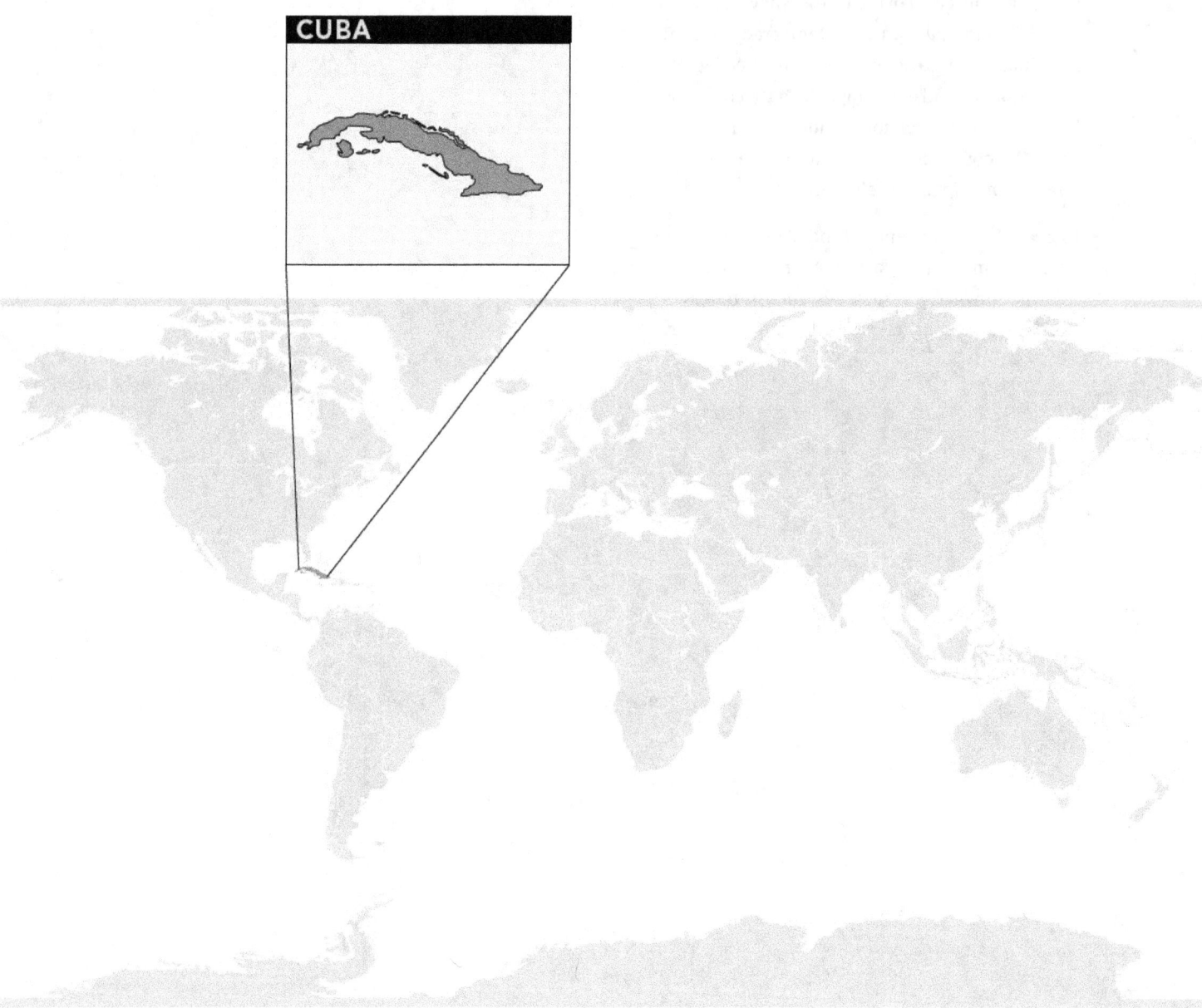

CUBA

CUBA

Key Findings

Serious religious freedom violations continue in Cuba, despite improvements for government-approved religious groups. The government continues to detain and harass religious leaders and laity, interfere in religious groups' internal affairs, and prevent democracy and human rights activists from participating in religious activities. Despite constitutional protections for religious freedom, the Cuban government actively limits, controls, and monitors religious practice through a restrictive system of laws and policies and government-authorized surveillance and harassment. Based on these concerns, USCIRF again places Cuba on Tier 2 in 2015. Cuba has been on USCIRF's Tier 2 since 2004.

Background

Religious adherence continues to grow in Cuba, although there are no reliable statistics of Cubans' religious affiliations. Sixty to 70 percent of the population is estimated to be Roman Catholic and five percent Protestant. According to the State Department, various religious communities approximate their membership numbers as follows: Assemblies of God, 110,000; the four Baptist conventions, 100,000; Jehovah's Witnesses, 96,000; Methodists, 36,000; Seventh-day Adventists, 35,000; Anglicans, 22,500; Presbyterians, 15,500; Muslims, 2,000-3,000; Jewish community, 1,500; Quakers, 300; and The Church of Jesus Christ of Latter-day Saints (Mormons), 50. An unknown number of Greek and Russian Orthodox, Buddhists, and Baha'is also live in Cuba.

The Cuban government controls religious activities through the Office of Religious Affairs of the Central Committee of the Cuban Communist Party and the Ministry of Justice. The government requires religious communities to undergo an invasive registration procedure with the Ministry of Justice. Only registered religious communities are legally allowed to receive foreign visitors, import religious materials, meet in approved houses of worship, and apply to travel abroad for religious purposes. Local Communist Party officials must approve all religious activities other than regular worship services of registered groups, such as repairing or building houses of worship and holding processions or events outside religious buildings. The government also restricts religious practices by denying, in many cases, access to state media and exit visas, requiring the registration of publications, and limiting the entry of foreign religious workers. The Cuban government in 2014 started restricting bank accounts to one per denomination or religious association, preventing individual churches from maintaining their finances independently. The Office of Religious Affairs continues to pressure denominations to make their internal governing structures, statutes, and constitutions more hierarchical, which would aid government efforts to control religious communities.

The government principally targets for arrest or harassment religious communities and leaders deemed too independent from government control or those who support democracy and human rights efforts. Government officials also regularly restrict the religious rights of democracy and human rights activists. All religious communities, including those with working relationships with the government, are subject to the control mechanisms listed above.

Religious Freedom Conditions 2014–2015
Positive Developments

As in previous years, positive developments continue for the Catholic Church and major registered Protestant denominations, including but not limited to Presbyterians, Episcopalians, and Methodists. These religious denominations continued to report increased opportunities to meet, worship, engage in public processions, receive exit visas, recruit new members, import religious materials, receive contributions from co-religionists outside Cuba, and conduct charitable, educational and community service projects. In October, the Cuban government announced that the Catholic Church will be allowed to build its first new church on the island in more than 55 years. This follows the building of a new Catholic seminary. Catholic and Protestant Sunday worship services continue to be held in prisons throughout the island.

Continued Targeting and Harassment

The government continued to harass the Apostolic Reformation, an independent and fast-growing religious community, during this reporting period. Such harassment includes: short-term arrests of leaders; government-organized mob attacks; confiscations, destruction of or threats to destroy church property; harassment and surveillance of church members and their relatives; fines on churches; and threats to leaders and members of loss of employment, housing, or educational opportunities.

Both the Eastern and the Western Baptist Conventions continued to report surveillance and harassment by state officials, including receiving death threats and being victims of "acts of repudiation." The two denominations also reported increased threats of church destruction or confiscation.

In three separate incidents, independent evangelical and interdenominational pastors were detained for short periods; several others received police summons and were questioned about their alleged role in "counter-revolutionary" activities.

As in previous reporting periods, the Cuban government continued to target human rights activists and particular religious communities. More than 100 separate incidents were reported in 2014 of Ladies in White members and other human rights and democracy activists being prevented from attending Sunday masses. In the majority of cases, these individuals were detained on their way to mass and released hours later. In other instances, police officers blockaded them from reaching their respective churches. Individuals reported being beaten and harassed during their detentions.

Prior to the Community of Latin American and Caribbean States summit in January 2014, two religious leaders and human rights activists – Independent Evangelical Church Pastor Yordani Santi and Ebenezer Baptist Church Pastor Mario Felix Lleonart Barasso – were harassed; Pastor Mario Felix was placed under house arrest until the summit ended. Several times during the reporting period Pastor Mario Felix and his wife were arrested and later released.

U.S. Policy

In December 2014, President Barack Obama announced a "New Course on Cuba" that starts a process of normalizing diplomatic relations between the countries and significantly lifting trade and travel restrictions. On the morning of the announcement, President Obama and Cuban President Raul Castro spoke on the phone for more than one hour, the first presidential-level communication between the countries since the Cuban revolution. For decades, U.S.-Cuban policies and relations have been dominated by the U.S. trade sanctions and travel embargo on Cuba imposed in 1960 and reinforced by the 1996 Helms-Burton Act. The U.S. government's imprisonment of five Cubans arrested in 1998 for spying (known as the "Cuban Five"), and Cuba's detention of USAID contractor Alan Gross, also significantly hampered the relationship.

The changes to U.S.-Cuba policy announced in December include: re-establishing a U.S. Embassy in Havana to be led by an Ambassador to Cuba; immediately reviewing the designation of Cuba as a State Sponsor of Terrorism; easing restrictions for passage to Cuba for travelers from 12 authorized categories; increasing remittance levels from $500 to $2,000 per quarter; increasing U.S.-led training opportunities for and exportation and/or sale of goods and services to Cuban private businesses and farmers; authorizing U.S. institutions to open banking accounts with Cuban financial institutions; allowing the use of U.S. credit and debit cards in Cuba; increasing the export to and establishment of telecommunications equipment on the island; easing the application of Cuba sanctions in third countries; and permitting U.S. citizens to import $400 of Cuban products (with a $100 limit on tobacco and alcohol).

In addition to the above changes, the Cuban government released USAID contractor Alan Gross, who was imprisoned in 2009 and later sentenced to 15 years imprisonment for crimes against the state, as well as a U.S. intelligence officer jailed in Cuba for more than 20 years. The U.S. government released the three remaining members of the Cuban Five. All the men were returned to their respective countries on the day of the announcement.

A number of Cuban and religious leaders welcomed the new Cuba policy. In particular, the Catholic Church has long advocated for lifting the embargo, and Pope Francis was a key initiator of and mediator to the U.S.-Cuba discussions.

President Obama's announcement to start a process to normalize U.S.-Cuba relations and review Cuba's placement on the State Sponsors of Terrorism list met with both approval and criticism from Congress. Supporters of the new policy argue that Cuban authorities will be held more accountable to their own people because they will no longer be able to blame the embargo for the country's poor economy, trade and travel will provide a new market for U.S. goods, and increased contact with U.S. citizens will bring person-to-person diplomacy that could lead to changes on the island. Critics of the new policy argue that the U.S. government did not get much in return for lifting trade and travel restrictions, the Cuban government remains repressive, and that any lifting of sanctions should be conditioned on improved human rights and democracy conditions on the island.

President Obama has said that the United States government will continue to strongly press for and support improved human rights conditions and democratic reforms in Cuba. For fiscal year 2016, the Administration is requesting $20 million to support humanitarian assistance to victims of political repression and their families, strengthen independent civil society, and improve freedom of expression in Cuba.

The Administration notes that as part of the December agreement, the Cuban government released 53 political prisoners who had long been the focus of concern among the human rights community, agreed to allow Internet access, and approved the return of International Committee of the Red Cross (ICRC) and UN human rights officials. At this writing, those visits have yet to take place.

This was the third time the Obama Administration eased U.S. sanctions on Cuba. In April 2009, the President lifted restrictions on the number of times Cubans in the United States can travel to Cuba to visit and the amount of money they can send to relatives in that country. On the same day, President Obama also announced that the United States would begin issuing licenses for companies to provide cellular telephone and television services in Cuba. In March 2010, President

Obama announced that technology companies would be permitted to export Internet services to Cuba to increase freedom of expression and allow human rights activists to collect and share information.

As part of the new U.S.-Cuba policy, Assistant Secretary of State Roberta S. Jacobson travelled to Havana in January and March 2015 for U.S.-Cuban migration talks. Migration talks have been ongoing for several years.

Recommendations

As part of the U.S.-Cuba ongoing discussions, USCIRF recommends that the U.S. government should:

- Press the Cuban government to:

  - stop arrests and harassment of religious leaders;

  - end the practice of preventing democracy and human rights activists from attending religious services, a practice which infringes on their religious freedom rights;

  - cease interference with religious activities and religious communities' internal affairs;

  - allow unregistered religious groups to operate freely and legally; revise government policies that restrict religious services in homes or other personal property;

  - lift restrictions on the building or repairing of houses of worship, holding of religious processions, importation of religious materials, and admittance of religious leaders; and

  - hold accountable police and other security personnel for actions that violate the human rights of non-violent religious practitioners;

- Use appropriated funds to advance Internet freedom and protect Cuban activists by supporting the development and accessibility of new technologies and programs to counter censorship and to facilitate the free flow of information in and out of Cuba; and

- Encourage international partners, including key Latin American and European countries and regional blocs, to ensure that violations of freedom of religion or belief and related human rights are part of all formal and informal multilateral or bilateral discussions with Cuba.

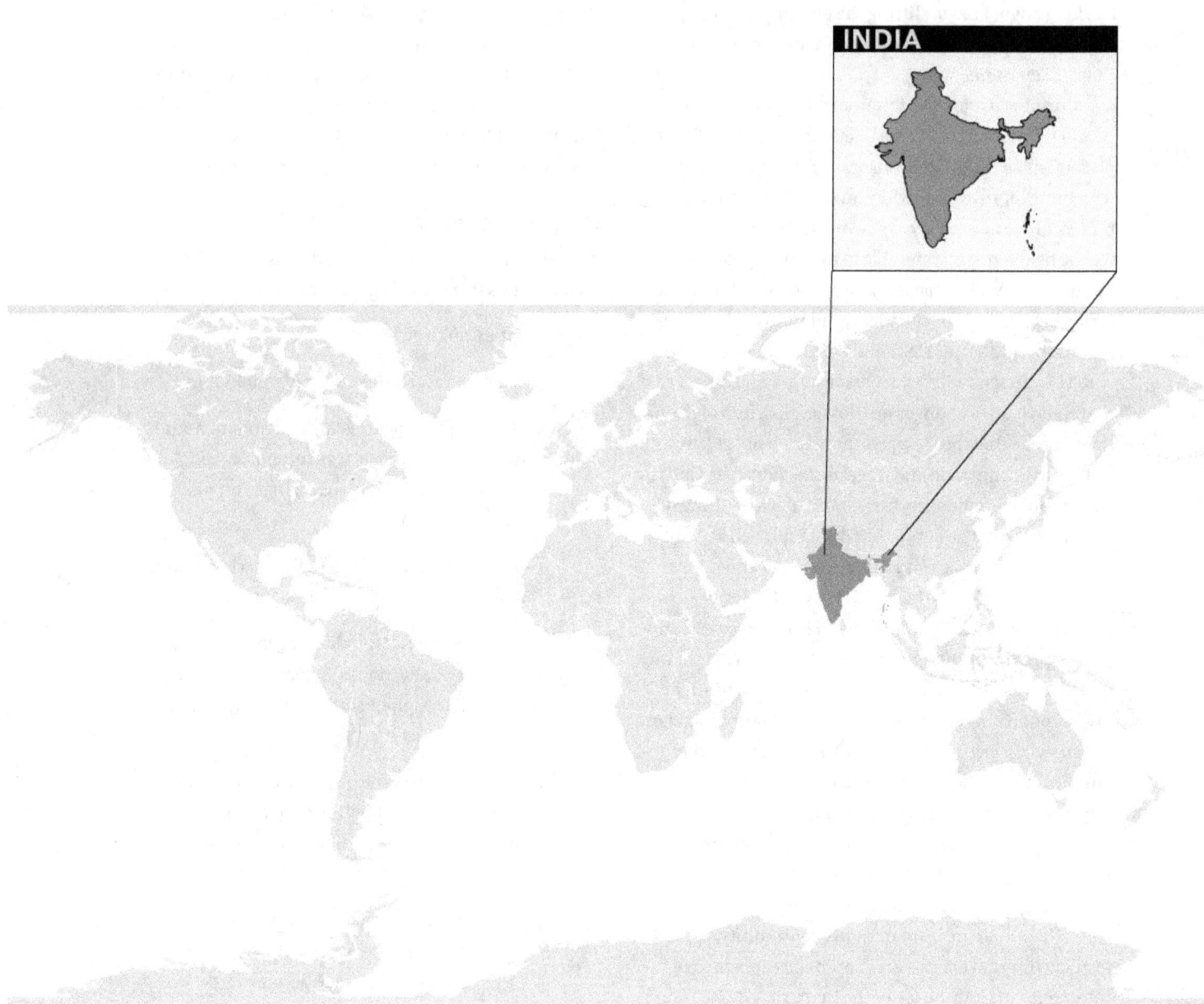

INDIA

Key Findings

Despite the country's status as a pluralistic, secular democracy, India has long struggled to protect minority religious communities or provide justice when crimes occur, which perpetuates a climate of impunity. Incidents of religiously-motivated and communal violence reportedly have increased for three consecutive years. The states of Andhra Pradesh, Uttar Pradesh, Bihar, Chattisgarhi, Gujarat, Odisha, Karnataka, Madhya Pradesh, Maharashtra, and Rajasthan tend to have the greatest number of religiously-motivated attacks and communal violence incidents. Non-governmental organizations (NGOs) and religious leaders, including from the Muslim, Christian, and Sikh communities, attributed the initial increase to religiously-divisive campaigning in advance of the country's 2014 general election. Since the election, religious minority communities have been subject to derogatory comments by politicians linked to the ruling Bharatiya Janata Party (BJP) and numerous violent attacks and forced conversions by Hindu nationalist groups, such as Rashtriya Swayamsevak Sangh (RSS) and Vishva Hindu Parishad (VHP).

Background

The world's largest democracy with about 1.22 billion people, India has a deeply religious, pluralistic society. A country with a Hindu majority, India is estimated to have the world's third largest Muslim population and over 25 million Christians. The country's religious diversity has been represented at the highest levels of government.

Despite these positive factors, India has long struggled with religious and communal harmony. Communal tensions between Muslims and Hindus have been a longstanding problem. Since 2008 and 2010 terrorist attacks, Muslim communities have reported facing undue scrutiny and arbitrary arrests and detentions, which the government justifies by the need to counter terrorism. In addition, for several years, Indian Christians, Christian missionary groups, and Hindus who convert to Christianity or another faith have reported more frequent harassment and violence, particularly in states with anti-conversion laws. Religious minority communities frequently accuse the RSS, VHP and other Hindu-nationalist groups and individuals of intolerance, discrimination, and violence against them. In addition, they cite police bias in failing to

> *Religious minority communities frequently accuse the RSS, VHP and other Hindu-nationalist groups and individuals of intolerance, discrimination, and violence against them.*

Christian NGOs and leaders report that their community is particularly at risk in states that have adopted "Freedom of Religion Act(s)," commonly referred to as anti-conversion laws. Based on these concerns, USCIRF again places India on its Tier 2 list of countries, where it has been since 2009.

investigate sufficiently and arrest perpetrators of violence. Moreover, religious minority communities voice concern that high-ranking BJP members protect or provide support to these groups. In light of these concerns, Prime Minister Narendra Modi's statement in support of religious freedom made after the close of the reporting period (discussed more fully below) was a positive development.

The country has experienced periodic outbreaks of large-scale communal violence against religious minorities, including in Uttar Pradesh in 2013, Odisha in 2007-2008, Gujarat in 2002, and Delhi in 1984. India has established special structures, such as Fast-Track Courts, Special Investigative Teams, and independent commissions, to investigate and adjudicate crimes stemming from these incidents. However, their impact has been hindered by limited capacity, an antiquated judiciary, inconsistent use, political corruption, and religious bias, particularly at the state and local levels. As a result, a climate of impunity continues to exist in some Indian states, exacerbating the social and religious tensions among communities.

Religious Freedom Conditions 2014–2015
Violations against Christians

Christian communities, across many denominations, report an increase of harassment and violence in the last year, including physical violence, arson, desecration of churches and Bibles, and disruption of religious services. The perpetrators are often individuals and groups associated with the RSS and VHP and operate with near impunity. Reportedly, local police seldom provide protection, refuse to accept complaints, rarely investigate,

by an estimated 25 Hindu nationalists for displaying images of Jesus in the storefront window.

Violations against Muslims

The Muslim community in India also has experienced increased harassment and violence. It faces significant hate campaigns perpetrated by Hindu nationalist groups and local and state politicians that include widespread media propaganda accusing Muslims of being terrorists; spying for Pakistan; forcibly kidnapping, converting, and marrying Hindu women; and disrespecting Hinduism by slaughtering cows. Additionally, the Muslim community reports that its mosques are monitored and young boys and men are detained indiscriminately under the pretext of countering terrorism. Muslims also complain that most Indian states violate their religious freedom by restricting or banning cow slaughter, which is required for Muslims during Eid al-Adha (Festival of the Sacrifice).

In addition, in the past year, there have been a number of violent incidents leading to deaths and displacement of Muslims. For example, in January 2015, a mob of more than 5,000 people attacked the majority-Muslim village of Azizpur, Bihar after a young Hindu man had been abducted and killed. Three Muslims were burned alive and about 25 houses set on fire. Police have arrested some perpetrators. In September 2014, police

> *Reportedly, local police seldom provide protection, refuse to accept complaints, rarely investigate, and in a few cases encourage Christians to move or hide their religion.*

and in a few cases encourage Christians to move or hide their religion. The Evangelical Fellowship of India has documented more than 38 incidents targeting Christians in November and December 2014 alone. Catholic communities in India also have documented a number of incidents, including at least six attacks on churches and a school between December 2014 and February 2015. For example, in December, St. Sebastian Catholic Church in Delhi was set on fire, Catholic Christmas carolers in Hyderabad were beaten badly by a mob, and a Catholic shopkeeper in Delhi was attacked brutally

arrested nearly 150 people in the state of Gujarat after violence left dozens, mostly Muslims, severely injured. Reportedly, the violence broke out after Hindu nationalists posted on the Internet images of the Hindu Goddess Maa Ambe and Lord Ram superimposed over images of Mecca and the Ka'aba.

Violations against Sikhs

India's Sikh community has long pursued a change to Article 25 of India's constitution which states, "Hindus shall be construed as including a reference to persons professing the Sikh, Jain or Buddhist religion, and the reference to Hindu religious institutions shall be construed accordingly." The lack of recognition of Sikhism as a distinct religion denies Sihks access to social services or employment and educational preferences that are available to other religious minority communities and to scheduled caste Hindus. (This is also true for the other faiths listed in Article 25.) Sikhs are often harassed and pressured to reject religious practices and beliefs that are distinct to Sikhism, such as dress, unshorn hair, and the carrying of religious items, including the *kirpan*.

Communal Violence

Communal violence, which generally occurs in states that have large minority communities, has been a long-standing issue in India. According to India's Union Home Ministry, in 2013 there were 823 incidents of communal violence nationwide, leaving 133 dead, and thousands injured, some critically. Uttar Pradesh had the highest number of incidents (247), followed by the states of Maharashtra (88), Madhya Pradesh (84), Karnataka (73) and Gujarat (68). According to Muslim and Christian NGOs that track communal incidents, 2014 statistics, yet to be released by the Ministry, will be likely higher.

Hindu Nationalist Groups and Forced Conversion

In December 2014, Hindu nationalist groups announced plans to forcibly "reconvert" at least 4,000 Christian families and 1,000 Muslim families to Hin-

"postponed" according to Mohan Bhagwat, a RSS leader. Hindu nationalist groups also reportedly give monetary incentives to Hindus to convert Christians and Muslims to Hinduism. In early December, hundreds of Muslims reportedly were forcibly "reconverted" to Hinduism in a mass ceremony in Agra, Uttar Pradesh. Members of the RSS allegedly tricked dozens of Muslims families into attending a meeting by telling them they would be provided financial help, but instead a Hindu religious leader performed a Hindu conversion ceremony; an investigation is underway. In September 2014, Dalit Seventh-day Adventists filed a report in Uttar Pradesh that they were forcibly converted to Hinduism and their church was converted to a Hindu temple. It is not known if a police investigation was conducted. The nationalist groups also allegedly target Dalits if they are believed to be considering conversion away from Hinduism.

Anti-Conversion Laws

Six Indian states – Chhattisgarh, Himachal Pradesh, Gujarat, Madhya Pradesh, Arunanchal Pradesh, and Odisha – have so-called "Freedom of Religion Act(s)," commonly referred to as anti-conversion laws, and Rajasthan's parliament passed an anti-conversion bill but it was never signed by the state's Chief Minister. These laws generally require government officials to assess the legality of conversions out of Hinduism only and provide for fines and imprisonment for anyone who uses force, fraud, or "inducement" to convert

These laws generally require government officials to assess the legality of conversions out of Hinduism only and provide for fines and imprisonment for anyone who uses force, fraud, or "inducement" to convert another.

duism in Uttar Pradesh on Christmas day as part of a so-called "Ghar Wapsi" (returning home) program. In advance of the program, the Hindu groups sought to raise money for their campaign, noting that it cost nearly 200,000 rupees (US $3,200) per Christian and 500,000 rupees (US $8,000) per Muslim. After both domestic and international criticism, the day was

another. While these laws purportedly protect religious minorities from forced conversions, they are one-sided, only concerned about conversions away from Hinduism but not towards Hinduism. Observers note they create a hostile, and on occasion violent, environment for religious minority communities because they do not require any evidence to support accusations of wrongdoing. In 2015, high-ranking members of the ruling BJP party, including the party's president Amit Shah, called for a nationwide anti-conversion law. There are reports that some evangelical groups use tactics that are unethical and insulting to Hinduism and Hindus, which exacerbate religious and communal tensions.

Redress for Past Large-Scale Violence

The Indian courts are still adjudicating cases stemming from large-scale Hindu-Muslim communal violence in Uttar Pradesh in 2013 and in Gujarat in 2002, Hindu-Christian communal violence in Odisha in 2007-2008, and Hindu-Sikh communal violence in Delhi in 1984. NGOs, religious leaders, and human rights activists allege religious bias and corruption in these investigations and adjudications. A one-member special judicial inquiry commission is still investigating the 2013 riots in Muzaffarnagar, Uttar Pradesh that left dozens, mostly Muslims, dead and tens of thousands, mostly Muslims, displaced. Cases stemming from the 2002 Gujarat violence also continue, including a special court case pertaining to the killing of 68 people, including former Congress Party Parliamentarian Ehsan Jafri. More than five years after the Odisha violence, cases are still being adjudicated. In July 2014, the national Supreme Court ruled that churches damaged during those riots are not entitled to additional compensation, because they receive sufficient foreign funds. Since 1984 there has been little progress in prosecuting perpetrators of crimes during the anti-Sikh riots, which allegedly occurred with the support or encouragement of government officials or prominent members of India's Congress Party. However, in late 2014 the central government established a committee to determine if a Special Investigation Team should be created to reinvestigate cases that had been previously closed.

U.S. Policy

Since the end of the Cold War, India and the United States have enjoyed increasingly closer ties, with India now described as a "strategic" and "natural" partner of the United States. In 2009, then Secretary of State Hillary Clinton launched the U.S.-India Strategic Dialogue, through which the countries discuss a wide range of bilateral, global, and regional issues, such as economic development, business and trade, education, technology, counter-terrorism and the environment. Five strategic dialogues have been held since 2009, none including issues related to religious freedom. The July 2014 dialogue included issues related to gender equality and urban safety, resulting in USAID, state governments of India, and the government of Japan partnering with UN Women to implement the "Safe Cities" program to monitor gender-based violence, strengthen systems to prevent and respond to it, and build women's confidence in the justice system.

As part of the initiative to build ties between the United States and India, the Obama Administration has made significant overtures to the Indian government. The first state visit President Barack Obama hosted after taking office was for then Prime Minister Manmohan Singh in November 2009. In November 2010, President Obama made a three-day state visit to India, and he returned in January 2015 to be the chief guest at India's annual Republic Day festivities, becoming the first U.S. President to travel to India twice.

During his 2015 visit, and again in February 2015 at the U.S. National Prayer Breakfast, President Obama made notable remarks on India's religious freedom issues. In his speech at a town hall event in New Delhi and again a few weeks later at the Prayer Breakfast, President Obama underscored the importance of religious freedom to India's success, urging the country to not be "splintered along the lines of religious faith" and stating, "Michelle and I returned from India - an incredible, beautiful country, full of magnificent diversity - but a place where, in past years, religious faiths of all types have, on occasion, been targeted by other people of faith, simply due to their heritage and their beliefs - acts of intolerance that would have shocked [Mahatma] Gandhiji, the person who helped to liberate that nation."

In mid-February 2015, at an event honoring Indian Catholic saints, Prime Minister Modi stated publicly, for the first time, that his government "will ensure that there is complete freedom of faith and that everyone has the undeniable right to retain or adopt the religion of his or her choice without coercion or undue influence." This statement is notable given longstanding allegations that, as Chief Minister of Gujarat in 2002, Mr. Modi was complicit in anti-Muslim riots in that state. In light of these allegations, in 2005, the State Department revoked a tourist visa he had been granted to visit the United States, under a provision in the Immigration and Nationality Act that makes any foreign government official who "was responsible for or directly carried out, at any time, particularly severe violations of religious freedom" ineligible for a U.S. visa. Prime Minister Modi remains the only person known to have been denied a visa based on this provision.

Recommendations

Since 2004, the United States and India have pursued a strategic relationship based on shared concerns about energy, security, and the growing threat of terrorism, as well as shared values of democracy and the rule of law. As part of this important relationship, USCIRF recommends that the U.S. government should:

- Integrate concern for religious freedom into bilateral contacts with India, including the framework of future Strategic Dialogues, at both the federal and provincial level, and encourage the strengthening of the capacity of state and central police to implement effective measures to prohibit and punish cases of religious violence and protect victims and witnesses;

- Increase the U.S. embassy's attention to issues of religious freedom and related human rights, including through visits by the Ambassador and other officials to areas where communal and religiously-motivated violence has occurred or is likely to occur and meetings with religious communities, local governmental leaders, and police;

- Encourage the establishment of a program similar to the "Safe Cities" program (described above) of impartial government officials, interfaith religious leaders, human rights advocates, and legal experts to discuss and recommend actions to promote religious tolerance and understanding, and protect religious minorities from intimidation and violence;

- Urge India to boost training on human rights and religious freedom standards and practices for the police and judiciary, particularly in states and areas with a history or likelihood of religious and communal violence;

- Urge the central Indian government to press states that have adopted anti-conversion laws to repeal

or amend them to conform with internationally-recognized human rights standards; make clear U.S. opposition to laws that restrict freedom of thought and association; and

- Urge the Indian government to publicly rebuke government officials and religious leaders that make derogatory statements about religious communities.

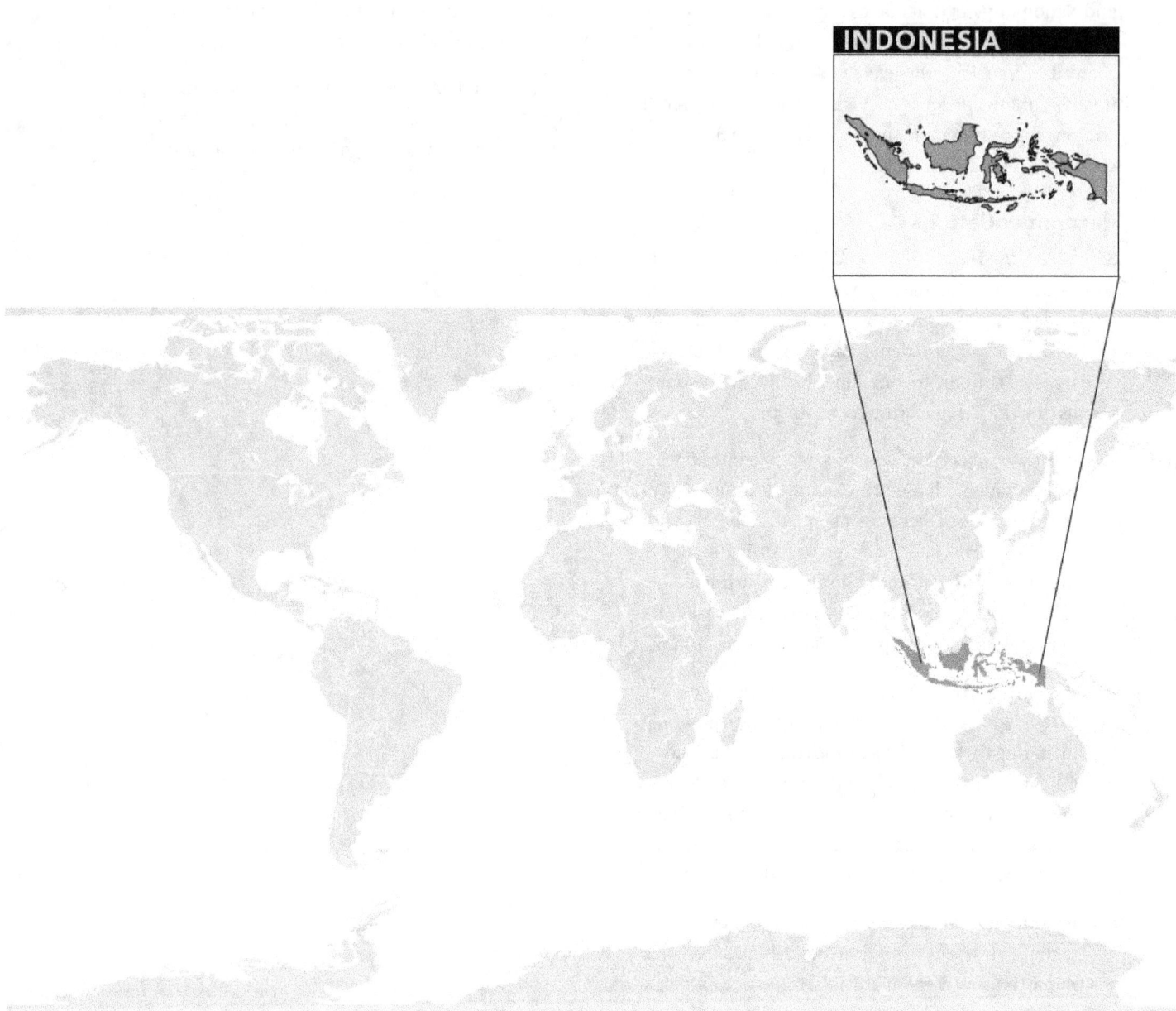

INDONESIA

Key Findings

As in previous years, internal pressures continued to diminish Indonesia's respect for religious freedom and tradition of tolerance and pluralism. Deteriorating religious freedom conditions in Indonesia in 2014 were somewhat overshadowed by legislative and presidential elections, but discrimination and violence against religious minorities continued, as well as the harassment and imprisonment of individuals accused of blasphemy. The announcement of President Joko "Jokowi" Widodo's intent to draft a law on religious tolerance that protects minority religious groups was welcomed, as its creation and passage could represent a major step forward in protecting religious freedom and living up to Indonesia's perceived reputation for tolerance. Yet the prospects for this unrealized commitment are threatened by the deeply entrenched legacy of the previous administration's discriminatory laws, policies, and practices against religious minorities and the relative impunity afforded to extremist groups. Based on these concerns, in 2015 USCIRF again places Indonesia on Tier 2, where it has been since 2003.

Background

The year 2014 capped off the decade-long presidency of Susilo Bambang Yudhoyono, under whose tenure religious extremism, and its expression through acts

in 2014. The Ministry itself has a history of implementing discriminatory practices and laws against non-Sunni Muslims, in particular Shi'a and Ahmadi Muslims. Hardline groups that incite violence against religious minorities or Muslims, with whom they disagree, continue to operate freely and with relative impunity.

Anti-Shi'a and anti-Christian attitudes came to the fore during the elections. Extremist groups heightened rhetoric in support of candidates who would "purge Shiites" from the country. Following a number of rallies, in early December, the extremist group the Islamic Defenders Front (FPI) "rejected" the newly-appointed Jakarta governor, Basuki "Ahok" Tjahaja Purnama, because he is an ethnic Chinese Christian, arguing that only a Muslim should be in charge of Jakarta; Ahok is the first non-Muslim Jakarta governor in 50 years. In addition, during the campaign, Jokowi's detractors falsely accused him of being both a Christian and of Chinese descent in an attempt to reduce his support among majority Muslim voters.

President Jokowi and the new Religious Affairs Minister, Lukman Hakim Saifuddin, have already struck a different, more inclusive tone in their statements. However, President Jokowi and Minister Lukman's planned new legislation protecting religious minorities has yet to be introduced. Moreover, it will take time to roll back deep-seated discrimination against religious

---

Hardline groups that incite violence against religious minorities or Muslims with whom they disagree continue to operate freely and with relative impunity.

---

of violence, grew with little government intervention. Religious Affairs Minister Suryadharma Ali, known for his support of Islamic extremist elements, also left office

minority groups, including Ahmadis, Christians, Shi'a, Sufi, Hindus, Baha'is, and followers of various indigenous and traditional beliefs. Indonesia has the world's largest Muslim population, 87 percent of its more than

250 million people. Approximately 10 percent of the country's population are Christian, three percent of whom are Catholic.

Indonesia's federal system and weak oversight gives provinces wide latitude to enforce negative interpretations of Indonesian law, ignore court decisions, and apply Shari'ah law in ways that violate constitutional protections. Consequently, to see durable and lasting improvements for religious freedom and minority rights, the government will need to ensure the broad coordination and cooperation of the complex layers of federal, provincial, and local officials spread across this vast chain of islands.

Religious Freedom Conditions 2014–2015
Forced Closures of and Violence against Religious Properties

Local government officials continue to harass religious minorities over religious sites, particularly in West Java. Local authorities justify church closures under a federal government decree requiring prior approval to build a house of worship from at least 60 local residents of different faiths, the local religious affairs department, and the government-sponsored Regional Interfaith Com-

congregation in Bogor spent Christmas locked out of their church building. After the church lost its permit in response to pressure from hardline groups, local authorities closed it in 2010. The Supreme Court has since ordered the church be reopened, but two mayoral administrations have ignored the order. Extremists, whom local Catholics identified as belonging to FPI and another similar group, also prevented the celebration of Mass at St. Charles Borromeo in West Java after first raiding the property and later sending threatening text messages to the parish priest.

Ahmadis

Followers of the minority Ahmadi faith continued to experience significant restrictions and abuses. A 2008 Joint Ministerial Decree bans Ahmadis from spreading their faith and provides the foundation for even harsher discriminatory measures and attacks against the community. On June 26, 2014, the Nur Khilafat Mosque, the house of worship for Ahmadis in Ciamis district in West Java, was closed just days prior to the month of Ramadan following the demands of approximately 300 FPI protestors. The following week, the congregation managed to reopen the mosque. More than 100 Ahmadis remain

---

A 2008 Joint Ministerial Decree bans Ahmadis from spreading their faith and provides the foundation for even harsher discriminatory measures and attacks against the community.

---

munication Forum. Although the rule is supposed to apply only to new construction, municipal authorities in West Java also have enforced it against long-established churches. In May 2014, government officials in Rancaekek, West Java issued a notice closing the Pentecost Church. In June, a Pentecostal church in Yogyakarta was attacked with stones, causing property damage, and an attack on a nearby Catholic prayer service resulted in several injuries. Also in June, Christian representatives in Cianjur, West Java filed complaints with the National Human Rights Commission, regarding the closure of seven churches on the pretext of permit violations between December 2013 and January 2014. This was the fifth consecutive year in which the GKI Yasmin

internally displaced in Mataram, West Nusa Tenggara after religious-based violence forced their eviction more than eight years ago.

Shi'a and Sufi Muslims

In April 2014, an estimated 1,000 or more people attended the first-ever Anti-Shi'a Convention. Organized by the Anti-Shi'a Alliance, the convention featured several high-profile clerics and called for "jihad" against Shi'a Muslims. Participants produced a declaration urging the government to ban the Shi'a faith. Sufi communities continue to face school closures and harassment from extremist groups with no protection from municipal authorities, particularly in Aceh.

Baha'is

Licenses and permits often are difficult to obtain for those without one of the country's six official religions on their ID cards. In July 2014, the new Minister of Religious Affairs, Lukman Hakim Saifuddin, stated that the Baha'i faith should be recognized as an official religion and adherents should be able to indicate Baha'ism as their religion on national identity cards. Despite the minister's encouraging announcement, the Ministry itself thus far has not taken action to add the Baha'i faith to the list of official religions.

Shari'ah Law in Aceh

In 2014, the local legislature in the province of Aceh passed a new bylaw that strengthened Shari'ah law and for the first time ever expanded it to non-Muslims, both Indonesians and foreigners; an estimated 90,000 non-Muslims reside in Aceh. The bylaw imposes Islamic law on persons of other faiths, establishes new crimes not found in the national criminal code, and potentially forces non-Muslims to be tried in Shari'ah courts. Some religious minorities have expressed concern that they will be punished under the bylaw for failing to conform to tra-

Local authorities in the city of Banda Aceh, and elsewhere throughout the province, banned all New Year's celebrations, deeming them contrary to Islam. The ban, issued via a fatwa from the Ulema Consultative Assembly, is similar to one delivered the previous year. Wilayatul Hisbah raided cafes, storefronts, and other locations where celebrations and paraphernalia were suspected.

Marriage Act under Judicial Review

In August 2014, a group of law graduates and students brought a case challenging the constitutionality of Article 2(1) of the 1974 Marriage Act, which, according to some interpretations, prohibits interfaith marriages. That provision legitimizes only those marriages conducted in accordance with the laws of the parties' religion, and has been interpreted by the Ministry of Religious Affairs, and some religious leaders and local municipalities, to mean that couples of different faiths cannot obtain marriage licenses or have their marriages officially recognized unless one spouse changes religions. The ambiguity and open interpretation of the Marriage Act adds onerous bureaucratic hurdles for some couples seeking interfaith

> The [Shari'ah] bylaw imposes Islamic law
> on persons of other faiths, establishes new crimes
> not found in the national criminal code, and
> potentially forces non-Muslims to be tried in Shari'ah courts.

ditional Islamic guidelines, even though those guidelines are not recognized by their own religions. Moreover, the bylaw entrenches Sunni Islam as the official religion in Aceh, thereby imposing Sunni traditions on all Muslims in the province, including Shia Muslims, as well as Ahmadis, overriding their right to practice their faiths freely. The new bylaw is enforced by Aceh's Shari'ah police force, known as Wilayatul Hisbah, which has seen its jurisdiction expand in recent years. Human rights advocates argue that Wilayatul Hisbah oversteps and unfairly targets women and the poor. They also have expressed concern that the growing breadth of crime and punishment under the bylaw has coincided with increased incidents of civilian vigilantism in parts of Aceh.

unions and, in practice, compels some individuals to convert to another faith solely to marry, which undermines the individual freedoms to practice a religion and marry a partner of one's choice.

Blasphemy Law

Indonesian laws criminalizing blasphemy and other forms of perceived religious insults continue to be used against individuals, often on trumped-up charges. For example, in 2014, Abraham Sujoko received a two-year prison sentence and fine for "defamation of religion" under Indonesia's Electronic Information and Transaction Law. In December 2014, police opened an investigation of Meidyatama Suryodiningrat, editor of The

Jakarta Post, for publishing what some believe to be a blasphemous cartoon criticizing the violence carried out by the terrorist group ISIL, the Islamic State of Iraq and the Levant.

U.S. Policy

An important U.S. partner in Southeast Asia, Indonesia is geopolitically strategic and often touted as an example of democracy in a Muslim-majority country.

Education and Training, and the U.S. Trade and Development Agency.

In 2010, the United States and Indonesia entered into a Comprehensive Partnership, a framework for cooperation on a variety of bilateral and regional issues, guided by three main pillars of cooperation and six issue-specific working groups, including one on democracy and civil society. The Partnership has elevated U.S. engagement with Indonesia and provided

---

Indonesian laws criminalizing blasphemy and other forms of perceived religious insults continue to be used against individuals, often on trumped-up charges.

Traditionally, Indonesia has been viewed as a leader in the Association of Southeast Asian Nations (ASEAN). Indonesia is also a member of the G20, the only ASEAN member in the group. At the November 2014 G20 Summit in Brisbane, Australia, President Jokowi outlined four economic priorities: business licensing, tax reform, fuel subsidies, and social infrastructure.

The United States provides a variety of assistance programs to Indonesia in areas such as education, the environment, criminal justice and anti-corruption, counterterrorism, military education and training, and democracy and governance, among others. The main conduits for this assistance are the State Department, the U.S. Agency for International Development (USAID), the Millennium Challenge Corporation (MCC), and the Peace Corps. For example, MCC's Indonesia Compact is a $600 million five-year program aimed at reducing poverty and expanding economic growth more broadly. In recent years, the U.S. government has shifted its USAID support to programs that are administered or conducted directly by Indonesian organizations and institutions, which includes civil society and local businesses. In its FY2016 Budget, the State Department noted Indonesia as a possible country of focus under its Countering Violent Extremism program; Indonesia was similarly noted in State's FY2015 Budget. Other specific U.S. funding programs include International Narcotics Control and Law Enforcement, Global Health, International Military

a clear pathway for dialogue on key issues of mutual interest. Thus far, human rights have not featured prominently in the engagement between the two countries under the Partnership, though related issues have, such as civil society consultations and peer-to-peer relationship-building. Prior to the Partnership, the United States and Indonesia co-sponsored a religious interfaith conference in Jakarta in 2010; similar dialogues were held in Bangladesh and at the Vatican.

Secretary of State John Kerry attended President Jokowi's inauguration in October 2014. At the first meeting between Presidents Obama and Jokowi in November 2014 during a summit of the Asia-Pacific Economic Cooperation forum, President Obama praised Indonesia for playing "an extraordinary role in promoting pluralism and respect for religious diversity."

Recommendations

Through increased engagement, the United States has both encouraged Indonesia and raised concerns about human rights conditions in the country, including the treatment of religious minorities. USCIRF encourages the U.S. government to continue to express these concerns both publicly and privately, particularly with respect to rising intolerance and extremism. In addition, USCIRF recommends that the U.S. government should:

- Encourage President Jokowi and Minister Lukman to fulfill their commitment to introduce new legislation protecting religious minorities and offer to provide technical assistance, if needed;

- Create specific bilateral working groups in the annual Comprehensive Partnership meetings with Indonesia to discuss human rights, religious freedom, and rule of law issues and establish concrete measures to address them;

- Raise in public and private with Indonesian officials the need to protect Indonesia's tradition of religious tolerance and pluralism by arresting and prosecuting individuals targeting religious groups for discrimination and violence;

- Urge the Indonesian government, at central, provincial, and local levels, to comply with the Indonesian constitution and international standards by: overturning the Joint Ministerial Decree on the Ahmadiyya community and any provincial bans on Ahmadiyya religious practice; amending or repealing Article 156(a) of the Penal Code and releasing anyone sentenced for "deviancy," "denigrating religion," or "blasphemy;" and amending the Joint Ministerial Decree No. 1/2006 (Regulation on Building Houses of Worship) to allow religious minorities the right to build and maintain their places of worship;

- Prioritize funding for governmental, civil society, and media programs that promote religious freedom, counter extremism, build interfaith alliances, expand the reporting ability of human rights defenders, train government and religious officials to mediate sectarian disputes, and build capacity for legal reform advocates, judicial officials, and parliamentarians to better fulfill Indonesia's obligations under international human rights law; and

- Help to train Indonesian police and counter-terrorism officials, at all levels, to better address sectarian conflict, religion-related violence and terrorism, including violence against places of worship, through practices consistent with international human rights standards, while ensuring those officers have not been implicated in past human rights abuses pursuant to Leahy Amendment vetting procedures.

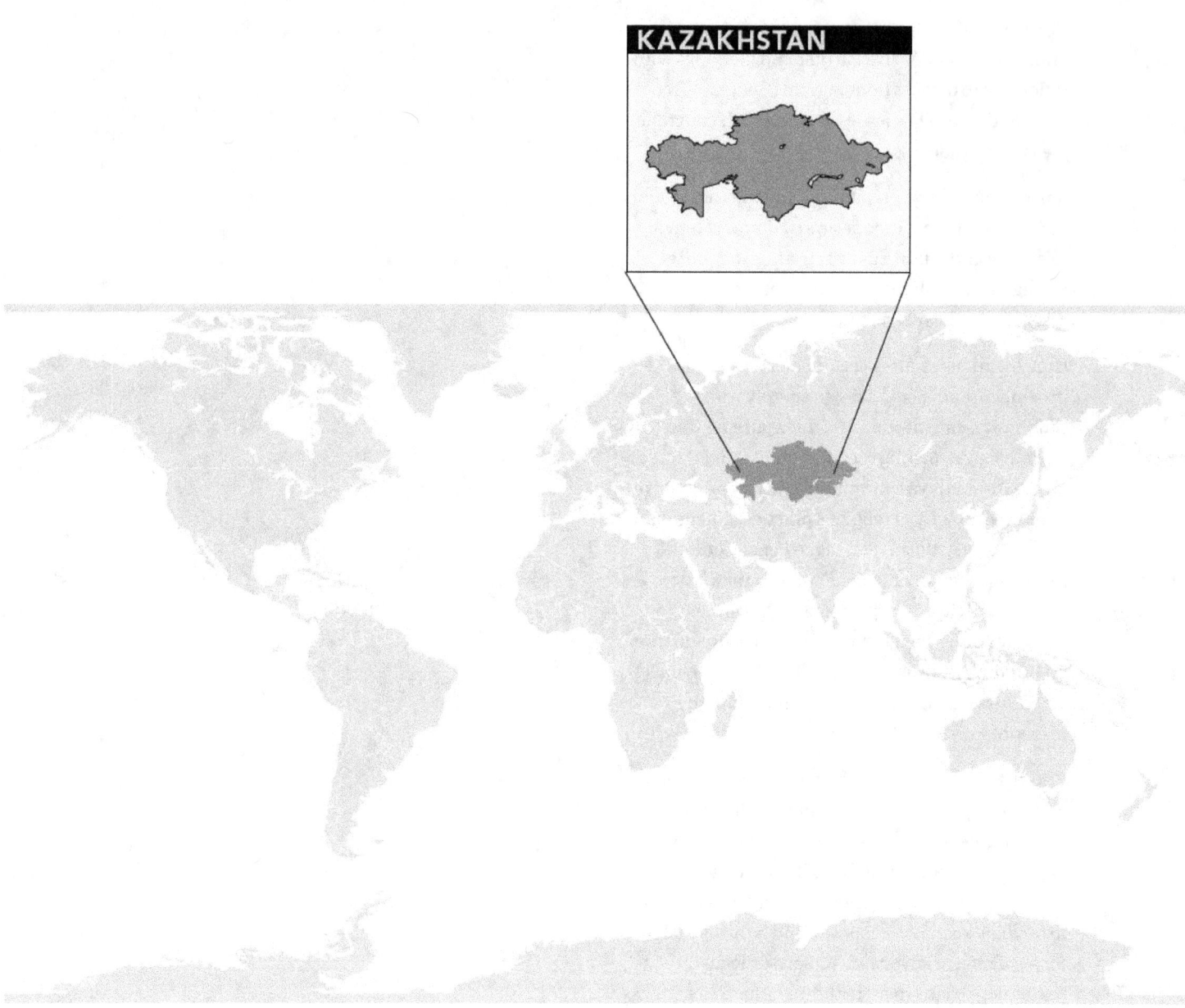

KAZAKHSTAN

KAZAKHSTAN

Key Findings

Although the government of Kazakhstan promotes religious tolerance at the international level, religious freedom conditions in the country continued to deteriorate in 2014. The country's restrictive 2011 religion law bans unregistered religious activity and has been enforced through the closing of religious organizations, police raids, detentions, and fines. The law's onerous registration requirements have led to a sharp drop in the number of registered religious groups, both Muslim and Protestant. Based on these concerns, in 2015 USCIRF again places Kazakhstan on Tier 2, where it has been since 2013.

Background

Kazakhstan's population is estimated to be 17.7 million, with about 65 percent Muslim, mostly Hannafi Sunni. Russian Orthodox Christians are about 25 percent of the country's population, with other groups under five percent including Jews, Roman and Greek Catholics, various Protestant denominations, and others. During the existence of the U.S.S.R., many non-Kazakh Soviet citizens (mostly Russians) moved to Kazakhstan to expand agricultural output, outnum-

tral Asia in regard to freedom of religion or belief. The 2011 law, however, sets complex registration requirements with high membership thresholds and bans unregistered religious activity; it restricts areas of permitted religious activity and teaching, distribution of religious materials, and training of clergy. The 2011 law also raised penalties for alleged violations. While the religion law declares that all religions have equal legal standing, its preamble "recognizes the historical role of Hanafi Islam and Orthodox Christianity," suggesting preferred official status. The government also supports "anti-sect centers" that promote intolerance against certain religious groups. Religious communities are subject to police and secret police surveillance, but due to fear of state reprisals, many hesitate to discuss this issue.

Under the 2011 law, all religious organizations were required to re-register pursuant to the complicated new rules. Depending on where they operate, groups had to register with national, regional, and/or local Ministry of Justice authorities, with different membership numbers required (50 for local registration, 500 in at least two regions for regional registration, 5,000 in each of the country's regions for national registration). Many

> *"Before its 2011 religion law, Kazakhstan was seen as one of the most liberal post-Soviet countries . . ."*

bering native Muslim Turkic Kazakhs. After Kazakhstan's independence, many of the non-Kazakhs left and official repatriation brought some one million ethnic Kazakhs to the country, increasing the percentage of Muslims.

Before the 2011 religion law, Kazakhstan was seen as one of the most liberal countries in post-Soviet Cen-

previously-registered groups could not meet the new thresholds and therefore lost their legal status. After the re-registration date of October 2012, the total of registered religious groups fell sharply. For example, of 48 "non-traditional" religious organizations, only 16 were re-registered. The 11,000 members of the Union of Evangelical Christian Baptists refuse to register as a matter of conscience. By 2013, only Muslim groups affiliated with the state-backed Muslim Board were registered. Shi'a and Ahmadi Muslims were denied legal status, as were mosques attended mainly by particular ethnic groups. Catholic communities were exempt because of an agreement with the Holy See.

In July 2014, President Nursultan Nazarbayev signed into law amendments to Kazakhstan's administrative and criminal implementation codes. The new administrative provisions largely repeat the previous penalties for alleged violations in regard to religion or belief, while the new criminal provisions place restrictions on convicts. The amended codes took effect on January 1, 2015.

Religious Freedom Conditions 2014–2015
Registration Issues

Kazakh officials continued to obstruct activities of unregistered religious groups, such as a Protestant church in Atyrau, and of certain registered communities including the registered Hare Krishna group in Kostanai, the NGO Forum 18 News Service noted. As of late 2014, the historic Din-Muhammad Mosque community – consisting mainly of ethnic Tatars in the northern city of Petropavl – again is applying for registration, although it was liquidated and its mosque confiscated. In late 2014, Almaty's Religious Affairs Department notified local registered religious groups that it is an offense to hold services outside of registered places of worship.

The Case of Pastor Kashkumbayev

On February 17, 2014, retired Presbyterian Pastor Bakhytzhan Kashkumbayev of Astana's Grace Church received a four-year suspended prison term for allegedly harming a parishioner's psychological health, although the alleged victim said she was not harmed. As of July 2014, however, he faced possible further punishment for allegedly harming a second

released from jail and then re-arrested for "terrorism." During one month of his nine-month term, in a return to methods observers described as "Soviet-style," the pastor was injected forcibly with psychotropic drugs. Observers consider the two-year-long criminal prosecution of the pastor and severe harassment of his family a symbol of the steep decline of respect for religious freedom in Kazakhstan.

Extremism Charges

Criminal charges of extremism regularly are brought against a range of individuals for peaceful religious activity. Court hearings on whether materials are "extremist" are not announced. There is an extensive list of banned texts on government websites. In February 2014, an Astana court banned as "extremist" a book partly written by Salafi Muslim Mohammed ibn Abdul-Wahhab. Christians Vyacheslav Cherkasov and Zhasulan Alzhanov were given 10-day prison terms and fined four months' wages in the Akmola region in October 2014 for offering on the street a book called "Jesus: More than a Prophet." Extremism charges remain pending against atheist writer Aleksandr Kharlamov. He was detained for five months in 2013, including one month of psychiatric exams. The Muslim missionary movement *Tabligh Jamaat* was banned in 2013, and trials of alleged members are secret. Forum 18 reported on a campaign against alleged *Tabligh Jamaat* members: in January 2015 Bakyt Nurmanbetov, Aykhan Kurmangaliyev, Sagyndyk Tatubayev, and Kairat Esmukhambetov were sentenced to 20-month terms; in late 2014 another received a three-year term, a trial began of five members and 20 others were detained.

Penalties for Unregistered Religious Activity

The most common violations of the 2011 religion law that result in fines are unlicensed distribution of religious texts, talking about religion without the required

---

It is an offense to hold services outside of registered places of worship.

---

church member's health. Just days after USCIRF met with the pastor's family in October 2013, he briefly was

"missionary" registration, and holding worship meetings without registration. The head of the presidential

Human Rights Commission said in September 2014 that 92 administrative cases were opened for unauthorized religious activity; as of October 2014 at least 14 were jailed for refusing to pay fines for not applying for state permits. A Baptist refused to pay three fines in two years for unauthorized worship meetings; he was jailed for

bans on 14 texts that courts deemed to "reject fundamental teachings of Christianity."

Concerns of UN Special Rapporteurs

UN Special Rapporteur on Freedom of Religion or Belief Heiner Bielefeldt visited Kazakhstan for 11 days

---

Criminal charges of extremism regularly are brought against a range of individuals for peaceful religious activity.

---

five days in 2014 and is banned from exiting the country. There are 25 Council of Churches Baptists who refuse to pay fines for unregistered religious activity and are on the Justice Ministry's list of debtors unable to leave Kazakhstan. Jehovah's Witnesses also have been prosecuted for committing this "offense." An Almaty-based Imam's fine of two months' average wages for leading an unregistered mosque was overturned in April 2014 because, although unregistered, the mosque was affiliated with the semi-official Muslim Board.

Increased Government Control of Muslims

The Muslim Board, which is closely tied to the Kazakh government, oversees mosque construction, theological exams and background checks for aspiring imams, and *hajj* travel. It reportedly requires aligned mosques to transfer one-third of their incomes to it and pressures non-aligned imams and congregations to join or face mosque closures. Increased official surveillance of mosques has fueled popular resentment and official discrimination, particularly in western Kazakhstan.

Restrictions on Religious Materials

There are few bookshops that in the government's view meet the religion law's strict requirements for selling religious texts. For example, only Hanafi Sunni materials can be sold. Cases against four Council of Churches Baptists in the Akmola Region for "illegally" distributing religious literature were dismissed in April 2014 due to tardy filings. In May 2014, a commercial bookseller in the Atyrau region was fined one month's average wages for the unlicensed selling of Islamic books. Jehovah's Witnesses failed in all their legal challenges of import

in March and April 2014. In a public statement at the end of the visit, he expressed concern "that non-registered religious groups can hardly exercise any collective religious functions in Kazakhstan." He also noted that he had heard "credible stories about police raids... of some non-registered groups, leading to confiscation of literature, computers and other property." In January 2014, Special Rapporteur Bielefeldt and five other UN human rights experts (on the promotion and protection of the right to freedom of opinion and expression; on the rights to freedom of peaceful assembly and of association; on the situation of human rights defenders; on the independence of judges and lawyers; and on minority issues) expressed concern about religious freedom abuses, such as punishments for missionary activity, police raids on religious communities, and bans on religious publications, with a particular focus on Jehovah's Witnesses. Special Rapporteur on Freedom of Assembly and Association Maina Kiai visited the country in January 2015 and noted that, although the right to freedom of association is constitutionally guaranteed, "a web of laws and practices limit the real-world freedom, . . . [including] of religious associations to operate."

U.S. Policy

After the Soviet Union's collapse, the United States was the first country to recognize Kazakhstan's independence, and is now the largest direct foreign investor in Kazakhstan's economy. Key bilateral issues include regional security, including stabilization efforts for Afghanistan, and nuclear nonproliferation. As the site of many Soviet nuclear tests, Kazakhstan plays a leading role in nuclear security; in 1991, President Nazarbayev closed down the Semipalatinsk nuclear test site. The two countries discuss these and other bilateral issues – such as regional cooperation, democratic reform, rule of law, human rights, civil society, economic development, energy, science, technology, and people-to-people contacts – through the U.S.-Kazakh Strategic Partnership Dialogue (SPD), which was set up in 2012. There are working groups on key issues.

The third SPD was held in December 2014, chaired by Kazakhstani Foreign Minister Erlan Idrissov and

three Yemenis and two Tunisians held for more than a decade at the U.S. military prison at Guantanamo Bay were flown to Kazakhstan for resettlement in December 2014, the Pentagon reported.

Recommendations for U.S. Policy

USCIRF recommends that the U.S. government should:

- Urge the Kazakh government to adopt the recommendations of UN Special Rapporteurs on Freedom of Religion or Belief and on Freedom of Association

---

The most common violations . . . that result in fines [include] unlicensed distribution of religious texts . . .

Secretary of State John Kerry. Both sides highlighted cooperation on counterterrorism and peacebuilding. The joint SPD statement noted that the United States welcomed Kazakhstan's hosting in Astana of the 5th Congress of Leaders of World and Traditional Religions in June 2015. The main theme of this Congress – held since 2003 – is the dialogue between political and religious leaders "in the name of development and peace." The statement also took positive note of its creation of a new Consultative and Advisory Body, "Dialogue Platform on Human Dimension," a government-civil society effort to recommend human rights improvements. The joint SPD statement affirmed cooperation on nuclear nonproliferation and security, democracy, and strengthening civil society; no mention was made of religious freedom.

Kazakhstan and the United States also have entered into a five-year plan to strengthen military cooperation through capacity-building programs. Deputy Assistant Secretary of State for South and Central Asia Affairs Dan Rosenblum said in a January 2015 VOA interview that Kazakhstan's government had shown interest in receiving excess U.S. military mine-resistant and armored vehicles. In 2014, Kazakhstan and the United States initialed a draft treaty on mutual legal assistance in criminal matters, which is supposed to be signed in 2015. In a move that may be part of such expanded law enforcement cooperation,

and Assembly issued after their recent visits to Kazakhstan regarding legal reform and change of enforcement policies;

- Call on the Kazakh government to use the Congress of Leaders of World and Traditional Religions to invite a representative array of religious communities peacefully residing within Kazakhstan, including minority religious groups;

- Urge the Kazakh government to agree to visits by the three OSCE Personal Representatives on Tolerance, set a specific date for a joint visit, and provide the full and necessary conditions for such visits;

- Ensure that the Strategic Partnership Dialogue includes discussion of concerns about freedom of religion or belief, and include in public statements and private interactions with the Kazakh government advocacy for the release of religious prisoners;

- Ensure that the U.S. Embassy maintains active contacts with human rights activists and press the Kazakh government to ensure that every prisoner has greater access to his or her family, human rights monitors, adequate medical care, and a lawyer;

- Encourage the Board for Broadcasting Governors to ensure continued U.S. funding for RFE/RL's Uzbek Service website, Muslims and Democracy, and consider translating this material into Kazakh; and

- Use funding allocated to the State Department
  under the Title VIII Program (established in the
  Soviet-Eastern European Research and Training
  Act of 1983) for research, including on human rights
  and religious freedom in former Soviet states, and
  language training.

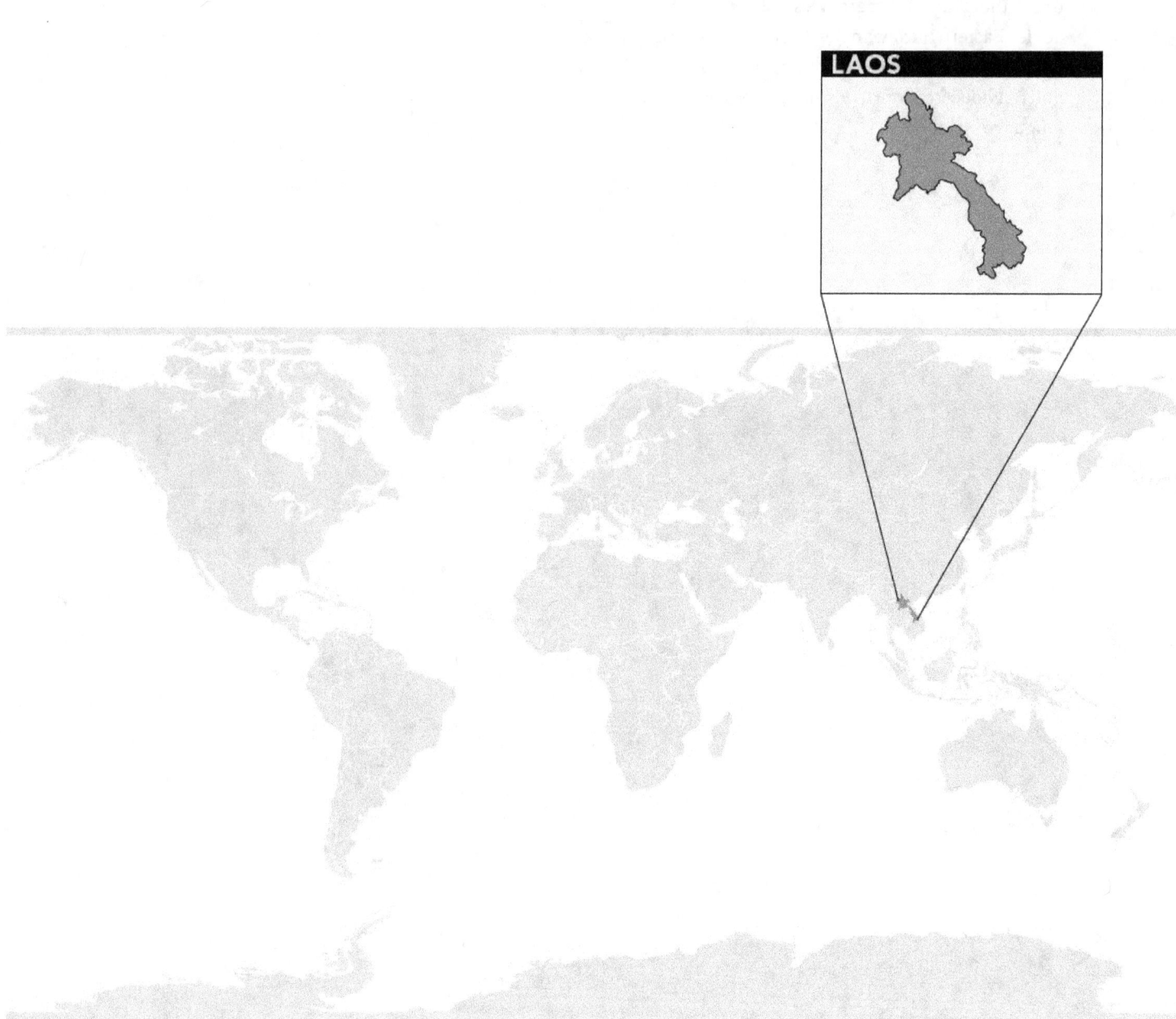

LAOS

Key Findings

The government of the ruling Lao People's Revolutionary Party (LPRP) continued to allow ongoing abuses against religious minority groups, abuses that are most prominent in remote, rural areas. Moreover, the government's suspicion of Protestant Christianity as a "Western" or "American" construct continued to result in discrimination, harassment, and arrests of Christians throughout the country, particularly in Savannakhet Province, where there were several reports of local officials ordering Christians to renounce their faith. The majority Buddhist community experiences religious freedom conditions that are generally free, as do some minority religious communities, such as animists, Baha'is, and Catholics. However, ethnic minorities tend to experience greater incidences of discrimination and harassment on many levels, including religious freedom. Based on these concerns, in 2015 USCIRF again places Laos on Tier 2, where it has been since 2009.

Background

Although the Lao constitution protects freedom of religion or belief, conflicting government decrees and policies routinely result in religious freedoms limitations. More than two-thirds of the population are Buddhists, while Christians are believed to comprise less than two percent. Animism, ancestor worship, and other traditional beliefs are common among ethnic minorities, and there are several other religious minority groups in the country.

A complicated web of government approvals is required for most religious practices and for the construction of houses of worship. The space to practice religion in the country has improved in some ways in recent years, but inconsistently so. Observers have noted reduced numbers of prisoners of conscience. However, some minority religious groups continue to face abuses

for not following the majority Buddhist faith. Overall, the varying and unpredictable application of the law in practice provides little meaningful protection to most religious groups.

Moreover, limitations on freedom of religion or belief take place in a climate where political space is largely limited. Civil society operates in a highly limited environment, and civil society and independent media face continued harassment and arbitrary arrest for exercising their rights to freedom of expression, association, or assembly. The suspicious disappearance of civil society leader Sombath Somphone is emblematic. Sombath, a well-known human rights defender, has not been seen since he disappeared in December 2012 after being stopped and detained by police, and the government has produced no meaningful information about his whereabouts. The government also tightly controls the print and broadcast media and recently increased restrictions on expression on the Internet, with new legislation that criminalizes criticizing the government or ruling party or circulating false information online.

Religious Freedom Conditions 2014–2015
Legal Restrictions on Religious Activities

The protections for freedom of religion or belief found in the Lao constitution are contradicted by the 2002 Decree on Religious Practice, otherwise known as Decree 92. Rather than strengthening and improving protections, particularly for minority religious communities, the Decree permits the government to control and interfere in all religious activities. This includes, for example, registration requirements for all religious groups, limits on proselytizing, and controls on the printing of religious materials. Approval requirements under Decree 92 are burdensome, and some religious groups have been unable to legally register, resulting in numerous challenges.

Abuses against Minorities

Discrimination against religious minority communities, particularly Christians, remains an ongoing problem in many parts of the country. Some of these communities attempt to operate discreetly to avoid harassment and threats from local authorities for not being formally recognized by the government. While suspicion is highest against Christianity, government officials in parts of the country hold a degree of similar mistrust of all non-Buddhist faiths. Detailed information about specific abuses against religious minority communities is often difficult to obtain, but given the Lao government's restrictive controls of information into and out of the country, there is no reason to believe that religious freedom abuses are not occurring.

In 2014, one of the most high-profile acts of discrimination against Lao Christians occurred in the remote village of Saisomboon in Savannakhet Province, where officials are known to be intolerant of minority religious faiths. A recent convert to Christianity was ill, and when she died in June 2014, her family obtained approval from the village chief to hold a Christian funeral. This approval was later revoked, and the family was forced to hold a Buddhist memorial and burial ceremony. Moreover, police arrested the family's pastor and four other Christians for allegedly contributing to the woman's death. In August 2014, the five Christians were found not guilty of murder. Despite their acquittal, all five remained in custody and faced new charges in February 2015, when a provincial court convicted them of practicing medicine without a license in connection with her death. Contrary to the charges, the five Christians deny administering medicine to the woman, stating instead that they prayed by her side. All five subsequently have been imprisoned and fined.

Additionally, in late September 2014, also in Savannakhet Province, a Christian pastor and six parishioners were arrested following a worship service in the pastor's home. Reportedly, local officials in Boukham Village had banned Christian worship gatherings and used the ban to justify arresting the seven Christians. The Christians spent a week in custody before being released.

Also in 2014, the central government banned all celebrations and observances of the Christmas holiday. The move was considered by some to be pointedly directed at ethnic minority Hmong Christians, who have been the target of government harassment for decades.

There also were reports throughout 2014 of Christian families being forced from their homes for refusing to renounce Christianity. Six Christian families left their homes in Savannakhet Province following pressure in their village to convert to Buddhism, and another six Hmong Christian families in Bolikhamxay Province were forcibly evicted for refusing to renounce Christianity and convert to animism.

U.S. Policy

Laos is among the few remaining communist countries in the world and takes many of its cues from neighboring Vietnam, a fellow communist country and close ally. There are multiple channels of cooperation between the two countries, religion among them. Cooperation on religious issues began in 2002 with the signing of a cooperative agreement on religious affairs, and in 2014, Laos and Vietnam re-committed to this arrangement through the year 2020.

Unlike Vietnam and Cambodia, Lao relations with the United States were never completely severed during the Vietnam War, though relations were downgraded and notably strained during this period, particularly after the communist takeover in 1975. The relationship has since improved, but the Lao government's ongoing mistreatment of ethnic Hmong is a source of enduring tensions. Both the Administration and Congress regularly have raised concerns. The Lao government's lasting wariness of the Hmong stems, in part, from their connection to the United States: thousands of ethnic Hmong were trained and armed by the United States and fought to prevent a communist takeover during the Vietnam War. Many since have fled to Thailand where they live in camps and/or face forced repatriation back to Laos. The United States has resettled approximately 250,000 Hmong refugees and continues to encourage Laos to improve transparency about the conditions of those forcibly returned from Thailand and to implement policies and practices to ensure the Hmong community no longer fears mistreatment.

Since restoring full diplomatic relations with Laos in 1992, the United States gradually has expanded its engagement with the country. Bilateral relations are conducted through several mechanisms, including the

U.S.-Laos Comprehensive Bilateral Dialogue and others focusing on specific sectors, such as trade or investment. This engagement has broadened further in recent years through U.S. support of the Lower Mekong Initiative (LMI), a partnership agreement between the United States, Cambodia, Laos, Thailand, Vietnam, and Burma to cooperate in areas such as environment, health, education, and infrastructure development, as well as women's and gender issues.

The United States provides foreign assistance to Laos in a number of key sectors: public health, the environment and climate change, economic growth and trade, and peace and security, including the removal of unexploded ordnance (from the Vietnam War period). For fiscal year 2016, the Department of State, the U.S. Agency for International Development, and related agencies are requesting funds through the following accounts: Development Assistance ($11.1 million); International Narcotics Control and Law Enforcement ($1 million); International Military Education and Training ($450,000); and Foreign Military Financing ($200,000). The requests also include funds for environment-related capacity-building in the LMI countries.

In 2014, the United States officially opened its new Embassy in the capital of Vientiane. The previous Embassy site is being outfitted to house a new American Center.

In 2016, Laos is scheduled to chair the Association of Southeast Asian Nations (ASEAN); the United States is a participant of the ASEAN Regional Forum and the East Asia Summit. Leading up to and during this period of amplified regional and international attention on Laos, the United States is in a position to leverage its influential position to encourage Laos to improve conditions for religious freedom and related human rights.

Recommendations

USCIRF recommends that, in addition to integrating concerns about religious freedom into its bilateral agenda when engaging with central government and provincial Lao authorities, the U.S. government should:

- Initiate a formal human rights mechanism, similar to existing U.S. human rights dialogues with Burma and Vietnam and the European Union's Working Group on Human Rights and Governance with Laos, to address regularly and consistently with the Lao government issues such as ethnic and religious discrimination, torture and other forms of ill-treatment in prisons, unlawful arrests and detentions, and the lack of due process and an independent judiciary;

- Continue to engage the Lao government on specific cases of religious freedom violations, including but not limited to forced evictions and/or forced renunciations relating to the practice of one's faith, and emphasizing the importance of consistent implementation, enforcement, and interpretation of the rule of law by both central government and local officials;

- Support technical assistance programs that reinforce the goals of protecting religious freedom, human rights defenders, and ethnic minorities, including: rule of law programs and legal exchanges that focus on revising Decree 92; training in human rights, the rule of law, and religious freedom and tolerance for Lao police and security forces, religious leaders, local officials, and lawyers and judges; and capacity-building for Lao civil society groups carrying out charitable, medical, and developmental activities;

- Continue to inquire consistently into the whereabouts of Sombath Somphone given that the Lao government's inability to provide any information from its investigation into his disappearance is emblematic of its overall approach to civil society and individual rights;

- Ensure that Lao police and security officials participating in training or technical assistance programs are thoroughly vetted, pursuant to the Leahy Amendment, to confirm that they are not implicated in human rights abuses, and deny U.S. training, visas, or assistance to any unit or personnel found to have engaged in a consistent pattern of violations of human rights, including religious freedom; and

- Encourage the Broadcasting Board of Governors to provide adequate funding for the Voice of America and Radio Free Asia Lao language broadcasts and increase efforts to provide uncensored Internet, and other information, into Laos.

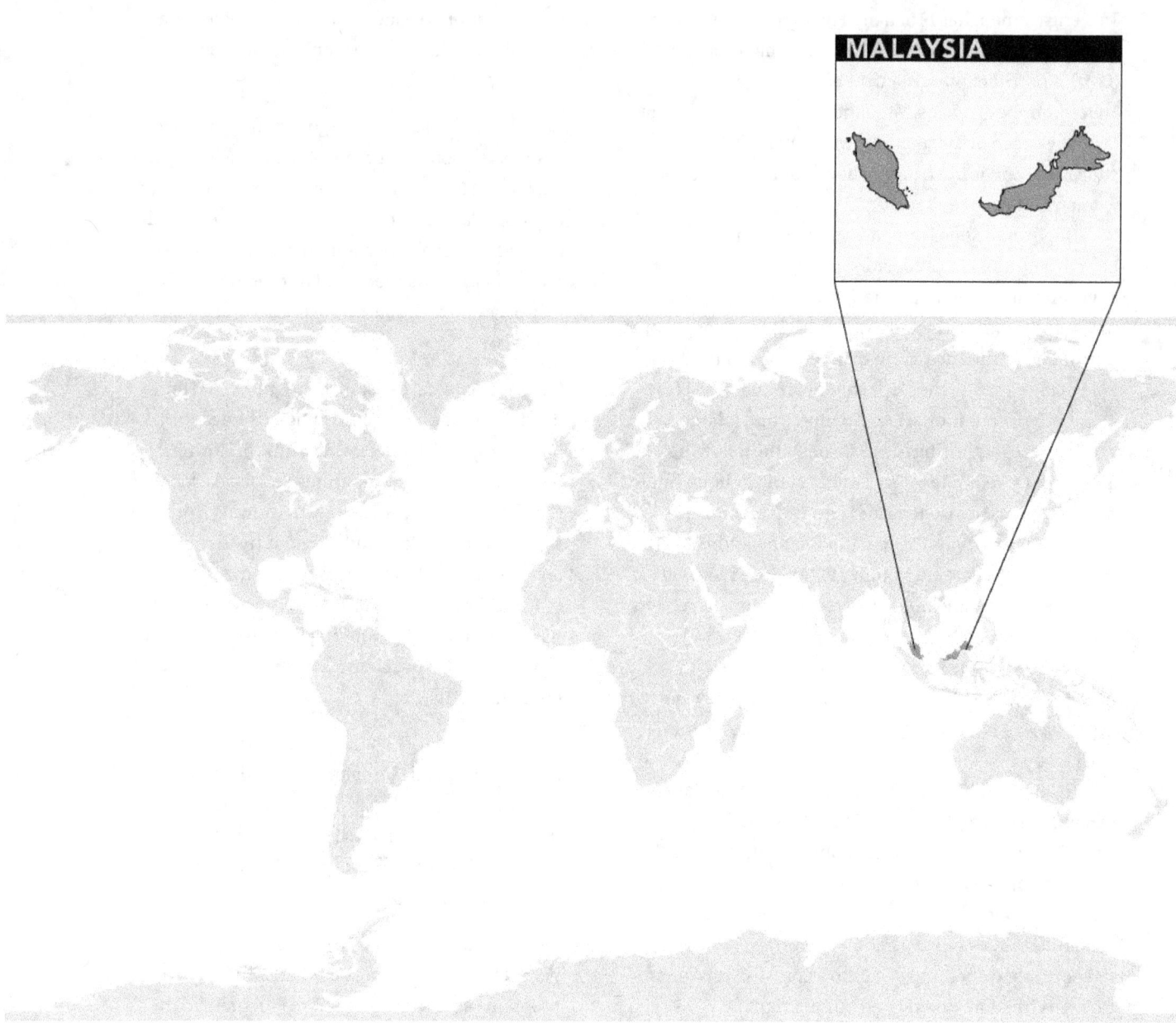

MALAYSIA

Key Findings

In 2014, the government, ruling party, and religious leaders put forth laws, policies, statements, and *fatwas* (religious edicts) broadening the application of Islam and potentially limiting religious freedom. Religious groups deemed "deviant," such as Shi'a, Ahmadiyya, and Baha'i, are banned. Both civil and Shari'ah courts have the power to police religious belief and expression; in 2014 the government sought to expand this power through the establishment of a religious police force and by amending the Sedition Act to restrict speech to prevent perceived insults to Islam. Moreover, the dual system of civil and Shari'ah courts creates legal ambiguity, and Shari'ah court jurisdiction over family and conversion cases places non-Muslims at a disadvantage. A ban on the use of the word "Allah" by a non-Muslim newspaper was upheld in 2014, and non-Muslim religious materials containing that word were confiscated. Collectively, these trends have resulted in diminished legal protections for religious minorities, non-Muslims and non-Sunni Muslims alike. Based on these concerns, in 2015 USCIRF again places Malaysia on Tier 2, where it has been since 2014. USCIRF will continue to monitor closely these troubling trends for religious freedom. Developments will influence how USCIRF will report on Malaysia in next year's annual report and may negatively impact its status.

Background

The intersection of the political sphere with religious- and ethnic-based interests has defined Malaysian politics over the last decade. The opposition Pakatan Rakyat has incrementally chipped away at the grip on power of the ruling Barisan Nasional (BN) coalition, causing both political groups to realign their messages to attract voters. Both coalitions sought to make strategic gains among key voting blocs, including voters who are young and technologically savvy, ethnic Chinese, and/or part of the increasing socially-conscious middle class. The BN government and its component political parties have put forth policies and statements

> *Religious groups deemed "deviant," such as Shi'a, Ahmadiyya, and Baha'i, are banned.*

asserting a more exacting interpretation of Islam that increasingly discriminates against religious and ethnic minorities. National and state-level efforts to address the perceived liberalization of Islam, particularly by non-Muslims and non-Sunni Muslims, have resulted in increased *fatwas* and even stronger appeals among Islamic political parties, both ruling and opposition, to their more conservative base.

In May 2014, Prime Minister Najib Razak warned of the threats posed by "human rightism," including humanism, secularism, liberalism, and human rights. According to Najib, this "new religion" is to be considered "deviant" for straying from the sanctity of Islam; Najib specifically noted that Sunni Islam is the only Islam in Malaysia, a comment directly targeting banned "deviant" sects and religious groups, such as Shi'a, Ahmadiyya, and Baha'i. Such groups continue to face crackdowns; for example, more than 100 Shi'a Muslims, including women and children, were arbitrarily arrested in Perak in March 2014 for attending a religious ceremony. By year's end, 25 prominent figures, including many former public officials, released an open letter calling on leaders to debate the relationship between Islamic law and the constitution.

The commingling of politics, religion, and ethnicity has a negative effect on religious freedom in Malaysia. The Malaysian constitution protects the right to freedom of religion, but also establishes Islam as the religion of the Federation and defines all ethnic Malays as Muslims. The majority of the population, approximately 61 percent, are Muslim. Twenty percent practice Buddhism, nine percent Christianity, six percent Hinduism, and the remainder follow minority religious faiths, such as Confucianism, Taoism, Shi'ism, and the Ahmadi and Baha'i faiths. Civil courts routinely cede jurisdiction to Shari'ah courts over family or conversion cases involving Muslims. Muslims are allowed to proselytize to non-Muslims, but not vice versa. Apostasy, considered a sin by Islamic authorities, has been criminalized in

progressed with its controversial proposal to establish a formal religious police force at both JAKIM and state-level religious departments. The new personnel will have authority to enforce Islamic laws against Muslims only. The move is the latest in a series of steps in recent years to expand JAKIM's powers.

Malaysia's vaguely-worded Sedition Act is frequently used as a means to suppress political and religious dissent. In November 2014, Prime Minister Najib announced that the government would strengthen the law to cover any insults to Islam; the amendments are expected in the spring of 2015. Approximately 40 people were investigated or charged under the Act in 2014, including civil society activists, religious leaders, politicians, journalists, and academics. Among them was human rights lawyer Erik Paulsen, who in February 2015 was charged with sedition for criticizing

> *Apostasy, considered a sin by Islamic authorities,has been criminalized in some states as a capital offense.*

some states as a capital offense. Those considered to have strayed from Sunni Islam, including individuals from "deviant" sects or those who seek to convert from Islam, can be forced into "rehabilitation" centers by the government or state-level Shari'ah courts, and/or face fines or prison sentences.

The role of the federal Department of Islamic Development Malaysia (JAKIM) in advancing Islamic affairs includes the authority to establish policies, monitor religious groups, and set guidelines for and maintain the official list of banned sects. In order to operate legally and be eligible for government funding, religious organizations and groups must register with the Home Ministry.

Religious Freedom Conditions 2014-2015
Policing Belief and Expression

In addition to the aforementioned restrictions on apostasy and proselytization, both civil and Shari'ah courts in Malaysia have the power to punish blasphemy and religious insult. In 2014, the prime minister's office

JAKIM for promoting extremism. Critics of the Act have noted that its use is one-sided. For example, in October 2014, the government refused to bring sedition charges against Ibrahim Ali, a former member of parliament and the founder and head of Perkasa, a Muslim rights group closely tied to BN. In 2013, Ibrahim had called for Bibles to be burned and has also said that the use of the word "Allah" in the Bible is a religious provocation against Muslims.

Ban on the Use of the Word "Allah"

The legal battle over the use of the word "Allah" by non-Muslims continued in 2014, with supporters of the ban asserting that Allah is exclusive to Islam. In June 2014, the Federal Court sided with the 2013 Court of Appeals decision that upheld a ban on the use of the word Allah by the Malay-language edition of *The Herald*, a weekly newspaper published by the Catholic Church in Malaysia. Soon thereafter, the central government issued a statement confirming that the court's decision only applied to *The Herald* newspaper. Nevertheless, concerns remain that the ban could still be applied to Bibles and other materials, and lawyers have noted that clarifying statements from the government have no legal effect. Pursuant to an appeals request from the Catholic Church, the Federal Court in January 2015 determined that an additional review of its June 2014 decision was not merited.

Confiscation of Bibles

The years-long debate over the use of the word Allah has coincided with the confiscation of tens of thousands of Bibles across the country. For example, in

tions undermine the ability of civil courts to effectively and consistently implement rulings. For example, those seeking to convert from Islam to another faith must apply through the Shari'ah court system and await the court's approval of their application. Both civil courts and Shari'ah courts can take jurisdiction in child custody battles in which one parent is Muslim and the other non-Muslim, with the possibility of conflicting judgments. Non-Muslims have no standing in Shari'ah courts, creating an inherent disadvantage. In two separate high-profile cases, two husbands who converted to Islam after marriage abducted and converted their

---

Malaysia's vaguely-worded Sedition Act is frequently used as a means to suppress political and religious dissent. . . . Approximately 40 people were investigated or charged under the Act in 2014, including civil society activists, religious leaders, politicians, journalists, and academics.

January 2014, the Selangor Islamic Department (JAIS) confiscated more than 300 Malay-language Bibles containing the word Allah from the Selangor office of the Bible Society of Malaysia. Within days of the Federal Court's June 2014 decision confirming the ban, the Attorney General determined that the seizure was not appropriate and the Bibles should be returned. However, the Selangor Islamic Religious Council (MAIS) refused to do so until November 2014 and only after surreptitiously stamping each Bible with a warning that they were prohibited from use by Muslims anywhere in the country and prohibited from use by anyone, including Christians, in the state of Selangor. In December 2014, police in Johor confiscated 31 hymnals containing the word Allah from a Catholic priest, and later questioned the priest for allegedly causing disharmony or ill-will on religious grounds.

Impact of Dual Court System

The rise of Islamic law and the Shari'ah court system in Malaysia has created legal ambiguity for Muslims and non-Muslims alike. The dual court system of Shari'ah courts and civil courts has resulted in a complicated, overlapping web of jurisdictions. These dueling jurisdic-

respective children. Although higher courts in the civil system granted custody to the non-Muslim mothers, both husbands have failed to return the children to their mothers, and police and other authorities thus far have refused to act on the court orders.

U.S. Policy

The United States and Malaysia have benefitted from a deepening relationship in recent years, with an eye toward longer-term bilateral and regional goals. In April 2014, President Barack Obama and Prime Minister Najib Razak entered into a Comprehensive Partnership, which was formally announced during President Obama's state visit to Malaysia, the first such visit by a U.S. president in nearly 50 years. The Partnership is aimed at strengthening bilateral cooperation on key issues, including trade and investment, education, and security and defense.

The two countries are also part of the 12-nation negotiations of the Trans-Pacific Partnership (TPP), a regional free trade agreement. While the TPP talks are ongoing, the Obama Administration and some in Congress are concurrently pursuing the renewal of Trade Promotion Authority (TPA), which could grant the president greater flexibility when negotiating and approving trade agreements such as the TPP. Others in Congress have raised concerns over some TPP com-

a non-permanent member of the UN Security Council. President Obama is expected to visit Malaysia in November 2015 for ASEAN and East Asia Summit meet-

---

The rise of Islamic law and the Shari'ah court system in Malaysia has created legal ambiguity for Muslims and non-Muslims alike. The dual court system of Shari'ah courts and civil courts has resulted in a complicated, overlapping web of jurisdictions.

---

ponents, including agriculture, automotive markets, worker rights, environmental protections, and human rights, among others, which are likely to be heavily debated during consideration of TPA. Congressional deliberation of both TPP and TPA provide crucial opportunities for robust dialogue about human rights concerns in a number of countries, Malaysia among them.

Malaysia is known for its efforts to prevent radicalism and violent extremism from taking root within its borders, particularly with respect to ISIL (the Islamic State of Iraq and the Levant), and is often praised for its moderation and pluralism. However, human rights advocates note that a moderate, pluralist approach is not applied when it comes to the tolerance of religious and ethnic minorities among its own people. Critics also point out that by expanding the Sedition Act and by allowing the conviction against Malaysian opposition leader Anwar Ibrahim to stand, Prime Minister Najib has eroded his country's reputation as moderate and tolerant. The BN-led government has a long history of politically targeting Anwar. Having already spent several years in prison following a conviction on charges of corruption and sodomy, Anwar is currently serving a five-year prison term following the court's February 2015 decision to uphold an earlier sentence; he will be banned from elected office for an additional five years thereafter. Indeed, in February 2015, a spokesperson for the National Security Council expressed the United States' disappointment with Anwar's conviction, noting specific concerns with rule of law and judicial fairness.

Beginning January 1, 2015, Malaysia began its one-year term as chair of the Association of Southeast Asian Nations (ASEAN), as well as its two-year term as

ings, and other high-level U.S. government delegations will visit throughout the year. The United States should take advantage of these bilateral and multilateral opportunities to initiate serious conversations with Malaysian leaders about the disturbing trends in religious freedom conditions in that country.

Recommendations

Restrictions of freedom of religion affecting non-Muslim and non-Sunni Muslim religious minorities are central to Malaysia's mounting human rights challenges. As such, any visit by Prime Minister Najib to Washington, DC, in 2015 should prominently feature discussions about improving religious freedom and related human rights in Malaysia. In addition, USCIRF recommends that the U.S. government should:

- Raise concerns regarding the conflation of religion and politics and the increasing limitation on rights for religious and ethnic minorities in the lead-up to and during the visits of President Obama and Secretary Kerry to Malaysia related to ASEAN and other high-level gatherings;

- Ensure that human rights and religious freedom are pursued consistently and publicly at every level of the U.S.-Malaysia relationship, including in the Comprehensive Partnership and other discussions relating to military, trade, or economic and security assistance, such as Malaysia's participation in the Trans-Pacific Partnership, as well as in programs that address freedom of speech and expression and civil society development, among others;

- Press the Malaysian government to bring all laws and policies into conformity with international commitments, especially with respect to freedom of religion or belief and freedom of religious expression, including the rights to use the word "Allah," and to possess religious materials;

- Urge the Malaysian government to cease the arrest, detention, or forced "rehabilitation" of individuals involved in peaceful religious activity, such as Shi'a, Ahmadi, and Al-Arqam groups, among others; and

- Encourage Malaysian elected leaders to address the human rights shortcomings of the parallel civil-Shari'ah justice systems, in order to guarantee that all Malaysians, regardless of ethnicity or religion, enjoy freedom of religion or belief.

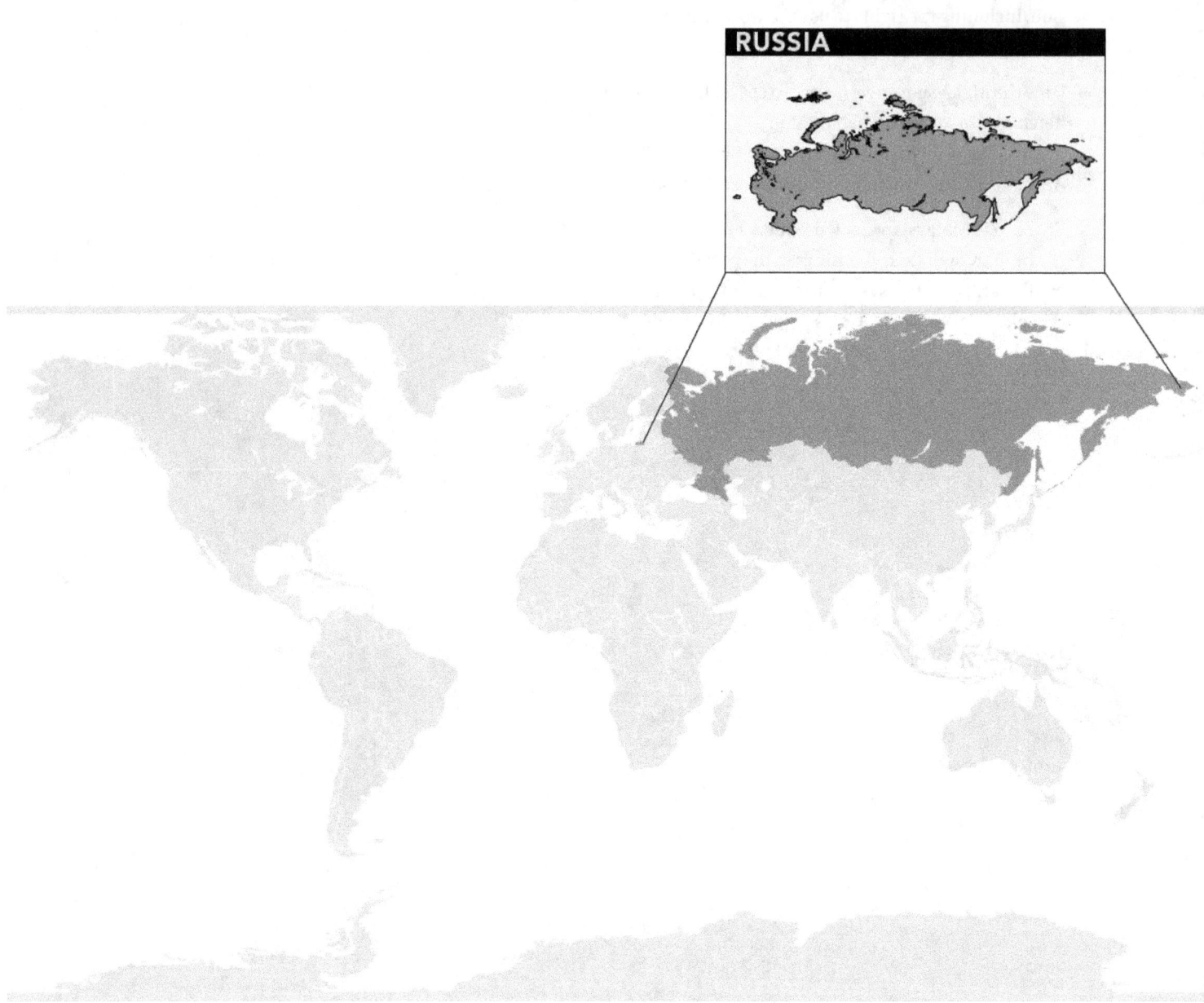

RUSSIA

RUSSIA

Key Findings

Amid a sharp increase in human rights abuses, serious violations of freedom of religion or belief continue in Russia. The government continues to bring criminal extremism charges against peaceful religious individuals and groups, particularly Muslim readers of Turkish theologian Said Nursi and Jehovah's Witnesses. Hundreds of Muslims are jailed, reportedly on false charges; many are denied due process and mistreated in detention. Increased legal restrictions on civil society have negative implications for religious groups. Rising xenophobia and intolerance, including anti-Semitism, are linked to violent and lethal hate crimes that often occur with impunity. Religious freedom violations are pervasive in the North Caucasus. There are growing religious freedom concerns in Russian-occupied Crimea and Russian-separatist regions of eastern Ukraine. For these reasons, in 2015 USCIRF again places Russia on Tier 2, where it has been since 2009.

Background

In 1991 the Russian Federation, the core of the former USSR, became the Soviet Union's sole legal successor. Russia is the world's largest country in terms of land

St. Petersburg and Siberia. Religious groups of under 5 percent each include Buddhists, Protestants, Roman Catholics, Jews, The Church of Jesus Christ of Latter-day Saints (Mormons), Jehovah's Witnesses, Hindus, Baha'is, Hare Krishnas, pagans, Tengrists, Scientologists, and Falun Gong adherents. While the 2010 census estimated there are 150,000 Jews, the Federation of Jewish Communities of Russia cites 750,000.

Russia's 1997 religion law sets onerous registration procedures and empowers state officials to impede registration or obstruct the construction or rental of worship buildings. Russia's weak and arbitrary legal system means that government respect for freedom of religion or belief varies widely, often depending on a religious group's relations with local officials. The religion law's preface, which is not legally binding, singles out Islam, Judaism, Buddhism, and Orthodox Christianity as the country's four "traditional" faiths. The Russian constitution guarantees a secular state and equal legal status for all religions. Yet the Moscow Patriarchate of the Russian Orthodox Church (MPROC) – which claims 60 percent of Russians as adherents – is especially favored; it has agreements with various state agencies and receives the most state subsidies of any

> *The 1997 [religion] law sets onerous registration procedures and empowers state officials to impede registration or obstruct the construction or rental of worship buildings.*

mass, with a population of 142.5 million. It is 81 percent ethnic Russian, with 160 various other ethnicities. A 2012 poll by the independent Levada Center reports 74 percent of Russians view themselves as Orthodox while 7 percent identify as Muslim. Most Muslims live in the Volga region, the North Caucasus, in Moscow,

religious group. "Non-traditional" religious groups do not receive state subsidies. Officials often refer negatively to religious and other minorities, abetting an intolerant climate.

The major threat to religious freedom remains the much-amended Russian anti-extremism law, which defines extremism in a religious context and does not require the threat or use of violence. If any Russian court rules any print or Web-based text extremist, it is added to the Justice Ministry's Federal List of Extremist Materials and banned throughout Russia; as of February 2015, that list totaled 2,634 items, including Jehovah's Witnesses' texts, writings of Turkish theologian

Religious Freedom Conditions 2014–2015

Possible New Legal Restrictions on Religious Groups

Although the 2012 "foreign agents" law exempts religious groups, in May 2014, President Vladimir Putin requested a new bill to increase scrutiny of foreign-funded religious groups. After the reporting

The major threat to religious freedom remains the much-amended Russian anti-extremism law, which defines extremism in a religious context and does not require the threat or use of violence.

Said Nursi, and a video of police-confiscated relics of the Russian Orthodox Autonomous Church. Possession of banned material can lead to fines; distribution, preparation, or storage of large amounts of these materials can result in a four-year prison term. February 2014 criminal code amendments increased the jail or forced labor terms for "extremism"-related offenses and eased surveillance criteria.

A 2013 blasphemy law sets fines of up to U.S. $15,000 and jail terms of up to three years for public actions in places of worship that disrespect or insult religious beliefs. Outside of houses of worship, such acts entail up to a year of jail and fines of up to U.S. $9,000. A 2012 public protest in Moscow's main Orthodox cathedral over the MPROC's close Kremlin ties served as the official impetus for the passage of this law. Increasing legal restrictions on civil society also impact religious groups. A 2012 law on "unauthorized" public meetings, with onerous fines, was used against a Protestant pastor for holding a religious service. Another 2012 law requires foreign-funded NGOs engaged in vaguely-defined political activity to register as "foreign agents" or face fines or two years' imprisonment. The treason law was amended in 2012, threatening with 20-year prison terms those Russian citizens who provide financial, material, technical, consultative, or other help to a foreign state or an international or foreign organization. In a statement likely meant to stoke Russian fears of Germans, the Kaluga governor in January 2015 compared the local registered Lutheran Church to an enemy element.

period there were reports that the Justice Ministry was drafting a bill that would authorize the state to request documents on religious activities and subject religious groups to unannounced inspections.

In January 2015, the Russian parliament approved on the first reading a draft law that would allow the government to identify and ban "undesirable" foreign and international organizations, including religious ones. In addition, President Putin recently called for a new agency to supervise inter-ethnic and inter-religious relations by increasing control over all religious groups, ensuring a uniform policy, and increasing religious leaders' responsibilities. It is unclear how this new agency's mandate would differ from that of the Ministry of Justice's 2009 Religious Expert Council, which underwent major personnel changes in March 2015.

Extremism Charges

Surveillance, investigations, and prosecutions of Muslims and Jehovah's Witnesses for alleged extremism continued during 2014, although many cases apparently were not linked to such activities. For example, a Yekaterinburg court upheld in 2014 a fine against a mosque for owning banned texts; its imam was warned against "extremist" activity. In addition, in late 2014, six Muslims in Perm and a Muslim in Rostov-on-Don were fined, in two separate cases, as alleged Nursi followers. Protracted "extremism" cases against alleged leaders of a Nursi women's group in Krasnoyarsk and against 16 members of the banned Jehovah's Witness community in Taganrog were repeatedly postponed. The

Russian Supreme Court in November 2014 confirmed the liquidation of the Jehovah's Witness community in Samara and one month later, it banned as "extremist" the Jehovah's Witness international Web site. Even before a court verdict, charges of extremism often

In June 2014, the ECtHR found against Russia in two cases involving a Jehovah's Witness and a Pentecostal, ruling that lack of registration status should not result in banning a religious group. The ECtHR requested Russia to bring its religion law into line with

Surveillance, investigations, and prosecutions of Muslims and Jehovah's Witnesses for alleged extremism continued . . .

involve house arrest, travel restrictions, and lengthy pre-trial detention.

In February 2015, after the reporting period, Bagir Kazikhanov, a Muslim from Ulyanovsk, was sentenced to a 3.5-year prison term for the "organization of extremist activity" in the first known conviction under the recently-increased penalties, according to the NGO Forum 18 News Service. Also after the reporting period, the Orenburg Regional Court in February 2015 overturned a lower court's 2012 ban of 50 of 65 Muslim religious texts. The lower court's ban gave rise to protests and numerous Muslims were fined for distributing these texts. In the last four months of 2014, many such texts were cited in charges in at least 18 administrative cases in 14 Russian regions brought against individuals or groups for owning "extremist" religious texts.

Legal Status Issues

Despite a 2009 European Court of Human Rights (ECtHR) finding that the 15-year existence rule for registration violated the European Convention on Human Rights, the Church of Scientology still is denied registration, as is an Armenian Catholic parish in Moscow. State officials obstruct construction or rental of worship buildings, particularly for allegedly "non-traditional" groups such as the Church of Jesus Christ of Latter-day Saints (Mormons), non-Moscow Patriarchate Orthodox, the Hare Krishna and Old Believers. Muslim groups in many urban areas, including in Moscow, encounter obstacles in obtaining permits to open mosques. In Kaliningrad, Muslims and Jews face official opposition to the construction or return of houses of worship.

international obligations and domestic case-law. As of late 2014, the Duma was considering religion law amendments which would end the 15-year registration waiting period, but problematically for the first time would also require registration of all small religious groups as well as large organizations.

Penalties for Public Religious Activities

In 2014, there were 23 known cases of fines for holding public religious activities without prior state permission, mostly against Jehovah's Witnesses and some Protestants, Forum 18 reported. In Sochi, a Protestant leader is appealing a fine for praying in a rented café; a Baptist preacher in Smolensk will appeal his fine for handing out religious texts in a public park, while a Baptist in Orel was fined for hymn singing in a public playground.

Violent Hate Crimes against Persons and Property

Chauvinist groups have stepped up violence against defenders of religious minorities and migrants, especially in Moscow and St. Petersburg. Moscow police have assisted some victims, but inconsistently and often ineffectively. Local officials often fail to investigate hate crimes against ethnic and religious minorities, mainly Muslim Central Asians and Jews. As of September 2014, fourteen have died and 77 been injured in hate crimes in 14 regions of Russia, according to the Russian NGO the SOVA Center for Information and Analysis; 31 received at least 13 sentences in 11 regions for racist violence. Moreover, 31 religious sites in 21 Russian regions had been vandalized as of September 2014, according to SOVA.

Violations in the North Caucasus

Human rights violators operate with almost total impunity in the North Caucasus. In Dagestan, its most violent region, alleged members of Salafi groups are banned, targeted and sentenced as suspected insurgents. Lawyers and religious rights activists are also the targets of violence in Dagestan. In one recent incident, defense lawyer and member of the "Memorial" Human Rights Center, Murad Magomedov, was brutally beaten in February 2015, the independent Russian news agency Caucasus Knot reported.

Chechnya's Kremlin-appointed president, Ramzan Kadyrov, oversees mass violations of human rights, including religious freedom. He and his militia practice collective "justice," distort Chechen Sufi traditions, and run a repressive state, including forcing women to wear Islamic headscarves. Kadyrov also is accused of murders, torture, and disappearances of critics and human

2014, the Spiritual Administration of Muslims of Crimea (the Muftiate), called on the Russian-installed local government to investigate disappearances and other crimes and prosecute perpetrators. In June 2014, a Molotov cocktail was thrown at the Chukurcha Jami mosque in Simferopol; no one was arrested. Two weeks after he took part in a peaceful protest, the corpse of Crimean Tatar activist, Reshat Ametov, was found in March 2014; no one has been held responsible.

After its takeover, Russia required that all religious communities in Crimea that had been registered with the Ukrainian state (some 1,500 groups) must register under Russia's more stringent requirements by January 2015. This deadline was later extended to January 2016. Large groups that function throughout Crimea must register with the Russian federal government, while local groups must register with local Russian authorities in Crimea. A Jewish group in Yalta has registered under

> *Chechnya's Kremlin-appointed president, Ramzan Kadyrov, oversees mass violations of human rights, including religious freedom. He and his militia practice collective "justice," distort Chechen Sufi traditions, and run a repressive state, including forcing women to wear Islamic headscarves.*

rights activists in Russia and abroad. In January 2015, Kadyrov presided over a protest by some 800,000 Chechens against the *Charlie Hebdo* cartoons; he publicly accused Western powers of being behind these cartoons to assist ISIL's recruiting.

Russia's Illegal Annexation of Crimea

In March 2014, Russia illegally annexed the Ukrainian Black Sea peninsula of Crimea, which has some two million people and a key Russian naval port. President Putin sought to justify this invasion as due to the shared Orthodox "culture, civilization, and human values" of Russia and Ukraine. The MPROC claims some 35 million followers or almost 70 percent of all Orthodox Christians throughout Ukraine, mostly in its central, eastern and southern regions. Almost all of the 300,000 Muslim Crimean Tatars, however, oppose Russian occupation and have been subject to particular persecution. In June

the new Russian rules, but 150 registration applications are still under consideration after initial rejection, Forum 18 reported. As of the end of the reporting period, only two centralized religious organizations (one Orthodox diocese and the Muftiate) and 12 local communities have been registered – about one percent of those that had Ukrainian registration. In March 2015, the Russian-installed vice prime minister of Crimea said that the 330 mosques in Crimea will be supervised by a single Muslim Spiritual Directorate. He claimed that this will prevent Muslim radical groups from trying to gain control of new mosques.

By late 2014, clergy without Russian citizenship were forced to leave Crimea, particularly Greek and Roman Catholics and Kiev Patriarchate Orthodox. Russia's Federal Migration Service is not extending residence permits for foreigners working for Crimean religious groups. Almost all Turkish Muslim imams and religious teachers were ordered to leave, ending a 20-year program. The Federal Migration Service in Crimea told Forum 18 that only registered religious groups can invite foreigners to work in the region. Ukrainian Catholic priests who are not Crimea natives can work for only three months before they must leave for a month and re-apply. Five of ten Kiev Patriarchate

Committee formed a working group to produce a new draft religion law by April 15, 2015.

Russia's Separatists In the Donbas

In those Donbas regions of eastern Ukraine controlled by Russian-backed separatists, Protestant and Kievan Patriarchate communities are the targets of violence, church damage, property confiscations, and

> *President Putin sought to justify [the Crimea] invasion as due to the shared Orthodox "culture, civilization, and human values" of Russia and Ukraine.*

priests were forced to leave Crimea. In June 2014, the leader of the Salvation Army in Crimea fled the region, as did Reform Rabbi Mikhail Kapustin of Simferopol in March 2014, after he denounced Russian actions and his synagogue was defaced. In April 2014, vandals defaced Sevastopol's monument to 4,200 Jews killed by Nazis. The Kiev Patriarchate's Crimea diocese, with about 200,000 members, has seen mob and arson attacks on its churches. The MPROC in Ukraine officially views other Orthodox churches, particularly the strongly pro-Ukraine Kiev Patriarchate, as "schismatic nationalist organizations."

Russian criminal and administrative codes now apply in Crimea. In October 2014, Crimea's Russian-installed acting Prime Minister Sergei Aksyonov issued a moratorium on raids, searches and literature confiscations until January 1, 2015. Previously, Russian-installed officials had raided many libraries, schools, Muslim homes, mosques and *madrassas*, and Jehovah's Witness Kingdom Halls, and issued fines for possession of Islamic and Jehovah's Witness texts, Forum 18 noted. During the moratorium, fewer raids and confiscation of religious texts were reported.

On October 15, 2014, acting Prime Minister Aksyonov presented a draft law "on freedom of conscience, religious associations as well as on prevention of religious extremism." The bill would limit missionary activity and restrict production of religious texts to registered religious groups. However, Crimea's Supreme Council rejected the draft law and its Culture

discrimination. For example, eight Ukrainian Orthodox churches in the Luhansk region were damaged and in separate incidents, a Protestant orphanage was raided and a rehabilitation center seized. A 4000-man pro-Russian armed group known as the Russian Orthodox Army (ROA) (once headed by a former Russian military intelligence officer) reportedly has been involved in such actions. In July 2014, the ROA reportedly held hostage for ten days Greek Catholic priest Father Tikhon Kulbaka. In May 2014, Russian-backed militants reportedly held captive for a day Roman Catholic priest Father Pawel Vitka. In June 2014, Russian militants reportedly tortured to death two Protestant pastors in Sloviansk. A Russian Orthodox philanthropist, Konstantin Malofeev, funds a Moscow-based charity that allegedly supports armed Donbas rebels. In July 2014, the Ukrainian government investigated Malofeev on these allegations; the United States and the European Union have sanctioned him.

U.S. Policy

In a key foreign policy initiative, President Obama sought to "reset" U.S.-Russia relations in 2010 to reverse what he called a "dangerous drift" in bilateral relations by engaging the Russian government on common foreign policy goals and by engaging directly with Russian civil society groups. The reset goals included promoting economic interests, enhancing mutual understanding, and advancing universal values. Arms control and foreign policy concerns took priority, but 16 working groups in a new U.S.-Russia Bilateral Commission also addressed civil society issues.

U.S.-Russian relations began to decline in September 2011, when then-Prime Minister Putin announced he would again run for the presidency in March 2012. The day before Putin's March 2012 inauguration, tens of thousands took to the Moscow streets; over 1,000 protestors were detained after clashes between the Moscow police and protestors. In October 2012, the Kremlin expelled the U.S. Agency for International Development and banned its Russia programs.

In December 2012, the U.S. Congress normalized trade with Russia by repealing the Jackson-Vanik Amendment, but also passed the Magnitsky Act sanctioning Russian officials responsible for gross human rights violations, including the 2009 death of lawyer Sergei Magnitsky in a Moscow prison; President Obama signed the Act later that month. In response, the Russian government denied Americans the opportunity to adopt Russian children, issued a list of U.S. officials prohibited from entering Russia, and posthumously convicted Magnitsky. In April 2013, the White House made public the names of 18 Russians sanctioned under the Magnitsky Act for egregious human rights abuses, particularly Magnitsky's death. There is also an unpublished list of sanctioned officials, reportedly including Ramzan Kadyrov, as USCIRF had recommended. Since then the U.S. State Department has continued to add relevant Russian officials to the Magnitsky list for U.S. visa bans and asset freezes.

The Russian annexation of Crimea in March 2014 marked a new low in Russia's foreign relations,

The United States has issued numerous sanctions against Russia, including banning various bilateral commercial transactions. It also has imposed sanctions against specific Russian officials and their proxies involved in the Crimean annexation and military support for separatists in the Donbas region of eastern Ukraine.

Recommendations

USCIRF recommends that the U.S. government should:

- Urge the Russian government to reform its extremism law to comply with international human rights standards, including by adding criteria related to the advocacy or use of violence, and to ensure that the law is not used against members of peaceful religious groups or disfavored communities;

- Press the Russian government to ensure that new laws, such as the expansion of the foreign agents law, do not limit the religious activities of peaceful religious communities; also encourage the Russian government to implement ECtHR decisions relating to religious freedom;

- Under the Magnitsky Act, continue to identify Russian government officials responsible for severe violations of religious freedom and human rights, freeze those individuals' assets, and bar their entry into the United States;

- Raise religious freedom concerns in multilateral settings, such as the OSCE, and urge the Russian

The Russian annexation of Crimea in March 2014 marked a new low in Russia's foreign relations, including with the United States.

including with the United States. The United States suspended its role in the U.S.-Russia Bilateral Commission, but the White House invited Russian Federal Security Bureau director Aleksandr Bortnikov to a February 2014 summit on countering violent extremism.

government to agree to visits by the UN Special Rapporteur on Freedom of Religion or Belief and the OSCE Representatives on Tolerance, set specific visit dates, and provide the full and necessary conditions for such visits;

- Call for the release of religious prisoners and ensure that the U.S. Embassy maintains appropriate contacts with human rights activists; press the Russian government to ensure that every prisoner has regular access to his or her family, human rights monitors, adequate medical care, and a lawyer;

- Encourage the Board of Broadcasting Governors to increase U.S. funding for the Voice of America's Russian and Ukrainian Services as well as for RFE/RL's Russian and Ukrainian Services and consider translating into Russian the RFE/RL Uzbek Web site, Muslims and Democracy;

- Use funding allocated to the State Department under the Title VIII Program (established in the Soviet-Eastern European Research and Training Act of 1983) for research, including on human rights and religious freedom in former Soviet states, and language training; and

- Regarding Russia's illegal military occupation of Crimea and its support of rebels in the Donbas, ensure that violations of freedom of religion or belief and related human rights are part of multilateral or bilateral discussions with the Russian government, and continue to work closely with European and other allies to apply pressure through advocacy, diplomacy, and targeted sanctions.

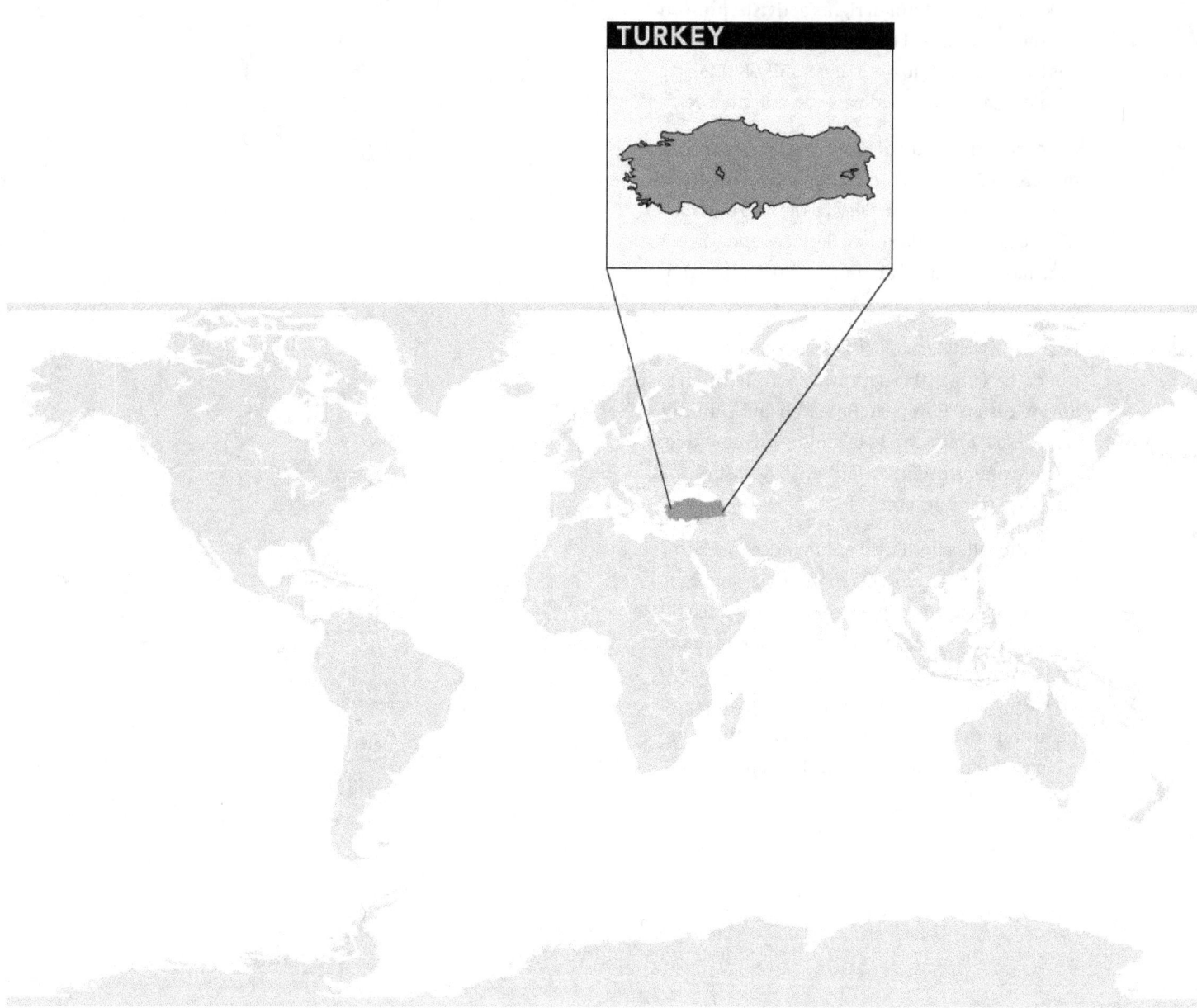

TURKEY

Key Findings

Turkish secularism historically has been particularly detrimental to the smallest religious minority communities and their ability to perpetuate their faiths. Per the 1982 constitution, the state has pervasive control over religion and denies full legal status to all religious communities. Other concerns exist, including the listing of religious affiliation on national identity cards, societal discrimination, anti-Semitism, and religious freedom violations in the Turkish-occupied northern part of Cyprus. In addition, the overall landscape for democracy and human rights has deteriorated significantly in the last two years, with troubling implications for freedom of religion or belief in Turkey. For these reasons USCIRF again places Turkey on Tier 2 in 2015.

Background

Turkey's 1982 constitution provides for freedom of belief, worship, and the private dissemination of religious ideas and prohibits discrimination on religious grounds. The Turkish constitution is based on the French model of *laïcité*, which requires the absence of religion in public life and in government. Therefore,

state control through the *Diyanet* (the Presidency of Religious Affairs) and all other faiths are subject to state control through the *Vakiflar* (the General Directorate for Foundations). Additionally, the 1923 Treaty of Lausanne, a peace treaty between Turkish military forces and several European powers, contains specific guarantees and protections for Greek and Armenian Orthodox and Jewish communities that are not afforded to other minority groups. Turkey's non-Muslim religious minority communities are small, comprising less than 1 percent of the country's current population, but are diverse and are historically and culturally significant.

Following his 2011 re-election as Prime Minister and his August 2014 election as President, Recep Tayyip Erdoğan pledged to revise the constitution. A parliamentary constitution drafting commission established after the 2011 election disbanded over disagreements unrelated to religious freedom, and since August 2014 no new actions to revise the constitution have been implemented. Nevertheless, despite the significant constitutional impediments to full religious freedom protections, the Turkish government has shown that improvements on property rights and

> *[N]o religious community, including the Sunni Muslim majority, has full legal status and all are subject to state control that limits all groups' rights to own and maintain places of worship, train clergy, and offer religious education.*

no religious community, including the Sunni Muslim majority, has full legal status and all are subject to state control that limits all groups' rights to own and maintain places of worship, train clergy, and offer religious education. Turkish policies subject Islam to

religious dress are possible without a new constitution when sufficient political will is present. This will, however, remains lacking on other issues, such as the long-promised reopening of the Greek Orthodox Halki Seminary, which has been closed since 1971.

Religious Freedom Conditions 2014–2015

Interference in Internal Religious Affairs

The Turkish government continues to require that only Turkish citizens can be members of the Greek Orthodox Church's Holy Synod. Although the Prime Minister in 2010 approved dual citizenship for 25 Metropolitans, others were denied. The government's role in deciding which individuals may be part of the Greek Orthodox Patriarchate represents interference in its internal affairs. The government also has interfered in the selection process of the Armenian Patriarchate's leadership. Generally, Turkey denies religious minority communities the ability to train clergy in the country. The Greek Orthodox Theological School of Halki remains closed, as it has been since 1971, despite promises and public

There have been some positive developments in the last year. In February 2014, 425,000 square feet of land in Istanbul was returned to the Holy Savior Armenian Hospital Foundation. In January 2015 the Turkish government approved the construction of a new Syriac Christian church in Yeşilköy district of Istanbul – the first such approval since the founding of the Turkish Republic in 1923. As USCIRF heard from Syriac religious leaders during a February 2014 trip to Turkey, the one existing Syriac church in Istanbul is not sufficient for the 18,000 Syriac Christians living there.

Additionally, in the last year the Turkish government has increased financial subsidies to minority religious communities to help pay utility bills, including electricity and water. According to the Turkish government,

The Greek Orthodox Theological School of Halki remains closed, as it has been since 1971, despite promises and public statements of support for its reopening by President Erdoğan and former President Gül.

statements of support for its reopening by President Erdoğan and former President Gül. The Armenian Orthodox community also lacks a seminary, however, there are 16 Armenian Orthodox parish schools.

Religious Minority Properties

The Turkish government throughout its history has expropriated religious minority properties. Beginning in 2003 and especially since the issuance of a 2011 decree, the government established a process to return some properties or pay compensation when return is not possible. The Turkish government reports that since 2003, more than 1,000 properties – valued, at more than 2.5 billion Turkish Lira (1 billion U.S. Dollars) – have been returned or compensated for. Hundreds more applications are still being processed. Nearly 1,000 applications reportedly were denied due to lack of proof of ownership or for other reasons. For example, the Turkish government reports that some applications are duplicates because different religious communities are claiming the same property. However, some communities allege bias, consider the process very slow, and claim that compensation has been insufficient.

387 non-Muslim places of worship recognized by the government are eligible for the subsidies. Additionally, the Turkish government reports that recognized places of worship are exempt from property and environmental sanitation taxes. The Turkish government also reported to USCIRF that in 2014 it had restored more than a dozen Christian and Jewish houses of worship and heritage sites, and said that other restorations were ongoing or planned. For example, in 2014, Izmir's Greater City Municipality restored a Greek Orthodox Church in Bornova and the 19th century Greek Orthodox Agios Voukolos Church. A liturgy service was celebrated in the latter church in August 2014 for the first time since 1922. The Beit Hillel Synagogue in Bornova was also restored, although reportedly the Jewish community does not control the property and services are not allowed. After the reporting year, in March 2015, the third largest synagogue in Europe, the Great Synagogue of Edirne located in the northwest region, was reopened and a service was held for the first time in nearly 50 years.

Since 2008, there had been an ongoing dispute over the Turkish government's attempted seizure of some territory of the 1,600-year-old Mor Gabriel Monastery, the Syriac Patriarch's residence from 1160 to 1932. In September 2013, the government announced that it would return Mor Gabriel to the appropriate Syriac Foundation and it has handed over the deed for 244,000 square meters (over 60 acres) of land. A case concerning an additional 320,000 square meters (nearly 80 acres) claimed by the community is pending before the European Court of Human Rights.

Education

The constitution makes religious and moral instruction compulsory in public primary and secondary schools, with a curriculum established by the Ministry of National Education. Non-Muslim children can be exempted, although there are reports of societal and teacher discrimination against children who opt out. Additionally, after complaints by religious minority communities, the Ministry of Education reported that it has made an effort to revise textbooks to not portray minorities in a derogatory manner. Alevis have complained that they are not allowed to have their children opt out of Sunni Islamic courses. In September 2014, the European Court of Human Rights ruled that Turkey's compulsory religious education for Muslim students violates the right of Alevi parents to have their children educated consistent with

sities, the parliament, courts, and schools. In the past, women who wore headscarves, and their advocates, were expelled from universities and lost public sector jobs, such as in nursing and teaching. In September 2013, the Turkish government lifted the headscarf ban for women in public institutions and universities. In September 2014, the headscarf ban was lifted in public middle schools and high schools. However, the ban still exists in areas that require a uniform, such as military and police offices, and in some courts. In addition, under Turkish law, only the titular head of any religious group may wear religious garb in public, but there have been no recent reports of government or local police enforcing this law in practice.

Alevis

Alevis comprise 15 to 25 percent of Turkey's total population. Although the Turkish government and many Alevis view them as heterodox Muslims, many Sunni Muslims do not accept that definition and consider them non-Muslims. Some Alevis identify as Shi'a Muslim, while others reject Islam and view themselves as a unique culture. Alevis worship in "gathering places" (*cemevi*), which the Turkish government does not consider legal houses of worship and thus cannot receive the legal and financial benefits associated with such status. In December 2014, the European Court of Human

> *In September 2014, the European Court of Human Rights ruled that Turkey's compulsory religious education for Muslim students violates the right of Alevi parents to have their children educated consistent with their own convictions.*

their own convictions. The court ruled that Turkey should institute a system whereby pupils could be exempted from religion classes without parents having to disclose their religious or philosophical convictions. The decision became final in February 2015 after the Court's Grand Chamber denied Turkey's request for review.

Religious Dress

Pursuant to Turkish secularism, the government has long banned religious dress, including the wearing of headscarves, in state buildings, public and private univer-

Rights ruled that Turkey discriminates against the Alevi community by failing to recognize *cemevis* as official places of worship. In the judgment the court "invited" the Turkish government to submit a proposal to resolve the longstanding issue of not recognizing *cemevis* as houses of worship.

Anti-Semitism

Representatives of the Jewish community in Turkey have told USCIRF that their situation is better than that of Jews in other majority Muslim countries and in parts of Western Europe. They are able to worship freely and their synagogues generally receive government protection when needed. Nevertheless, they remain concerned about rising anti-Semitism in society and in the media and occasional derogatory comments by government officials. During the summer of 2014, the Jewish community reported that it faced increased harassment and discrimination that it viewed as related to the Israel-Gaza conflict, and was increasingly fearful of violence.

The Ergenekon Conspiracy and Violence against Religious Minorities

Justice remains elusive in several high-profile past cases of violence against religious minorities. In January 2015, three suspects in the 2007 killing of three Protestant Christians at a Bible publisher in Malayta were released after having been held for more than five years without a final court decision. Early in 2014, five other suspects had been released. Only one suspect remains in jail. The suspects reportedly were members of the "Ergenekon" conspiracy, in which secularist "deep state" officials and elites allegedly plotted to overthrow the AKP government and to carry out violence against religious minorities.

Cases concerning the 2007 killing of Hrant Dink – the founder and editor of the weekly *Agos* and an advocate for democracy and Turkish-Armenian reconciliation – also continue. Two individuals, Ogun Samast

on national identity cards violates the European Convention, all individuals are still required to do so. Some religious groups, such as the Baha'is, are unable to state their religion because it is not on the official list of options. While a 2006 law allowed individuals to leave the religion section blank or change the religious designation, some communities have reported that they face intimidation or harassment when choosing either of these options.

Northern part of the Republic of Cyprus

Turkey has occupied nearly one-third of the northern part of Cyprus since 1974. As in past years, minority communities continued to be denied access to their religious places of worship and cemeteries that are within the boundaries of Turkish military zones or bases during 2014. In May 2014, the European Court of Human Rights ordered Turkey to pay 90 million Euros (100 million U.S. dollars) in compensation for its 1974 illegal invasion and occupation of the northern part of Cyprus.

U.S. Policy

Turkey is an important strategic partner of the United States; it is a NATO ally and there is a U.S. airbase in Incirlik, Turkey. The U.S.-Turkey relationship includes many matters, most importantly regional stability and security due to Turkey's shared borders with Syria, Iraq, and Iran, and the emergence of the Islamic State of Syria and the Levant (ISIL). The United States

---

Despite the 2010 European Court of Human Rights' ruling that the requirement to list religious affiliation on national identity cards violates the European Convention, all individuals are still required to do so.

---

and Yasin Hayal, were convicted in 2011 and 2012 of involvement in his killing; 19 other suspects were acquitted. In October 2014, Istanbul's 5th High Criminal Court overturned the acquittal of the 19 individuals, on the grounds that it overlooked possible links to a "criminal organization."

National Identity Cards

Despite the 2010 European Court of Human Rights' ruling that the requirement to list religious affiliation

continues to support Turkish accession to the European Union (EU), encouraging Turkey to continue the reforms necessary to complete the membership process, and arguing that a Turkey that meets EU membership criteria would be good for the United States, for the EU, and for Turkey. In addition, in the past, the United States worked to criminalize the sources of material support for the Kurdish Workers' Party (PKK) by designating the PKK a Foreign Terrorist Organization and supported the Turkish military against the PKK in northern Iraq. However, in 2014, relations between Turkey and the United States soured over a number of issues, including, differences in their Syria policies and approaches to dealing with the ISIL threat, anti-democratic moves in Turkey, and the Israeli-Palestinian conflict during the summer. Nevertheless, the United States and Turkey continue to be partners, especially regarding the Syrian and Iraq crises.

Since President Jimmy Carter, every U.S. president has called consistently for Turkey to reopen the Greek Orthodox Theological School of Halki under the auspices of the Ecumenical Patriarchate and to take specific steps to address concerns of the ethnic Kurdish population and other minority communities. The U.S. government also cooperates with Turkey to assist in the advancement of freedom of expression, respect for individual human rights, civil society, and promotion of ethnic diversity. Like every country except Turkey, the United States does not officially recognize the "Turkish Republic of Northern Cyprus." However, the United States government does discuss religious freedom with Turkish Cypriot authorities and supports international efforts to reunify the island.

Recommendations

In its engagement with Turkey, the U.S. government, at the highest levels, should continue to raise religious freedom issues with Turkish government counterparts. Specifically, USCIRF recommends that the U.S. government should urge the Turkish government to:

- Revive the multi-party constitutional drafting commission with the goal of drafting a new constitution consistent with international human rights standards on freedom of religion or belief;

- Fully implement the Universal Declaration of Human Rights and the International Covenant on Civil and Political Rights by withdrawing reservations that negatively impact religious freedom, and interpret the 1923 Lausanne Treaty so as to provide equal rights to all religious minority communities;

- Comply with decisions made by the European Court of Human Rights, including by

  - removing the space listing religious affiliation on official identification cards;

- recognizing Alevi *cemevis* as official places of worship; and

  - instituting a system whereby pupils can be exempted from religion classes without parents having to disclose their religious or philosophical convictions;

- Fulfill private- and publicly-stated promises that the Greek Orthodox Halki Seminary would be reopened, and permit other religious communities to open and operate their seminaries;

- Permit religious communities to select and appoint their leadership in accordance with their internal guidelines and beliefs;

- Publicly rebuke government officials who make anti-Semitic or derogatory statements about religious communities in Turkey; and

- Ensure that, with respect to the northern part of the Republic of Cyprus, Turkish military authorities and Turkish-controlled local authorities end all restrictions on the access, use, and restoration of places of worship and cemeteries for religious minorities.

OTHER COUNTRIES MONITORED

- BAHRAIN

- BANGLADESH

- BELARUS

- CYPRUS

- KYRGYZSTAN

- SRI LANKA

BAHRAIN

USCIRF has concluded that the Bahraini government has made demonstrable progress in rebuilding mosques and religious structures it destroyed during unrest in the spring of 2011. Nevertheless, more needs to be done to implement recommendations from the Bahrain Independent Commission of Inquiry (BICI) to redress past abuses against Shi'a Muslims and further improve religious freedom conditions. In addition, Shi'a Muslims continued to be detained and arrested arbitrarily throughout the year. In December 2014, a USCIRF staff member traveled to Manama; in addition to visiting almost all of the destroyed religious sites identified in the BICI report, he met with U.S. Embassy personnel, civil society representatives, members of religious communities, human rights groups, and human rights defenders.

Background

Bahrain is a diverse country and Bahraini citizens have a deep sense of their culture and history going back centuries. With a population of approximately 1.3 million, approximately half are Bahraini citizens and half are expatriate workers, primarily from South Asian countries.

community, Hindus, and Sikhs, as well as a small Baha'i community that it recognizes as a social organization. Most Bahrainis acknowledge that their society has been historically tolerant of all faiths and religiously pluralistic to a degree that is notable in the region.

Progress and Concerns Related to Accountability for Past Abuses

Of the more than 4,600 public and private workers dismissed in 2011 as a consequence of the unrest, the vast majority were Shi'a Muslims. According to non-governmental interlocutors, only 80-90 cases remain unresolved. In a February 2014 BICI follow-up report, the Bahraini government stated that only 49 cases remain unresolved. A March 2014 agreement between the Bahraini government and the International Labor Organization (ILO) included a commitment to resolve all remaining cases. Among those that have been resolved, hundreds were not reinstated in their original jobs, but in lower level jobs and some in different private companies. According to interlocutors, the most important element of the ILO agreement is to ensure mechanisms

USCIRF has concluded that the Bahraini government has made demonstrable progress in rebuilding mosques and religious structures it destroyed during unrest in the spring of 2011.

Almost half of the expatriate workers are non-Muslim (approximately 250,000-300,000). The religious demography of Bahraini citizens is estimated at 60-65 percent Shi'a and 30-35 percent Sunni, with approximately 1-2 percent non-Muslims, including Christians, Hindus, Sikhs, Jews, and Baha'is. Compared to other countries in the region, Bahrain is among the most tolerant of non-Muslim religious minority communities. The government officially recognizes several Christian denominations, a tiny Jewish

that would prevent future discriminatory dismissals and improve transparency in recruiting and hiring.

The government created the Civilian Settlement Office to compensate families of victims who were killed and individuals who were physically harmed in the 2011 unrest, as well as an Office of the Ombudsman in the Ministry of Interior to ensure compliance with standards of policing and to receive reports of misconduct. However, the government still has not adequately held high-level security officials accountable for serious abuses, which included targeting, imprisoning, torturing, and killing predominantly Shi'a demonstrators. Bahraini courts have tried, prosecuted, and convicted

> *Most Bahrainis acknowledge that their society has been historically tolerant of all faiths and religiously pluralistic to a degree that is notable in the region.*

only a few lower-level police officers, with little or no transparency about the trials, convictions, and length of prison terms. The government has stated that there are ongoing investigations of commanding officers related to the 2011 abuses, but has not disclosed details.

Ongoing Abuses and Discrimination

In 2014, Shi'a Muslims continued to be detained and arrested arbitrarily. In December 2014, Shi'a cleric and prominent opposition leader Ali Salman was arrested and charged with several security-related crimes that could carry prison terms ranging from three years to life. Human rights defenders have said the charges are baseless, and UN experts have criticized them as violations of the freedoms of expression, association, and religion. At the end of the reporting period, Salman remains in detention. In April 2014, the government forced Shi'a cleric Hussain Mirza Abdelbaqi Najati to leave the country after revoking his Bahraini citizenship in November 2012. According to the UN Special Rapporteur on Freedom of Religion or Belief, the authorities expelled Najati on account of "religiously motivated discrimination."

Furthermore, government and pro-government media continued to use inflammatory, sectarian rhetoric. New media laws that would curb anti-Shi'a incitement, as recommended in the BICI report, have not been passed. According to interlocutors, members of the Shi'a community still cannot serve in the active military, only in administrative positions, and there are no Shi'a in the upper levels of the Bahrain government security apparatus, including the military and police.

Progress in Rebuilding Shi'a Mosques and Religious Structures

While the Bahraini government did not meet its end-of-2014 deadline, it made significant progress in rebuilding the destroyed structures over the past year. In early 2014, the government increased to approximately $8 million the amount to rebuild Shi'a mosques and religious structures, nearly twice what it pledged in 2012. It also moved the deadline from 2018 to the end of 2014 to complete the construction of the 30 destroyed structures identified in the BICI report. As of December 2014, 14 mosques had been rebuilt, eight by the government and six by the Shi'a community, and 13 others were approximately 80-90 percent complete. The government helped secure legal permits for the six structures built by the Shi'a community, however, despite indicating a willingness in the past, officials have not committed to reimbursing the community.

There has been no progress on three of the 30 sites due to ongoing procedural and legal hurdles. Of the 27 completed or nearly complete, one mosque – the Mohamad Al Barbaghi mosque, which is religiously and historically significant to the Shi'a community – is nearly completed, but was rebuilt some 200 meters from its original site. The government says this was for security reasons, since the original mosque site is next to a major highway, but some members of the Shi'a community continue to insist that the mosque can only be built on the original location. In the past, Bahraini officials have committed to an ongoing dialogue with the Shi'a community to resolve the remaining disputed cases, although representatives from the Shi'a community do not believe the government is fully committed to the negotiations.

Recommendations

USCIRF urges the United States government to continue to press the Bahraini government to implement fully the BICI recommendations, including those related to freedom of religion and belief and accountability for past abuses against the Shi'a community. In addition, USCIRF continues to encourage the Bahraini government to reimburse the Shi'a community for expending its own funds to rebuild six mosques and religious structures that were demolished in 2011.

BANGLADESH

In 2014, societal discrimination, harassment, intimidation, and occasional violence against religious minority communities, especially the Hindu minority population, continued in Bangladesh. In addition, illegal land appropriations, commonly referred to as land-grabbing, and ownership disputes remain widespread, with a disproportionate number of religious minorities being targeted. Additionally, while the government has made some progress in complying with the Chittagong Hill Tracts Peace Accord, the ruling Awami League and other political parties use religiously-divisive language and, on occasion, act in ways that exacerbate rather than diminish religious and communal tensions. In September 2014, a USCIRF staff member travelled to the country to assess the religious freedom situation.

Background

On January 5, 2014, Bangladesh held its parliamentary election, which was not free or fair, with more than half of the seats uncontested. The main opposition party, the Bangladesh Nationalist Party (BNP), and 18 other political parties boycotted the election. Post-election violence occurred in 16 out 64 districts in Bangladesh, with most attacks attributed to individuals and groups associated with the BNP and the main religious party Jamaat-e-Islami (Jamaat). The worst attacks occurred in minority-dominated villages. Dozens of Hindu properties were looted, vandalized, or set ablaze, and

> *Dozens of Hindu properties were looted, vandalized, or set ablaze, and hundreds of Hindus fled their homes.*

hundreds of Hindus fled their homes. Christian and Buddhist communities also were targeted. Prime Minister Sheikh Hasina made public statements in support of religious minority communities after the violence, but reports emerged that police and security forces dispatched by the government to affected areas did not actively stop the violence and, in some cases, participated in it.

According to the country's 2011 census, approximately 90 percent of the population is Sunni Muslim. Hindus are 9.5 percent of the total population, and all other faiths, including Christians and Buddhists, are less than one percent.

Murder of Bloggers and Charges of Blasphemy

After the reporting period, two self-professed secular bloggers were brutally murdered in separate incidents on public streets in Dhaka. Avijit Roy, an American citizen of Bangladeshi dissent, was hacked to death on February 26, 2015; Roy's wife was critically injured. One suspect was arrested and charged in early March 2015. On March 30, 2015, Washiqur Rahman also was hacked to death; four men have been arrested and charged. During the reporting period, three self-professed atheists were released from detention; they had been arrested and charged with "offending religious sensitivities" in April 2013 after they blogged about Bangladesh's 1971 War Crimes Tribunals. In 2013, individuals associated with Jamaat reportedly gave the government a list naming 84 other individuals they wanted to see investigated for blasphemy.

Property Returns

In 2011, the Vested Property Return Act established an application process for families or individuals to apply for the return of, or compensation for, Hindu property seized prior to Bangladesh's independence from Pakistan in 1971. However, Hindu communities and NGOs complain that the Act is too narrowly defined, the application process too cumbersome and convoluted, and only a small percentage of eligible properties have been returned.

Land Grabbing

Representatives of minority communities told USCIRF that land-grabbing is a significant concern and is widespread throughout Bangladesh. Land-grabbing affects all communities, although religious minorities, particularly Hindus, appear disproportionately targeted

> *Land-grabbing affects all communities, although religious minorities, particularly Hindus, appear disproportionately targeted for displacement from land they have claimed for generations.*

for displacement from land they have claimed for generations. Reportedly, local police and political leaders, including some members of the national parliament, are occasionally involved in land-grabbing and/or shielding politically-influential individuals from prosecution. Land-grabbing is most frequent near roads or in industrial zones where land is at a premium; therefore, it is difficult to determine if minorities are targeted due to their religious faith, their vulnerable status as minorities, or the value of the property.

Chittagong Hill Tracts Peace Accord (CHT Accord)

The CHT Accord is a political agreement and peace treaty between the Bangladeshi government and the political party representing the ethnic and indigenous people of the area, of whom nearly 50 percent are followers of Theravada Buddhism. According to information provided to USCIRF by the Bangladeshi government, out of 72 articles of the CHT Accord, 48 have been fully implemented, 15 have been partially implemented, and nine have yet to be implemented. However, individuals representing the area assert that only 25 articles have been fully implemented. In February 2015, the Home Ministry restricted access to the area by foreign visitors and both national and international organizations,

apparently to limit reporting on disputes between the local people and the military.

Rohingya Muslims

The Bangladeshi government considers the estimated 30,000 Rohingya Muslims residing in two government-run camps in Cox's Bazaar near the Bangladesh-Burmese border as refugees from Burma, while the estimated 200,000 to 500,000 Rohingya Muslims living outside of the camps elsewhere in Bangladesh are treated as illegal immigrants. In February 2014, Bangladesh adopted a national strategy to respond to the Rohingya Muslim population in the country, which includes providing more humanitarian assistance and engaging Burma. In November 2014, Prime Minister Hasina announced that the two refugee camps, which are supported by the UNHCR, would be moved to improve the current living conditions of the refugees, which she described as inhumane. While UNHCR welcomed the announcement, it also indicated that the move would be costly and could lead to fear and tension in the Rohingya community. UNHCR reports that the Rohingya Muslims living outside the camps receive no support from the agency and live in deplorable conditions.

Recommendations

In its engagement with Bangladesh, USCIRF recommends that the U.S. government should: urge Prime Minister Hasina and all government officials to frequently and publicly denounce religiously-divisive language and acts of religiously-motivated violence and harassment; assist the Bangladeshi government to provide local government officials, police officers and judges with training on international human rights standards, as well as how to investigate and adjudicated religiously-motivated violent acts; and urge the government of Bangladesh to investigate claims of land-grabbing, rescind the order restricting NGO access to the Chittagong area, and revoke its blasphemy law.

BELARUS

USCIRF continues to monitor the situation in Belarus, where the government tightly regulates religious communities through an extensive security and religious affairs bureaucracy, which has driven some groups underground. Officials are particularly hostile towards religious groups viewed as political opponents, such as Protestants. The government strictly controls foreign citizens who conduct religious activity, particularly Catholic priests. While close cooperation between the state and the majority Orthodox Church has led to reli-

in the city of Gomel, a city court fined four Baptists in January 2014; their fines were upheld one month later. Use of houses of worship and any public exercise of religion requires state permission, which is rarely granted for disfavored groups, particularly Protestants. Orthodox and Catholic communities are less affected, partly due to the state's more positive view of them, but also because they are more likely to occupy historic churches. The New Life Church, a 1,000-member Pentecostal congregation in Minsk, has struggled since 2002

> *The government strictly controls*
> *foreign . . . Catholic priests*

gious freedom violations, citizens reportedly do not suffer religious discrimination in access to public services. There is no legal provision for conscientious objection to military service, and the religious rights of prisoners – even those on death row – are routinely denied.

Government control

A government agency, headed by the Plenipotentiary for Religious and Ethnic Affairs, oversees an extensive bureaucracy to regulate religious groups; each of the country's six regions employs multiple religious affairs officials, as does Minsk city. Officials from local Ideology Departments and the Belarusian secret police (which retains the Soviet-era title of Committee for State Security (KGB)) are also involved in religious controls. The 2002 religion law, which includes compulsory state registration of all communities and geographical limits on religious activity, is central to a wide web of regulations which tethers all registered religious groups.

Religious meetings in private homes must not occur regularly or involve large numbers. After a late 2013 police raid on a Baptist Sunday worship meeting

to keep control of its private church property, a renovated cow barn that authorities claim cannot officially be used as a church.

Unregistered religious activity is usually treated as an administrative offense punishable by a fine. Since registration is compulsory, the religion law makes no provision for those which do not wish to register, such as the Council of Churches Baptists and a similar Pentecostal group. A religious group found to have violated the religion law must correct the alleged violation within six months and not repeat it for one year or face closure. There is no legal avenue for religious groups to challenge such warnings, as the Belarus Constitutional Court noted in April 2007. After that court's decision, Jehovah's Witnesses have often tried, but failed, to establish the legal right to challenge such rulings.

Actions against Foreign Religious Leaders

In his annual report released in January 2014, the Plenipotentiary for Religious and Ethnic Affairs, Leonid Gulyako, accused unnamed foreign Catholic priests working in Belarus of holding services outside regions of official registration, failing to understand the state languages (Russian and Belarusian), and drunken driving. He also threatened not to prolong their visas, according

Unregistered religious activity is usually treated as an administrative offense.

to Forum 18 News Service. The Belarusian Catholic community called these accusations "slanderous." The number of foreign Catholic priests (who are mostly from Poland) declined from 126 to 113 between September 2014 and January 2015. Polish priest Fr. Roman Schulz's permit to remain in his Mogilev parish was extended by six months, until June 2015, only after members of the parish protested. The government also has refused to allow a Baptist seminary to invite religious lecturers from the United States. A court warned two Jehovah's Witnesses that as foreigners they had no right to speak publicly about their faith.

Fr. Vladislav Lazar of the Descent of the Holy Spirit Catholic parish in Minsk Region's Borisov was arrested for espionage in May 2013. He was held six months almost incommunicado at the Minsk KGB secret police investigation prison before being transferred to house arrest in December 2013. During his imprisonment, Fr. Lazar was denied a Bible, prayer book, rosary, and family visits; he was finally allowed one visit from the Apostolic Nuncio to Belarus. The investigation against Fr. Lazar seems to have been dropped in June 2014 due to lack of evidence, but no official announcement was made; he has been allowed to return to work in his parish.

Recommendations

Since Ukraine was invaded by Russian forces in 2014, Belarus has hosted several high level international meetings on the crisis. These meetings have included State Department representatives, even though the United States has not had an ambassador in Belarus since 2008. With such increased U.S. government engagement with Belarus, USCIRF recommends the State Department raise concerns about religious freedom and related human rights with them. In addition,

the U.S. government should publicly raise Belarusian religious freedom violations at appropriate international fora, such as the OSCE and the UN, particularly the need to reform the religion law.

CYPRUS

For several years, USCIRF has monitored religious freedom conditions in Cyprus, reporting only on the northern region since 2011, in accordance with U.S. House Resolution 1631 that called on USCIRF "to investigate and make recommendations on violations of religious freedom in the areas of northern Cyprus under control of the Turkish military." However, recent efforts by the United Nations and the Swedish government have led to notable improvements regarding religious freedom and bi-communal harmony. A UN-backed Swedish initiative brought together the Republic of Cyprus government, Turkish Cypriot authorities, Archbishop Chrysostomos II, and Grand Mufti Dr. Talip Atalay to advance interfaith understanding, religious freedom, and access to religious sites.

Eased Movement of Religious Leaders and Laity

In October 2013, longstanding restrictions were lifted that prevented the Archbishop of the Greek Orthodox Church of Cyprus in the south and the Muslim Grand Mufti in the north from crossing the Green Line. The Archbishop led two services at Apostolos Andreas Monastery in the northern part of Cyprus, attended by 5,000 Greek Cypriots from the area under the effective control of the government of the Republic of Cyprus, and the Grand Mufti led a service at the Hala Sultan Tekke mosque in the government-controlled area, attended by hundreds of northern Turkish Cypriot Muslims. In February 2014, after the first-ever joint statement by the island's five religious leaders (the Archbishop of the Church of Cyprus, the Grand Mufti of Cyprus, the Maronite Archbishop, the Armenian Archbishop, and the Patriarchal Latin Vicar), religious leaders and laity were permitted several more cross-area movements for worship, some for the first time since 1974. Between mid-December 2013 and late June 2014, the UN facilitated an unprecedented level of engagement, including 48 religious services and commemorative events and 98

bi-communal harmony civil society events, with more than 20,000 people crossing from both sides. In several instances, the Greek Orthodox Archbishop and the Muslim Grand Mufti participated in religious events and

> *Recent efforts by the United Nations and the Swedish government have led to notable improvements regarding religious freedom and bi-communal harmony.*

ceremonies together, further strengthening religious and bi-communal harmony.

Greek Cypriots and Turkish Cypriots indigenous to the island can generally cross the Green Line with no approval process needed. Nevertheless, a UN-facilitated application process to visit religious sites is required on occasion, and reports continue that individuals or groups still are periodically restricted from crossing the Green Line. Under European and Republic of Cyprus national law, however, Turkish settlers and other persons without proper documentation cannot cross into the government-controlled areas. The Grand Mufti, not being a citizen of the Republic of Cyprus, is subject to these regulations; however, as noted above the Republic of Cyprus did make exceptions for him in the last year.

Access to Houses of Worship

While there have been improvements in north-south relations relating to religious freedom, access to houses of worship remains a work in progress. Since USCIRF's February 2011 visit, an increasing number of Christian religious services were successfully conducted in places of worship in the Turkish-occupied part of the Republic of Cyprus.

Between January 2013 and May 2014, the Republic of Cyprus reported to USCIRF that Turkish Cypriot authorities rejected 15 applications for permission for services in the north. For the same period, representatives of Turkish Cypriot authorities based in Washington, DC reported to USCIRF that the north approved 33 applications. In addition, between January 2013 and May 2014 the Republic of Cyprus reported to USCIRF that the Turkish military denied two applications for access to religious sites located in Turkish military bases or zones. For the same period, representatives of Turkish Cypriot authorities based in Washington, DC reported to USCIRF that 17 such applications were approved. In the government-controlled Republic of Cyprus, all but two mosques are open only on Fridays and cannot be accessed for worship or repair work on other days. The two mosques in Larnaca and Limassol are open on weekdays during regular business hours, making two of the five required prayers for Muslims impossible. In the north, religious minority communities must seek permission to worship in churches other than eight that require no such permission. The application process in the north was eased following USCIRF's 2011 visit to the island.

Official Discrimination and Harassment

In the Turkish-occupied part of Cyprus, plain-clothed police monitor, videotape, or question religious minorities regularly, including at their houses of worship, although USCIRF is not aware of individuals being detained or arrested. Reportedly, officials in the south frequently harass and discriminate against individuals thought to be non-Greek Orthodox, including those attending mosques. Small religious communities in the south, such as Buddhists, Baha'is, and Jehovah's Witnesses have faced problems securing licenses to build places of worship. Additionally, there are reports that textbooks originating from both the north and the south include negative information about each other's religious community. In the south, non-Greek Orthodox students may be exempted from religious classes, but reportedly some who opt out experience social harassment. In the north, religious education is required and there is no exemption allowance; therefore minority religious communities run their own schools, largely out of homes. There also have been some reports, including by Amnesty International, of the Republic of Cyprus detaining or deporting asylum seekers fleeing religious persecution, including Baha'is from Iran.

Religious and Cultural Heritage

Many of the 500-plus churches and cemeteries in the north have been or are nearly destroyed from years of neglect or intentional damage by the Turkish military, looters of priceless religious artifacts, and desecrators. Some churches now are used as mosques, community halls, sporting venues, stables for animals, or storage. In the south, dozens of mosques are also in extremely poor condition from neglect or intentional damage. Under UN auspices, the joint Technical Committee on Cultural Heritage reached an agreement in 2012 on restoring and repairing a number of churches in the north and mosques in the south. Notably, at least two mosques in the south and four churches in the north have been restored. Additionally, the restoration of Apostolos Andreas Monastery has begun, with completion slated for April 2016.

Recommendations

The Swedish initiative presents a unique opportunity to address longstanding issues impacting religious freedom and bi-communal harmony. The U.S. government should urge the Republic of Cyprus and Turkish Cypriot authorities to: implement the recommendations suggested by the United Nations and the Swedish embassy, including creating and/or expanding bi-communal harmony dialogues among political officials, religious leaders and laity, and civil society in both the north and the south; while respecting Republic of Cyprus national legislation and EU regulations, remove any restrictions on religious leaders and laity crossing the Green Line for religious worship or to visit religious sites; permit unrestricted access to houses of worship; train teachers on religious and cultural sensitivities; ensure that textbooks do not contain negative information about religious groups; and eliminate official harassment or discrimination towards religious minority communities in the north and the south, including those communities not considered native to the island.

KYRGYZSTAN

The Kyrgyz government restricts religious freedom through its 2008 religion law and other laws and policies, and draft October 2014 amendments would sharply

> *The 2008 religion law imposes burdensome registration requirements*

increase these controls. USCIRF has been monitoring conditions in Kyrgyzstan for a number of years. A USCIRF staff member visited the country in October 2014 to assess the religious freedom situation.

Background

Over 80 percent of Kyrgyzstan's population is Sunni Muslim. There is also a very small Shi'a community. Fifteen percent of the population is Christian, mostly Russian Orthodox; there are about 11,000 Protestants and a small number of Catholics. The Jewish, Buddhist and Baha'i communities are estimated at 1,000 each. The country's large ethnic Uzbek community (up to 40 percent of the south Kyrgyz population) mostly adheres to traditional Hanafi Sunni Islam. The Kyrgyz constitution purports to provide for religious freedom for all citizens. In February 2014, President Almazbek Atambayev said it had been a "mistake" to remove state agencies from regulating religious practice. In September 2014, the Kyrgyz Supreme Court Constitutional Chamber ruled that activities of a registered religious group cannot be limited geographically.

2008 Religion Law

Kyrgyzstan's 2008 religion law imposes burdensome registration requirements for religious organizations, including having 200 resident citizen founders and at least 10 members, of whom at least one must have been

in Kyrgyzstan for 15 years. International organizations, including the Organization for Security and Cooperation in Europe (OSCE), the Council of Europe's Venice Commission, and the UN Human Rights Committee, have noted the law violates international standards; its flaws include strict registration requirements, criminal penalties for unregistered religious activities, vague restrictions on "fanaticism and extremism," and limitations on missionary activities and the dissemination of religious materials.

Proposed 2014 Amendments

On October 9, 2014, draft amendments to the religion law and administrative code suddenly were distributed to a roundtable arranged by the State Committee on Religious Affairs (SCRA) with the United Nations Development Program (UNDP) in Bishkek. The SCRA-led government working group that wrote the drafts, the UNDP, local human rights groups, and clergy from the state-backed Muslim Board, the Russian Orthodox Church, and several Protestant churches took part. At the roundtable USCIRF staff encouraged the involvement of international legal specialists in the drafting. SCRA promised to hold a second roundtable; the drafts were issued the night before the session.

Religious Freedom Prospects in 2015

These amendments, if enacted in 2015, would markedly change the environment for religious freedom in Kyrgyzstan and could warrant a change in Kyrgyzstan's tier status in next year's USCIRF annual report. The amendments would sharply increase SCRA authority; privilege Islam and the Russian Orthodox Church, and define other religious groups as "non-traditional;" require 500 founders for all religious groups to re-register by December 31, 2015; require an annual SCRA license for any official or worker in a religious group or religious educational institution; and further limit sites where religious texts can be distributed. Another set of draft proposals would increase the maximum administrative code fines for religious offenses to the equivalent of 14 months' average salary.

Increased State Control of Muslim Board and Banning Groups

A February 2014 Presidential Decree increased state control over the semi-autonomous Muslim Board, directing it to "improve the system" to elect imams and the Chief Mufti; to include government officials in internal exams for imams; to organize material rewards for those Muslim clergy who have excelled in meeting internal criteria; and to check with local and national government law enforcement agencies to ascertain if clerical candidates are members of extremist organizations, Forum 18 reported. The Muslim Board was also instructed to choose the Mufti, imams, regional imams, religious judges and members of the Council of Ulema only from the Hanafi school of Islam that the government deems "traditional" for Kyrgyzstan's Muslims. Unlike elsewhere in Central Asia, Kyrgyzstan also has programs for local members of Tabligh Jamaat, an international Muslim proselytizing movement.

In March 2014, a Bishkek court banned the Uzbek Islamic religious movement Akromiya as an extremist organization. Lists of prohibited religious organizations reportedly are coordinated with intergovernmental regional security organizations, in particular, the Shanghai Cooperation Organization and the Collective Security Treaty Organization.

Registration Issues

In 2014, nearly 700 of the country's unregistered mosques were identified as "illegal," Forum 18 reported. Ahmadi Muslims have not been able to hold

refusal to register Ahmadi Muslims. The Church of Scientology's registration was denied in 2014. Jehovah's Witnesses are registered in one city but are denied national registration despite numerous attempts. In June 2014, Russian Orthodox Bishop Feodosy was forced to leave the country after the SCRA refused to renew his missionary registration, alleging he was a threat to public security and sowed religious discord, allegations that members of his community denied.

In a potentially positive development, in September 2014, the Constitutional Chamber of the Supreme Court ruled that a religious organization cannot be limited to carrying out its activity only in the place where it has its legal address. The Constitutional Chamber also found that it is unconstitutional for local councils to approve the list of 200 founders of a religious group required for legal status. The Jehovah's Witnesses who brought the case think this will, if implemented, help stop harassment of their community.

Other Legal Issues

Other restrictions in current Kyrgyz religion law include restricting conscientious objection to military service to young men who belong to registered religious groups. In addition, SCRA authority to censor religious materials – increased by 2012 amendments to the religion law – seem particularly to apply to non-traditional Muslim, Protestant, and other minority religions.

Recommendation

USCIRF recommends that the U.S. government urge Kyrgyzstan to seek expert advice from the UN Special Rapporteur on Freedom of Religion or Belief as well as relevant OSCE entities on the October 2014 draft religion law and include international legal experts in a second

---

In 2014, nearly 700 unregistered mosques were identified as "illegal."

---

worship meetings since July 2011, when the SCRA refused to re-register them in Bishkek and three other cities. In July 2014 the Supreme Court rejected an appeal of two lower courts' support of the SCRA's

roundtable. The United States should also publicly raise Kyrgyzstan's religious freedom violations at appropriate international fora, such as the OSCE and the UN.

SRI LANKA

During 2014, the now former Rajapaksa government permitted extremist monks and laity affiliated with Sinhalese Buddhist nationalist groups to perpetrate numerous attacks against religious minority communities in Sri Lanka. In September 2014, a USCIRF staff member visited the country and heard multiple reports that officials in the previous government tacitly supported these groups and their actions against Muslims, Christians, and Hindus. Interlocutors also reported that some local police harassed religious minorities at their houses of worship, did not stop religiously-motivated attacks and sometimes participated in them, and did not adequately protect minorities. In March 2015, USCIRF Commissioner Eric Schwartz and USCIRF staff travelled to Sri Lanka to reassess the situation following the January 2015 election. While some religious freedom concerns remain, USCIRF is encouraged by the new government's statements and actions to promote religious freedom, national reconciliation and unity.

Background

Sri Lanka is a religiously pluralistic country, with a population estimated, as of 2012, to be 70 percent Buddhist, 12.6 percent Hindu, 9 percent Muslim, and 7.5 percent Christian. Until 2009, the country was ravaged by a 26-year civil war with the Liberation Tigers of Tamil Eelam (LTTE), an ethnically-based movement seeking an independent state. During the war, both sides failed to prevent communal violence involving Sinhalese Buddhists, Hindus, Muslims, and Christians. Both the former Rajapaksa government and the LTTE are alleged to have committed war crimes, and the former government refused calls for investigations into these allegations for years.

On January 9, 2015 Maithripala Sirisena was sworn in as Sri Lanka's new president after defeating Mahinda Rajapaksa, who held the office since 2005. Sirisena, who left the Rajapaksa government to run in opposition, put forward a platform that included fighting governmen-

tal corruption and nepotism, as well seeking national reconciliation and harmony. In a February 2015 speech President Sirisena stated, "While protecting the country's main religion Buddhism, we also protect the rights and freedom of Hindu, Muslim, and Catholic people in practicing their religion and create consensus among them to build up this country." Sri Lankan officials repeated those sentiments about tolerance and respect for religious freedom to a USCIRF mission to Sri Lanka in March 2015, and indeed, USCIRF has found that reports of abuses diminished significantly in the first months of 2015.

Violence against Religious Minorities

Individuals associated with Buddhist nationalist groups, particularly Bodu Bala Sena (BBS) and Sinhala Ravaya, perpetrated violence against religious minority communities during 2014. In the largest incident, a mob of an estimated 500 Buddhist nationalists attacked Muslims in the towns of Aluthgama, Beruwala and Dharga in the southwestern Kalutara district in June 2014. At least four people were killed, dozens severely injured, an estimated 10,000 people fled the area, and mosques and Muslim-owned shops and homes were destroyed. Officials in the Rajapaksa government who were associated with BBS were

> *Officials in the Rajapaksa government who were associated with BBS were accused of complicity in the attack*

accused of complicity in the attack, for example, by shutting down media Web sites so they could not show the extent of the violence or that local police were not stopping it. Moreover, former President Rajapaksa made remarks at the UN Human Rights Council that seemed to blame the Muslim victims. However, the then-government did provide assistance to affected people and began to rebuild destroyed properties. Numerous other violent incidents against Muslims also occurred throughout the year.

Dozens of attacks against Christian churches and individuals were reported. For example, in January 2014, a mob attacked the Assembly of God and Calvary churches in Hikkaduwa. Local police reportedly were warned in advance but arrived after the attack. Eighteen individuals, including seven Buddhist monks, were arrested and are facing trial. In February 2014 a Buddhist nationalist mob of more than 200 individuals, including several Buddhist monks, attacked and damaged the Holy Family Church in Kandy district, injuring its pastor and his family. Dozens of similar attacks against Christian churches and individuals were reported in 2014.

Hindu communities also faced intimidation and harassment. While Hindus generally do not face the same level of violent persecution as the other minority communities, local police reportedly conduct surveillance of Hindu individuals and temples suspected of supporting the LTTE or advocating for an international war crimes tribunal.

Intolerant Propaganda

In 2014, BBS propaganda cast religious minority communities in a negative light, exacerbating religious tensions. For example, Buddhist nationalist monks accused Muslims of seeking to wipe out Buddhism in the country by secretly sterilizing Buddhist women. Additionally, BBS pressured the former government to ban Muslim headscarves and halal slaughter. BBS used similar propaganda campaigns against Christians, and called for the country to adopt a nationwide anti-conversion law and ban missionary groups.

Governmental Restrictions on Houses of Worship

A 2008 circular, still being implemented, issued by the Ministry of Buddha Sasana and Religious Affairs causes problems for Christian communities viewed as new to the country, such as Evangelical and Pentecostal denominations and Jehovah's Witnesses. The circular requires religious communities to register houses of worship

with the Ministry and seek advance approval of new construction. While the requirements appear to apply to all religious groups, reportedly they are only enforced against Christians and Muslims. In addition, minorities

> *The circular requires religious communities to register houses of worship with the Ministry and seek advance approval of new construction.*

complain that the registration process is opaque and slow; that registration results in monitoring and harassment by local police; and that they are often forced to register as NGOs and not religious groups. Unregistered houses of worship have been closed. For example, the National Evangelical Christian Alliance of Sri Lanka reported that 30 churches were forced to close in 2014.

Discrimination in Public Schools

During USCIRF's 2014 and 2015 visits, Muslim, Christian and Hindu communities reported discrimination in government-run schools. Teachers and administrators harass non-Buddhist students, including by throwing out of class Muslim girls who cover their hair. Reportedly teachers quiz minority students about Buddhism and, if a student cannot answer, the parents are fined and/or the student barred from school until s/he shows knowledge of Buddhism. Religious education is a required course, and religious knowledge is assessed on the national university entrance exam. If a school has more than 15 non-Buddhist students, it is supposed to provide a religious education class on the relevant religion, taught by a member of that religion, and assess that knowledge on the university entrance exam. However, these requirements are often not met, forcing non-Buddhist students to either take the class on Buddhism or skip the religious section of the national test, which lowers their scores and adversely affects their entrance to university.

Religious Police

In April 2014 the former government formed a special police unit purportedly to handle complaints by religious communities. However, the unit of approximately 500 officers was comprised almost exclusively of Buddhists, raising concerns among religious minorities that the then-government and its BBS allies would use the unit to curtail their rights and intimidate and harass them.

Religious Freedom Prospects in 2015

Since President Sirisena took office in January, he has taken several steps to improve religious unity and religious freedom. For example, he created three new ministries to handle religious affairs for the Muslim, Christian, and Hindu communities respectively. Additionally, the new Ministry of Christian Affairs appointed a special coordinator for Charismatic, Evangelical and Pentecostal Christian churches. The special police unit created by the former government has been disbanded, according to officials and religious communities with whom USCIRF met in March 2015.

President Sirisena's public statements on the need for national unity, reconciliation, harmony, and improved religious freedom have been encouraging, as were the comments by government officials with whom

President Sirisena's public statements on the need for national unity, reconciliation, harmony, and improved religious freedom have been encouraging, as were the comments by government officials with whom USCIRF met in March 2015.

USCIRF met in March 2015. Additionally, while the President continues to oppose an international investigation into alleged war crimes by the former government and the LTTE at the end of the civil war, he has made public statements in favor of accepting United Nations support on these issues, including advice on how a Sri Lankan investigation should be conducted. Finally, and perhaps most importantly, reports of abuses against religious minorities have diminished in the first months of 2015, though concerns remain.

Recommendations

USCIRF recommends that the U.S. government should: strongly encourage the positive movement that has occurred in recent months; encourage the Sri Lankan government to allow a transparent and independent investigation into alleged war crimes, including targeted attacks on religious minorities; ensure that a portion of U.S. humanitarian aid to Sri Lanka is used to help protect minorities from religiously-motivated violence; assist the Sri Lankan government to train local government officials, police officers, and judges on international religious freedom standards and on how to investigate and prosecute violent attacks; and urge Sri Lankan government officials to provide minority students an equal opportunity to learn their faiths in public schools and to rescind policies and practices – often driven at local levels – that restrict religious communities' ability to build houses of worship or practice their faith.

APPENDIX 1
COMMISSIONER BIOGRAPHIES

Dr. Katrina Lantos Swett, Chair

Dr. Katrina Lantos Swett established the Lantos Foundation for Human Rights and Justice in 2008 and serves as its President and Chief Executive Officer. This human rights organization is proudly carrying on the unique legacy of the late Congressman Tom Lantos who, as the only survivor of the Holocaust ever elected to Congress, was one of our nation's most eloquent and forceful leaders on behalf of human rights and justice. In addition to managing the Lantos Foundation, Dr. Lantos Swett teaches human rights and American foreign policy at Tufts University. She also taught at the University of Southern Denmark while her husband, former Congressman Richard Swett, was serving as the U.S. Ambassador in Copenhagen.

Her varied professional experiences include working on Capitol Hill as Deputy Counsel to the Criminal Justice Sub-Committee of the Senate Judiciary Committee for then Senator Joe Biden and as a consultant to businesses, charitable foundations, and political campaigns.

Dr. Lantos Swett also has experience in broadcasting, having co-hosted the highly regarded political talk show "Beyond Politics" for many years on WMUR TV, New Hampshire's only network affiliated television station. As co-host, she interviewed state, national, and international figures, including Prime Minister Benjamin Netanyahu, Vice President Al Gore, First Lady Hillary Clinton, Members of the United States Congress, and George Stephanopoulos on the issues of the day.

From 2003-2006 Dr. Lantos Swett served as the Director of the Graduate program in Public Policy at New England College. She is also a member of the Board of HRNK Human Rights in North Korea and the Tom Lantos Institute in Budapest. She has served on numerous Boards in the past, including the Christa McAuliffe Planetarium Foundation, the Institute for Justice Sector Development, the Granite State Coalition Against Expanded Gambling (co-Chair), and the NH Citizen's Commission on the State Courts. She has also been active in Democratic politics for over three decades. In 2002, she was the Democratic nominee for Congress in New Hampshire's 2nd District, and she was chosen as a Presidential elector in 1992. She has been a member of the New Hampshire Democratic Party (NHDP) Executive Committee and served as Vice-Chair of the NHDP Finance Committee.

Under Dr. Lantos Swett's leadership as President and CEO, the Lantos Foundation has quickly become a distinguished and respected voice on many key human rights concerns ranging from rule of law in Russia and Internet freedom in closed societies to the on-going threat of anti-Semitism and Holocaust denial. The Foundation also supports human rights defenders around the globe through its Front Line Fund and runs the Lantos Congressional Fellows program in conjunction with Humanity in Action. Each year the Lantos Foundation awards the Lantos Human Rights Prize to an individual who has demonstrated a commitment to standing up for decency, dignity, freedom, and justice. Past recipients have included His Holiness the Dalai Lama, Professor Elie Wiesel, and Paul Rusesabagina.

Dr. Lantos Swett graduated from Yale University in 1974 at the age of 18 and earned her Juris Doctor at the University of California, Hastings College of the Law in 1976. She received her Ph.D. in History from the University of Southern Denmark in 2001. Dr. Lantos Swett has been married for 31 years to former Congressman and Ambassador Richard Swett and they are parents of 7 children and 2 grandchildren. She resides in Bow, New Hampshire.

Dr. Lantos Swett was appointed to the Commission on March 26, 2012 by Senate Majority Leader Harry Reid (D-NV) and reappointed to a second term in 2014.

Dr. Robert P. George, Vice Chair

Robert P. George is McCormick Professor of Jurisprudence and Director of the James Madison Program in American Ideals and Institutions at Princeton University. He has been a Visiting Professor at Harvard Law School, and is a Senior Fellow of the Hoover Institution at Stanford University.

He has served on the President's Council on Bioethics and as a presidential appointee to the United States Commission on Civil Rights. He has also served on UNESCO's World Commission on the Ethics of Scientific Knowledge and Technology (COMEST), of which he remains a corresponding member.

A graduate of Swarthmore College and Harvard Law School, Professor George also earned a master's degree in theology from Harvard and a doctorate in philosophy of law from Oxford University, which he attended on a Knox Scholarship from Harvard. He holds honorary doctorates of law, letters, science, ethics, divinity, humane letters, civil law, and juridical science.

He is the author of Making Men Moral: Civil Liberties and Public Morality and In Defense of Natural Law, among other books. His articles and review essays have appeared in the Harvard Law Review, the Yale Law Journal, the Columbia Law Review, the Review of Politics, the Review of Metaphysics, the American Journal of Jurisprudence, and Law and Philosophy. He has also written for the New York Times, the Wall Street Journal, the Washington Post, First Things magazine, National Review, the Boston Review, and the Times Literary Supplement.

Professor George is a former Judicial Fellow at the Supreme Court of the United States, where he received the Justice Tom C. Clark Award.

His other honors include the United States Presidential Citizens Medal, the Honorific Medal for the Defense of Human Rights of the Republic of Poland, the Bradley Prize for Intellectual and Civic Achievement, the Phillip Merrill Award for Outstanding Contributions to the Liberal Arts of the American Council of Trustees and Alumni, a Silver Gavel Award of the American Bar Association, the Paul Bator Award of the Federalist Society for Law and Public Policy, and the Canterbury Medal of the Becket Fund for Religious Liberty.

He is a member of the Council on Foreign Relations and is Of Counsel to the law firm of Robinson & McElwee.

Dr. George was appointed to the Commission on March 22, 2012 by Speaker of the House John Boehner (R-OH) and was reappointed in 2014 for a second term.

Dr. James J. Zogby, Vice Chair

Dr. James J. Zogby is the founder and president of the Arab American Institute (AAI), a Washington, D.C.-based organization which serves as the political and policy research arm of the Arab American community. He is also Managing Director of Zogby Research Services, which specializes in public opinion polling across the Arab world.

Since 1985, Dr. Zogby and AAI have led Arab American efforts to secure political empowerment in the U.S. Through voter registration, education and mobilization, AAI has moved Arab Americans into the political mainstream.

For the past three decades, Dr. Zogby has been involved in a full range of Arab American issues. A co-founder and chairman of the Palestine Human Rights Campaign in the late 1970s, he later co-founded and served as the Executive Director of the American-Arab Anti-Discrimination Committee. In 1982, he co-founded Save Lebanon, Inc., a relief organization which provided health care for Palestinian and Lebanese victims of war. In 1985, Zogby founded AAI.

In 1993, following the signing of the Israeli-Palestinian peace accord in Washington, he was asked by Vice President Al Gore to lead Builders for Peace, an effort to promote U.S. business investment in the West Bank and Gaza. In his capacity as co-president of Builders, Zogby frequently traveled to the Middle East with delegations led by Vice President Gore and late Secretary of Commerce Ron Brown.

Dr. Zogby has also been active in U.S. politics for many years. Since 1995 he has played a leadership role in the National Democratic Ethnic Coordinating Committee (NDECC), an umbrella organization of leaders of European and Mediterranean descent. In 2001, he was appointed to the Executive Committee of the Democratic National Committee (DNC), and in 2006 was also named Co-Chair of the DNC's Resolutions Committee.

A lecturer and scholar on Middle East issues, U.S.-Arab relations, and the history of the Arab American community, Dr. Zogby has an extensive media profile in the U.S. and across the Arab World. He currently serves as Chairman of the Editorial Advisory Committee for SkyNewsArabia. Since 1992, Dr. Zogby has also written a weekly column published in 14 Arab and South Asian countries.

He has authored a number of books, including: Looking at Iran (2013), Arab Voices (2010), What Ethnic Americans Really Think (2002), and What Arabs Think: Values, Beliefs and Concerns (2001).

In 1975, Dr. Zogby received his doctorate from Temple University's Department of Religion. He was a Post-Doctoral Fellow at Princeton University in 1976, and has been awarded numerous grants and honorary degrees.

Dr. Zogby is married to Eileen Patricia McMahon.

Dr. Zogby was appointed to the Commission on September 6, 2013 by President Obama.

Ambassador Mary Ann Glendon, Commissioner

Mary Ann Glendon is the Learned Hand Professor of Law at Harvard University, and former U.S. Ambassador to the Holy See. She writes and teaches in the fields of human rights, comparative law, constitutional law, and political theory.

Glendon is a member of the American Academy of Arts and Sciences since 1991, the International Academy of Comparative Law, and the Pontifical Academy of Social Sciences which she served as President from 2004-2014. She is also a past president of the UNESCO-sponsored International Association of Legal Science. She served two terms as a member of the U.S. President's Council on Bioethics (2001-2004), and has represented the Holy See at various conferences including the 1995 U.N. Women's conference in Beijing where she headed the Vatican delegation.

Glendon has contributed to legal and social thought in several articles and books, and has lectured widely in this country and in Europe. Her widely translated books, bringing a comparative approach to a variety of subjects, include The Forum and the Tower (2011), a series of biographical essays exploring the relation between political philosophy and politics-in-action; Traditions in Turmoil (2006), a collection of essays on law, culture and human rights; A World Made New: Eleanor Roosevelt and the Universal Declaration of Human Rights (2001), which the New York Times reviewer said should be the definitive study of the framing of the UDHR; A Nation

Under Lawyers (1996), a portrait of turbulence in the legal profession, analyzing the implications of changes in legal culture for a democratic polity that entrusts crucial roles to legally trained men and women; Seedbeds of Virtue (co-edited with David Blankenhorn) (1995); Rights Talk (1991), a critique of the impoverishment of political discourse; The Transformation of Family Law (1989), winner of the legal academy's highest honor, the Order of the Coif Triennial Book Award; Abortion and Divorce in Western Law (1987), winner of the Scribes Book Award for best writing on a legal subject; The New Family and the New Property (1981), and textbooks on comparative legal traditions.

Her prizes and honors include the National Humanities Medal, the Bradley Foundation Prize, and honorary doctorates from numerous universities including the Universities of Chicago and Louvain.

Glendon taught at Boston College Law School from 1968 to 1986, and has been a visiting professor at the University of Chicago Law School and the Gregorian University in Rome.

She received her bachelor of arts, juris doctor, and master of comparative law degrees from the University of Chicago. During a post-graduate fellowship for the study of European law, she studied at the Université Libre de Bruxelles and was a legal intern with the European Economic Community. From 1963 to 1968, she practiced law with the Chicago firm of Mayer, Brown & Platt, and served as a volunteer civil rights attorney in Mississippi during "Freedom Summer" 1964.

A native of Berkshire County, she lives in Chestnut Hill, Massachusetts.

Ambassador Glendon was appointed to the Commission on May 23, 2012 by Senate Minority Leader Mitch McConnell (R-KY) and reappointed to a second term in 2014.

Dr. M. Zuhdi Jasser, Commissioner

M. Zuhdi Jasser, M.D. is the President of the American Islamic Forum for Democracy (AIFD) based in Phoenix, Arizona. A first generation American Muslim, Dr. Jasser's parents fled the oppressive Baath regime of Syria in the mid-1960's for American freedom. A devout Muslim, he and his family have strong ties to the American Muslim community having helped lead mosques in Wisconsin, Arkansas, Virginia and Arizona.

In the wake of the 9/11 attacks on the United States, Dr. Jasser and a group of American Muslims founded AIFD which promotes Muslim voices for liberty and freedom through the separation of mosque and state in order to counter the root cause of Islamist terrorism--the ideology of political Islam (Islamism) and a belief in the supremacy of the Islamic state. AIFD's primary projects include the Muslim Liberty Project, the American Islamic Leadership Coalition and Save Syria Now!

An internationally recognized expert on Islamism, Dr. Jasser is widely published on domestic and foreign issues related to Islam, Islamism, and modernity. He has spoken at hundreds of national and international events including testimony to the U.S. Congress on the centrality of religious liberty in countering Muslim radicalization within the "House of Islam". He is a contributing writer to a number of books and the author of The Battle for the Soul of Islam: An American Muslim Patriot's Fight to Save His Faith (Simon & Schuster, 2012).

Dr. Jasser earned his medical degree on a U.S. Navy scholarship at the Medical College of Wisconsin in 1992. He served 11 years as a medical officer in the U. S. Navy, achieving the rank of Lieutenant Commander. His tours of duty included Medical Department Head aboard the U.S.S. El Paso, Chief Resident at Bethesda Naval Hospital, and Staff Internist for the Office of the Attending Physician to the U. S. Congress. He is a recipient of the Meritorious Service Medal.

Dr. Jasser is a respected physician currently in private practice specializing in internal medicine and nuclear cardiology. He is a Past-President of the Arizona Medical Association. He and his wife Gada and their three children reside in Arizona.

Dr. Jasser was appointed to the Commission on March 22, 2012 by Senate Minority Leader Mitch McConnell (R-KY) and was reappointed to a second term in 2014.

Dr. Daniel I. Mark, Commissioner

Dr. Daniel Mark is an assistant professor of political science at Villanova University in Pennsylvania. He teaches political theory, philosophy of law, American government, and politics and religion. At Villanova, he is a faculty associate of the Matthew J. Ryan Center for the Study of Free Institutions and the Public Good. He also holds the rank of Battalion Professor and serves as the university representative to the performance review board for Villanova's Navy Reserve Officers' Training Corps unit. He is the faculty adviser to the mock trial team and to the men's club lacrosse team, and he is a mentor in the university's Faith and Learning Scholars Program. Dr. Mark serves on the Jewish Religion and Culture Lecture Committee and the Graduate Committee of the Department of Political Science.

In addition, Dr. Mark is an assistant editor of Interpretation: A Journal of Political Philosophy; a fellow of the Witherspoon Institute in Princeton, NJ; and a contributor to Arc of the Universe: Ethics and Global Justice. He has been published recently in US News & World Report, Investor's Business Daily, and the Philadelphia Inquirer, and he recently appeared on CNN, Al Jazeera America, and CBS radio in Philadelphia.

He holds a BA (magna cum laude), MA, and PhD from the Department of Politics at Princeton University. He wrote his dissertation under the direction of Professor Robert P. George on the subject of "Authority and Legal Obligation." There, he participated in the Program in Law and Public Affairs and the Penn-Princeton Bioethics Forum. He was also affiliated with the James Madison Program in American Ideals and Institutions and served as coordinator of its Undergraduate Fellows Forum.

Dr. Mark works with the Tikvah Fund in New York and the Hertog Foundation in Washington, DC, and he has taught at the Straus Center for Torah and Western Thought at Yeshiva University. He speaks frequently for wide a variety of groups, including the Archdiocese of Denver, the Eastern University Philosophical Society, the Neumann Forum, the Love and Fidelity Network, the Becket Fund for Religious Liberty, the US Military Academy (West Point), the American Enterprise Institute, the Jewish Heritage Center, Chabad at Dartmouth, and the Rae Kushner Yeshiva High School. Before graduate school, Dr. Mark spent four years as a high school teacher in New York City, and he received the New Jersey Department of Education Commissioner's Distinguished Teacher Candidate Award while earning his teaching certification.

For the 2015-16 academic year, Dr. Mark will be on sabbatical from Villanova University as a visiting fellow in the Department of Politics at Princeton University under the sponsorship of the department's James Madison Program in American Ideals and Institutions.

Dr. Mark was appointed to the Commission on May 9, 2014 by Speaker of the House John Boehner (R-OH).

Rev. Thomas J. Reese, S.J., Commissioner

Rev. Thomas J. Reese, S.J. is a Senior Analyst for the National Catholic Reporter, a position he has held since 2014. Previously, he was a Senior Fellow at the Woodstock Theological Center from 2006 to 2013 and from 1988 to 1998. He joined the Center as a Visiting Fellow in 1985. He was Editor-in-Chief of America magazine from 1998 to 2005 and an associate editor from 1978 to 1985. As an associate editor, he covered politics, economics, and the Catholic Church. Rev. Reese entered the Jesuits in 1962 and was ordained in 1974. He received a B.A. and an M.A. from St. Louis University, an M.Div. from the Jesuit School of Theology at Berkeley, and a Ph.D. in Political Science from the University of California, Berkeley.

Rev. Reese was appointed to the Commission on May 14, 2014 by President Obama.

Hon. Hannah Rosenthal, Commissioner

Hannah Rosenthal is the CEO and president of the Milwaukee Jewish Federation. Prior to joining the Milwaukee Jewish Federation, Hannah served as: Special Envoy to Monitor and Combat Anti-Semitism, U.S. State Department; Executive Director, Chicago Foundation for Women (CFW); Executive Director, Jewish Council for Public Affairs (JCPA); and Executive Director, Wisconsin Women's Council.

In these positions, Rosenthal has demonstrated an ability to build relationships within and between communities, creating unique connections with local, national and international influencers. She has been honored for her achievements throughout her career, with distinctions including: the National Council for Jewish Women Building Bridges Award (2013); Pearls for Teen Girls, Women Inspired to Lead (2013); RUMI Forum Peace and Dialogue Award for extraordinary contributions (2012); National Council for Jewish Women Faith and Humanity Award for advancing human rights and advocacy (2011); 2010 – Forward Fifty's Top 5, national Jewish weekly's list of the world's most influential Jews (2010); Haiti Holocaust Committee award for advocacy for historical memory (2010); and Women to Watch, Jewish Women International's list of outstanding leaders (2005). Hannah has also received the Wisconsin State Civil Rights Award and the Wisconsin Community Action Advocacy Award.

Rosenthal currently represents the at-large community on the United States National Commission for the United Nations Educational, Scientific, and Cultural Organization (UNESCO), and on the Committee on Holocaust Denial and State-Sponsored Anti-Semitism of the United States Holocaust Memorial Museum.

As an agent for change, Rosenthal was responsible for a significant new approach to combating anti-Semitism in her most recent position with the State Department, and successfully led CFW through its transition into an advocacy organization. She is leading the reorganization of the Milwaukee Jewish Federation following the agency's strategic reimagining process.

Rosenthal is a graduate of the University of Wisconsin-Madison and studied for the rabbinate in Jerusalem and California. She has long been active in public policy in Wisconsin, serving in support roles to a Wisconsin State Representative and a Wisconsin Member of Congress, as well as heading a Wisconsin state agency and a regional federal agency. Rosenthal also is a former member of the Madison Jewish Federation Board of Directors.

Ms. Rosenthal was appointed to the Commission on June 17, 2014 by the Honorable Nancy Pelosi.

Hon. Eric Schwartz, Commissioner

Eric Schwartz became dean of the Hubert H. Humphrey School of Public Affairs at the University of Minnesota in October 2011, after serving for 25 years in senior public service positions in government, at the United Nations and in the philanthropic and non-governmental communities.

Prior to his arrival in Minnesota, he was U.S. Assistant Secretary of State for Population, Refugees, and Migration, having been nominated by President Obama and confirmed by the U.S. Senate in 2009. Working with Secretary of State Hillary Clinton, he served as the Department of State's principal humanitarian official, managing a $1.85 billion budget, as well as State Department policy and programs for U.S. refugee admissions and U.S. international assistance worldwide.

From 2006 through 2009, he directed the Connect U.S. Fund, a multi-foundation – NGO collaborative seeking to promote responsible U.S. engagement overseas, and which included the Hewlett Foundation, the

Rockefeller Brothers Fund, the Open Society Institute, the Ford Foundation, the Atlantic Philanthropies and the Mott Foundation.

From August 2005 through January 2007, he served as the UN Secretary-General Kofi Annan's Deputy Special Envoy for Tsunami Recovery. In that capacity, he worked with the Special Envoy, former President Clinton, to promote an effective recovery effort. Before that appointment, he was a lead expert for the congressionally mandated Mitchell-Gingrich Task Force on UN Reform. Prior to that, in 2003 and 2004, he served as the second-ranking official at the Office of the UN High Commissioner for Human Rights in Geneva.

From 1993 to 2001, he served at the National Security Council at the White House, ultimately as Senior Director and Special Assistant to the President for Multilateral and Humanitarian Affairs. He managed responses on international humanitarian, human rights and rule of law issues, as well as United Nations affairs, including peacekeeping.

From 2001 through 2003, he held fellowships at the Woodrow Wilson Center, the U.S. Institute of Peace and the Council on Foreign Relations. During this period, he also served as a contributor to the Responsibility to Protect Project of the International Commission on Intervention and State Sovereignty.

From 1989 to 1993, he served as Staff Consultant to the U.S. House of Representatives Foreign Affairs Subcommittee on Asian and Pacific Affairs. Prior to his work on the Subcommittee, he was Washington Director of the human rights organization Asia Watch (now known as Human Rights Watch-Asia). He holds a law degree from New York University School of Law, where he was a recipient of a Root-Tilden-Snow Scholarship for commitment to public service through law; a Master of Public Affairs degree from the Woodrow Wilson School of Public and International Affairs Princeton University; and a Bachelor of Arts degree, with honors, in Political Science from the State University of New York at Binghamton. Between 2001 and 2009, he also was a visiting lecturer of public and international affairs at the Woodrow Wilson School, teaching both undergraduate and graduate seminars, taskforces and workshops.

He was appointed to the Commission on April 25, 2013 by President Obama and reappointed in 2014.

APPENDIX 2
ERITREAN PRISONER LIST 2015

Jehovah's Witness Prisoner List 2015

NAME	AGE AT ARREST	SEX	LOCATION	DATE OF ARREST	REASON
Paulos Eyassu	41	Male	Sawa Camp	9/24/1994	Conscientious Objection
Isaac Mogos	38	Male	Sawa Camp	9/24/1994	Conscientious Objection
Negede Teklemariam	40	Male	Sawa Camp	9/24/1994	Conscientious Objection
Aron Abraha	40	Male	Sawa Camp	5/9/2001	Conscientious Objection
Mussie Fessehaya	42	Male	Sawa Camp	6/2003	Conscientious Objection
Ambakom Tsegezab	38	Male	Sawa Camp	2/2004	Conscientious Objection
Bemnet Fessehaye	43	Male	Sawa Camp	2/2005	Conscientious Objection
Henok Ghebru	30	Male	Sawa Camp	2/2005	Conscientious Objection
Worede Kiros	57	Male	Sawa Camp	5/4/2005	Religious Activity
Yonathan Yonas	28	Male	Sawa Camp	11/12/2005	Religious Activity
Kibreab Fessehaye	36	Male	Sawa Camp	12/27/2005	Conscientious Objection
Bereket Abraha Oqbagabir	46	Male	Sawa Camp	1/1/2006	Conscientious Objection
Yosief Fessehaye	25	Male	Sawa Camp	2007	Conscientious Objection
Mogos Gebremeskel	68	Male	Adi-Abieto	7/3/2008	Unknown
Bereket Abraha	67	Male	Meitir Camp	7/8/2008	Unknown
Ermias Ashgedom	24	Male	Meitir Camp	7/11/2008	Unknown
Habtemichael Mekonen	73	Male	Meitir Camp	7/17/2008	Unknown
Tareke Tesfamariam	63	Male	Meitir Camp	8/4/2008	Unknown
Tesfai Teklemariam	61	Male	Meitir Camp	8/8/2004	Unknown
Goitom Aradom	70	Male	Meitir Camp	8/8/2008	Unknown
Habtemichael Tesfamariam	66	Male	Meitir Camp	8/8/2008	Unknown
Tewoldemedhin Habtezion	55	Male	Meitir Camp	8/9/2008	Unknown
Teferi Beyene	73	Male	Meitir Camp	9/23/2008	Unknown
Beyene Abraham	62	Male	Karen Police Station	10/23/2008	Unknown
Asfaha Haile	80	Male	Meitir Camp	12/2/2008	Unknown
Tsehaye Leghesse	75	Male	Karen Police Station	12/23/2008	Unknown
Tsegezeab Tesfazghi	65	Male	Meitir Camp	12/23/2008	Unknown
Tsehaye Tesfamariam	73	Male	Meitir Camp	1/5/2009	Unknown
Yoab Tecle	63	Male	Meitir Camp	4/23/2009	Unknown
Yoel Tsegezab	38	Male	Meitir Camp	8/26/2008	Conscientious Objection
Nehemiah Hagos	28	Male	Meitir Camp	8/26/2008	Conscientious Objection
Samuel Ghirmay	32	Male	Meitir Camp	3/2009	Conscientious Objection
Teklu Gebrehiwot	39	Male	Meitir Camp	6/28/2009	Religious Meeting

NAME	AGE AT ARREST	SEX	LOCATION	DATE OF ARREST	REASON
Isaias Afeworki	29	Male	Meitir Camp	6/28/2009	Religious Meeting
Isaac Milen	24	Female	Meitir Camp	6/28/2009	Religious Meeting
Faiza Seid	29	Female	Meitir Camp	6/28/2009	Religious Meeting
Tesfazion Gebremichael	72	Male	5th Police Station	7/20/2011	Unknown
Hagos Woldemichael	62	Male	Meitir Camp	4/21/2012	Preaching at a Funeral
Araia Ghebremariam	60	Male	Meitir Camp	4/21/2012	Preaching at a Funeral
Tsegabirhan Berhe	51	Male	Meitir Camp	4/21/2012	Preaching at a Funeral
Daniel Meharizghi	37	Male	Meitir Camp	4/21/2012	Preaching at a Funeral
Yoseph Tesfarmaiam	50	Male	Around Keren	5/2012	Conscientious Objection
Wogahta Dawit	29	Female	Mai-Serwa	7/3/2013	Religious Activity
Gebru Berane	64	Male	2nd Police Station	4/14/2014	Religious Meeting
Tekle Gebrehiwot	58	Male	2nd Police Station	4/14/2014	Religious Meeting
Thomas Tesfagabir	32	Male	5th Police Station	4/27/2014	Religious Meeting
Mordochai Estifanos	20	Male	5th Police Station	4/27/2014	Religious Meeting
Mehari Tewolde	*	Male	5th Police Station	4/27/2014	Religious Meeting
Michael Gashazghi	22	Male	5th Police Station	4/27/2014	Religious Meeting
Liya Hidry	*	Female	5th Police Station	4/27/2014	Religious Meeting
Nigisti Asfaha	48	Female	5th Police Station	4/27/2014	Religious Meeting
Wintana Shiwaseged	25	Female	5th Police Station	4/27/2014	Religious Meeting
Mikaal Taddessee	23	Female	5th Police Station	4/27/2014	Religious Meeting
Emnet Woldai	35	Female	5th Police Station	4/27/2014	Religious Meeting
Salem Ghebrehiwot	19	Female	5th Police Station	4/27/2014	Religious Meeting
Senait Berhane	*	Female	5th Police Station	4/27/2014	Religious Meeting
Bereket Habteyesus	22	Male	2nd Police Station	5/26/2014	Conscientious Objection
Melaku Kahsai	*	Male	2nd Police Station	Unknown	Unkown

APPENDIX 3
PAKISTANI PRISIONER LIST 2015

Individuals with pending death sentences or in the process of appeal in Pakistan

NAME(S)	RELIGION	SEX	LOCATION	DATE OF SENTENCE	SECTION	ALLEGATION	SENTENCE
Mohammad Zulfiqar Ali	*	Male	Lahore	7/14/2014		Writing blasphemous messages on walls in 2008	Death and 1 million Rs.
Shafqat Emmanuel	Christian	Male	Toba Tek Singh	4/4/2014	295-B, C, D	Sending blasphemous text messages on June 18, 2013	Death
Shugufta Emmanuel	Christian	Female	Toba Tek Singh	4/4/2014	295-B, C, D	Sending blasphemous text messages on June 18, 2013	Death
Savan Masih	Christian	Male	Joseph Colony, Punjab	3/27/2014	295-C	Blasphemy	Death and 200,000 Rs.
Muhammad Asghar	*	Male	Sadiqabad	1/24/2014	295-C	Claiming to be a prophet	Death
Hazrat Ali Shah	*	Male	Barenis Village, Khyber-Pakhtunkhwa	12/15/2012	295	Blasphemy	Death and 10 years in prison
Soofi Mohammad Ishaq	Muslim	Male	Talagang/Chakwal	1/20/2012	295-A, C	Claiming to be a prophet	Death and Fined Rs. 200,000
Abdul Sattar	*	Male	Larkana	6/22/11	*	Blasphemy	Death & fined Rs. 50,000
Rafiq	*	Male	Jalalpur Peerwala	2/2/11	*	Blasphemy	Death
Malik Muhammad Ashraf	Muslim	Male	Central Jail (Adiala) Rawalpindi	2/17/10	295-C, 298-A	Derogatory remarks against the Prophet	Death sentence pending
Malik Ashraf	Muslim	Male	Pind Dadan Khan (Punjab)	3/9/10	*	Blasphemy	Death
Ms. Aasia Noreen (Bibi)	Christian	Female	District Jail Sheikhupura	6/19/09	295-C	Derogatory remarks against the Prophet	Death, Rs. 100,000 fine, appeal pending
Muhammad Shafeeq Latif	*	Male	Sialkot, Punjab	6/18/08	*	Blasphemy	Death
Liaqat	Muslim	Male	District Jail Faisalabad	3/21/06	295-C	Blasphemy	Death & life imprisonment, confined in central jail Faisalabad
Muhammad Shafiq	Muslim	Male	District Jail Sahiwal	3/17/06	295-B, C	Passing derogatory remarks about Prophet and burning Quran	Death, 6 months jail, fine Rs. 500,000 -appeal pending
Abdul Hameed	Muslim	Male	District Jail Sahiwal	3/3/06	295-A,B&C	Proclaimed himself a prophet of Islam, built model of Kaaba in yard	Death & 35 years, fined Rs. 80,000
Anwar Kenneth	Christian	Male	New Central Jail Multan (Multan Jail)	6/15/01	295-C	Distributing pamphlet containing Bible verses	Death and Rs. 500K fine,
Wajihul Hassan aka Murshid Masih	Christian - convert	Male	District Jail Sheikhupura	3/3/99	295-A, C, 298 & 298-A	Writing/passing derogatory remarks	Death, appeal pending

Individuals sentenced to life in prison for violation of blasphemy laws

NAME	RELIGION	SEX	LOCATION	DATE OF SENTENCE	PENAL CODE SECTION	ALLEGATION	SENTENCE
Malik Mohammad Farooq	*	Male	Karachi district sessions	05/08/2014	*	Tearing up a banner inscribed with Muhammed's name	Life in prison
Sajjad Masih	Christian	Male	Station City Gojra	07/13/2013	295-C	Blasphemy	Life - appeal pending
Manzarul Haq Shah Jahan	*	Male	Kasur	03/17/2012	295-C	Blasphemy	Life and Fined 200,000
Muhammad Mushtaq alias Masta	Muslim	Male	New Central Jail Multan	8/1/11	295-B	Disgracing Qur'an	Life - appeal pending
Imran Ghafoor	Christian	Male	District Jail Faisalabad	7/1/11	295-A, B	Burning pages of Qur'an in front of his shop	Life
Muhammad Ishaq	*	Male	Uch Sharif, Mohallah Qadirabad	1/5/11	*	Blasphemy	Life
Muhammad Safdar	Muslim	Male	New Central Jail Multan	10/1/10	295-B	Blasphemy	Life - appeal pending
Muhammad Shafi	Muslim	Male	New Central Jail Multan	4/8/10	*	Vandalizing poster with Qur'an verses on it	Life, Rs. 200,000 fine, appealed
Muhammad Aslam (son)	*	Male	New Central Jail Multan	4/8/10	*	Vandalizing poster with Qur'an verses on it	Life, Rs. 200,000 fine, appeal pending
Imran Masih	Christian	Male	District Jail Faisalabad	1/1/10	295-A, B	Blasphemy	10 years rigorous, life and fined 100,000/appeal pending
Abdul Kareem	Muslim	Male	District Jail Sahiwal	6/21/07	295-B	Blasphemy	Life - appeal pending
Inayat Rasool	Muslim	Male	District Jail Sahiwal	6/23/06	295-B	Putting Qur'an in canal water	Life - appeal pending
Asif	Muslim	Male	District Jail Sahiwal	6/18/06	295-B	Burning the Qur'an	Life - appeal pending
Arif Mahdi	Muslim	Male	New Central Jail Multan	4/18/06	295-B	Disgracing Islamic booklets.	Life - appeal pending
Imran	Muslim	Male	District Jail Faisalabad	7/1/05	295-B	Blasphemy - after property dispute	Life imprisonment
Shamas ud Din	Muslim	Male	District Jail Sahiwal	7/1/05	295-A, C	Writing blasphemous letter	Life and 150,000 Rs fine - appeal pending
Maqsood Ahmad	Muslim	Male	District Jail Sahiwal	6/28/05	295-C	Put Qur'an on floor	Life, fined Rs. 20,000 - appeal pending
Muhammad Shahzad	Muslim	Male	District Jail Sahiwal	3/24/03	295-B	Assisting Muhammad Yousaf - burning Qur'an	Life - appeal pending
Muhammad Yousaf	Muslim	Male	District Jail Sahiwal	3/24/03	295-B	Burning the Qur'an	Life - appeal pending
Rehmat Ali	Muslim	Male	District Jail Faisalabad	*	295-A, B	Blasphemy	Life

APPENDIX 4
AZERBAIJANI PRISIONER LIST 2015

Prominent Muslim leaders and teachers caught up in a government campaign against independent and/or prominent activists, including some who were part of the official Azerbaijani Islamic establishment

	NAME	DATES OF ARREST	ARTICLES OF THE CRIMINAL CODE	PLACE OF DETENTION	STATUS
1	Tale Kamil Bagirov (Bagirzade)	31 Mar 2013	234.1	Labor Camp #12	On 24 March 2013, a week before his arrest, Bagirov gave a speech at a mosque, blaming the authorities for corruption and false arrests, calling on religious followers not to be afraid of "the oppression of a dictator," and posting the speech to social media. On 1 November 2013, Sabunchu District Court sentenced him to a two year term; In August 2014, his prison term was extended by four months; he is still imprisoned as of this writing.
2	Abdul Neymat Suleymanov	12 Aug 2011	228.1, 233, 234.1, 234.4.3, 283.2.1	Prison #8	Suleymanov is a leader of the Jafari Heylyat (Life of Jafar) Muslim religious congregation in Baku. He was arrested in an official sweep against popular Muslim leaders. He was sentenced to an 11-year term in 10 August 2012 by Baku Court of Grave Crimes. Baku Court of Appeals upheld the sentence on 23 January 2013.
3	Jeyhun Jafarov	10 Mar 2015	Accusations of treason		Jafarov, 42, has led hajj groups to Mecca; led a series on Space TV on religion; translated books by late Iranian Ayatollah Mohammadreza Mahdavi Kani; and led the Evolution Translation Center. On 4 March, he returned with his brother from an 8-day visit to Iran. After their return, Jafarov was ordered to the Ministry of National Security (MNS) secret police on 10 March 2015 and arrested. On 12 March 2015, Baku's Sabail District Court ordered him held in pre-trial detention in the MNS secret police Investigation Prison in Baku for four months. He was told he is under investigation under Criminal Code Article 274 ("Treason") with a term ranging from 12 years to life.
4	Elshan Mustafaoglu	Dec 2014	Reportedly accused of treason		On 17 December 2014, the MNS detained theologian Elshan Mustafaoglu. Two days later, the court arrested him for four months. According to some reports, he is charged with treason. Until his arrest, he was press spokesman for the Caucasus Muslim Board, which has not commented on his arrest.

Religious activists arrested with journalist Nijat Alieyev, editor of www.azad.xeber.az, a Muslim website. Alieyev, other journalists, and young activists were arrested in 2012–2013 for campaigning against the arrests of religious believers as well as for distributing discs with religious materials, including sermons by imprisoned Muslim leaders Abdul Suleymanov and Tale Bagirov.

	NAME	DATES OF ARREST	ARTICLES OF THE CRIMINAL CODE	PLACE OF DETENTION	STATUS
5	Valeh Mammadaga Abdullayev	9 Dec 2013	167.2.2.1, 281.2, 283.2.3	Baku Investigative Prison (Kurdakhani Detention Center)	Abdullayev was sentenced to 8 years in jail under a decision issued by Baku Court of Grave Crimes Judge Zeynal Agayev on 9 December 2013.
6	Gorkhmaz Huseyn Jamalov	18 Jan 2013	167.2.2.1, 281.2, 283.2.3	Baku Investigative Prison (Kurdakhani Detention Center)	Jamalov was sentenced to 7 years in jail under a decision issued by Baku Court of Grave Crimes Judge Zeynal Agayev on 9 December 2013.
7	Ali Etibar Aliyev	9 Dec 2013	167.2.2.1, 283.2.3	Baku Investigative Prison (Kurdakhani Detention Center)	Aliyev was sentenced to 4 years in jail under a decision issued by Baku Court of Grave Crimes Judge Zeynal Agayev on 9 December 2013.
8	Elimkhan Gurbankhan Huseynov	22 May 2012	167.2.2.1, 283.2.3	Baku Investigative Prison (Kurdakhani Detention Center)	Huseynov was sentenced to 7 years in jail under a decision issued by Baku Court of Grave Crimes Judge Zeynal Agayev on 9 December 2013.
9	Samir Khanpasha Huseynov	23 May 2012	167.2.2.1, 228.1, 228.4, 283.2.3	Baku Investigative Prison (Kurdakhani Detention Center)	Huseynov was sentenced to 6 years in jail under a decision issued by Baku Court of Grave Crimes Judge Zeynal Agayev on 9 December 2013. Baku Court of Appeals upheld the decision on 27 June 2014.
10	Safar Rovshan Mammadov	9 Dec 2013	167.2.2.1, 283.2.3	Baku Investigative Prison (Kurdakhani Detention Center)	Mammadov was sentenced to 3 years and 4 months in jail under a decision issued by Baku Court of Grave Crimes Judge Zeynal Agayev on 9 December 2013. Baku Court of Appeals upheld the ruling on 27 June 2014
11	Elvin Nuraddin Nasirov	20 May 2012	167.2.2.1, 234.4.1, 234.4.3, 281.2, 283.2.3	Baku Investigative Prison (Kurdakhani Detention Center)	Nasirov was sentenced to 9 years in jail under a decision issued by Baku Court of Grave Crimes Judge Zeynal Agayev on 9 December 2013.
12	Jeyhun Zabil Safarli	20 May 2012	167.2.2.1, 234.4.1, 234.4.3, 281.2, 283.2.3	Baku Investigative Prison (Kurdakhani Detention Center)	Safarli was sentenced to 9 years in jail under a decision issued by Baku Court of Grave Crimes Judge Zeynal Agayev on 9 December 2013. The Baku Court of Appeals upheld the ruling on 27 June 2014.
13	Emin Yadigar Tofidi	16 Jan 2013	167.2.2.1, 283.2.3	Baku Investigative Prison (Kurdakhani Detention Center)	Tofidi was sentenced to 3.5 years in jail under a decision issued by Baku Court of Grave Crimes Judge Zeynal Agayev on 9 December 2013. Baku Court of Appeals upheld the ruling on 27 June 2014.

Religious activists arrested in the Masalli region along with journalist Araz Guliyev, editor of www.xeber44.com, a website critical of Azerbaijani religion policy. The defendants assisted Guliyev's journalist activity. In 2012, six Muslims from Masalli were arrested on various false charges, including stoning people during a local folk festival.

	NAME	DATES OF ARREST	ARTICLES OF THE CRIMINAL CODE	PLACE OF DETENTION	STATUS
14	Rza Gorkhmaz Agali	9 Dec 2012	233, 315.2, 324	Prison #14	On 5 April 2013, Agali was sentenced to 7 years in prison under a decision issued by Lankaran Court of Grave Crimes Judge Nizami Guliyev. Shirvan Court of Appeals Judge Kamran Akbarov upheld this ruling on 9 January 2014.
15	Suraj Valeh Agayev	15 Sept 2012	233, 315.2, 324	Prison #5	On 5 April 2013, Agayev was sentenced to 5 years in jail under a decision issued by Lankaran Court of Grave Crimes Judge Nizami Guliyev. Shirvan Court of Appeals Judge Kamran Akbarov upheld this ruling on 9 January 2014.
16	Nijat Yaser Aliyev	18 Sept 2012	233, 315.2, 324	Prison #16	On 5 April 2013, Aliyev was sentenced to 4.5 years in jail under a decision issued by Lankaran Court of Grave Crimes Judge Nizami Guliyev. Shirvan Court of Appeals Judge Kamran Akbarov upheld this ruling on 9 January 2014.
17	Khalid Nofal Kazimov	14 Sept 2012	233, 234.4.3, 315.2, 324	Prison #6	On 5 April 2013, Kazimov was sentenced to 8 years in jail under a decision issued by Lankaran Court of Grave Crimes Judge Nizami Guliyev. Shirvan Court of Appeals Judge Kamran Akbarov upheld this ruling on 9 January 2014.
18	Namig Alisa Kishiyev	18 Sept 2012	233, 315.2, 324	Prison #5	On 5 April 2013, Kishiyev was sentenced to 4.5 years in jail under a decision issued by Lankaran Court of Grave Crimes Judge Nizami Guliyev. Shirvan Court of Appeals Judge Kamran Akbarov upheld this ruling on 9 January 2014.
19	Ziya Ibrahim Tahirov	9 Sept 2012	233, 315.2, 324	Prison #5	On 5 April 2013, Tahirov was sentenced to 7 years in jail under a decision issued by Lankaran Court of Grave Crimes Judge Nizami Guliyev. Shirvan Court of Appeals Judge Kamran Akbarov upheld this ruling on 9 January 2014.

Cases of those arrested for participation in the 5 October 2012 "Freedom for hijab" public protest. On 10 December 2010, Azerbaijan's Education Ministry offered that school uniforms had to be worn, thereby in effect banning the hijab (Islamic headscarf.) A May 2011 mass protest was violently dispersed; a second protest in October resulted in mass arrests. There are reports that government provocateurs initiated a confrontation with police that lead to violence and arrests.

	NAME	DATES OF ARREST	ARTICLES OF THE CRIMINAL CODE	PLACE OF DETENTION	STATUS
20	Tarlan Faiq Agadadashov	5 Oct 2012	233, 315.2	Prison #16	Agadadashov was sentenced to 5.5 years in jail under a 22 April 2013 decision of the Narimanov District Court. The Baku Court of Appeals upheld this ruling on 19 December 2013.
21	Rovshan Huseyn Allahverdiyev	5 Oct 2012	233, 315.2	Prison #16	Allahverdiyev was sentenced to 5.5 years of imprisonment under a 22 April 2013 decision of the Narimanov District Court. The Baku Court of Appeals upheld this ruling on 19 December 2013.
22	Nasimi Yusif Hasanov	6 Oct 2012	228.1, 234.1	Prison #16	Hasanov was arrested in connection with his participation in the "Freedom for hijab" protest but unlike other defendants was not charged with taking part in an unauthorized public demonstration. He was sentenced to 4 years in jail on 27 July 2013.
23	Ilham Bahman Hatamov	5 Oct 2012	233, 315.2	Prison #14	Hatamov was sentenced to 5.5 years in jail under a 22 April 2013 decision of Narimanov District Court. Baku Court of Appeals upheld the ruling on 19 December 2013.
24	David Tarlan Karimov	5 Oct 2012	233, 315.2	Prison #16	Karimov was sentenced to 6 years in jail under a 22 April 2013 decision of Narimanov District Court. Baku Court of Appeals upheld this ruling on 19 December 2013.
25	Anar Asgar Gasimli	5 Oct 2012	233, 315.2	Prison #14	Gasimli was sentenced to 5.5 years in jail under a 22 April 2013 decision of Narimanov District Court. The Baku Court of Appeals upheld this ruling on 19 December 2013.
26	Aydin Janbakhish Mammadov	5 Oct 2012	233	Prison #17	Mammadov was sentenced to 2 years and 3 months in jail under a 4 June 2013 decision of Narimanov District Court. Baku Court of Appeals upheld this ruling in July 2013.
27	Elshad Fikrat Rzayev	23 Feb 2013	233, 315.2	Prison #16	Rzayev was sentenced to 6 years in jail under a 3 June 2013 decision of Narimanov District Court. The Baku Court of Appeals upheld the decision in August 2013.
28	Telman Shirali Shiraliyev	5 Oct 2012	233, 315.2	Prison #16	Shiraliyev was sentenced to 6 years in jail under a 22 April 2013 decision of Narimanov District Court. Baku Court of Appeals upheld the decision on 19 December 2013.
29	Ramil Rahim Valiyev	5 Oct 2012	167.2.1, 233, 315.2	Prison #5	Valiyev was sentenced to 6.5 years in jail under a 3 June 2013 decision of the Narimanov District Court. Baku Court of Appeals upheld the decision in August 2013.

Imam and members of the Sunni Lezgin Mosque in Baku's Old City who work in the Burhan bookshop. As of August 2014, the Lezgin mosque community was told it must vacate its mosque so it can be renovated; In February 2015, Imam Qarayev and four others were arrested on charges of selling texts that had not been officially approved.

	NAME	DATES OF ARREST	ARTICLES OF THE CRIMINAL CODE	PLACE OF DETEN-TION	STATUS
30	Mubariz Qarayev	Feb 2015	167.2.1	Pre-trial detention at MNS secret police	Imam of the Sunni Lezgin Mosque in Baku's Old City, and owner of Burhan Muslim book-shop. Arrested with several other bookstore workers.
31	Habibulla Omarov	26 Feb 2015	167.2.2.1	Pre-trial detention at MNS secret police	Bookstore worker.
32	Salim Qasimov	26 Feb 2015	167.2.1	Pre-trial detention at MNS secret police	Bookstore worker.
33	Eyvaz (last name unknown)	26 Feb 2015	167.2.1	Pre-trial detention at MNS secret police	Bookstore worker.
34	Azad Gafarov	26 Feb 2015	167.2.2.1	Pre-trial detention at MNS secret police	Bookstore worker.

Two readers of Turkish theologian Said Nursi, whose texts are banned in Azerbaijan

	NAME	PRETRIAL DETENTION	ARTICLES OF THE CRIMINAL CODE	PLACE OF DETENTION	STATUS
35	Zakariyya Isakh Mammadov	14 Apr 2014	168.1, 167.2.2.1, 299.0.2	MNS Detention Facility	Accused of conducting private religious classes on banned Turkish theologian Said Nursi.
36	Shahin Hasanov	14 Apr 2014	168.1, 167.2.2.1, 299.0.2	MNS Detention Facility	Accused of conducting private religious classes on banned Turkish theologian Said Nursi.

Jehovah's Witnesses detained for distributing religious texts not approved by the state

	NAME	PRETRIAL DETENTION	ARTICLES OF THE CRIMINAL CODE	PLACE OF DETENTION	STATUS
37	Valida Jabrayilova	17 Feb 2015	167.2.2.1	MNS jail, Baku	Charged with distributing religious texts not approved by the state.
38	Irina Zakharchenko	17 Feb 2015	167.2.2.1	MNS jail, Baku	Charged with distributing religious texts not approved by the state.

Jehovah's Witness jailed for conscientious objection to compulsory military service

	NAME	DATE OF ARREST	ARTICLES OF THE CRIMINAL CODE	PLACE OF DETENTION	STATUS
39	Kamran Shikhaliyev	10 Oct 2013	335.1	Disciplinary battalion, Salyan	Conscientious objector to compulsory military service, Jehovah's Witness. In April 2014 Jalilabad Military Court sentenced him to one year in prison. On 16 July 2014 Shirvan Appeal Court denied his appeal.

Other cases

	NAME	DATE OF ARREST	ARTICLES OF THE CRIMINAL CODE	PLACE OF DETENTION	STATUS
40	Zohrab Shikhaliyev	13 Nov 2014	228.1	Prison #1	A Sunni Muslim given a six month jail term for hosting a public prayer room in his home by Judge Azer Ismayilov at Sumgait City Court.

Religious freedom/Human rights defenders

	NAME	DATES OF ARREST	ARTICLES OF THE CRIMINAL CODE	PLACE OF DETENTION	STATUS
41	Leyla Yunus (Leyla Islam Yunusova)	30 Jul 2014	274, 178.3.2, 192.2.2, 213.2.2, 320.1, 320.2	Baku Detention Facility	Yunus runs the Institute of Peace and Democracy. She has worked on numerous projects relating to human rights, religious freedom, political persecution, corruption, human trafficking, gender issues, violations of property rights, monitoring of court proceedings, peace initiatives, and more. She has studied the cases of more than 100 political prisoners and revealed their illegal arrest to be entirely politically motivated.
42	Arif Yunus (Arif Seyfulla Yunusov)	30 Jul 2014	274, 178.3.2	Baku Investigative Facility (Kurdakhani prison)	A historian, academic, and expert on Islam, he is the husband of Leyla Yunus. He worked at the Institute of Peace and Democracy.
43	Rasul Agahasan Jafarov	2 Aug 2014	192.2.2, 213.1, 308.2, 179.3.2, 313	Baku Detention Facility (Kurdakhani prison)	Jafarov is a lawyer at the Institute for Reporters' Freedom and Safety. In 2010, he co-founded the Human Rights Club. A month after presenting a list of political prisoners to a session of the Parliamentary Assembly of the Council of Europe (PACE), and immediately following the arrest of Leyla Yunus, Jafarov was taken into custody. On 16 April 2015 he was sentenced to 6.5 in prison by the Baku Grave Crimes Court.
44	Intiqam Kamil Aliyev	8 Aug 2014	179.3.2, 192.2.2, 213.1, 308.2	Baku Detention Facility (Kurdakhani Prison)	Head of the Legal Education Society, Aliyev has been involved in human rights advocacy for nearly 20 years, including on religious freedom issues. As a lawyer, he has filed over 300 complaints with the European Court of Human Rights. During a 2014 speech at a PACE session, he criticized the government for political prisoners, attacks on independent NGOs, false charges, arrests of government critics, and mass violations of property rights. He was sentenced to 7.5 years in prison and deprived of holding any position for 3 years by Baku Court on Grave Crimes.

Criminal Code Articles:

28.2 – the criminal liability shall be instituted only for preparation of semi-serious, and serious crimes;

167.2.1 – import, sale, and distribution of religious literature, religious items and other informational materials of a religious nature with the aim of reproduction, sale and distribution without appropriate authorization;

167.2.2.1 – import, sale and distribution of religious literature, religious items and other informational materials of a religious nature with the intent to reproduce, sell and distribute without appropriate authorization, committed with advance agreement by a group of persons or an organized group;

168 – creation of a group carrying out activity under the pretext of spreading a religious faith and carrying out religious activity and by this illegally harming social order, or harming the health of citizens or violating the rights of citizens irrespective of the form of infringement, as well as distracting citizens from performance of duties established by law, as well as leadership of such a group or participation in it;

168.2 – implementation of religious activities and thus infringing rights of the citizens (involving minors in commitment of these acts);

178.3.2 – fraud, with a large amount of damage;

179.3.2 – assignment or waste, through plunder of property entrusted to the guilty party by another person, in a large amount;

180.3.1 – robbery by an organized group;

182.2.2 – Extortion, is requirement to transfer another's property or right on property or commitment of other actions which is admitted as in property nature under threat of application of violence, distribution of data, dishonoring a victim or his close relatives, as well as by threat of destruction of property belonging to them, repeatedly;

192.2.2 – illegal business committed through derivation of income in a large amount;

204.3.1 – manufacturing or selling of counterfeit money or securities by an organized group;

204.3.2 – manufacturing or selling of counterfeit money or securities in a large amount;

213.1 – evasion of taxes or obligatory state social insurance payments in a large amount;

214.2.1 – preparation of a crime committed with advance arrangement by a group of persons, an orga-

nized group, or a criminal community or organization;

213.2.2 – tax evasion, in large amounts;

214.2.3 – preparation of a crime committed with the application of firearms or objects used as a weapon;

218.1 – creation of a criminal organization in order to commit semi-serious or serious crimes, as well as a management of such organizations, structural divisions included, and also the creation of organizers' associations, heads or other representatives of the organized groups with plans to develop and conditions for committing of semi-serious or serious crimes;

218.2 – participation in criminal community (criminal organization) or in association of organizers, heads or other representatives of the organized groups;

221.3 – hooliganism, committed with a weapon or use of items as weapons;

228.1 – illegal purchase, transfer, selling, storage, transportation or carrying of firearms, accessories to it, supplies (except for the smooth-bore hunting weapons and ammunition), and explosives;

228.4 – acquiring, selling, or carrying a weapon;

228.2.1 – illegal purchase, transfer, selling, storage, transportation or carrying of fire-arms, accessories to it, supplies (except for the smooth-bore hunting weapon and ammunition to it), explosives on preliminary arrangement by group of persons;

228.3 – illegal purchase, transfer, sale, storage, transportation, or carrying of firearms, accessories, supplies (except for smooth-bore hunting weapons and ammunition), or explosives, and facilities, committed by an organized group;

228.4 – illegal purchase, selling or carrying of gas weapons, cold steel, including throwing weapon, except for districts where carrying of a cold steel is an accessory of a national suit or connected to hunting;

233 – organization of actions promoting infringement of a social order or active participation in such actions;

234.1 – illegal purchase or storage without a purpose of selling of narcotics or psychotropic substances exceeding an amount necessary for personal consumption;

234.4.1 – illegal purchase or storage without intent to sell of narcotics or psychotropic substances in a quantity exceeding the amount necessary for personal consumption, committed with preliminary arrangement by a group of persons or an organized group;

234.4.3 – illegal purchase or storage without intent to sell of narcotics or psychotropic substances in a quantity exceeding the amount necessary for personal consumption, in a large amount;

263.1 – violation of traffic rules and rules of operation of vehicles;

274 – treason against the State;

299.1 – payment of money to a witness or victim, with intent to influence them to give false testimonies; to an expert with intent to influence him/her to give a false report or testimony; or to a translator with the intent to influence them to translate incorrectly;

274 – deliberate action committed by a citizen of the Azerbaijan Republic to the detriment of the sovereignty, territorial integrity, state security or defensibility of the Azerbaijan Republic: changeover to enemy side, espionage, distribution of state secrets to foreign state, rendering assistance to a foreign state, foreign organization or their representatives resulting in hostile activity against the Azerbaijan Republic;

278 – actions towards the violent capture of power or violent deduction power that infringes on the Constitution of the Azerbaijan Republic, as well as actions directed taken towards violent changes of constitutional grounds of the states;

281.2 – public appeals for the violent capture of authority, violent deduction of authority, violent change to constitutional grounds, or infringement of the territorial integrity of the Azerbaijan Republic, as well as distribution of materials of such content, committed by a group of persons;

283.1 – actions directed to incite national, racial or religious hatred or humiliation of national advantage, or actions directed to restrict citizens' rights, or establish the superiority of citizens on the basis of their national or racial belonging or creed, committed publicly or with the use of mass media;

283.2.1 – actions directed to incite national, racial or religious hostility, or humiliation of national advantage, as well as actions directed to restrict citizens' rights, or establish the superiority of citizens on the basis of their national or racial belonging or creed, committed publicly or with the use of mass media committed with the application of violence or with the threat of violence;

283.2.3 – actions directed to incite national, racial, or religious hostility, or humiliation of national advantage, as well as actions directed to restrict citizens' rights,

or establish the superiority of citizens on the basis of their national or racial belonging or creed, committed publicly or with the use of mass media, committed by an organized group;

299.0.2 – violating legislation on holding religious meetings, marches, and other religious ceremonies;

308.2 – abuse of power committed with the intent of affecting the results of an election or referendum;

312.2 – the presentation of a bribe to official for commitment of obviously illegal actions (inaction) by him or repeated presentation of a bribe;

313 – service forgery, that is submission by an official person of official documents containing clearly false data, or amending such documents to invalidate their contents, committed as a mercenary or through other personal interest;

315.2 – resistance or use of force against a representative of authority;

320.1 – forging of official documents;

320.2 – use of forged documents;

324 – actions insulting the state flag or state emblem of the Republic of Azerbaijan;

335.1 – evasion of military service by causing harm to health or in another way;

APPENDIX 5
DEFENDING FREEDOMS PROJECT PRISONER LIST

Defending Freedoms Project Prisoners List

The Tom Lantos Human Rights Commission, in conjunction with the U.S. Commission on International Religious Freedom and Amnesty International USA, in 2012 launched the Defending Freedoms Project with the aim of supporting human rights and religious freedom throughout the world with a particular focus on prisoners of conscience.

Specifically, Members of Congress "adopt" prisoners of conscience, standing in solidarity with these brave men and women, while committing to advocate for their release.

The individuals below have been imprisoned for their religious beliefs or actions or their religious freedom advocacy. They are part of a longer list of prisoners of conscience, detained for other reasons, who are included in the Defending Freedoms Project.

CHINA
Gao Zhisheng

Gao Zhisheng (m, currently under house arrest) is one of the most respected human rights lawyers in China. He has defended activists and religious minorities and documented human rights abuses in China. This award-winning lawyer has handled a number of high-profile human rights cases, including those of Christians in Xinjiang and Falun Gong practitioners. In August 2006, after numerous death threats and continued harassment, Gao disappeared. In 2006, Gao was convicted of "subversion," and was sentenced to three years in prison. He was incarcerated in December 2011 for allegedly violating the conditions of his suspended three-year sentence. Gao was released from prison on August 7, 2014, and he is now kept under house arrest.

Chen Zhenping

Chen Zhenping (f) is a Falun Gong practitioner who was detained in August 2008 for "using a heretical organization to subvert the law." She is currently serving an eight-year prison sentence in Henan Provincial Women's prison. Repeated attempts by her lawyer to visit her since her imprisonment have all been blocked by the authorities. Her family has not been able to see her since March 2009. She has been subjected to regular beatings, been forcibly injected with drugs, and given electric shocks on sensitive parts of her body. Since her imprisonment, authorities have blocked visits from her lawyer, and since November 2009, they have denied information on Chen's wellbeing.

Guo Quan

Guo Quan (m) is a former professor who has been in prison since 2008 under a ten-year sentence for calling for political reform. In 2008, Guo played a leading role in a campaign to protect the rights of demobilized military officers. He also published criticism about the government's response to the Sichuan earthquake and exposed international human rights violations committed by the Party. He wrote letters to the government throughout 2007 calling for reforms and in December 2007, he announced that China People's Livelihood Party, an opposition party established by Guo, was renamed as the "New People's Party of China." On December 6, 2007, Quan was stripped of his associate professorship at Nanjing Normal University and relocated to the university library to serve as a data management officer.

On November 13, 2008, he was taken into custody by Nanjing police, who also raided his home, where Guo and his wife hosted regular Protestant "house church" activities. His family was informed that he was being criminally detained on suspicion of "inciting subversion of state power." On June 10, 2009, Guo's case was recorded on the docket of the Suqian Municipal Intermediate People's Court in Jiangsu province, and his trial was held on August 7, 2009. On October 16, 2009, the court convicted Guo of "subversion of state power" and sentenced him to a ten-year prison term. Guo's wife and son fled to the United Sates on January 23, 2012, where they are appealing for international help in winning his early release.

Alimujiang Yimiti

Alimujiang Yimiti (m) is a Uyghur Christian who converted from Islam in 1995. He and his wife, Gulinuer, were the leaders of a house church ministry in Kashgar, Xinjiang in the Uyghur Autonomous Region of China. Targeted for his minority faith and ethnicity, on January 12, 2008, the Kashgar police detained Alimujiang on "suspicion of inciting subversion of state power" and "leaking state secrets overseas." He was formally arrested on those charges on February 28, 2008. Later, the charges were changed to "divulging state secrets to foreign individuals" based on a private conversation the Uyghur Christian pastor held with an American Christian friend.

In 2009, he was sentenced during secret trials to 15 years in prison and 5 years deprivation of political rights. In September 2008, the United Nations Human Rights Council Working Group on Arbitrary Detention stated that 'the deprivation of liberty of Mr Alimujiang Yimiti is arbitrary, being in contravention of [...] the Universal Declaration of Human Rights' and that he 'is being kept in detention solely for his religious faith'. For the past several years, Yimiti's wife has petitioned police officers, government officials, and state agencies, but the officers refused to see them, even barring Alimujiang's lawyers from visiting him in prison. Yimiti's quality of life in prison is poor; he was hospitalized in 2009, but prison authorities claimed that it was for a routine health check, even though witnesses claimed that there were signs of brutality. Moreover, on January 23, 2013, prison authorities informed his wife that her monthly visits were being reduced to once every three months, without providing a reason.

Pastor Yang Rongli

Pastor Yang Rongli (f) has been serving a seven-and-a-half-year prison term since 2009 for leading the 50,000-member Linfen Church in Shaanxi province. Yang is a 1982 graduate of the Linfen Normal College's Chinese department. Because of her excellent academic record, she was retained by the college to teach. She also worked as an editor and reporter. She and her husband, Wang Xiaoguang, were the leaders of the Jindengtai (Golden Lampstand) Church, a house church in Linfen, Shaanxi province. In 1998, they became the church's full-time clergy and in the following two decades, the church grew to 50,000 members. On September 13, 2009 at 3 a.m., the local Fushan county government dispatched more than 400 police officers and plainclothes police, led by government officials, to the meeting site of the Fushan Christians and the Gospel Shoe Factory, where they brutally beat Christians staying in a dormitory. More than 100 people were seriously injured. On September 23, armed police surrounded the main Jindengtai church building, and on September 25, Yang and six other church leaders were arrested while traveling to the provincial capital of Taiyuan to petition the government. On November 25, the Yaodu District Court convicted Yang and her husband of "illegal occupation of farmland" and "gathering a mob to create a traffic disturbance." Yang was sentenced to a seven-year prison term and fined 30,000 yuan (US$4,755); her husband was sentenced to a three-year term and fined 10,000 yuan (US$1,585). Yang is currently suffering from diabetes, high blood pressure, and hepatitis, and despite her aliments, she has been denied medical assistance.

Tenzin Delek Rinpoche

Tenzin Delek Rinpoche (m) is a Tibetan Buddhist leader from Garze, Sichuan. Delek has advocated for the protection and preservation of Tibetan culture, religion, and way of life. Over the years, he has built monasteries, provided education for children in remote rural areas, established Buddhist institutions, and promoted social activism in Tibet. In the 1980s, his Holiness the Dalai Lama recognized him as a reincarnated Lama, a title given to those are permitted to teach the Dharma, for his commitment as a Buddhist monk. On April 7, 2002, the government claimed that Delek was involved in bomb blast that occurred on April 3rd in Chengdu, the capital of China's Sichuan. The evidence linking him to this crime was based on a confession made by a relative of Delek's during a torture session. However, the relative later retracted his statement, claiming that Delek was not involved in the attack. Despite this claim, Delek was charged with of "inciting Splittism," and for his alleged actions in the event he was sentenced to death in December 2, 2002. However, due to international pressure, on

January 26, 2005, Delek's sentence was commuted to life in prison. In efforts to free Delek, 40,000 Tibetans, in November 2009, signed a petition asking for a re-trial. Additionally, during that same month, 70 Tibetans were arrested for their participation in a hunger strike that was conducted county seat of Lithang. The case has stirred international controversy for its procedural violations and lack of transparency.

According to the Tibetan Center for Human Rights and Democracy, Delek is in poor health with a worsening heart condition and having suffered nervous breakdowns. He carries a walking stick as a result of his feet becoming injured in prison.

Kunchok Tsephel

Kunchok Tsephel (m) is an official in a Chinese government environmental department and the founder of the first Tibetan literary website, Chodme or Butter Lamp. This website, with assistance from poet Kyabchen Dedrol, was founded in 2005 for the purpose of promoting Tibetan literature and culture in China. The Chinese government actively monitored the website since its beginnings, and on several occasions, authorities have shut down public access to the website. In March 2008, the Chinese authorities began to crackdown in the Tibet Autonomous Region following the anti-government protests in Lhasa and other areas; since the onslaught, over 40 Tibetans have been taken into custody for their works on issues contrary to the party's position. On February 26, 2009, Chinese authorities targeted and detained Kunchok. While being held in their custody, officers searched his home and seized his computer, cell phone, and other personal belongings. For nine months, the government failed to inform Kunchok's family about his arrest and condition. Then on November 12, 2009, his family was summoned to attend the trial at the Intermediate People's Court of Kanlho, only hear that he had been sentenced to 15 years in prison on the charges of disclosing state secrets. Kunchok trial was conducted behind closed doors and he was denied access to a lawyer.

Many believe that published content on his website, especially information regarding the 2008 protests that occurred across the Tibetan plateau, led to his arrest and conviction.

Lobsang Tsering

Lobsang Tsering (m) is a monk from Kirti monastery in Tibet who was detained by the Chinese police in August 2012. In December, the police announced that they had accused Lobsang of inciting the self-immolation of eight Tibetans, even though five of the self-immolations never occurred. While under arrest, the Supreme Court of China, on December 5, 2012, stated that "criminals behind the scenes who plan, incite, aide, abet... and help those perpetrating self-immolations will be investigated for criminal liability in the crime of intentional murder." On January 31, 2013, Lobsang was charged with the "intentional homicide" of eight Tibetans in Ngaba, and as a result, he was sentenced to death with a two year reprieve.

Lobsang was denied the right to a fair trial, according to Xinhua, a state run news agency, acknowledged that Lobsang was not represented by a lawyer during the court proceedings. Additionally, despite a claim made by a judge who told the Global Times that: "authorities obtained sufficient evidence showing it [the alleged crimes] had been instructed by 'forces from abroad." According to Xinhua, the only documented form of evidence presented by the court was two confessions made by Lobsang and his nephew, Lobsang Tsering, who was also arrested and tried under the same charges as his uncle. In their statements, they admitted to encouraging Tibetans to self-immolate under the instructions of the Dali Lama. Many question the accuracy of these confessions because Chinese authorities are known to use torture to extract information out of detainees, and it is feared this may have happened in this case.

Gedhun Choekyi Nyima, the Panchen Lama

Gedhun Choekyi Nyima, the Panchen Lama (m) has been held by Chinese authorities in a secret location since 1995 when he was six years old, allegedly to keep him safe from "Tibetan Nationalists." China refuses all requests, both domestic and international to see Nyima. The Panchen Lama is a high ranking spiritual leader in the Tibetan Buddhist hierarchy and is passed down by reincarnation. The Dalai Lama selected Gendun Choekyi Nyima in 1995 to be the next Panchen Lama, while Chinese authorities decreed Gyaltsen Norbu to be the next. As the Panchen Lama traditionally is held responsible for the selection of the Dalai Lama, The

Chinese authorities believe it is important to control the Panchen Lama's fate.

According to Chinese government claims, he is attending school and leading a normal life somewhere in China. Chinese officials have stated that Gedhun Choekyi Nyima is a "perfectly ordinary boy" who is in "protective custody," growing up in an "excellent state of health." However, no outside party has been allowed to visit Nyima because state officials claim to keep his whereabouts undisclosed in order to protect him.

Bishop James Su Zhimin

Bishop James Su Zhimin (m) was an unregistered Bishop in the city of Baoding in the Chinese province of Hebei. In 1996, the bishop was arrested during a religious procession for conducting unregistered religious activities. In November 2003, his family discovered him by chance at a hospital in Baoding, surrounded by police and public security. He has not been heard or seen from since, despite repeated international inquiries. In all, he has spent 40 years in prison, without charge, without trial. Before being arrested in 1996, Bishop Su Zhimin was held off and on for 26 years either in prison or forced labor camps. The Chinese government deemed him as "counterrevolutionary" because, since the 1950s, he has refused to join the Patriotic Association, the national Chinese Catholic Church which has detached themselves from the Pope's authority. To this day, if one attempts at identifying or memorializing him or holding public events in his honor have met with hostile police action.

Wang Zhiwen

Wang Zhiwen (m, currently under house arrest) is a former Peoples Republic of China Ministry of Railways engineer, who was seized from bed on July 20, 1999 for his involvement and leadership in Falun Gong. Falun Gong promotes the practice of meditation and slow-moving qigong exercises with a moral philosophy. The movement was banned two days after Wang's arrest, and those who continue to practice are now considered to be dissidents of the state. On December 26, 1999, Wang was sentenced by the Beijing No. 1 Intermediate People's Court to 16 years in prison and four years deprivation of political rights on the charges of, "organizing and using a heretical organization to undermine imple-

mentation of the law," "organizing and using a heretical organization to cause death," and "illegally obtaining state secrets."

On October 18th, 2014, he was released from a Chinese prison after serving 5,475 days in jail. While incarcerated, Wang developed diabetes and high blood pressure, and suffered from a stroke immediately prior to his release. Upon Wang's release from prison, he was immediately sent to what his family describes as a "brainwashing center" for 10 days, and on the 24th of October he was released to house arrest. Wang Zhiwen's family is still pursuing his release from in-home detention, so that he is allowed to leave the country.

Li Chang

Li Chang (m) is a former high-ranking governmental official in the Ministry of Public Security, belonged to the Chinese Communist Party for over 39 years before becoming a member of Falun Gong. Falun Gong is the practice of meditation and slow-moving qigong exercises with a moral philosophy. The practice is not accepted by Party and those who practice it are considered to be dissidents.

Li originally joined the organization to improve his health, but over time he become more involved and eventually took a leading position in the Falun Dafa Research Society, considered to be vocal point for all of Falun Gong operations. Li is linked to organizing a sit-in protest on April 25, 1999 at the housing compound for the highest-level Communist Party leaders. The protest received a significant amount of attention, and consequently, the Party started to take a hard line against its members.

Li Chang put under house arrest for three months on July 20, 1999, two days before the banning of Falun Gong in China. On October 19, 1999 Li was arrested formally and brought to trial on December 26, 1999. He was sentenced to 25 years in prison and five years of deprivation of rights and charged for "Organizing and using a heretical organization to cause death," "Illegally obtaining state secrets," and "Organizing and using a heretical organization to undermine implementation of the law." The courts decided to commute his sentence to 18 years, since he confessed to his involvement with Falun Gong. He is currently being held at Qianjin Prison in Tianjin and is expected to be released in 2017.

Ilham Tohti

Ilham Tohti (m) is a Uyghur economics professor at Beijing's Minzu University, where he was known for his research on Uyghur-Han relations as well as his activism for the implementation of regional autonomy laws in China.

In 2006, Tohti founded UighurOnline, a Chinese-language website devoted to fostering understanding between Uighur and Han people, China's dominant ethnic group. In 2008, authorities shut down his website citing the websites links to Uyghur "extremists" abroad. After the July 5, 2009 ethnic rioting between Uyghurs and Han in Ürümqi, Tohti's whereabouts were unknown after he had been summoned from his home in Beijing. Tohti was subsequently released on August 23, 2009 after international pressure and condemnation.

Tohti was again arrested in January 2014, after police raided his apartment and confiscated his laptops, books, and papers. In September 2014, after a two-day trial, Tohti was found guilty of "separatism" and sentenced to life imprisonment in addition to all of his assets being frozen.

Adopted by Representative Lynn Jenkins (R-KS), Alimujiang Yimiti

Adopted by Representative Lynn Jenkins (R-KS), Alimujiang Yimiti (m) is a Uyghur Christian from Xinjiang Province now serving a fifteen-year prison term. His home is in Urumqi, capital of Xinjiang, and he and his wife have two young sons. While working at a British agri-food company, Alimujiang was the leader of a house church in the city of Kashgar. On September 13, 2007, the Kashgar Religious Affairs Bureau ruled that "Alimujiang Yimiti since 2002 has illegally engaged in religious infiltration under the guise of work, spreading Christianity among the Uyghur people, distributing Christian propaganda and growing [the number of] Christian believers." On January 12, 2008, the Kashgar police criminally detained Alimujiang on "suspicion of inciting subversion of state power" and "leaking state secrets overseas." He was formally arrested on those charges on February 20, 2008. On September 12, 2008, the United Nations Working Group on Arbitrary Detention ruled in its No. 28 document that Alimujiang's arrest and detention had been arbitrary. In a secret trial on 6 August, the Kashgar Intermediate People's Court sentenced Alimuji-

ang to fifteen years in prison for the crime of "leaking state secrets to foreigners." On March 16, 2010, the Xinjiang Uyghur Autonomous Region Higher People's Court, without holding a hearing and barring lawyers from court, upheld the Intermediate Court's sentence and added a five-year sentence of deprivation of political rights.

Adopted by Representative Mark Meadows (R-NC), Zhang Shaojie

Adopted by Representative Mark Meadows (R-NC), Zhang Shaojie (m) is a Three-Self church pastor from Nanle County in China's central Henan and former Nanle County Three-Self leader, was detained on Nov. 16, 2013, after a series of land disputes with local authorities. Zhang and more than 20 members of his congregation were charged with "gathering a crowd to disrupt the public order." Zhang was also charged with fraud; the fabricated charge was based on help he gave to another detainee when her son was killed. On July 4, 2014, Zhang was sentenced to 12 years in prison. His final appeal was rejected on August 21, 2014.

ERITREA
Eritrean Patriarch Abune Antonios

Eritrean Patriarch Abune Antonios (m) was deposed by the government in 2006 and placed under house arrest after he protested the Eritrean Department of Religious Affairs' interference in his church's affairs. In January 2005, the Patriarch's annual Nativity message was not broadcast or televised and the Eritrean Holy Synod met in August 2005 with the main purpose of removing all executive authority from the Patriarch. He was allowed to officiate at church services but prohibited from having any administrative role in church affairs. Among the accusations brought against the Patriarch, were his reluctance to excommunicate 3,000 members of the Medhane Alem, an Orthodox Sunday School movement and his demands that the government release imprisoned Christians accused of treason. In January 2006, he was officially removed from his position as head of the Eritrean Orthodox Church and spiritual leader of more than two-million persons and placed under house arrest. On May 27, 2007, the government installed Bishop Dioscoros of Mendefera as the new Patriarch. That same day, Abune Antonios was forcibly removed from his residence and transported to an undisclosed location. Since then, he has been prevented from communicating with the outside world and reportedly denied medical care.

IRAN

Behnam Irani

Behnam Irani (m) is an evangelical Christian leader from Iran who led a 300-member Church of Iran in Karaj, a city less than 15 minutes outside the capital of Tehran.

In 2011, Irani was sentenced to six years imprisonment for his Christian activities after a raid on a house church in Karaj. In September 2014, Mr. Irani was hit with 18 additional charges, including "Mofsed-e-filarz", which means "spreading corruption on Earth", a crime punishable by death. However, in October 2014, this charge was dropped and Irani was sentenced instead to six years imprisonment due to his alleged "acting against national security" and forming "a group to overthrow the government." In total, Pastor Irani is expected to serve a total of twelve years in prison and is therefore due for release in 2023.

Mr. Irani has faced numerous health problems while in prison, including severe bleeding due to stomach ulcers and colon complications. Mr. Irani is married and has a daughter and son.

The Baha'i Seven

The Baha'i Seven are former Baha'i leaders in Iran who have been deprived of the rights accorded to prisoners under Iran's own laws and regulations. Prior to their arrests in 2008, the seven were members of an ad hoc national-level group that attended to the spiritual and social needs of Iran's Baha'i community. In September 2010 they were told that their sentences had been reduced to 10 years after an appeal court acquitted them of some of the charges, including espionage, but they have never been given a written copy of either of the court verdicts. It was first reported on 18 March, 2011 that the 20-year sentence had been reinstated.

Jamaloddin Khanjani

Jamaloddin Khanjani (m) was a successful factory owner who, because he was Baha'i, lost his business after the 1979 Islamic revolution. Khanjani's volunteer service to his religious community included membership on the National Spiritual Assembly of the Baha'is of Iran in 1984, a year in which four of its nine members were executed by the government. Khanjani was arrested and imprisoned at least three times before this most recent incarceration in 2008. He has four children and six grandchildren. His wife, Ashraf Sobhani, passed away on March 10, 2010 while Khanjani was still in prison. On January 5th, 2015, Khanjani was transferred to a hospital in Tehran for health treatment.

Afif Naeimi

Afif Naeimi (m) is an industrialist who was unable to pursue his dream of becoming a doctor because as a Baha'i he was denied access to university. Born in Yazd, he lived part of his youth with relatives in Jordan after the death of his father. He was long active in volunteer Baha'i service, teaching classes for both children and adults and serving as a member of the Auxiliary Board, an appointed position with the function of inspiring, encouraging and promoting learning among Baha'is.

Behrouz Tavakkoli

Behrouz Tavakkoli (m) was a social worker who lost his government job in the early 1980's because of his Baha'i belief. Prior to his most recent imprisonment, he experienced intermittent detainment and harassment and three years ago, was jailed for four months without charge, spending most of that time in solitary confinement and developing serious kidney and orthotic problems. Mr. Tavakkoli was elected to the local Baha'i governing council in Mashhad while a student at the university there and later served on a similar council in Sari before such institutions were banned in the early 1980's.

Vahid Tizfahm

Vahid Tizfahm (m) is an optometrist and owner of an optical shop in Tabriz, where he lived until early 2008 when he moved to Tehran. He was born and spent his youth in the city of Urumiyyih and went to Tabriz at age eighteen to study to become an optician. He later also studied sociology at the Advanced Baha'i Studies Institute, an affiliate of the Baha'i Institute for Higher Education. Since his youth, Mr. Tizfahm has served the Baha'i community in a variety of capacities – for a time as a member of the Baha'i National Youth Committee and later as part of the Auxiliary Board, an advisory group that serves to uplift and inspire Baha'i communities.

Adopted by Representative Suzanne Bonamici (D-OR), Fariba Kamalabadi

Adopted by Representative Suzanne Bonamici (D-OR), Fariba Kamalabadi (f) is a developmental psychologist and mother of three who was arrested twice previously because of her involvement with the Baha'i community. On one of those occasions she was held incommunicado for 10 days. As a youth, Mrs. Kamalabadi was denied the opportunity to study at a public university. In her mid-30s, she embarked on an eight-year period of study and ultimately received an advanced degree from the Baha'i Institute of Higher Education, an alternative institution established by the Baha'i community of Iran to serve young people who were barred from university.

Adopted by Representative Jan Schakowsky (D-IL), Mahvash Sabet

Adopted by Representative Jan Schakowsky (D-IL), Mahvash Sabet (f) is a teacher and school principal who was dismissed from public education for being a Baha'i. Before her arrest, she served for 15 years as director of the Baha'i Institute for Higher Education, which provides alternative higher education for Baha'i youth. She began her professional career as a teacher and also worked as a principal at several schools. In her professional role, she also collaborated with the National Literacy Committee of Iran. After the Islamic revolution, like thousands of other Iranian Baha'i educators, she was fired from her job and blocked from working in public education.

Adopted by Representative Lynn Jenkins (R-KS), Saeid Rezaie

Adopted by Representative Lynn Jenkins (R-KS), Saeid Rezaie (m) is an agricultural engineer who has run a successful farming equipment business for more than twenty years. During the early 1980's, when persecution of Baha'is was intense, he moved first to northern Iran and worked as a farming manager and then to Kerman to work as a carpenter, in part because of the difficulties Baha'is faced in finding formal employment or operating businesses. His two daughters, both in their twenties, were among a group of fifty-four young Baha'is

arrested in Shiraz in 2006 while working on a project aimed at helping underprivileged young people. In 2006, before his latest incarceration in 2008, Mr. Rezaie was arrested and detained for a period that included forty days in solitary confinement.

Sima Eshraghi

Sima Eshraghi (f) – A member of the Baha'I community in Iran, she was summoned by the Mashhad Revolutionary court in November of 2010 and was transferred to Vakilabad Prison. Sima was sentenced to five years in prison. She has two children and one of her children, Sina Aghdaszadeh, was recently released on bail by the Mashhad Intelligence Office after two months in custody and is currently awaiting trial.

Adopted by Representative Keith Ellison (D-MN), Ayatollah Mohammad Kazemeini Boroujerdi

Adopted by Representative Keith Ellison (D-MN), Ayatollah Mohammad Kazemeini Boroujerdi (m) is a Shi'a cleric who advocates for the separation of religion and state and has spoken out on behalf of the rights of Iran's religious minorities as well as those of its Shi'a Muslim majority. In October 2006, he was arrested and imprisoned without charge. He and seventeen of his followers were tried by a special court with jurisdiction over Shi'a clerics and sentenced to death on spurious charges, including "enmity against God" and spreading propaganda against the regime. After an appeal, the death sentence was withdrawn and Ayatollah Boroujerdi was sentenced to eleven years in prison. He currently is serving his prison term, and the government has banned him from practicing his clerical duties and confiscated his home and belongings. He has suffered physical and mental abuse while in prison.

Adopted by Representative Trent Franks (R-AZ), Saeed Abedini

Adopted by Representative Trent Franks (R-AZ), Saeed Abedini (m) is a father and husband from Idaho who currently is imprisoned in Evin Prison. Saeed is a dual national of the United States (via naturalization) and Iran (by birth). He has broken no codified Iranian law, but has been sentenced to eight years in prison for practicing his Christian faith. In the last year, he has been arrested, given a sham trial before a notoriously biased judge, threatened with death, beaten, and denied life-saving medical treatment. [Also adopted by Representatives Raul Labrador (R-ID) and Henry Waxman (D-CA)]

Adopted by Representative Jeff Duncan (R-SC), Farshid Fathi

Adopted by Representative Jeff Duncan (R-SC), Farshid Fathi (m) is a Christian pastor who ran a network of house churches in Tehran. Iranian officials arrested him on December 26, 2010. Pastor Fathi currently is serving a 6-year sentence in Iran's notorious Evin prison. Farshid left Iran to attend seminary in Turkey and then pursued additional training in London with his wife before returning to Iran. Farshid reportedly is imprisoned alongside Saeed Abedini (see above). Though his crime is being a Christian and spreading his faith, Iranian authorities have cast his Christian activity as "political offenses," arguing that his Christian activities were equivalent to "actions against national security." He also was charged with possessing religious propaganda. At trial, the regime offered as evidence that Pastor Fathi had Bibles printed in Farsi, unlawfully distributed them, and possessed Christian literature. The regime also made it difficult for his lawyers to present a defense by denying them full access to the case until just a few days before trial.

KAZAKHSTAN

Bakhytzhan Kashkumbayev

Bakhytzhan Kashkumbayev (m) led the Presbyterian Grace Church in Astana. He has been jailed since May 2013. For a period of time he was detained in a psychiatric hospital where he was forcibly administered psychotropic drugs, a notorious Soviet form of punishment. While he was released from the psychiatric hospital, he was rearrested on charges of extremism. These serious charges carry a possible prison term of three to seven years, with grave implications for both Pastor Kashkumbayev and the Grace Church. The Pastor was arrested on May 17, 2013 on charges of "intentional infliction of serious harm to health" to parishioner Lyazzat Almenova but her mother called for the case against the pastor to be dropped. The pastor's pre-trial detention was extended on October 7 until November 17 and he was then supposed to be transferred from prison to house arrest. Finally, after the Pastor's very brief reunion

in prison with his family he was re-arrested and charged with acts of "propaganda of terrorism or extremism or public calls to commit an act of terrorism or extremism as well as the distribution of material of the content indicated." Pastor Bakhytzhan Kashkumbaev was released on Feb. 17, 2014 after spending nine months in jail awaiting trial. He was convicted of the charge and received a four-year suspended sentence. Although four other charges were dropped, some fear that new charges could be filed. Pastor Kashkumbaev was freed after court proceedings and returned to the home he shares with his wife, Alfiya. He plans to appeal the conviction.

PAKISTAN

Adopted by Representative Joseph Pitts (R-PA), Asia Bibi

Adopted by Representative Joseph Pitts (R-PA), Asia Bibi is a Catholic mother of five and was a farmhand from the village of Ittan Wali in Sheikhupura District of Punjab province. In June 2009, an argument arose with her fellow labors over whether the water she brought was "unclean" because she was Christian and they Muslim. Later coworkers complained to a cleric that Bibi made derogatory comments about Prophet Muhammad. Police investigated her remarks, which resulted in her arrest and prosecution under Section 295 C of the Pakistan Penal Code for blasphemy. She spent more than a year in jail. On November 8, 2010, a district court in Nankana Sahib, Punjab, sentenced her to death for blasphemy, the first such sentence for blasphemy handed down against a woman. The death penalty is permissible under Pakistani law. On October 16, 2014, the Lahore High Court dismissed her appeal and upheld her death sentence. Her lawyers plan to appeal to the Supreme Court.

SAUDI ARABIA

Hamad al-Naqi

Hamad al-Naqi (m) is a Shia Muslim who in February and March 2012 allegedly made a series of posts on Twitter critical of the Prophet Muhammad, his wife, his followers, and the rulers of Saudi Arabia and Bahrain. Several members of the National Assembly of Kuwait called for his death. Al-Naqi pled not guilty, arguing that he had not posted the messages, and that his account had been hacked. In June 2012, Al-Naqi was found guilty of "insulting the Prophet, the Prophet's wife and companions, mocking Islam, provoking sectarian tensions, insulting the rulers of Saudi Arabia and Bahrain and misusing his mobile phone to spread the comments" and sentenced to ten years in prison. Al-Naqi was attacked within weeks of entering prison and has been held in solitary confinement for safety reasons. His lawyers appealed his sentence but, in July 2014, Kuwait's top court upheld his ten-year sentence.

Dr. Medani previously served as head of the Office of the High Commissioner for Human Rights (OHCHR) office in the West Bank and Gaza, Chief of Mission of the OHCHR in Zagreb, Croatia, legal advisor to the Special Representative of the U.N Secretary-General in Iraq as well as Afghanistan, and a Regional Representative for the OHCHR in Beirut, Lebanon. He holds a Ph.D. from the University of Edinburgh in comparative Criminal Law.

VIETNAM

Francis Jang Xuan Dieu

Francis Jang Xuan Dieu (m) is a Catholic intellectual and activist. Dieu is well known in Vietnam for his efforts to advocate for increased child education access and awareness of political prisoners in Vietnamese jails. In August of 2011, Dieu was arrested along with a group of other Vietnamese Catholics and charged with trying to "overthrow the people's administration." He was sentenced to 13 years in prison, plus five years under supervision. Dieu's family has been denied access to Dieu.

Adopted by Representative Chris Smith (R-NJ), Father Nguyen Van Ly

Adopted by Representative Chris Smith (R-NJ), Father Nguyen Van Ly has spent over 15 years in prison for the causes of religious freedom, democracy, and human rights. Initially arrested in September 1977 and sentenced to 20 years in a labor camp near Hue, he was later released but prohibited from engaging in religious activities. He was returned to jail in 2001 when he submitted testimony to the U.S. Congress and the U.S. Commission on International Religious Freedom opposing a U.S.-Vietnam Bilateral Trade Act. On March 30, 2007, in a broadcasted show trial, authorities muzzled him while he tried to defend himself. He is a one of the founders of Bloc 8406 and past editor of an underground publication.

Adopted by Representative Zoe Lofgren (D-CA), Nguyen Van Lia

Adopted by Representative Zoe Lofgren (D-CA), Nguyen Van Lia (m) is a longtime adherent of Hoa Hao Buddhism, a religious group often suppressed by the government, and the co-author of several Hoa Hao Buddhist religious instruction texts and books. He is charged with violating article 258 of the penal code for "abusing democratic freedoms to infringe upon the interests of the state," a crime that could result in a sentence of up to seven years. According to state media, he possessed printed materials, CD's, and DVD's criticizing the Vietnamese government's religious record. He had previously met with the U.S. Consulate and USCIRF officials in Saigon. He was sentenced to a five-year term on December 13, 2011 on the charge of "abusing democratic freedoms."

Adopted by Representative Ted Poe, (R-TX), Duong Kim Khai Duong

Adopted by Representative Ted Poe, (R-TX), Duong Kim Khai Duong (m) is a pastor for the Mennonite Church in Vietnam, a long-time advocate for aggrieved farmers, a democracy activist and member of Viet Tan, an organization advocating for democracy. Since the early 1990's, he has been detained or arrested thirteen times, often while trying to organize prayer sessions. He was jailed in 2004 for starting an "illegal" religious group. Upon his release in 2006, he founded the Mennonite Cattle Shed Congregation in order to advocate for religious freedom and social justice, particularly to provide assistance to farmers so they could petition the government for redress in land disputes or corruption cases in Ben Tre and Dong Thap provinces. He also joined Viet Tan during this period. Pastor Duong Kim Khai was arrested on August 10, 2010 on the charge of "attempting to overthrow the government." The condition of his health and place of detention were kept from his family by authorities until October 12, 2010, when it received written confirmation of his arrest. On May 30, 2011, he was sentenced to a six-year prison term (later reduced to five years) followed by five-year term of house arrest. In 2011, the UN Working Group on Arbitrary Detention ruled that the Hanoi government's detention and conviction of Pastor Duong Kim Khai and six other land activists were in violation of international law.